Bolshevism, syndicalism and the general strike

BOLSHEVISM AND THE BRITISH LEFT

Part Three

Bolshevism, syndicalism and the general strike

The lost internationalist world of A.A. Purcell

Kevin Morgan

Lawrence & Wishart
LONDON 2013

Lawrence and Wishart Limited
99a Wallis Road
London
E9 5LN

© Lawrence & Wishart 2013

Cover photos courtesy Working Class Movement Library.

The author has asserted his rights under the Copyright, Design and Patents Act, 1998 to be identified as the author of this work.

All rights reserved. Apart from fair dealing for the purpose of private study, research, criticism or review, no part of this publication may be reproduced, stored in a retrieval system, or transmitted, in any form or by any means, electronic, electrical, chemical, mechanical, optical, photocopying, recording or otherwise, without the prior permission of the copyright owner.

ISBN 978 1 905007 27 1

British Library Cataloguing in Publication Data.
A catalogue record for this book is available from the British Library

Contents

Acknowledgements	7
Abbreviations	8
Introduction: around a life	10
1. Syndicalism, internationalism and the furnishing trades	23
2. Roads to freedom in the 1920s	64
3. Labour's Russian delegations	106
4. 'Swimming against a flood': Emma Goldman in London	156
5. The other future?	196
6. The General Strike	233
7. Internationalist swansong	281
Epilogue: a claim-making performer	305
Bibliography	310
Timeline	326
Index	335
Bolshevism and the British left: concluding thoughts	349

Acknowledgements

The idea of a study of Purcell was first suggested to me by Edmund and Ruth Frow. The friendship and encouragement of the Frows are greatly missed, and the early chapters here make extensive use of the Furnishing Trades' materials held by the Working Class Movement Library which they founded. In using this and other materials at the WCML I should particularly like to thank the librarians Alain Kahan and Lynette Cawthra, and similarly would like to thank the several archivists over the years at the People's History Museum and also Christine Coates and colleagues at the TUC Library Collections. Indispensable in tracking Purcell round the country was the assistance of local history librarians in Accrington, Cinderford, Coventry and Salford. For assistance with the Baikalov papers and a massive photocopying order I should like to thank Tanya Chebotarev at Columbia University Library. Research at Warwick's Modern Records Centre was made much easier and pleasanter thanks to the hospitality of Nazima Rahimkhan, and for guidance and support in Amsterdam and at the International Institute of Social History I would like to thank Mieke Ijzermans. Francis King and Julie Johnson (to whom very special thanks) helped on trips to Moscow. Norry LaPorte provided invaluable assistance with references in German, particularly those used in chapter five. My Manchester colleague Paul Kelemen assisted with the references to Krishna Menon papers in chapter seven. Many others provided help or advice on particular points including the late Nina Fishman, David Howell, Ed Johanningsmeier, Neville Kirk, Barry McLoughlin, Nick Mansfield, John Peet, Andrew Thorpe, Reiner Tostorff and John Carter Wood. Thanks too to Sally Davison for her great patience as editor and publisher. Sam and Jane have lived with Purcell all their lives without acquiring an exaggerated view of his importance. My thanks to them for that and much else.

Kevin Morgan
September 2012

Abbreviations

ACIQ	(Labour Party) Advisory Committee on International Questions
ACMA	Alliance Cabinet-Makers' Association
ADGB	Allgemeiner Deutscher Gewerkschaftbund (German conferderation of trade unions)
AEU	Amalgamated Engineering Union
AFL	American Federation of Labour
AITUC	All-Indian Trades Union Congress
ARCCTU	All-Russian Central Council of Trade Unions
Arcos	All-Russian Co-operative Society
ARPC	Anglo-Russian Parliamentary Committee
ASE	Amalgamated Society of Engineers
ASW	Amalgamated Society of Woodworkers
AUBTW	Amalgamated Union of Building Trade Workers
BSP	British Socialist Party
BWD	Beatrice Webb diaries
CGT	*Conféderation générale du travail*
CI	Communist International or Comintern
CP(GB)	Communist Party (of Great Britain)
CPSU	Communist Party of the Soviet Union
DLB	*Dictionary of Labour Biography*, vols 1-10, ed. Joyce M. Bellamy and John Saville, 1972-2000; vols 11-13, ed. Keith Gildart, David Howell and Neville Kirk, 2003-2010
ECCI	Executive Committee of the Communist International
ETU	Electrical Trades Union
FFG	Furniture and Furnishing Guild
FRD	Fabian Research Department
GARF	State Archive of the Russian Federation
GLDS	*Emma Goldman. A Guide to her Life and Documentary Sources* (see note 8, p184)
GFTU	General Federation of Trade Unions
ICWPA	International Class War Prisoners' Aid
IFTU	International Federation of Trade Unions
IISH	International Institute for Social History
ILO	International Labour Organisation

Abbreviations

ILP	Independent Labour Party
ISEL	Industrial Syndicalist Education League
ITF	International Transportworkers' Federation
ITS	International Trade Secretariat
IUW	International Union of Woodworkers
KPD	German Communist Party
LCC	London County Council
LRD	Labour Research Department
LSI	Labour and Socialist International
MFGB	Miners' Federation of Great Britain
MSTC	Manchester and Salford Trades Council
NA	National Archives, Kew
NAFTA	National Amalgamated Furnishing Trades Association
NFBTO	National Federation of Building Trades Operatives
NEP	New Economic Policy
NGL	National Guilds League
NUGMW	National Union of General and Municipal Workers
NUR	National Union of Railwaymen
NUWCM	National Unemployed Workers' Committee Movement
PB	(Communist Party) Political Bureau
PCF	French Communist Party
RGASPI	Russian State Archive of Socio-Political History
RILU	Red International of Labour Unions or Profintern
SAI	Sozialiste Arbeiter Internationale (Labour and Socialist International)
SDAP	Social Democratic Labour Party
SDF	Social Democratic Federation
SDP	Social Democratic Party
SIC	(TUC) Special Industrial Committee
SOC	(TUC) Strike Organisation Committee
SPD	German Social Democratic Party
SRC	Socialist Representation Committee
TGWU	Transport and General Workers' Union
TUC (GC)	Trades Union Congress (General Council)
UDC	Union of Democratic Control
WCML	Working Class Movement Library
WMC	(TUC) Ways and Means Committee

Introduction: around a life

In March 1926, the communist-edited *Sunday Worker* ran a poll to identify the labour movement leaders most popular with its readers. Topping the list with nearly 4500 votes was the unofficial leader of the Labour left, George Lansbury. Also making the readers' top ten, as the coal crisis loomed, were three militant miners' officials, A.J. Cook, Robert Smillie and Herbert Smith. Two further Labour politicians, John Wheatley and Ramsay MacDonald, were separated by three communist ones, Tom Mann, Harry Pollitt and the MP Shapurji Saklatvala. Sandwiched between Mann and Pollitt in sixth place was a name nowadays more difficult to place, that of Albert Arthur, or 'Alf', Purcell.[1] Alone of the ten, Purcell and Smillie await some sort of biographer – and even Smillie found a ghost-writer to recount his 'life for Labour'. Again according to the *Sunday Worker*, Purcell was the labour movement leader most abused by the movement's opponents. But who is there now that can remember why?

There seemed reason enough at the time. Not only did Purcell combine membership of the House of Commons with honorary membership of the Moscow Soviet; he was notably more enthusiastic about the latter. Twice he had taken part in official Labour delegations to the new workers' Russia. The second time he provoked an international outcry, to which in due course even the Tintin adventures contributed. Purcell had moved the resolution that brought into being the British communist party (CPGB). He also assisted in the declaration of a 'Red Trade Union International' and founded one of the handful of working guilds inspired by guild socialism. When he was elected MP for the Forest of Dean, a constituent wrote to King Rama VI of Siam warning of a looming global conflagration that would lay waste property, law and religion, and which did not spare even Gloucestershire.[2] For three years Purcell was president of the International Federation of Trade Unions (IFTU), in which time he managed to antagonise every one of its sections but the British. When a Russian cartoon depicted him as a muzhik with a concertina, he commented, 'A desirable caricature. Not unlikely! Anything possible today.'[3] *Izvestia* gave him front-page accolades, but in America the *Washington Post* demanded his deportation. The anarchist Emma Goldman called him the 'fake Purcelle'; the communist Dutt warned of his genial militant fuzz; MacDonald as Labour leader disowned him; for the establishment he was the epitome of the irresponsible rabble-rouser. For *Sunday Worker* readers, on the other hand, Purcell was one of their own; and when American leftists for the first time sent their own delegation to Russia, its vehicle was a so-called Purcell Fund. If the Webbs can personify the intellectual pro-Sovietism of the 1930s, none better than Purcell encapsulates the pro-Bolshevik disposition of British Labour in the years immediately after the revolution.

More Andy Warhol than Labour's forward march, Purcell's passing celebrity now appears a mere five minutes in the spotlight – from the shadows of a provincial union office and back again, all within a decade. Contrasting with the longevity of a Mann, a Lansbury or a MacDonald, this mayfly-like appearance must partly explain his subsequent obscurity. But there is also an obvious political consideration. In all its disparate manifestations, Purcell's notoriety was that of the foremost of the TUC 'lefts' who aroused such foreboding and expectation in the years of crisis and disaffection that followed the First World War. Even the communists extended him their credit – as one wrote from Fife, he had at least 'more or less stirred the Boss'.[4] It was the General Strike of 1926 that proved his moment of reckoning. As chairman of the central strike organisation committee, Purcell was at its heart, and when the strike was called off while still unbroken, and with its objects unachieved, the precipitancy of his descent was matched only by its comprehensiveness. Even as the miners battled on in 1926, competing narratives of the strike were being promulgated that would underpin the sharper delineation of Labour reformism and a stalinised revolutionary tradition. Purcell's career had flourished in the indeterminate space between these emerging forces; now he had a place in neither.

Purcell had had a good deal in common with the miners' leader Cook. Cook's awareness of the mobilising power of rhetoric, which some thought simple demagogy, did not preclude a capacity for undeceived political calculation and some well-documented manoeuvring in 1926. Though liable to caricature by more mainstream historians, his public persona nevertheless emerged unscathed for those supportive of his militant stance, and decades later Cook was still being lionised as embodiment of the miners' cause.[5] Industrially, Purcell has lacked this identification with any key group of workers or moment of struggle. Politically, moreover, he has had the further liability of personifying the hopes which the emerging stalinist leadership of the Soviet communist party briefly vested in the TUC, and which were symbolised by the short-lived Anglo-Russian trade-union committee (1925-7), in whose formation Purcell was instrumental. Trotsky in his autobiography noted that 'the behaviour of the General Council during the general strike signified the collapse of Stalin's hopes of Purcell', who thus appeared a sort of empty vessel whether viewed from the left or from the right.[6] Just once in the 1970s, a later generation caught a glimpse of Purcell in Jim Allen's BBC docudrama *Days of Hope*. His role, through imaginary dialogue, was to symbolise the bureaucratic affectation of militancy which the denouement of the strike then exposed as spurious and self-deceiving. With the additional licence afforded the dramatist, the image of Purcell which Allen presented more or less reproduced that to be found in a wider literature, whether political or academic.

There is no lost leader here waiting to be discovered by a later generation. There is, on the other hand, a sort of lost world of A.A. Purcell, more deeply buried even than Raphael Samuel's lost world of the communists, but one which illuminates many aspects of the wider relationship of Bolshevism and the British left.[7] In seeking to contextualise the attraction to Soviet communism of the Webbs, an earlier volume retraced the diverse 'roads to Russia' that were followed at different times by planners, co-operators and revolutionary elitists. Purcell introduces us to a fourth such road, at least as congested as the others, by which the active trade unionist and trade-union official might come to see in Soviet Russia the attempted realisation of a shared aspiration to the good society. Like the co-operators' road, but unlike that of the Webbs and other planners, this one dated from the earliest years of the revolution, and the insufficiency of a 'Russian gold' type of explanation is once again apparent. On the other hand, Purcell does offer a fresh perspective on the issues of political funding and resourcing that were the focus of the first volume of this study. In particular, he exemplifies the trade-union career path that was central to Labour's emergence as a national political force and crucially underpinned its claim to represent the new democracy. Though such a career was itself of relatively recent growth, it may be contrasted with both the traditional forms of patronage and social advantage that were finding their way into the labour movement and the trend to professionalisation that developed so rapidly between in the wars. Politically, Purcell may be seen a casualty of the pincer movement of managerial social democracy and communism, which some have referred to as the double closure.[8] But he also represents the incursion of the manual worker into conventional politics, which for a moment seemed so full of promise, but which was itself squeezed out by the further double closure of a corporatist trade unionism on the one hand and the professional politician on the other. More remarkable even than Purcell's temporary ubiquity was the precipitateness of his exclusion or self-exclusion from every national or international platform within just a year or two of the General Strike.

It would be absurd to suggest that the unions' history is a lost world in itself. Through books like Coates and Topham's magisterial *Making of the Labour Movement*, parts of it have been comprehensively charted; and an informed and empathetic study also exists of Purcell's own union, the Furnishing Trades.[9] What this largest of British social movements has nevertheless lacked is, with a very few exceptions, any significant corpus of biographical writing. The smaller-scale studies of the *Dictionary of Labour Biography* are, of course, indispensable. These apart, significant studies of Purcell's generation of trade-union leaders scarcely exist except where they attained some political or other external eminence. Lansbury and MacDonald, of the *Sunday Worker*'s list, have attracted numerous biographers. Even Pollitt, Mann and Saklatvala have a couple each, and there is, exceptionally, a distinct genre of miners' leaders' lives that reflects the enduring fascination of coalfield history.[10] But in a period in which the unions figured centrally in Britain's social and political life, their leaders otherwise muster scarcely a biography between them. Conley-Elvin-Findlay-Poulton-Beard-Quaile-Purcell – a 1920s' TUC roll-call conveys almost nothing to us, though each name must conceal varieties of industrial experience, political engagement, cultural formation and personal circumstance. One of the objects of the present study is to see how far that can be put right.

The paucity of any such literature is in part a matter of external preconceptions and social prejudice. Keith Middlemas once observed that 'even' the history of the unions could be 'written in terms of leaders like Ernest Bevin when the personality is large enough'.[11] As the 'even' implied, it apparently rarely was; indeed, with Bevin alone excepted, all these leaders together could until very recently barely muster the thousand or more pages Middlemas devoted to their Conservative nemesis Stanley Baldwin.[12] In a pregnant passage from 1921, the Webbs deplored the absence in such movements, 'not of men of good conduct or high character, but of men of distinguished intellect and magnetic personality':

> And if no small part of the failure to achieve artistic excellence or intellectual distinction, or even far-extended and well co-ordinated administration, is attributed to the fact that so little desire is felt to obtain the services of men of superior talent and education, and that the brain-working employees are selected and governed in ways characteristic of constituencies and committees of manual workers, this, too, is common to Trade Unions and 'self-governing workshops', as well as to consumers' Co-operative societies. The characteristic psychological imperfections ... [of] working-class movements in Great Britain are due, in fact, simply to [their] being ... a working-class movement.[13]

As biography more and more flourishes, and shelves buckle under the lives of second-order politicians and bellettrists, personality, distinction or some other biographically indispensable quality evidently remains lacking in the grey, uneducated mass of British trade unionists.

But this is just as much a matter of the self-presentation of the unions themselves. In the institutionalist historiography which the

Webbs pioneered, the union as collective actor was dominant, and the individual traced only as a career path through the institution. Hugh Clegg, who was the author or co-author of definitive works within this tradition, restricted his biographical summaries to strings of offices either within or directly deriving from the British trade-union movement.[14] This was entirely consistent with the bias of official union histories towards experience and service in one's trade, one's trade society, or perhaps, at its most expansive, in the wider labour movement. From the portrait photographs that stare impassively from these volumes, one would imagine that no collar had ever been loosened, as Cook's famously was, nor fist ever clenched, shoulder shrugged or head bowed in resignation or defeat. A 'career ... full of useful service to trade-unionism'; 'an indefatigable worker for our organisation'; 'unflagging efforts at General Office'; 'vigorous participation in the affairs of the society'; this admittedly is not the stuff of biography.[15]

With the 'new' labour history that emerged from the 1960s, diverse forms of grassroots and shopfloor activism were recovered from the teleology of the institution. But while alternatives to the development of the union bureaucracy were thus painstakingly excavated, the identification of the dominant leadership stratum with the institution was if anything reinforced. Forty years after its appearance in English, Zygmunt Bauman's *Between Class and Elite* remains one of the few serious studies of British labour movement elites.[16] Its periodisation includes a phase characterised as the 'evolution of a mass labour movement' (1890-1924), which maps almost perfectly onto Purcell's career, from his first achieving union office in the 1890s to his attainment of its highest levels in the mid-1920s. According to Bauman, this phase signified the displacement of the union 'agitator', whose charismatic attributes had helped bring the unions into being, by the less compelling and also more anonymous figure of the 'administrator'. To the agitator like Tom Mann, the organisation had always been secondary and subordinate: pared down by Clegg to positions officially held, all but two of the last forty-one years of Mann's life are entirely unaccounted for.[17] Administrators, on the other hand, not only found the organisation already established, but were its 'product' and 'owe[d] their being to it'. Preferring a well-ordered desk to the platform spotlight, and 'hard-headed ... statistics' to 'fiery speeches', the leaders of Purcell's generation formed 'a new category of elite' that was 'colourless, dry and dull'.[18]

The lives of writers and cabinet ministers carry no guarantee of singularity or iridescence. In the case of the trade unionist, however, the materials are apparently lacking for a conventional biographical treatment that penetrates beneath the surface dullness. Prospective biographers of Arthur Henderson, whom Bauman saw as an archetype of the new class of administrator, have either conceded the impression of dullness and one-dimensionality or been deterred by it.[19] Andrew Thorpe, who does intend a full biography, notes that even where the lives of such figures include a significant trade-union component, this tends to be passed over quickly 'to get to the interesting bit'.[20] At least Henderson maintained his office correspondence, and as a national political figure he can be traced through the papers of elite correspondents. There is, as Thorpe puts it, an archival footprint. For most of Henderson's trade-union contemporaries even this is not usually possible, and if biography has to depend on such sources it is likely to remain a restricted domain, and one that replicates traditional forms of social and historiographical exclusiveness. How revealing it is that Henry Pelling, whose career was largely devoted to labour history, should have found his only worthy biographical subject in the person of Winston Churchill. Within the field of industrial relations, Clegg, very properly, is to have his own biography, and among his predecessors as students of trade unionism L.T. Hobhouse, the Webbs and lately Allan Flanders already have theirs. Important as is this literature in itself, the sense of occlusion is irresistible. Labour biographers like Douglas Cole have labour biographer biographers like Margaret Cole, who in turn has a biographer biographer biographer of her own.[21] From the chain thus established, the shadowy collective agent of labour itself seems alone excluded.[22]

Where self-representation through print and archive lends itself so reluctantly to such an enterprise, it seems appropriate as well as unavoidable to adapt the writing of life-histories to the different ways in which these were documented within different cultures. The anarchist Kropotkin originally wanted the title *Autour de sa vie* for his memoirs. In Kropotkin's case this apparently represented an instinct of privacy and personal reticence, for his *Memoirs of a Revolutionist* do not at all provide a biographically decentred narrative.[23] In a case like Purcell's, however, it is around rather than through the individual that such an account can alone be constructed. Mann, an irresistible biographical subject, has thus given rise to both the life-and-times approach of Dona Torr and the elements of collective biography drawn upon by Chushichi Tsuzuki.[24] In Mann's case, however, a substantial body of personal papers has been preserved. More directly comparable with Purcell as biographical subject is the nineteenth-century radical shipwright John Gast, who, even more than Purcell, combined wide associations with a paucity of such personal documentation. In taking Gast as his organising subject, Iorwerth Prothero thus conceded the impossibility of a conventional biographical treatment while employing painstaking research to reconstruct the diverse aspects of a public life and the interconnections between them.[25] A sphere of intimacies and personal confidences will, in a case like this, remain elusive. Indeed, in Purcell's case even the defining moment of the General Strike gave rise to some deeper predicament on which the only light to be thrown is that of inference, circumstantial evidence and a sort of biographical behaviourism.

This does not mean that only superficial insight is possible, or an unachieved version of the fuller biography that one would prefer to write. A communist document of the early 1920s describes leaders like Purcell as 'like banners', that is, as symbols or 'rallying centres' of particular policies or programmes.[26] One is reminded of Philip Williamson's argument that politics is crucially a public activity, and that those engaged in this activity like Baldwin – Williamson's subject – are for this reason appropriately studied through the public sphere in which alone they existed for this wider population.[27] It was as a rallying centre that Purcell received the votes of the *Sunday Worker*'s readers, and these, as their votes demonstrated, were quite capable of particularising between different individuals in ways conforming to no overriding party or factional pattern. They did so, moreover, on the basis of well-developed forms of communication, by word and other forms of action, which remain substantially accessible to the historian. While only a handful of Purcell's personal letters have been traced, for nearly twenty years he published a monthly report in his union's journal that was at once personalised in tone and addressed to a collective subject on terms of an easy sociality. According to its conventions, Purcell's failure to account for himself after the General Strike was not a private affair or a matter for his future biographers, but an eloquent retreat into 'silence' that occasioned wide and damaging comment. Such personal sources as have survived, like the TUC secretary Walter Citrine's diary of the strike, have in some respects had a distinctly distorting effect. Given a culture that set little store by the personal archive and what it represented, there is a compelling case for engaging with the forms of interlocution and address that did define it as a collectivity.

A presentation like Williamson's, thematically organised and focusing on the public persona, is expressly intended as an alternative to biography. It is also an avowedly top-down approach, one that effectively reconceives the individual as a public institution, and which may therefore be denied those deemed neither original nor important enough to repay such examination. Within a Conservative Party context overloaded by conventional biographies, in which the party leader undoubtedly was a sort of institution, Williamson's approach has its own distinct advantages. Within a labour movement context dominated by institutional narratives, on the other hand, the case for a biographical or prosopographical approach lies in the insight that it offers into the delimited scope of the institution itself.

Prothero's rationale in organising a study around Gast was to get beyond the 'artificial' compartmentalisation of activities into the political, industrial, co-operative and educational fields.[28] Purcell is similarly approached here, not so much for the elusive glimpse of personality, nor even for a more outward-facing life and times, but to seek out the connections and transitions by which even the seemingly straightforward trade-union life was shaped. To the extent that such an approach remains valid for a subject postdating Gast by a century, the notion that a figure like Purcell owed his being to any one employing organisation will be called more sharply into question. As the subject moves through diverse movements that are typically conceived of compartmentally, the advantage of an individualised approach to collective movements is that the parameters of individual life-history take us beyond those boundaries of period and institution which from other angles can have an ineluctable framing effect. There were myriad cross-currents between movements like syndicalism, communism and labour socialism, both concurrently and over time. The approach adopted here aims to bring out the complex interaction of agency, opportunity and constraint that is so easily obscured when these movements are conceived of only generically.

It is not an intellectual history, if that means the history of intellectuals. But in the spirit of other recent work in the field, it does recognise that the 'context' of Skinnerian intellectual history was itself a generator of ideas whose reconstruction is no less demanding of critical reading and textual analysis.[29] It also takes us beyond the stereotypes of agitator and administrator. A key debating point in the exchanges between 'rank-and-filist' and 'neo-institutionalist' approaches to British industrial relations has been the character of the role of union officers, and how far and in what circumstances these were either more or less militant than the members they represented.[30] Bauman's view was that the agitator and the administrator were mutually exclusive roles, displaying different skills, character traits, and psychological and intellectual make-up, and representing 'very different sociological types' rarely found in combination.[31] This is consistent with the critique of officialdom long ago advanced from within the syndicalist movement, and subsequently reflected in an extensive marxisant academic literature on the incorporating effects of the bureaucracy.[32]

Recent accounts have stressed the limitations of this focus solely on the structural determinants of union leaders' conduct. The view that leaders were necessarily more disposed to conciliation than the members they represented has come in for particular criticism.[33] Given the prominence of the issue, it is nevertheless surprising how little attempt there has been to explore these issues through either individual or collective biography.[34] Differences of occupational culture and union structure – almost invisible in some constructions of 'labourism' – were one crucial influence.[35] Kelly and Heery have also urged a greater recognition of the ways in which union roles and internal relations were shaped by the values which different generations of officers 'imported' into these activities.[36] This is particularly applicable to those of Purcell's generation, who encountered British socialism in its formative years and whose conception of trade-union activity was strongly conditioned by, as it helped to shape, its values and aspirations. In some cases an ideological residue seemed to be given little more than ceremonial expression as circumstances required. In a case like Purcell's, on the other hand, the socialism of the trade-union officer was expressed in terms of multiple roles and commitments, whose active performance continued to be combined with official union responsibilities. Kelly and Heery particularly emphasise the role of formative phases of industrial activity. In this period, when the union was often not the initial vehicle of social activism, the importation of values nevertheless went beyond the ebb and flow of industrial militancy.

Born in London in 1872, Purcell's personal history of activism begins at a local level as early as his mid-teens. Fuller research would doubtless recover more extensive traces of his involvement in the various currents of metropolitan radicalism. The account provided here nevertheless picks up, as it did with the Webbs, at the turn of the century, and with Purcell's employment in the role of full-time union officer that was to provide the basis for the disparate attachments and enthusiasms that followed.

Chapter one examines Purcell's early activities as a syndicalist and a Furnishing Trades organiser, within a specific union characterised by an internationalist outlook of remarkable articulacy. The following chapter then explores his involvement with diverse social and political movements in the years following the First World War, notably including communism, guild socialism and the Parliamentary Labour Party. The broadly chronological treatment is picked up again in the book's sixth chapter, which focuses on Purcell's central role in the General Strike and the challenge to conventional narratives of the strike which this perspective suggests.

Sandwiched in between is an extended discussion of the international commitments through which Purcell emerged for a time as a key actor in the relationship between Bolshevism and the British left. In these chapters especially, the discussion broadens beyond the particular case of Purcell to consider the wider political choices which he faced and the tensions and sometimes open conflict to which these gave rise. Eric Hobsbawm commented that it would be more interesting for researchers to investigate the positive appeal of 'working-class operational internationalism' than to demonstrate once again its obvious limitations.[37] A study of Purcell allows us to do the first without losing sight of the second.

Following the discussion of the roots of Purcell's labour internationalism in earlier chapters, his participation in the Labour and TUC delegations to Russia in 1920 and 1924 is revisited in its wider labour movement context in chapter three. Chapters four and five then provide comparative context. The first describes the frustrations of the American anarchist Emma Goldman as she sought to dispel the 'Russian superstition' of the British left during her time in

Britain in 1924-6. The second examines the competing future vision of Americanism, and asks why this proved so much less attractive to Purcell and the contemporary British left than it did to their counterparts in some other European countries. In each chapter Purcell is approached as the Webbs were, as the organising principle of the study and not its sole point of focus. The greater predilection of the British labour activist for a broadly pro-Soviet and anti-American conception of the good society is explicable only on the basis of its wider cultural and political frame of reference, which the account provided here seeks to illuminate from its particular perspective.

The final chapter marks Purcell's passing from the national scene. Purcell resembles Lansbury or Mann in carrying forward a spirit of latitudarianism into the tighter confines of an age of party. But whereas both of these eventually found a final political resting place, one in the Labour Party and one as a communist, Purcell spent the last years of his life in the backwaters of the Manchester and Salford Trades Council. In a history of competing partisan traditions, projected and mythologised through Lansbury and Mann by the time of their deaths in 1940-1, this may help explain the very different purchase these figures have had on the collective memory of the left. Perhaps Purcell's return to obscurity also represents the displacement at last of the agitator, whose role he had sought but ultimately failed to reconcile with that of administrator. If so, it was according to a more uneven and extended process than established conventions allow. It would be too much to view Purcell's passing from the national scene as marking an era in trade-union politics. Nevertheless, whether in respect of Bolshevism, Americanism or the role of the unions in Britain itself, a clear change of direction was epitomised by the ascendancy within the TUC from 1926 of its new secretary Walter Citrine. It is with this note of only seeming resolution that the account here closes.

First, however, it is necessary to turn to Purcell's early years as a union activist and to his union, the National Amalgamated Furnishing Trades Association or NAFTA. NAFTA, as we shall see, was only a fraction of the size of the unions' big battalions. Nevertheless, in the shape of Purcell and the TUC's first full-time secretary, Fred Bramley, it provided the two most important British initiators of the extraordinary endeavour in the mid-1920s to establish Anglo-Russian trade-union unity. Both Purcell and Bramley were of that generation that saw the world as if anew through the new social gospel of socialism. Not only did the established organisations of the working class seem the obvious vehicle for this movement of social reckoning and emancipation. For the working-class activist, deprived of resources of time and income, the emergence of a new class of union officers would have seemed not an impediment to the role of agitator but a possible means of pursuing it. Not only were there parallels in this respect with Lansbury's timber-yards or Mann's subvention from Moscow;[38]

it was also true that what for the time being were often relatively weak bureaucratic command structures allowed socialist-inclined union officers a degree of independent initiative which should not be underestimated. A whole cohort of such figures deserves rescuing from neglect, and an individual study of this type may be taken as a sort of instalment.

In their *History of Trade Unionism* in 1894, the Webbs cited the characterisation of the new breed of union organiser by the ILP socialist Katherine Bruce Glasier. 'He has his offices, but he is generally conspicuous there for his absence', Glasier wrote:

> Walter Crane's 'Triumph of Labour' hangs on the wall, and copies of *The Fabian Essays*, and the greater proportion of the tracts issues by the Manchester or Glasgow Labour Presses lie scattered over the room ... John Stuart Mill's *Political Economy*, side by side with a *Student's Marx* give proof of a laudable determination to go to the roots of the matter ... But the call to action is never-ceasing, and train-travelling ... affords but little opportunity for serious reading. 'The daily newspapers are constantly filled with lies, which one ought to know how to refute', and the situation all over the globe 'may develop at any moment'.[39]

In Purcell's office, which for many years was in his home, the *Student's Marx* was better thumbed than Mill, and the pamphlets were mostly not Fabian ones. Nevertheless, his early career exemplified this social type, and his later career represented its attempted transferral to the national stage. It is with the Triumph of Labour to guide us that we must begin.

NOTES

1. *Sunday Worker*, 21 March 1926. The paper's readers were asked to choose from twenty names, those receiving fewer votes being Ernest Bevin, Margaret Bondfield, John Bromley, J.R. Clynes, William Gallacher, Arthur Henderson, George Hicks, James Maxton, A.B. Swales and Ellen Wilkinson.
2. Gloucestershire Record Office D37/1/583, Maynard Colchester-Wemyss to Rama VI, n.d. but July 1925.
3. *Daily Herald*, 27 November 1924.
4. David Proudfoot to Allen Hutt, 20 July 1925 in Ian MacDougall, ed., *Militant Miners*, Edinburgh: Polygon, 1981, p. 225.
5. See for example Paul Foot, *An Agitator of the Worst Type*, Socialist Workers Party, 1986. A more complex picture is presented in Paul Davies, *A.J. Cook*, Manchester: MUP, 1987.
6. Trotsky, *My Life. An attempt at an autobiography*, Harmondsworth: Penguin edn, 1975, pp. 549-50.
7. Samuel, *The Lost World of British Communism*, Verso, 2006.
8. *Bolshevism and the British Left*, I, p. 12.

9. Ken Coates and Tony Topham, *The Making of the Labour Movement. The formation of the Transport and General Workers' Union, 1870-1922*, Nottingham: Spokesman, 1994; Hew Reid, *The Furniture Makers. A history of trade unionism in the furniture trade 1865-1972*, Oxford: Malthouse Press, 1986.
10. The most recent and extensively researched example is Nina Fishman, *Arthur Horner: a political biography*, Lawrence & Wishart, 2 vols, 2010. To a more limited extent, the same may be said of trade unionism on the railways, e.g. David Howell, *Respectable Radicals. Studies in the politics of railway trade unionism*, Aldershot: Ashgate, 1999, chs 5 and 7.
11. Robert Keith Middlemass, *The Clydesiders. A left wing struggle for parliamentary power*, Hutchinsons, 1965, p. 16.
12. Keith Middlemas and John Barnes, *Baldwin. A biography*, Weidenfeld & Nicolson, 1969.
13. Sidney and Beatrice Webb, *The Consumers' Co-operative Movement*, Longmans, 1921, pp. 379-80.
14. Hugh Armstrong Clegg, *A History of British Trade Unions Since 1889. Volume 2: 1911-1933*, Oxford: OUP, 1987 edn, pp. 572-81.
15. S. Higenbottam, *Our Society's History*, Manchester: Amalgamated Society of Woodworkers, 1939, pp. 298-308. This example is chosen in the absence of any official history of Purcell's own union.
16. Zygmunt Bauman, trans. Sheila Patterson, *Between Class and Elite. The evolution of the British Labour movement: a sociological study*, Manchester: MUP, 1972.
17. Clegg, *History*, p. 577.
18. Bauman, *Between Class and Elite*, pp. 192-204.
19. Mary Agnes Hamilton, *Arthur Henderson. A biography*, Heinemann, 1938, p. viii; Chris Wrigley, *Arthur Henderson*, Cardiff: GPC Books, 1990, pp. 204-5; McKibbin, 'Arthur Henderson as Labour leader' in idem, *The Ideologies of Class. Social relations in Britain 1880-1950*, Oxford: OUP, 1991, pp. 42-65.
20. Andrew Thorpe, 'Nina Fishman's *Arthur Horner* and labour and political biography', *Socialist History*, 38, 2011, p. 77.
21. See for example John E. Kelly, *Ethical Socialism and the Trade Unions: Allan Flanders and British industrial relations reform*, Routledge, 2010; Peter Ackers, 'More Marxism than Methodism: Hugh Clegg at Kingswood School, Bath (1932-39)', *Socialist History*, 38, 2011, pp. 23-46. A full biography of Clegg by Ackers in in preparation. For details of the other biographies, see *Bolshevism and the British Left*, II.
22. Notable exceptions include large-scale studies of two of Bevin's successors as general secretary of the TGWU: V.L. Allen, *Trade Union Leadership: based on a study of Arthur Deakin*, Longmans, Green & Co, 1957; Geoffrey Goodman, *The Awkward Warrior: Frank Cousins, his life and times*, Davis-Poynter, 1979. For a wider discussion see Kevin Morgan, '"Colourless, dry and dull": why British trade unionists lack biographers and what (if anything) should be done about it', *Journal for the History of Social Movements/Zeitschrift für die Geschichte sozialer Bewegungen*, 2013.
23. P. Kropotkin, *Memoirs of a Revolutionist* (1899), New York: Dover edn, 1971, p. v and passim.

24. Dona Torr, *Tom Mann and his Times. Volume one: 1856-1890*, Lawrence & Wishart, 1956; Chushichi Tsuzuki, *Tom Mann, 1856-1941. The challenges of Labour*, Oxford: OUP, 1991.
25. I.J. Prothero, *Artisans and Politics in Early Nineteenth-Century London: John Gast and his times*, Folkestone: Dawson, 1979, p. 4 and passim.
26. RGASPI 495/100/96, typescript report (by Borodin?) on work of RILU British Bureau, n.d., c. mid-1923.
27. Philip Williamson, *Stanley Baldwin. Conservative Leadership and National Values*, Cambridge: CUP, 1999, pp. 14-15.
28. I.J. Prothero, *Artisans and Politics in early Nineteenth-Century London: John Gast and his times*, Folkestone: Dawson, 1979, p. 4 and passim.
29. See for example Logie Barrow and Ian Bullock, *Democratic Ideas and the British Labour Movement 1880-1914*, Cambridge: CUP, 1996; Ben Jackson, *Equality and the British Left. A study in progressive thought 1900-64*, Manchester: MUP, 2007.
30. See for example Jonathan Zeitlin, '"Rank and filism" in British labour history: a critique', *International Review of Social History*, 34, 1989, pp. 54-8; Richard Price, '"What's in a name?" Workplace history and "rank and filism"', ibid, pp. 72-3; Zeitlin, '"Rank and filism" and labour history: a rejoinder to Price and Cronin', ibid, pp. 95-8.
31. Bauman, *Between Class and Elite*, p. 201.
32. For a discussion of the former see Ralph Darlington, 'British syndicalism and trade union officialdom', *Historical Studies in Industrial Relations*, 25/26, 2008; for an example of the latter, James E. Cronin, 'Coping with Labour, 1918-1926' in James E. Cronin and Jonathan Schneer, eds, *Social Conflict and the Political Order in Modern Britain*, Croom Helm, 1982, e.g. pp. 114-15, 128.
33. Roy Church and Quentin Outram, *Strikes and Solidarity. Coalfield conflict in Britain 1889-1996*, Cambridge: CUP, 1998, pp. 70 ff.
34. See for example the somewhat cursory and impressionistic discussion of this aspect in Church and Outram, *Strikes and Solidarity*.
35. See discussion in *Bolshevism and the British Left*, I, p. 14.
36. John Kelly and Edmund Heery, *Working for the Union: British trade union officers*, Cambridge: CUP, 1994, ch. 2.
37. Eric Hobsbawm, 'Working-class internationalism' in Fritz van Holthoon and Marcel van der Linden, eds, *Internationalism in the Labour Movement 1830-1940*, Leiden: Brill, 1988, vol. 1, p. 9.
38. For which see *Bolshevism and the British Left*, I.
39. Sidney and Beatrice Webb, *The History of Trade Unionism*, Longmans, Green & Co, 1896 edn, pp. 463-4.

Chapter one

Syndicalism, internationalism and the furnishing trades

1.1 SYNDICALISTS WITHOUT SYNDICALISM?

In the spring of 1924, Alf Purcell was entering into the period of his fame and notoriety. The previous December, aged fifty-one, he had been returned to parliament in the election that produced the first Labour government. When Ramsay MacDonald included the trade unionist Margaret Bondfield in his administration, it was Purcell who succeeded her as TUC chairman. He also took over the IFTU responsibilities of another of MacDonald's appointees, J.H. Thomas, and at its Vienna congress in June was confirmed as IFTU's president. MacDonald's preferment of such moderate figures had thus created unanticipated openings for the left. Differences between the Labour Party and TUC leaderships were sharply accentuated, and by the end of the year TUC radicals like Purcell were enjoying a temporary ascendancy.

Beatrice Webb referred to them as 'Communist trade union leaders'.[1] They are difficult to place more precisely than that. This was epitomised by a *Labour Monthly* symposium, 'Towards a new policy', to which several of these figures contributed in the early months of 1924. Best known of them was A.J. Cook, who in replacing Frank Hodges as secretary of the Mineworkers' Federation was another unintended beneficiary of MacDonald's ministerial appointments. Other contributors included the Transport Workers' secretary Robert Williams, who had been among Purcell's companions on Labour's 1920 Russian delegation; the Locomen's secretary John Bromley, who travelled with him in 1924; and the Builders' secretary George Hicks, who made the Russian trip in 1925 and who in this period was Purcell's closest political ally. Their formulation of a 'new policy' was faltering at best, and in Purcell's case openly disregardful of matters of practical detail. Those 'desperately anxious' for a new policy, he said, were welcome to get on with it. Purcell, however, preferred what he called the old and trusted maxim of the militant activist: that of 'preaching, urging, quietly, noisily, in season and out, undiluted working-class solidarity'.[2] It was the nearest that he ever came to a statement of his political philosophy. No wonder that Palme Dutt, the journal's editor, referred to it as a general genial fuzz and despaired of what he saw as a manifest incapacity for political leadership.[3]

One word to describe this outlook is syndicalism. Usually syndicalism is discussed as a movement or relatively well-defined tendency within the labour movement. Studies of syndicalism are typically of the 'narrative-institutional' type, Marcel van der Linden notes, and as a movement it has been identified internationally with particular organisations or agitations whose ebb and flow provide it with a sort of corporate chronology.[4] Understood in this way, as a discrete form of allegiance and identity, syndicalism could be no more than a phase in the life of its activists. Within Dutt's symposium, Williams grouped it with a succession of socialist panaceas that had had their day and disappeared.[5] Purcell's response was that any 'good-looking peg' was of value if it was 'momentarily strong enough to hang your young or old advocacy upon'.[6] Even so, syndicalism in its formal sense was by 1924 just such a discarded peg, and its adepts could now be found gravitating to Bolshevism, reformism, even fascism, or lapsing into relative inactivity. In Dutt's symposium it was referred to only in the past tense.

On the other hand, syndicalism can also be thought of as a 'mood', an attitude, a mentality: one never successfully defined in any prescriptive way and consequently colouring quite disparate affiliations and career trajectories. This too was a common contemporary usage. Journalists for a time unearthed a syndicalist in every strike; communists later used the term as a pejorative connoting 'economism'. Historians attempting a more exacting typology will necessarily reject such colloquialisms. In the British case, however, even van der Linden and Thorpe, in their tabulation of what were otherwise broadly syndicalist organisations, have nothing to fall back on but the unsatisfactory surrogate of the 'labour unrest'.[7] If 'unrest' sounds more like a mood than a movement, this does not have to imply the 'psychological' explanation for the phenomenon to which Richard Price has rightly taken exception.[8] Rather, it can be located within Price's own notion of a 'longer term tradition of a proletarian public discourse in the public sphere', of which syndicalism was but one variant, in a particular phase of labour history.[9] Wrestling with the same conundrum, Bob Holton used the notion of 'proto-syndicalism' to capture the idea of '"ordinary" workers ... tending through their behaviour towards a syndicalist perspective'.[10]

'Ordinary' workers were by no means inarticulate, even if their opinions are not usually documented. There need therefore be no confusion here with the syndicalist shibboleth of 'spontaneity': in tending to syndicalism in their behaviour, 'ordinary' workers certainly had recourse to notions of social justice, independence and self-representation, but in ways that often were not otherwise recorded than through their behaviour. As a full-time official conversant in syndicalist terminology, Purcell can hardly be thought of as a proto-syndicalist of this type. Nevertheless, a similar issue is posed of how one should distinguish between the avowed syndicalism he briefly espoused and the implicit perspective to which his extensive non-syndicalist activities tended. In practice these issues of definition meant little to activists of Purcell's type. Nevertheless, the qualifier 'syndicalistic' is employed here to connote ideas and practices deriving from, or expressed through, the culture of syndicalism, but without satisfactorily attaining the discrete coherence that a full-fledged ism might imply.

This does not mean that syndicalism, any more than Fabianism, simply vanishes under the logic of permeation. In Purcell's case, one can identify its distinct and formative impact, and the construction of his whole future political identity in some sense depended upon it. There was, even so, no way of joining or leaving the syndicalist movement, no subscription fee or test of commitment, no requirement to abandon old associations or to forego the establishment of new ones. Britain's one important syndicalist body was the Industrial Syndicalist Education League (ISEL), to whose initiation Purcell contributed significantly. Nevertheless, even this lacked any real organisation or leadership structure, and it disintegrated when it sought to establish one.[11] To paraphrase Eric Hobsbawm's well-known essay on the 1970s, Britain in this earlier period offers the spectacle of syndicalists without syndicalism: a cadre of activists espousing syndicalistic precepts, but without establishing, or for the most part seeking to establish, a significant organisational identity.[12] Elusive and yet ubiquitous, the movement was 'mostly not institutionalized' nor even embodied in a durable programme or periodical.[13] *Faute de mieux*, its chronology has frequently been derived from the movements of a single individual, Tom Mann.

This did not signify depreciation of organisation per se. If syndicalism in Britain took no separate institutional form, it was because institutions already existed which seemed to offer a surer route to syndicalist goals, and to a degree had helped to stimulate them.[14] Even the syndicalist theorist Georges Sorel, not an anglophile, had in earlier writings offered a vision of the *syndicats* as a form of self-government influenced by the example of the British unions.[15] He did not however retain this rosy view, and syndicalism meant nothing if not at very least the unions' transformation. On the other hand, from the 'New Unionism' emerging in 1889 to the reviving militancy of the pre-1914 period, there were not lacking signs that just such a transformation might be underway. For British syndicalists, as later for the communists, the unions therefore continued to provide a vehicle for struggle and emancipation to which activists remained deeply and almost unconditionally committed, and which structured their roles, commitments and priorities. Within US syndicalism there was also a minority 'boring from within' tendency influenced by European examples.[16] In Sorel's France, the *Confédération générale du travail* (CGT), though formally committed to revolutionary syndicalist goals, combined these with immediate trade-union functions and the incorporating pressures of a bureaucratic career structure.[17] Only in Britain, however, did the method of working through unions of no revolutionary pretensions command such general support among the majority of professed syndicalists.

In what then, if not mere militancy of behaviour, did the specificity of syndicalism lie? Discussing the CGT's drift into reformism, Barbara Mitchell salvages continuity through a minimalist definition of its objects as those of improving conditions, raising consciousness and maintaining organisation.[18] This is very much *le trade unionisme* done into French, at the expense of syndicalism's distinct significance. Far more helpful is Van der Linden and Thorpe's specification of attributes of class war and direct action as well as union organisation. In Britain, the latter in particular – 'Direct Action, or Syndicalism as it has come to be known' – was seen as synonymous with the new movement.[19] Repeatedly Mann linked Direct Action and Industrial Solidarity as syndicalism's watchwords, and described as its mission the demonstration to the workers of the 'full meaning of their organic tendency to Industrial Solidarity' on both a national and an international scale.[20]

The Direct Action formula nevertheless concealed potential ambiguities. According to the French syndicalist Emile Pouget, it meant 'the putting into operation, directly, without intermediaries, without intervention from outside, of the strength which lies within the working class'.[21] In France this clearly meant reliance on syndicalism's own organisations. In Britain, however, it signified working through the established unions and the affirmation of an encompassing trade-union identity as the key to social emancipation. For Purcell, the grounding in a particular trade environment provided the foundation for a wider career embracing these intermediary roles but with a syndicalistic sense of having appropriated them.

This persistence of a form of proletarian discourse was not without its incongruities. In Dutt's symposium Purcell observed how: 'Thirty-four years continuous membership of the Union in a trade gathers within its four corners the experiences of quite a mass of "new" and "forward" policies.' As if this later comment were its half-remembered echo, at his first international socialist congress in 1896 Purcell had heard the Lib-Lab Yorkshire Miners' president Ned Cowey salute 'the emancipation of the working class' as one who had 'been a trade unionist for thirty-five years ... but whilst .. a trade unionist ... have never yet closed my mind to the views of other progressive people who have the same object in view'.[22] Between Cowey and Purcell there were dramatic discontinuities, but equally there were the elements of a shared trade-union identity. It was in any case through his thirty-four years in a union barely twenty thousand strong that Purcell came to speak for a movement numbering millions, both nationally and internationally.

1.2 SOCIALIST AND SYNDICALIST

Where institutions are weak, the role of personality is accentuated. From such sweeping generalisations many exceptions must be made; syndicalism in its British variant is not one of them. In labour history and folklore, the movement is not only inseparable from the figure of Tom Mann, but frequently dated with precision from Mann's return from eight-and-a-half years in Australasia in the spring of 1910.[23] Australia, Mann explained, had persuaded him of the inadequacy of party-political ambitions as realised in its pioneering Labour governments.[24] A visit to Paris shortly after his return provided the more positive example of the CGT. Within weeks Mann had launched the monthly *Industrial Syndicalist*, and by the end of 1910 he was presiding over the foundation of the ISEL. Further frenetic agitation culminated in his playing a leading role in the transport workers' strikes the following summer, and directing a 'quasi-general strike' in Liverpool.[25] G.D.H. Cole insisted that timing, not personality, was the key to the impact that he made. Even Cole, however, conceded that Mann was the 'spark' that 'set the train alight'.[26] In signal contrast with other fields of union history, Mann has as many biographers as British syndicalism has historians. One of them describes his arrival in London as marking the end of the movement's 'pre-history'.[27]

Some of his collaborators were already familiar with these ideas. John Turner, the anarchist Shop Assistants' official with whom Purcell later travelled to Russia, had thus in 1907 launched the short-lived *Voice of Labour* to promote the same cause of Direct Action. Purcell, on the other hand, was one of those on whom Mann had a more dramatic impact. 'What you taught me to say then I am saying out here', he wrote to Mann from India some eighteen years later, recalling their first shared platform in the summer of Mann's return.[28] By 1910 Purcell was already a socialist of twenty years standing and a figure well known in the Manchester region. Nevertheless, it is only after Mann's appearance there that his hitherto conventional understanding of social democracy gave way to the syndicalistic mindset that in some sense he then retained through all his subsequent vicissitudes.

Of Irish extraction, Purcell had been born in Hoxton, London on 3 November 1872.[29] His family had moved for a time to Keighley and he began work as a half-timer in a woollen mill before taking up his father's trade as a French polisher. Once more in London, he worked for a time in the piano trade, whose seasonal patterns of work were to leave a lasting mark on his views of work and employment issues.[30]

A trade unionist from 1891, Purcell progressed rapidly through the offices of treasurer, president and finally general secretary of the London French Polishers, which in 1898 was amalgamated into the Amalgamated Society of French Polishers. In 1900 he moved with the union to Manchester, still as general secretary, and with brief interruptions he remained there for the rest of his life. Three years earlier he had married Sarah Fidler, a domestic servant and the daughter of an Edmonton engine driver.[31] It was a typical trade-union marriage in this respect, that almost nothing was heard of Sarah until a widow's fund was established after her husband's death.

Purcell's formative years in London left a lasting mark. Keighley was one of the early Yorkshire strongholds of independent labour organisation, even predating the ILP's establishment nationally.[32] In such an environment there is no knowing how Purcell's commitments might have been influenced by an ethical socialist or radical liberal tradition. Even in London he was briefly attached to the temperance movement, regarding whose precepts he was notably relaxed in later life. More suggestive of his later persona was the budding prizefighter: one associate recalled that he had been 'a six-round performer in boxing rings for a purse of 7/6', another that as a combative trade unionist he remained 'as ready with his fists as with his tongue'.[33] More consequentially, Purcell was drawn into the marxist circles that had one of their strongest bases in the capital. According to the dockers' leader Ben Tillett, he was a convert 'to the Movement' in 1888, and 'as a lad ... was a propagandist in the roughest school of rebels in Hoxton'.[34] In 1893, aged just twenty, he became involved in propaganda work for the Legal Eight Hours and International Labour League, of which Eleanor Marx and Edward Aveling were among the leading lights. It was an issue to which he would return throughout his career, and it was by the criteria of its working hours that he later acclaimed Soviet labour standards as the world's most advanced.[35] Also while in London, Purcell had his first experience of elected public office, as a Shoreditch borough councillor; and in 1895 or 1896 he took the fateful step of joining the Social Democratic Federation (SDF).

At the same early date he had his first exposure to the movement at an international level. In July 1896, the third of the international congresses convened by the Second International was held over five days in London. Almost two-thirds of the 746 delegates were British; of these over half were from London, among them the twenty-three year old delegate of the French Polishers' society. Like most of his compatriots, Purcell made no intervention in the proceedings. He did, however, share a Hyde Park platform with Bernard Shaw, Marx's son-in-law Paul Lafargue and the Dutch socialist P.J. Troelstra. It was a typically British occasion: sunshine gave way to heavy rain, banners were redeployed as improvised tents, and as the park took on the appearance of a boating lake Purcell had his moment centre-stage with scarcely a soul to witness it.[36]

The congress itself was a salutary initiation into the challenges of internationalism. Four sittings were devoted to disputes over credentials; the Germans wanted discipline, the French formed into two delegations and the anarchists at one point sought to mount the platform. Cowey, who understood neither continental theories nor any other language than English (and that, H.M. Hyndman added meanly, 'no more than imperfectly') threatened to call in the police.[37] Vainly Mann and Keir Hardie, both then representing the ILP, put the case for tolerance, even of anarchists, and for a 'many-sided' movement united by its common aims. 'Any shade of opinion can come under the head of trade unionism', Mann insisted. 'How shall we draw a line without being inconsistent? ... We are all striving for the same ideal, and ... we should not dispute about method'.[38] Hyndman, by contrast, led the SDF delegates in supporting the dominant view that opponents of political action should be ejected. MacDonald was among twenty-six ILPers who shared that view and circulated a note of 'emphatic protest' at the position of Hardie and Mann.[39] Purcell represented his union, not the SDF, and we do not know how he voted. It was nevertheless the Hardie-Mann minority position to which he would consistently adhere in his own later international activities.[40]

For the time being, he remained a relatively orthodox follower of Hyndman's adaptation of continental social democracy. According to Joe Toole, later a Labour MP, Purcell's arrival in Salford in 1900 had brought a 'ray of hope' to the local SDF after years of uphill struggle. 'A man of fine physique, a first-class speaker, and possessed of a good knowledge of working-class life, he threw himself into our propaganda work and rallied thousands to our standard.'[41] Purcell was soon active on the trades council; and at his third attempt was returned as city councillor for the St Paul's ward in Pendleton in 1906. His record as councillor was said to be not 'shy or retiring' and Toole described him as a force in municipal life.[42] If there was anything distinctive in this environment, it was its impatience with factional dividing lines. In 1901 it was agreed that the ILP should organise in West Salford and the SDF in the neighbouring South Salford division, and when the Irish marxist James Connolly paid a successful propaganda visit the expenses were shared between the two.[43] Active in the West Salford ILP, Purcell remained a member of both parties, and according to one obituary was 'mainly instrumental' in effecting an understanding between them.[44]

For many of the region's activists, commitment to socialist unity went with a growing disillusionment in the Labour Party. Purcell himself was originally adopted as a Labour parliamentary candidate for West Salford but in mid-1909 he withdrew from the nomination and in the following January's general election stood on behalf of the 'West Salford Socialist Representation Committee'. Supporting him morally though not financially was what was now the Social Democratic Party (SDP).[45] Assisted by SDP speakers like Hyndman and the Countess of Warwick, Purcell gave no hint of syndicalism or workers' control in his address. Instead, he propounded a vigorous state collectivism directed, not yet at industrial servitude, but at the poverty on which Fabian campaigning had so successfully focused radical energies.[46] His leading slogan, 'Political Action is but the Means, Abolition of Poverty the Objective', might have been approved by the Webbs themselves. Demanding state maintenance of children, co-operative organisation of the unemployed and a 'wholesome transition to a better social organisation', Purcell rejected contributory state insurance schemes, as the Webbs did, and supported nationalisation of the land in the interests of rural employment and self-sufficiency in food.[47] Dismissing the issue of the House of Lords over which the election had been called, he apparently took votes from both the Liberals and Tories, though without threatening to overtake either.[48] Undaunted by his defeat, he helped sponsor a 'Provisional Committee for the Promotion of Common Action among Socialists' that aimed to establish similar 'socialist representation committees' (SRCs).[49] Though he lacked the financial means to fight the second election that ensued that year, he had indicated his intention of standing and he did proceed to a second term as councillor.[50] Purcell's initial encounter with Mann had not, therefore, entailed the immediate displacement of other associations.

Even so, he needed only a spark to set him alight. For the union officer with little faith in the Labour alliance, syndicalism provided a reconciliation of industrial agency and socialist object which Hyndman at least had never even attempted. When Mann spoke at the Free Trade Hall, Purcell was in the chair and moved a very mild resolution regarding the meeting's object of increased representation on boards of guardians. Mann, who followed on the subject of 'Socialism, political action, industrial activism', simply swept aside such pettifogging electoral preoccupations:

> Parliament was not made by the workers for the workers, but by the workers' enemies to control the workers. It was a machine that had always been in the hands of the ruling classes, and it was as completely in those hands now as it had ever been. The agency to which he looked with the greatest hope was industrial organisation.[51]

It was this meeting that Purcell remembered long afterwards as 'the best thing I was ever associated with'.[52] Indeed, shortly after the meeting he moved that Mann be invited to address the local trades council on industrial unionism.[53]

Even Mann did not resign from the SDP until the following May.

Purcell, meanwhile, honoured an existing commitment to address another Free Trade Hall meeting alongside Hyndman. 'Officially representing the Social-Democratic Party', Hyndman recorded, 'Purcell and I formally stated … that we are ready now, as we have always been, to sink minor differences in a strenuous effort to bring about a united Socialist Party….' These minor differences, however, included Hyndman's open distaste for the SRCs, and his dismissal of the unions as 'merely sentient automata' and an 'unconscious element' barely comprehending the meaning of their own actions. In seeking to channel the desire for unity through the pre-eminent institution of the party, Hyndman was aptly enough supported by the future CPGB secretary Albert Inkpin.[54] It was an entirely different perspective from Mann's, and by the end of the year Purcell had publicly cast in his lot with the latter.

If Mann was the spark, that meant nothing without tinder. In setting up the *Industrial Syndicalist* he could hardly have managed without the support of Guy Bowman, link to the CGT and manager of the SDP's Twentieth Century Press.[55] In promoting the idea of a National Transport Workers' Federation, Tillett's support was similarly indispensable.[56] Though at first a largely paper exercise, the ISEL also relied on existing networks of contacts, of which in this instance Purcell was at the centre. Initially the league's founding conference was to have been held in London. However, Purcell and some 'Lancashire comrades' pushed Manchester's stronger claims and rescheduled the event to a Saturday afternoon to allow a genuine industrial representation. Labour bodies within twenty miles were circulated details, and provided over three-quarters of the nearly two hundred delegates at what was almost entirely an affair of the English north and midlands.[57] Though now on an industrial basis, it thus revived the spirit of Mann's involvement with the ILP in the years of its initial revolt against the metropolitan bias of parliamentary radicalism. In 1912 or 1913, Mann himself removed to Manchester, as if in symbolic reversal of the relocation to the capital of his former party.[58]

Convenor of the ISEL conference was Arthur Stewart, about whom little is apparently known except his garden suburb address and lack of an industrial affiliation. Purcell took the chair and 'as a trade unionist, and one who knew much about Trade Unionism' argued that their energies had contracted by depending so much upon political action:

> He looked upon Industrial Unionism as a movement which was far more important than the political Labour movement. The Industrial Workers themselves were the propelling force that would impel politics to be what they desired them to be. … If the principles which many of them held dear with regard to the Class War meant anything at all, they meant that the workers were to emancipate themselves.[59]

The following weekend Purcell was still advertised as speaking on the hoarier topic of 'Socialism or tariff reform'.[60] That very month he was re-elected as a local councillor, and he was 'heartily cheered' when he outlined the programme on which he intended standing again for parliament.[61] It is not clear that he ever actually left the SDP, and when he attended the CPGB's founding congress a decade later it was as one of the South Salford delegates from its successor the British Socialist Party (BSP). Nevertheless, the vision which henceforth moved him was that of the workers themselves 'impelling politics' in the spirit and interest of their own emancipation. The workers themselves meant the unions, and Purcell did not again seek re-election as a councillor.[62] The basis of his theory and practice alike was his position as an organiser for the Furnishing Trades.

1.3 'LET ALL ELSE GO HANG': SYNDICALISM AND THE FURNISHING TRADES

This in itself was a source of ambiguity. At the heart of much syndicalist rhetoric was a searing critique of officialdom, classically expounded in the Rhondda militants' manifesto of 1912, *The Miners' Next Step*. Here union leaders were depicted as an autocratic grouping whose function was to 'keep the men in order' for the benefit of employer, consumer and 'public'. Presented as a 'scheme for the reorganisation of the [Miners'] Federation', *The Miners' Next Step* therefore urged the subjection of these officers to 'free and rapid control by the rank and file', and the prevention of their hardening into a caste by restrictions on tenure in office.[63] The miners' unions had distinctively oligarchical features which helped provoke such a reaction. Nevertheless, the critique of bureaucracy was voiced wherever syndicalism had an influence. According to the metalworker J.T. Murphy, a transitional figure between syndicalism and communism, syndicalism itself as a movement represented 'a repudiation of leadership'.[64]

Like almost everything in syndicalism, these ideas can be located within a longer tradition, partly originating in Engels and afterwards continued in a marxist-leaning academic literature.[65] Reviewing this literature, John Kelly notes that it offers explanation for leadership conservatism at rather different levels of sophistication.[66] Probably the commonest theme in contemporary critique was the transformation of social location through bureaucratic advancement. In the words of a characteristic assessment from the shop stewards' movement, the salaries paid such officials enabled them to 'live in a social strata far above the working class' and become 'more Bourgeois than the Bourgeoise themselves'. A second line of argument, found in the same document, stressed differences of work environment and function: through the 'constant intercourse with the employers and the extra work and worry involved in conducting trade disputes' officials developed an innately 'conservative' state of mind.[67]

Closer to Purcell's own immediate field of activities, Price's work on the building industry depicted syndicalism very much in these terms, as a rank-and-file response to the incorporation of a 'bureaucratic, professional elite' within an increasingly insulated system of industrial bargaining. Syndicalism was not, Price argued, just another stage of 'simple union militancy'; its 'central benchmark' was the revolt against union institutions and procedures, among which Price instances the appointment of full-time union organisers in the 1890s and early 1900s.[68] While this clearly takes us further than the emphasis on immediate social relations, Kelly observes that such an analysis leaves the phenomenon of the militant trade-union leader unexplained.[69]

According to the Webbs' figures, there was a quintupling in the number of full-time officers between 1892 and 1920.[70] Was syndicalism really just a reaction against such figures? Or was it not in part also the expression of a radical element among them, or at least a formative phase through which they passed? Precisely in the period identified by Price, a cohort of full-timers can be identified who were clearly influenced by syndicalism and yet spent longer or shorter periods on a union payroll. As well as Mann and Purcell, Richard Coppock, James Larkin and Noah Ablett are other prominent names recorded at Britain's first syndicalist conference in 1910, and they all either then or later held significant full-time positions of responsibility. How extensive this cohort was is a question unanswerable on the basis of our present knowledge. Often the strike wave of the 1910s is depicted as a revolt against this leadership stratum in the form of 'aggressive worker activity'.[71] However, it is an empirical phenomenon at the very least worthy of further reflection that the aggressiveness and the leadership stratum had to a very marked extent developed together.

If syndicalism is regarded as a repudiation of leadership, then leadership in turn might be seen as a repudiation of syndicalism and the acceptance of such positions as the evidence of syndicalism's decline or degeneration.[72] On the other hand, possible foundations for this development are clearly discernible within syndicalism itself. Within its repertoire of argument there were two distinct conceptions of leadership which even the same individual might draw upon according to circumstance. According to Murphy or *The Miners' Next Step*, the assumption of a directive role by the few implied for the many a state of passivity calling to mind a shepherd's flock, a football crowd or 'pliable goods, to be moulded and formed'.[73] There was, however, another strain within syndicalism that drew directly on the elitist tenets that in this period were so pervasive in European culture. Almost simultaneously with *The Miners' Next Step*, the US labour agitator W.Z. Foster published an account of syndicalist precepts that posited the emergence in every society of a certain few 'directing forces' of superior intellect, energy or organising ability. The labour movement, according to Foster, was especially conducive to such minorities, of which the syndicalists were the most effective and ultimately irresistible.[74] The previous year the sometime syndicalist Michels had formulated his 'iron law of oligarchies', while the current syndicalist publicist Emma Goldman issued a manifesto for 'Minorities versus majorities' that was not for the democratically squeamish.[75] British trade-union activists were rarely so outspoken.[76] Nevertheless, in syndicalism, as in almost every variant of left-wing politics, democratic impulses coexisted with the ready assumption of leadership roles. Syndicalist responses to the concentration of state and capital included not just 'localist autonomy', as is sometimes suggested, but a countervailing centralisation of authority within the 'army' of labour.[77] The role of existing elites was similarly countered by the projection of alternative leaders or leadership structures, with the sorts of tensions and inconsistencies that were so evident in the early communist movement.[78] As militants sought at once to harness and transform the unions, the plasticity of these concepts is easily comprehensible.

The unions themselves represented an extraordinary diversity of cultures and traditions. As these are ironed and folded into the analytical drawer of 'labourism', only laziness and prejudice would deny them the differentiation allowed more conventional articulations of individual and group identity. The Furnishing Trades, more particularly, represented a singular mix of craft-based radicalism and industrial unionism leavened by a formidable cadre of activist-organisers variously located within the wider socialist movement. Founded in 1902 as an amalgamation of English and Scottish Cabinetmakers' societies, and subsequently absorbing Purcell's French Polishers, NAFTA itself was a trade-union minnow.[79] It had around 14,000 members at the start of the First World War, and some 22,000 at its end, or about a quarter of the workers in the furnishing trades. In 1924, when the figure had fallen back to 20,000, it was only thirty-fourth in size of the TUC's affiliates, and fourth even in its own sector of the building and woodworking trades. On the other hand, furnishing workers had a long record of continuous organisation, and a tradition of political engagement that was epitomised by the moral-force radical and Chartist William Lovett, a sometime Cabinetmakers' president.

Lovett in his autobiography rightly described his fellows as 'a very respectable body of journeymen'.[80] In the decades after Chartism the trade was nevertheless subject to the several challenges of mechanisation, geographical dispersal and undercutting. NAFTA's immediate parent body, the Alliance Cabinet-Makers' Association (ACMA), consequently represented a more inclusive model of organisation and it almost quadrupled in size during the heyday of 'new unionism' in

1887-91.[81] NAFTA thus had credible ambitions as an industrial union of the furnishing trades, confirmed by later accretions like the French Polishers. At the same time, within so small, dispersed and strategically marginal a trade it was difficult to harbour notions of NAFTA itself as an engine of the social revolution. Within a comparative industrial monoculture like the South Wales coalfield, collective identities, including the syndicalist aspiration to workers' control, were plausibly articulated at an industrial level.[82] Within the furnishing trades, on the other hand, politicisation meant being drawn outwards, to a class-based or at least a pan-industrial perspective. In the spirit of William Lovett, NAFTA produced what for its size was a remarkable group of activists whose political horizons went beyond the union, and whose careers could not ultimately be contained within it.

Three other figures stand out among Purcell's contemporaries. All were cabinet-makers by trade; all had socialist affiliations that did not translate into disciplined party attachments. The oldest of them, born in Cupar, Fife in 1862, was the union's general secretary Alex Gossip. An ILP foundation member, strongly influenced by Keir Hardie, Gossip shared Hardie's fluency in the language of ethical socialism and was a pioneer of the Socialist Sunday School movement. Without any sense of a rupture, he was later a steadfast supporter of communist causes, though never a CPGB member.[83] The union's trade organiser, James O'Grady, was a Bristolian, born in 1866, whom the local predominance of marxian socialism drew towards the SDF, as it did Dan Irving and the young Ernie Bevin. Unusually, O'Grady combined this with membership of the Fabian Society and the Roman Catholic church, doubtless to the enhancement of his reputation for independent-mindedness as NAFTA's sole MP from 1906.[84] With the introduction of parliamentary salaries in 1911, O'Grady made way as trade organiser for the Yorkshireman Fred Bramley.[85] Born in Otley in 1874, Bramley was also active in the ILP and had spent some years as a full-time socialist propagandist with the Clarion Van.[86] On his death in 1925, Bramley was described by one obituarist as a transitional figure between older trade-union values and the 'new world of culture and education' which in this period so often meant socialism.[87] The same might have been said of any of Bramley's NAFTA collaborators.

Purcell found his place within this vibrant milieu with NAFTA's absorption of the French Polishers at the end of 1910. Trade conditions were improving, labour was rediscovering its combativity and the looming 'great unrest' was also felt in the furnishing trades. Gossip, rather like Hardie, welcomed what he called a 'divine discontent', in revolt against the ugly and hateful and yearning after a 'fuller and a freer life'.[88] Even Bramley, always more cautious, described the stirring from below as the condition for the unions' future advance.[89] It was nevertheless Purcell who, as Bramley's fellow trade organiser based in Manchester, consistently urged the unions' responsibility to fan the simmering class war into a 'conscious and well disciplined revolt'.[90]

Though the language he used would have been recognised by any syndicalist, there was no binding syndicalist programme and Purcell's presentation of syndicalist argument was shaped by the specificities of his trade and his particular perspective as a full-time officer. Three particular themes were to persist in some form or other beyond the moment of syndicalism itself. One was that of unity, both at the industrial level and beyond it. A second was a basic defining antagonism to the employers and their state. The third was the indispensable function of trade-union leadership.

Unity, for British syndicalists, was primarily identified with the object of industrial unionism. Ambiguously in this regard, NAFTA combined ambitions as the 'one big union' of the furnishing trades with a persisting craft identity underpinning claims beyond the scope of the furnishing industry itself.[91] Price, in depicting union federation and amalgamation as distinct and competing strategies, identified the former with official interests and the latter with the rank and file.[92] In practice, different officials in different unions had divergent interests, and NAFTA's calls to industrial unity did not preclude recurrent conflict with unions in the construction and transport sectors where it had traditionally organised on a craft basis.[93] Purcell certainly spoke like a true syndicalist in ascribing resistance to amalgamation to 'Union Officialism' and its 'determination to '"govern" and not represent those who elect them'.[94] He was not, however, jeopardising his own position lately secured within the industry's largest union. The French Polishers at the time of amalgamation had fewer than a thousand members and their offices were located in Purcell's own home. One of the provisions of amalgamation was the creation of a second general official based in the north, and for four years at least Purcell himself was guaranteed this position.[95] An official with the most conventional notions of leadership might have seen the case for amalgamation on these terms.

Equally, different positions were possible that cannot always be reduced to bureaucratic self-interest. Within NAFTA, it was Purcell who consistently put the case for amalgamation, with the long-term perspective of a 'huge joint organisation' with a single membership card.[96] In Mann's paper the *Syndicalist*, lately renamed the *Syndicalist and Amalgamation News*, his one substantial contribution was an account of such developments within the Furnishing Trades.[97] It was Bramley, conversely, who tended to speak for NAFTA in the demarcation disputes with the Railwaymen and the Co-operative Employees which persisted until the General Strike and beyond.[98] This was consistent with Bramley's strong personal commitment to a craft or vocational basis of organisation, which he later voiced with considerable eloquence.[99] Though Purcell too used the language of

Syndicalism, internationalism and the furnishing trades

craft, primarily it was as a weapon that could be brandished in the class war.

Unity was an imperative that went beyond amalgamation or even the wider co-ordination of industrial activities. At a time of endemic industrial conflict, the Furnishing Trades union was not well placed for the flexing of industrial muscle. Even protracted disputes offered little prospect of wider social or economic disruption. Given the industry's uneven geographical spread and modest union density, they were usually localised in character and susceptible to the ready availability of blackleg labour. The need to generate a wider solidarity was consequently hardly less than for the mining or transport unions, whose independent capacity for a wider effect was so much greater. In Purcell's earliest union reports there is stress on the need for joint union deputations corresponding to the scope of employers' organisations.[100] For the Furnishing Trades, however, there was no real counterpart to the Triple Alliance type of arrangement established by the principal mining and transport unions in 1913. Indeed, NAFTA did not even secure affiliation to the National Federation of Building Trades Operatives (NFBTO) after its formation in 1918.

In its place, the union placed unusual stress on the organised consumer and forms of community action. One of the earliest and most acrimonious disputes in which Purcell was involved for NAFTA was an action for union recognition at the Accrington billiard table manufacturers E.J. Riley's in 1911. Though of several months' duration, even in Accrington the dispute was instantly overshadowed when the town was brought to a halt by a national transport strike. Solidarity action alone offered any realistic prospect of success, and Purcell in a public lecture drew the moral for the Riley's dispute:

> If railway men would refuse to let 'blacklegs' pass the wicket, if cabmen would refuse to carry 'blacklegs', if people would refuse to house them, and if people would refuse to sell them beer, and if men would refuse to drink in the same 'pub' as 'blacklegs', trade unionists would soon get what they wanted.[101]

The weapon of the boycott would not just extend to imported labour but to the items of domestic consumption in which the furnishing industry specialised. Riley's tables were particularly dependent on the workers' collective patronage, and Purcell conceived of the entire dispute as one of boycott against boycott, of unionised workers by the employers and of non-unionised work by the unions. 'The employer boycotts and persecutes trade unionists, therefore the trade unionist must boycott the employer's goods.'[102] Despite the action's failure, Purcell continued to advocate the boycott as a weapon as powerful as the strike, and sometimes as the only weapon available to the workers.[103]

Purcell's strong commitment to the trades councils as the vehicle of such forms of solidarity is understandable in such a context.[104] He also urged involvement in the co-operative movement, not merely as providing a working-class commissariat, still less because he idealised its working conditions, but as promising the solidarity of the organised consumer. This was his rationale in 1915 for lobbying the annual Co-operative Congress:

> It can make and unmake firms according to the willingness or otherwise to comply with our conditions without the withdrawal of a solitary man from work; it can help pursue the boycott in the highest and most relentless manner, simply because it has the power to refuse or give work. There are cases in which ... it would completely close the firm, and yet it is a working-class institution, which is just the reason why no time should be lost in making the very best use of all our own and its machinery.[105]

In this light one may also appreciate Bramley's distinctive emphasis on co-operative control as a surer route than industrial militancy to the elimination of capitalism.[106]

The need for demonstrative forms of action could also make for a more inclusive union culture than those focused solely on the workplace. Price, like most other commentators, rightly describes syndicalism as a 'masculine ideology' of the producer.[107] However, syndicalists' failure (again according to Price) to spawn 'satellite cultural organisations' was in Britain at least a reflection of their general orientation towards existing organisational structures rather than the proliferation of new ones. Purcell's ideal of the NAFTA social as a 'huge family party' reflected the centrality of the male wage-worker. It did not however imply the denial of family relations that Foster in the States expressed in dramatic and even misogynistic terms:

> Many a man's conduct in the workshop and elsewhere is determined by the measure of interest exhibited and the amount of encouragement rendered in his home. Yet more important still, why should the remaining members of a family be kept in ignorance as to the work of the organisation to which the father, brother or sister is connected with? The truth is that industrial action involves the home circle in its entirety.... [108]

In theory industrial unionism also implied the organisation of women workers within the union itself. At the time of its absorption into NAFTA there were forty women members of the French Polishers (to 'get rid of their unfair competition') and on just these grounds Purcell continued to advocate women workers' organisation within the union.[109] His ideas of camaraderie were traditional and masculine. After one morning-after demonstration, he paid a heartfelt tribute to the accompanying band as 'washing the refuse from the regions of the liver, forcing the heart to beat uniformly, pushing the mental fog away, jerking the limbs and revitalising the muscles'.[110] Nevertheless, and despite Purcell's often strident rhetoric, the relative weakness of the Furnishing Trades compelled some recognition of unity as inclusiveness. This was epitomised in 1913 by the bank-holiday gathering some five hundred-strong which Purcell organised at the West Riding beauty spot of Hardcastle Crags.[111]

Hostility to the state can be seen as the mirror-image of this expansive view of working-class activity. Nothing in Purcell's immediate experience compared with the firing upon demonstrators at Tonypandy in 1910, or the 'Don't Shoot' prosecution which in 1912 landed Mann in Salford gaol. Syndicalist precepts, however, combined with the increasing bitterness of trade disputes to disabuse him of illusions regarding a liberal political order. In actions pivoting on the use of blackleg labour, picketing was both crucial to a successful outcome and a visible enactment of the idea of class struggle. Though peaceful picketing in theory was recognised under the 1906 Trades Disputes Act, diverse charges ranging from conspiracy to the calling of 'derisive names' were made to stick by a magistracy of 'capitalist and political hacks'.[112] Where employers deemed it necessary, as in Accrington, Purcell also saw how elaborate police protection was extended to blackleg labour; in Manchester he himself received summonses for intimidation, never brought to court.[113] As a local councillor Purcell had shown a surprising evenhandedness towards the police, even extolling those in Salford against those in Manchester.[114] Now, however, he insisted that anyone joining their ranks thereby forfeited his manhood and 'automatically becomes a traitor to his fellows'.[115]

NAFTA's most important pre-war dispute did not immediately involve the defence of existing union strongholds, but a campaign to extend its organisation in the union blackspot of High Wycombe in Buckinghamshire. Leading to an employers' lockout in November 1913, this saw the drafting in of police from London and the free use by the employers of their powers as local magistrates. In a town in which uniquely the furnishing trade predominated, the syndicalist language of 'industrial dictators' had the sort of plausibility it had in the coalfield. The normally moderate Bramley, whose responsibility as union organiser the action was, put together an Anti-Violence Brigade led by two former army sergeants and described *The Battle of Bucks* with a relish that any militant syndicalist would have applauded. 'I have seen the mounted police deliberately rush on to the pavement at crowds of helpless men and women time after time', he reported:

> I have seen the foot police make deliberate and unprovoked attacks upon our pickets, and I have also seen some of our High Wycombe

members respond heartily to the call, and prove by many a vigorous reply that uniformed hooliganism is not going to be tolerated in this district unless at a greater cost and with a greater risk to those responsible than ever before.[116]

After thirteen weeks the union achieved a famous victory. Purcell, who particularly commended the contribution of the 'A.V.B.'s', described it as one of the greatest in the History of the Working Class.[117]

One response to this use of the state, and to the limited industrial effectiveness of a union like NAFTA, was the argument for parliamentary redress. This, of course, was the rationale of the emerging Labour Party, and within NAFTA it was expressed in just these terms by O'Grady.[118] At this stage, however, Purcell was hardly less hostile to the state in its constructive aspects. His response to destitution was transformed in less than a year, from the promotion of Fabian-style remedial action to the striking of 'blow after blow' of working-class militancy so that everything else could 'go hang'.[119] The only public ownership worth having was that of the workers themselves, not 'municipal or national capitalism' by means of a 'rate relieving' public sector.[120] When a Manchester distress committee was formed during the war, Purcell was quick to warn against 'the usual busybodies ... [and] professional paul prys ... who would search through and through a working class home for fog dust prior to deciding upon parting with a shilling relief ticket'.[121] Although a longstanding supporter of shorter working hours, at his first TUC in 1918 Purcell opposed the interference of the state in such matters.[122] On similar grounds, he retained throughout his life an instinctive suspicion of state benefits like old age pensions and family allowances, and he held their purpose and effect to be the undermining of union conditions.[123]

In deprecating political activity Purcell could invoke the rank-and-filist argument that it was 'where the work was done' that mattered.[124] He did not, however, translate this into the critique of union bureaucracy which in other versions of syndicalism might have extended to his own salaried status. Purcell's conception of 'conscious and well disciplined revolt' was one to which the maintenance of effective union organisation was indispensable. Even at the height of the syndicalist agitation, he never brought into question the prerogatives of the established unions, nor gave his sanction to wildcat strikes or union branches 'playing the game off their own bat'. Without discipline, he insisted, 'orderly attack and defence' were impossible.[125] Bramley too deprecated 'disorganised enthusiasm' and warned against actions 'outside the spirit and provision of our Rules'.[126] Though its dampening potential is apparent, such a position also allowed the official who sought it a considerable degree of initiative as surrogate or enabler of the rank and file. Purcell himself, more impatient than Bramley, thus had to be reminded by the NAFTA executive of the need to secure its sanction for the incurring of expenditure and promotion of official strike action.[127]

The greatest test of this philosophy occurred just after the war when the employers' federation extended a dispute originating in Manchester to a partial national lockout affecting a quarter of NAFTA's membership.[128] Purcell was at his most combative industrially and held that the union was strong enough to compel the employers to retreat.[129] Nevertheless, there had the previous year been established a Joint Industrial Council (JIC) for the furnishing trades, and with the agreement of its NAFTA representatives a committee of the JIC settled the dispute in defiance of a ballot of Manchester members. Purcell responded with vehement invective, and Gossip, who had a major hand in the negotiations, never quite forgot his free use of 'personalities' and innuendo.[130] Even so, while rousing opinion against the union's 'London executive' – 'I must record my amazement that men who do not understand the make-up of the northern trade unionist ... should have the temerity to try and impose conditions altogether alien to their custom and practice'[131] – Purcell ultimately sought redress through constructive amendment of the union rule book. His comprehensive proposals for reorganisation on a district basis included limited district autonomy, a system of district organisers, election by the districts of the union executive, and the introduction of 'properly arranged scales' for branch officers' salaries. When provisions in this spirit were agreed by the union in October 1921, Purcell for the time being took his place among a new stratum of eight full-time district organisers.[132]

Despite its syndicalist trappings, this had much in common with the Webbian ideal of the salaried officer and the communist one of the professional revolutionary. Purcell had earlier written of High Wycombe that a 'good plodding man on the spot' would treble the membership and put 'pence upon pence on the present miserable labour price of the district'.[133] When subsequently the town's employers 'set the pace' for the post-war lockout he returned to the need for a full-time secretary, 'free from the workshop completely', and for a 'well-equipped office' from which activities in the town could be directed. 'There are over 3,000 men and women in High Wycombe, and that will easily be one man's job to care for ...'[134] Urging adequate payment for NAFTA officials, he also described theirs as 'a full seven days week job' involving 'at all hours, all the work we are called upon to do in the time at our disposal, within the limits of Sunday night to the following Sunday night'.[135] Lenin could hardly have asked more of his professional revolutionaries. In contrast to some other industries, shop stewards' activities figured little in discussions in the furnishing trades.[136] Instead, it was the full-time officer whom Purcell envisaged as providing a continuity of application impossible for the lay activist or visiting agitator.

Both the strength and the limitations of his generation of trade-union leaders derived from this conflation of rank-and-filism and officialdom. Purcell's later TUC colleague Herbert Smith once said that he remained a rank-and-filer even as Miners' national president: 'I go down the pits to see what there is in the pits and the conditions under which the men are working. I talk as a miner ... and not as a Trade Union official...'[137] Price describes the role of such officers as one 'structured around the *quid pro quo* of discipline in return for the right to bargain'.[138] This is unexceptionable if it is understood that bargaining did not necessarily mean bargaining away. But in NAFTA's case, it was the members, not the leaders, who voted for participation in the JIC and a subsequent conciliation board, to the open dismay and disapproval of officers like Gossip and Purcell. 'Frankly, it is not our business to aid in organising those we have to be continually opposing', the union's executive reported gloomily as proceedings began.[139] Aggressively as he believed it could be used, the union's right to bargain was at the centre of Purcell's conception of controlled trade-union militancy. As he put it in his 1924 presidential address to the TUC: 'A well-disciplined industrial organisation is the principal weapon of the workers – a weapon to strike with, if need be, or to use as an instrument of peaceful persuasion as occasions arise and circumstances demand.'[140]

As circumstances required, Purcell, whether through the trades council or later the TUC, was thus also a skilled and if necessary tenacious negotiator. In Manchester once he headed continuous negotiations with co-operative employers over twenty-four hours, and was commended by his interlocutors as the architect of the settlement reached.[141] This, moreover, was not regarded as detracting from his industrial credentials, and his TUC biographical profile highlighted his achievements as successful arbitrator, not the organisation of strikes and solidarity actions.[142] Even joint industrial councils were defensible where they allowed a closer grip on issues of employment and industrial organisation, albeit – in an echo of Hyndman's reconciliation of palliatives and catastrophism – pending the 'great wave of emotion' that would sweep capitalist society from end to end.[143]

To this extent, Purcell's syndicalism may be regarded as in large part a rhetorical strategy, to be deployed or discarded as a weapon as 'circumstances' allowed. On one illuminating occasion Bramley and Purcell recorded the same encounter with a recalcitrant employer of whom both disapproved. 'The reply was direct and clear', Bramley acknowledged; but Purcell described it as 'a grunting, groaning, yet whining sort of a *NO*'.[144] He also described employers as 'lying and filthy dogs', police detectives as 'the most inhuman cads and brutal curs that breath ever oozed from the nostrils of' and newspaper reports as 'heavy ladles of pottage from the putrid wells of the British capitalist class press'.[145] The use of language straight out of Robert

Tressell was as much a rhetorical device as Smith's laconic 'nowt' when asked what the miners had to give away.[146] It did not therefore have to signify Purcell becoming overpowered by his own loquacity. Employed in the context of the class war, it did however betray the classic deficiencies of war propaganda, where claims as weapons resonated long after their uses as rallying cry or negotiating lever had been exhausted. Unattainable trade-union demands might certainly set the framework for what could be achieved. The aspiration to a rank-and-filist style of leadership was nevertheless an inherently unstable one that either constrained the room for manoeuvre or else gave it the appearance of betrayal. When the TUC in 1926 demanded discipline in defeat, Smith's nowt was turned against Purcell himself and his credibility never recovered.

1.4 'AN INTERNATIONAL CLASS'

Despite the central role of Bramley and Purcell in the Anglo-Russian trade union committee of the 1920s, mention is never made of their common socialisation within the same trade union.[147] This characteristic neglect of trade-union biography makes for a shallow understanding of motive and the denial of a personal history and complex rationality. It also dislocates these Russian attachments from a longer discourse of labour internationalism more consistently upheld within NAFTA than in possibly any other British union. The socialist political commitments of NAFTA's leading officers provide part of the explanation. Nevertheless, the TUC's adoption of a radical foreign-policy stance was also rooted in a distinct concept of labour internationalism whose ethos of solidarity, national and international, was grounded in notions of mutuality and collective self-interest generated from within the unions themselves. If Purcell and Bramley stand out from received ideas of British trade-union parochialism, this can be traced to a common organisational culture in which internationalist values were pervasive.

Labour internationalism, as we shall see, has been linked with the input of 'foreign variables' into domestic environments.[148] Even within the confines of such an environment, however, relative mobility of product or labour could pose the logic of extrinsic threat, provoking responses that could be generalised beyond its boundaries. Unlike its near relation the building trade, production in the furnishing trade was not tied to the locality in which it was required. Nor was it bound by natural resources as in the extractive industries. No great investment was tied up in plant or site development, and there were no obvious advantages of location except in proximity to domestic markets. Even the availability of skilled labour, inasmuch as this underpinned union strength and conditions, meant that deskilling and the undermining of conditions were felicitously achieved by employment in 'cheap labour districts' beyond their reach.[149] Centrifugal pressures were particularly apparent in the London area. The rapid development of the sweated trade in the capital's northern and eastern districts had been a major factor in the ACMA's establishment in 1865, and fifty years later Bramley described as a primary industrial objective the sweeping away of the 'City Road border line'.[150] The same pattern was repeated on a nation scale; in purely economic terms its extension internationally was a difference of degree rather than kind. During the 1920s much was to be made of the distinction between industries exposed to foreign competition and so-called 'sheltered' trades. If Furnishing Trades unionists proved especially responsive to foreign variables, it was because theirs was not a sheltered trade even within its national borders.

Already in the decades before the First World War, the internationalisation of labour and product markets was giving rise to increasing if faltering endeavours towards a trade-union internationalism. With Gossip to the fore, NAFTA played an active part in the establishment of an International Union of Woodworkers (IUW) in 1904 and it may be grouped with the smaller, older craft unions which Susan Milner notes were most drawn by such affiliations.[151] For some of these unions, solidarity issues were posed primarily in terms of labour mobility, whether through migration or the calculating use of strikebreakers. This had been the original stimulus to the British unions' involvement in the First International, and was already set out in George Odger's address 'to the working men of France' during the building workers' lockout of 1857-8.[152] The importation of strikebreakers was also, as we have seen, a major headache for the Furnishing Trades. Nevertheless, the primary underlying issue was that of the mobility of raw materials and finished product, and it was this which allowed the establishment of the cheap labour districts from which the strikebreakers were usually drawn.

This was exemplified by High Wycombe, not thirty miles from Charing Cross and mixing primitive forms of outworking with modern machine production. In each case these were largely unprotected by union agreements, to the particular detriment of the better organised London trades. 'At the close of the working-day motor wagons, drays and conveyances of all kinds, are loaded up, and goods are sent, load after load, direct to the London Market', Bramley reported during the lockout in 1913-14, 'dispatched like farm produce daily to the consumer in the great City'.[153] The interplay of interests as between unionised and non-unionised localities was in these circumstances anything but an abstraction, and Purcell in Manchester was tireless in raising members' levies, establishing relief committees and seeking to organise a co-operative boycott.[154] While the union prevailed on this occasion, by the end of the decade Wycombe was once again a 'fouling nest' used by the employers against conditions elsewhere. 'It sends chairs to every town in the Kingdom', Purcell again complained. 'It therefore competes against every town. Strengthen it and correspondingly we strengthen every other centre.'[155] Replace 'town' with 'nation' and the logic of Purcell's trade-union internationalism is already apparent.

Mobility of labour was not just a matter of labour supply, or of the moving about of blacklegs. It also helped define the forms of association through which the sense of the national and international was constructed. In NAFTA's case, analogies between the two were underpinned by the interplay of ethnic as well as geographical factors in the shaping of the labour market. With the entry into the trade of sizeable numbers of Jewish workers towards the close of the nineteenth century, existing tensions between its 'honourable' and 'dishonourable' sections acquired a significant ethnic dimension. By 1901, around eleven per cent of London males described as of 'Russian or Russian-Polish' origin worked in the furnishing industry. Over just a decade this represented a near twofold increase in relation to the overall Jewish working population and a fourfold increase in absolute terms.[156] Within the northern counties for which Purcell was responsible, cities with significant concentrations of Jewish furnishing workers included Manchester, Liverpool and Leeds.

Students of US labour history, where the issue of ethnicity was so much more pervasive, are well aware that such encounters did not automatically translate into the language of solidarity. Within the NAFTA leadership, a response of exclusion and even anathematisation was particularly identified with O'Grady. Of Irish origin himself, O'Grady had mobilised a large Irish vote in his Leeds parliamentary constituency and could be vehement in his commitment to Irish interests.[157] If the Irish were nevertheless seen, as O'Grady saw them, as 'the only white people under the British flag', this need not necessarily conflict with the anti-alien note which O'Grady contributed to the Royal Commission on Alien Immigration (1903) and the subsequent implementation of the Aliens Act.[158] This all-too-common ethnic construction of labour movement factionalism would resurface in NAFTA during the war. Particularly at the smaller-scale and sweated end of the trade, it was not just an issue of labour supply but of undercutting employers, and even Bramley could resort to populist images of the conniving Jew.[159] Within the SDF, the use of such language had been particularly widespread; and, as late as his 1910 election campaign, when Purcell sought to conjure up the threat to the small shopkeeper he almost casually invoked the example of the chain tobacconists Salmon & Gluckstein.[160]

Despite such stereotypes, the predominant note of the union's activist cadre was one of class as the alternative to ethnic division. Under pressure for implying anti-Jewish prejudice, Bramley took pains to reaffirm the basic class principle of 'no distinction of race, colour, or creed'.[161] As he also observed, the moral was reinforced by the employers' evident willingness to put their own class interest above such petty differences:

> To all of them my mission has been the same, to ask them to pay something and 'tis true, wonderfully true, that where interests are identical, racial sentiments or religious feeling makes no difference. An employer is the same person every time, they buy labour like wood, in the cheapest market ...[162]

Purcell too, when the employers' association sought to break the union in 1912, described it with characteristic finesse as a 'Jew-Gentile octopus' hypocritically playing on ethnic tensions and needing to be beaten 'to a frazzle'.[163]

Syndicalism and the amalgamation movement, from this perspective, implied the overcoming of ethnic divisions as well as those of craft and function. In London, Manchester and Liverpool, 'Hebrew branches' represented the incorporation within the union of what might otherwise have survived as separate ethnic organisations. In London's East End, the Independent Jewish Cabinet Makers' Association was incorporated as the radical East London United branch while retaining the right to organise Jewish workers.[164] Organisation around ethnic difference could also allow the expression of ethnic hostility, particularly with the targeting of aliens after the outbreak of war. On Merseyside, where NAFTA members condoned the victimisation of Jewish workers by the War Office, Purcell warned of 'a tacit support of the idea of extermination, or, what some are pleased to call, anti-semitism'.[165] Perhaps for this reason, he set great store by activities going beyond the individual branch, such as the 'meet' at Hardcastle Crags. With some five hundred in attendance, of all sectors, both sexes, 'Jews, Gentile, German and Pole', the 'fraternising of all districts and grades' was seen as a contribution to mutual understanding and the perfecting of the 'Industrial Union Movement'.[166]

The scope for slippages between the national and international was vividly attested in the ambiguous case of Ireland. Like O'Grady, Purcell supported Irish self-government and during the war of independence he shared a Manchester platform with Countess Markiewicz and roused audiences with the Bolsheviks' support for Ireland's cause.[167] In the industrial sphere, on the other hand, Purcell had little time for the Sinn Fein motto 'ourselves alone'. Extolling the TUC's support for locked-out Dublin workers in 1913, he held that the corollary to such actions was a union organisation as little respecting the Irish Sea as it did the City Road.[168] Pending NAFTA's appointment of a temporary Irish organiser in 1921, Purcell took responsibility for its Irish branches; indeed, had he sailed as he intended with the torpedoed ship the *Leinster* in 1918, he might never have troubled the historian further.[169] Undeterred by his escape, Purcell spent increasing amounts of time in Ireland, assisting in a nearly six-month long dispute in the 'old-world' one-street village of Richhill in County Armagh. Just as at High Wycombe, one of the principal objects was to protect the 'higher paid districts', notably Belfast and Liverpool, whose solidarity was the more imperative given the physical isolation of the Richhill strikers and their lack of previous strike experience.[170] Figuring in a small way in the Belfast general strike the following February, Purcell described it as a 'tremendous act of class unity' in the face of 'terrible inter-class strife'.[171] Again in 1920, when he attended a 'harmonious and industrially loyalist' gathering of branches in Dublin he described the demonstration of workers' unity as the one dependable way out of Ireland's present 'cataclysm'.[172]

Issues of solidarity were not always straightforward. In a reversal of the stock union argument regarding the undercutting worker, Richhill employers described NAFTA as an Englishman's tool to steal the Irish trade.[173] Irish historian Emmet O'Connor has also described the presence of British unions in Ireland as a form of colonialism and contested the framing of the issue confronting trade unionists as one between internationalism and an 'introspective' nationalism.[174] Whatever the form of organisation developed to address the issue, it is nevertheless clear that labour and commodity markets in this example were not confined by national borders. Wherever the products of labour were moved as easily as from Wycombe to London, the issue of a union 'Common Rule' would necessarily be posed as one to be safeguarded across political boundaries. The formulation of the Common Rule had been that of the Webbs in *Industrial Democracy*, but Purcell did not need to learn it there. As a matter of simple class instinct he held that the Irish capitalist class was 'just as sordid and brutal as the British capitalist class' and that no distinction should be drawn between them.[175]

Prioritising the interests of higher paid districts, which at this level were nationalities, could clearly embed advantages which were not merely the fruits of trade-union organisation. Moreover, if the state was conceived of as collective consumer, as it was by many socialists, the alternative instrument of the boycott might take a state-protectionist form for the maintenance of conditions through the exclusion of goods produced by undercutting. Even as between the different English regions, NAFTA lobbying of the London County Council to have work done only in the capital showed how a form of labour protectionism could derive from the same essential logic without necessarily representing purely local interests, as opposed to the upholding of a basic common rule.[176] Purcell's later inconsistencies indicate that there was no absolute distinction between arguments of labour internationalism and labour protectionism as variations on the core union object of control of the labour supply. The syndicalist distrust of politicians extended to nationalist politicians, as likewise nationalist employers, and a particular construction of class-based economic common interest remained at the centre of Purcell's worldview. Whatever Ireland's political destiny, he wrote in 1918, its future lay in a vigorous trade-union movement, unrestricted by sex and ethnicity. 'Complete industrial organisation and solidarity first and the rest follow quite easily.'[177]

The ambiguities of Purcell's internationalism will be revisited in a later chapter. That particular interests could be articulated in general terms should not, however, detract from the challenge this internationalism posed to dominant social values that went beyond mere calculations of sectional advantage. Nor should the minority status of such a position be confused, as it sometimes is, with the 'impossibility' of any such alternative.[178] In 1913, Purcell paid tribute to a German-born NAFTA veteran, Gus Smith. 'They say he was a German, just because he was born there he was not a foreigner, because he was a loyal member of the working class, and there can be no foreigners in the work class because it is a non-national, that is an international class.'[179] Decades earlier, the Chartist Lovett had also insisted on the 'identity of interests' of the world's workers and the 'common cause of nations identical in the great brotherhood of man'.[180] As if vaulting the century between them, Purcell closed his epitaph to Smith with Tom Paine's motto: 'The world is my country, mankind are my brethren, to do good is my religion.' Such sentiments were tested as never before when twelve months later Europe descended into war.

1.5 WAR AND REVOLUTION

Reconstructions of working-class internationalism are fatally compromised if they exclude the conflicts which posed its greatest challenge.[181] This is not just an issue of balance or comprehensiveness. Susceptibilities to nationalism on the part of professed internationalists not only reveal discontinuities and alleged 'betrayals' but expose tensions and ambiguities within the discourse of internationalism itself. As importantly, it was at just these testing and formative moments that internationalism as the rejection of nationalism was most obviously dissenting, contrary and divisive, with enduring consequences for the politics of the left.

There can be few better examples of this than the Furnishing Trades' union. Internationally, the IUW maintained a more continuous activity than any other trade secretariat, and its German secretary Theodor Leipart included notices from all the belligerent countries in the thirty-six wartime issues of its international bulletin.[182] Within Britain, NAFTA's consistency in opposing the 1914-18 war was second to none, and as early as March 1915 was expressed in an outspoken manifesto endorsed by a membership ballot. At the same time, the furnishing workers, like the South Wales miners, produced particularly high levels of recruitment to Britain's pre-conscript army.[183] The same cause was vigorously promoted in opposition to his fellow officers by James O'Grady, who amidst considerable acrimony effectively defected to another union. As Ross McKibbin notes, 'it is too easy to say that the unions supported the war and the socialists did not'; of socialist union activists such as officered the Furnishing Trades, it is problematic even to formulate the argument in this way.[184] Through Gossip, Bramley, O'Grady and Purcell himself, a tangle of socialist traditions can be identified that was anything but economistic in its consideration of the war.

Gossip's opening notes in the union journal set the tone. Unyielding opposition to the war and to the interests in which it was waged was matched by bafflement and despair at the response of most working-class organisations.[185] Gossip as general secretary was not subject to re-election and he had no hesitation in also speaking out against tendencies to chauvinism within NAFTA's own ranks, particularly as directed towards members of German or Austro-Hungarian origin.[186] Bramley was initially more reticent, pending his re-election as trade organiser at the end of 1914. Once this uncertainty was removed, he also expressed his frank opposition to the 'present horrible war' and together with Gossip gave the union a compelling political lead.[187] It was under their joint names that the manifesto was issued in March 1915 attributing the conflict to secret diplomacy, national aggrandisement and the corrupting influence of a 'lying' capitalist press. If militarism was more prevalent in Germany than in Britain, that meant a greater responsibility still to 'use the power of organised labour to promote a clearer vision, and attempt to build up a universal desire for peace and goodwill strong enough to prevent such crimes as at present are being committed on humanity being repeated by the rulers of any country'. As one later Labour leader might have put it, they were tough on war and tough on 'the causes and consequences of war', without being led astray by issues of which power was most responsible for which atrocities.[188] It was a remarkable document, and, on an admittedly low poll representing barely a tenth of the membership, NAFTA approved it by a two-to-one majority.[189]

Discussion of such dissenting opinion tends to focus on the predominantly middle-class progressivism of the Union of Democratic Control (UDC). Not only was this was the 'most important organisation of opposition' to government policy, but leading figures within it, like E.D. Morel and H.N. Brailsford, were, as Liberal converts, to have an important role in shaping Labour's Russian policies after 1917.[190] Bramley, however, not only represented a minority working-class presence within bodies like the UDC and the No Conscription Fellowship, at whose convention in April 1916 he was described as the one representative trade unionist present.[191] He also put forward a distinctively working-class view of internationalism rooted in his trade-union values. This was most fully expounded in his admirable pamphlet elaborating upon the NAFTA manifesto, *Class Cohesion versus Spurious Patriotism*.[192] Class cohesion was here identified with Europe's ruling classes in their continuing solicitude for their own kind even as commercial rivalry dragged them into war. But it was also invoked as an ideal to be set against the spurious patriotism of union leaders and sometime class-war socialists in their support for the general slaughter. Recalling the 'thrill of pleasure' he had experienced on hearing of fraternisation across the lines on the first Christmas of the war, Bramley insisted that these were not issues 'outside the province of Trade Union activity' and linked them with the spontaneous enthusiasm and fellow-feeling shown the German trade unionist Carl Legien when he addressed the Manchester TUC in 1913.

There were several legacies here that help explain Bramley's commitment to the TUC's Russian delegation a decade later. One was a recognition of the symbolic value of such exchanges across the lines of a class-based diplomacy as well as outright war. Internationalism, Bramley wrote in his pamphlet, would be realised by a 'closer contact and clearer understanding as between the common people', who had for too long let themselves be led astray by 'academic meddlers'. A second common theme was the right and obligation of trade unionists to have their full say in foreign-policy issues of which they bore the consequences. A third, in reaction to the vicious propaganda of the yellow press, was a reluctance to lend credence to materials liable to excite national animosities. At the General Federation of Trade Unions (GFTU) in 1915, one delegate told of children's hands being nailed to window sills; another wanted to 'wipe out every German. He would exterminate them'.[193] Amid considerable commotion, Bramley was the sole dissenter. The proper function of a trade union, he argued, was 'to publish and emphasise points of agreement between the working classes of the different countries', not items liable to raise 'a keen hatred of anything German'.[194] The later unwillingness to credit anti-Bolshevik propaganda is impossible to understand if not in part as a reaction against the construction of such figures of the enemy and the role these played in a culture of militarism.

O'Grady was on the side of the exterminators. Bramley had attended the GFTU only because O'Grady felt unable to uphold his union's view of the war. Over recruitment and conscription he was continuously out on a limb, and on industrial conscription his own position was defeated by a thirty-to-one majority in a members' ballot.[195] One could not have accused O'Grady of parochialism. His recreations, according to the later *Labour Who's Who*, were 'travelling and foreign politics'.[196] As an MP he had taken a particular interest in Indian affairs and he had represented the Labour Party on the British

Committee of the Indian National Congress.[197] Raising a vigorous parliamentary protest against Edward VII's state visit to the Tsar in 1908, he urged Labour's special responsibility as 'the only movement of a political character which was also of an international character'.[198] At once a Hyndmanite loyalist and a Fabian collectivist, O'Grady was nevertheless a keen supporter of the citizens' army proposals to which the SDF in particular was committed. A formative personal influence was Thomas Carlyle, whose enthusiasm for 'drilling' must have been contagious, as likewise the commitment to what O'Grady called 'the expansion of Empire'.[199]

Following Hyndman into his pro-war breakaway, the National Socialist Party, O'Grady expressed a sense almost of exhilaration at the idea of the nation in arms. There can certainly have been few more uncompromising professions of state socialism than the 'fundamental principle' which O'Grady enunciated in defence of conscription:

> that all we are in temperament, brains, and capacity, and what we possess in the world's goods, we owe to the State. That the State is the super-man, so to speak; the greater life; the totality of us all. That we are of the State; that we could not exist without the State; and that any aggressor seeking to cripple or end the existence of the State of which we are units, ought to be resisted at the expense, not only of material, individual possessions or wealth, but if need be with the sacrifice of our lives.[200]

On the same grounds of 'Socialist doctrine' O'Grady also advocated the internment or deportation of conscientious objectors.[201] His position as NAFTA's political mouthpiece was thus clearly becoming untenable, and when NAFTA for the first time decided to ballot for its GFTU delegate, it placed O'Grady, who was the federation's chairman, in an invidious position. Purcell was later to face a similar predicament regarding his responsibilities for the TUC and it effectively put an end to his national career.[202] O'Grady, however, had support within the wider labour movement, and through his friend and ally Ben Tillett he was quickly engineered an alternative GFTU mandate from the Dockers' Union.[203] He was also elected paid general secretary of the National Federation of General Workers, apparently as a precaution against the loss of NAFTA's parliamentary nomination.[204] O'Grady's role in NATFA from this point on was of little importance.

Purcell's position was less clear-cut than any of these. Although initially holding that the workers of the warring powers had no quarrel with each other, just three days into the conflict he presided over a discussion at Manchester's Clarion Café that led to the cancellation of a protest meeting due to have been addressed by Ramsay MacDonald.[205] Describing alleged German atrocities as both 'sordid and cannibal-like' and 'scientifically developed ... organised murder', Purcell was not the only syndicalist to lose his bearings, and at this stage he urged the prosecution of the war 'to the bitter end'.[206] Even as he railed against Germany's 'Blood and Iron Autocracy', recognition of the domestic class war nevertheless provided an unbroken thread. Until well into 1918 Purcell avoided overt opposition to the war, and the absence of his name from the Gossip-Bramley manifesto can hardly have been an oversight. He was nevertheless at one with his colleagues in opposing the Treasury Agreements, Munitions Act and other such efforts to demobilise the workers on the home front.[207] He thus achieved a consistency of sorts by urging the primacy of the workplace, to which the distractions of war and peace alike could appear as but a further intrusion of the snares of politics. The 'highest virtue and the noblest patriotism' he stated in October 1914, was that of 'absolute loyalty to working-class interests', and the greatest vice, conversely, disloyalty to those interests, 'all other interests and conditions notwithstanding'.[208] This was not exactly an exemplary war record, and in Russia in 1920 it is interesting that Purcell and his fellow left-winger Robert Williams seemed reluctant to enter into a discussion of the British unions' attitudes to the war.[209] Support for militant industrial action, against the trend to unforced concessions to 'Governmental and political prigs', was nevertheless consistently expressed from the outset.[210]

In August 1918 Gossip provided a stirring revival of the class cohesion theme. 'Small issues' of territorial rivalry were raised only to obscure the hidden designs of the 'money-power'. The 'forces of capitalism', in reality, 'reach[ed] in an unbroken line around the world', whilst the workers' forces were broken up and scattered. 'The industrial workers in all nations must be linked together if ever they are going to get rid of the slavery and oppression of our class.'[211] Nothing Purcell wrote during the war could compare with this. Nevertheless, the influence it had upon him should not be discounted. Jeremy Jennings writes of syndicalism as an open-ended tradition without fixed parameters and thus allowing not only for internal diversity but for those impelled by it to 'change sides without necessarily realising the distance they have covered'.[212] In just this way one may allow for borrowings and appropriations from a common stock of ideas to which the contribution of any particular individual was sometimes faltering or uneven. Purcell at this time never voiced internationalist principles with the sort of feeling and cogency which Gossip and Bramley communicated. Nevertheless, he was to draw on these ideas in the post-war campaign for international unity, and in successive international addresses of the 1920s he made his own contribution to a shared culture of internationalism.

Russia in this latter period had become the litmus test, not so much of internationalism, as of irreconcilable views as to what internationalist principle implied. At first it seemed less complicated. For internationalists everywhere, the Russian revolutions of 1917 provided vindication as well as inspiration. Representing NAFTA at the famous Leeds anti-war convention of June 1917, Gossip described the renewal of faith in internationalism as testimony to the 'cruelly misrepresented and vilified minority' who by their loyalty and strength of purpose had maintained the same ideal in adversity.[213] Presiding over a similar gathering at Manchester's Free Trade Hall, Purcell too hailed the revolution as 'full of potentialities'.[214] When the second Russian revolution led to the Bolsheviks' prompt withdrawal from the war, several NAFTA branches urged that the example of an immediate peace be followed.[215] Even O'Grady came to oppose outside intervention, and he was later to act as chief commissioner when the International Federation of Trade Unions organised a Russian relief mission.[216]

Over time the revolution in Russia came to function as surrogate or compensation for its absence elsewhere. At the moment that Purcell embraced it, however, it was more as a crystallisation of wider tendencies, or else, as he put it to cheers at the Free Trade Hall, as 'an indication of what might easily happen elsewhere'.[217] The revival of militancy at home produced record days lost in stoppages even in the furnishing industry.[218] In Belfast Purcell saw the city-wide general strike of February 1919 as the harbinger of greater things to come. Four months later his NAFTA branch urged support of Sylvia Pankhurst's People's Russian Information Bureau; and when a national Hands Off Russia (HOR) committee was established Purcell was a supporter from the start.[219] Feelings of solidarity were cemented by his participation in British Labour's Russian delegation of May–June 1920. In preparation for the trip, Purcell expressly recorded his debt to NAFTA's Manchester Hebrew branch for practical information and advice.[220] On his return, he was one of five delegates calling for direct action against anti-Soviet intervention.[221] He was the only one, however, urging emulation as well as solidarity at a homecoming Albert Hall rally, so that 'workers in this country might speedily follow the pace set by the Russian workers'.[222]

For Purcell this proved an irrevocable commitment. When HOR became the Anglo-Russian Parliamentary Committee, he was again its chairman, and until his death he was steadfast in his support for the USSR. Sidney Webb described him simply as 'Purcell the Communist'.[223] Communistic leanings, however, were combined in this case with diverse connections and expectations established over a period of some thirty years. George Hardy, a syndicalist some twelve years Purcell's junior, was to describe the impact of Bolshevism as marking the end of one lifetime and the beginning of another.[224] Such an idea is problematic even for many communists. For an activist of Purcell's accumulated interests and associations, it would have required a sort of felo de se of which he had not the slightest intention. No more than Webb himself could Purcell have become a communist in any sense that Hardy would have recognised. What was distinctive about the British case was the delaying of any such definitive moment of reckoning. The new mass formations of communism and social democracy were taking shape around Purcell, and by the end of his life he appears as one of their casualties. For the time being, however, fluid political relations and a respect for established credentials allowed him room for manoeuvre and an unexpected moment of ascendancy. Even the head of the Comintern wondered whether Britain's best prospects lay through the CPGB itself or 'some other door' – one might almost say the Purcell-Bramley door.[225] Before returning to Purcell's Russian attachments, the disparate commitments with which he managed to reconcile them will repay attention in their own right.

NOTES

1. BWD 17 August 1925.
2. Purcell, 'Towards a new policy: V', *Labour Monthly*, May 1924, pp. 268-70.
3. Dutt, 'A postscript', *Labour Monthly*, August 1924, p. 465.
4. Marcel van der Linden, 'Second thoughts on revolutionary syndicalism', *Labour History Review*, 63, 2, 1998, p. 183; Marcel van der Linden and Wayne Thorpe, 'The rise and fall of revolutionary syndicalism' in Marcel van der Linden and Wayne Thorpe, eds, *Revolutionary Syndicalism*, Aldershot: Scolar Press, 1990, p. 5.
5. Robert Williams, 'Towards a new policy: IV', *Labour Monthly*, April 1924, p. 212.
6. Purcell, 'Towards a new policy: V', p. 268.
7. Van der Linden and Thorpe, 'Rise and fall', pp. 5-6.
8. Richard Price, 'Contextualising British syndicalism, c.1907-c.1920', *Labour History Review*, 63, 3, 1998, pp. 262 and 274 n. 4.
9. Price, 'Contextualising', pp. 261 and 266-9.
10. Bob Holton, *British Syndicalism 1900-1914: myths and realities*, Pluto, 1976, p. 208.
11. Joseph White, 'Syndicalism in a mature industrial setting: the case of Britain' in van der Linden and Thorpe, *Revolutionary Syndicalism*, p. 109.
12. E. J. Hobsbawm, 'The 1970s. Syndicalism without syndicalists' in idem, *Worlds of Labour. Further studies in the history of Labour*, Weidenfeld & Nicolson, 1984, pp. 273-81.
13. Van der Linden and Thorpe, 'Rise and fall', p. 5.
14. See *Bolshevism and British Left*, I, p. 112; van der Linden and Thorpe, *Revolutionary Syndicalism*, p. 5.
15. Jeremy Jennings, *Syndicalism in France. A study of ideas*, Basingstoke: Macmillan, 1990, pp. 57-71.
16. Edward P. Johanningsmeier, *The Forging of American Communism. The life of William Z. Foster*, Princeton, N.J.: Princeton University Press, 1994.

Syndicalism, internationalism and the furnishing trades 55

17. In the van der Linden/Thorpe collection (p. 5) this is covered by the formula 'no longer syndicalist'.
18. Barbara Mitchell, 'French syndicalism: an experiment in practical anarchism' in van der Linden and Thorpe, *Revolutionary Syndicalism*, p. 38.
19. 'The legacy of 1911 to 1912', *Syndicalist*, January 1912.
20. 'Workers of the World Unite! May Day, 1912', *Syndicalist*, May 1912.
21. Cited Jennings, *Syndicalism in France*, p. 44.
22. Ned Cowey in *International Socialist Workers and Trade Union Congress. London, 1896. Report of proceedings, list of British and foreign delegates, and balance sheet*, Twentieth Century Press, n.d. but 1896, p. 7.
23. See Chushichi Tsuzuki, *Tom Mann, 1856-1941. The challenges of Labour*, Oxford: OUP, 1991, chs 6-7.
24. Speech in Battersea, reported *Syndicalist*, February 1912. The Australian example would frequently be used by syndicalists in this way; see for example John Turner, *Syndicalist*, December 1913.
25. For contrasting accounts, see White, *Tom Mann*, pp. 173-9; Hugh Armstrong Clegg, *A History of British Trade Unions since 1889. Volume 2: 1911-1933*, Oxford: OUP, 1985, pp. 33-41.
26. G.D.H. Cole, *The World of Labour. A discussion of the present and future of trade unionism*, Bell, 1913, p. 40.
27. White, 'Syndicalism in a mature setting', p. 103.
28. Torr papers CP/Ind/Torr/8/3, Purcell to Mann, 23 January 1928.
29. Biographical information presumably provided by Purcell was collected in a profile for the *Salford Reporter*, first published 8 June 1907 and reprinted 15 January 1910. This is the principal source of the summary provided here.
30. 173 Hansard fifth series, 13 May 1924, cols 1239-44.
31. There are brief family details in GARF 5451/13a/55/37, biography of May Purcell, 1925.
32. David Howell, *British Workers and the Independent Labour Party 1888-1906*, Manchester: MUP, 1983, pp. 216-27.
33. Joe Toole, *Fighting Through Life*, Rich & Cowan, 1935, p. 89; S.G. Hobson, *Pilgrim to the Left. Memoirs of a modern revolutionist*, Edward Arnold: 1938, p. 246.
34. Anglo-Russian Parliamentary Committee *News Bulletin*, 4 January 1936.
35. Purcell, 'The importance of May Day', *Labour Monthly*, April 1926, p. 210.
36. Purcell, 'Four great demonstrations, *Labour Magazine*, July 1924, p. 182; Augustin Hamon, *Le Socialisme et le congrès de Londres. Étude historique*, Paris: Stock, 1897, pp. 89-96.
37. *International Socialist Workers and Trade Union Congress. London, 1896. Report of proceedings, list of British and foreign delegates, and balance sheet*, Twentieth Century Press, n.d. but 1896; H.M. Hyndman, *Further Reminiscences*, Macmillan, 1912, pp. 103-16.
38. *International Socialist Workers and Trade Union Congress*, pp. 9-10.
39. Hamon, *Le Socialisme et le congrès de Londres*, pp. 241-2, n. 59; Tom Mann, *Tom Mann's Memoirs*, Labour Publishing Co, 1923, p. 104.
40. At a meeting of the British section, the voting was 223: 104 in favour of the 'Zurich resolution' effectively excluding the anarchists; but there is no indication of how the minority was composed.
41. Toole, *Fighting Through Life*, p. 89.

42. W.J. Munro, 'Albert Arthur Purcell: a short biography', Manchester and Salford Trades Council *Annual Report and Directory*, 1935-6, p. 12; Toole, *Fighting*, p. 89.
43. Dylan Morris, 'Labour or socialism: opposition and dissent within the Independent Labour Party 1906-1914 with special reference to the Lancashire division', Manchester, PhD, 1982, p. 100; C. Desmond Greaves, *The Life and Times of James Connolly*, Lawrence & Wishart, 1972 edn, pp. 133-4.
44. *Salford City Reporter*, 27 December 1935.
45. Morris, 'Labour or socialism', pp. 92, 239-40.
46. See *Bolshevism and the British Left*, II, pp. 30-2.
47. Purcell, West Salford election address, January 1910, WCML; *Salford Reporter*, 8 January 1910.
48. G.W. Agnew (Lib.): 6,216; C.W. Bellairs (Cons.): 5,239; A.A. Purcell (Soc.): 2,394.
49. *Justice*, 16 July 1910.
50. *Manchester Guardian*, 1 December 1910.
51. *Justice*, 16 July 1910; *Manchester Guardian*, 22 July 1910.
52. Purcell to Mann, 23 January 1928.
53. *Manchester Guardian*, 18 August 1910.
54. *Justice*, 1 October 1910; also 17 and 24 September, 3 and 10 October 1910 for preliminary discussions and correspondence and Morris, 'Labour or socialism', p. 246 for criticisms of Purcell locally.
55. Tsuzuki, *Tom Mann*, pp. 142-3.
56. White, *Tom Mann*, pp. 160-1; Jonathan Schneer, *Ben Tillett. Portrait of a Labour leader*, Croom Helm, 1982, pp. 149-51.
57. 'Conference on industrial syndicalism', *Industrial Syndicalist*, September 1910, pp. 24-8 and October 1910, pp. 23-4.
58. See conflicting suggestions given in White, *Tom Mann*, p. 162 and Tsuzuki, *Tom Mann*, pp. 148 and 167.
59. Purcell, opening address, 'First conference on industrial syndicalism', *Industrial Syndicalist*, December 1910, pp. 12-13.
60. *Justice*, 4 December 1910.
61. *Manchester Guardian*, 1 December 1910.
62. *Salford City Reporter*, 27 December 1935.
63. *The Miners' Next Step: being a suggested scheme for the reorganisations of the Federation*, Tonypandy: Unofficial Reform Committee, 1912.
64. Cited Ralph Darlington, *Revolutionary Syndicalism. An international comparative analysis*, Salford Papers in Sociology, 2001, p. 53.
65. See John Kelly, *Trade Unions and Socialist Politics*, Verso, 1988, ch. 7.
66. Kelly, *Trade Unions*, pp. 150-1.
67. Tanner papers, thesis on 'British trade unionism and the revolution', probably produced for Shop Stewards and Workers' Committee Movement, n.d., c. 1920?.
68. Richard Price, *Masters, Unions and Men: work control in building and the rise of labour 1830-1914*, Cambridge: CUP, 1980, chs 6 and 7 passim.
69. Kelly, *Trade Unions*, pp. 151-2, 155.
70. Cited Ralph Darlington, 'British syndicalism and trade union officialdom', *Historical Studies in Industrial Relations*, 25/26, 2008, p. 108.
71. For arguments and figures see James E. Cronin, 'Strikes and the struggle

Syndicalism, internationalism and the furnishing trades 57

for union organization: Britain and Europe' in Wolfgang J. Mommsen and Hans-Gerhard Husung, eds, *The Development of Trade Unionism in Great Britain and Europe 1880-1914*, Allen & Unwin, 1985, pp. 55-77.
72. As for example in Darlington, 'British syndicalism' which notes its extraordinarily brief history as an 'organisational entity' but identifies its more durable influence with the hostility to 'the entire layer of officialdom' (pp. 103-6, 119).
73. *Miners' Next Step*, ch. 2; Murphy cited Darlington, *Revolutionary Syndicalismh*, p. 53.
74. Earl C. Ford and William Z. Foster, *Syndicalism* (1912), Chicago: Charles H. Kerr, 1990 edn, ed. James R. Barrett, pp. 43-4.
75. See Robert Michels, *Political Parties. A sociological study of the oligarchical tendencies of modern democracy* (1915), New York: Transaction Publishers edn, 1999 (original German edition: 1911). For Goldman see chapter 4 below.
76. For the wide circulation of such ideas see nevertheless *Bolshevism and the British Left*, II, pp. 158-9; or e.g. Jack Tanner, *The Social General Strike*, WSF, 1919, p. 3: 'It has ever been the intelligent, energetic, and enthusiastic minority that has revolted against tyranny and oppression, and given the lead to the indolent mass ... In every strike and revolution it is the force and initiative of the minority that moves the mass.'
77. Compare with Price, 'Contextualising', p. 268.
78. *Bolshevism and the British Left*, I, pp. 198-206.
79. The one published history is Hew Reid, *The Furniture Makers. A history of trade unionism in the furniture trade 1865-1972*, Oxford: Malthouse Press, 1986.
80. Lovett, *Life and Struggles of William Lovett in his Pursuit of Bread, Knowledge and Freedom* (1876), MacGibbon & Kee, 1967 edn, p. 26.
81. David Blankenhorn, '"Our class of workmen". The Cabinet-makers revisited' in Royden Harrison and Jonathan Zeitlin, eds, *Divisions of Labour. Skilled workers and technological change in nineteenth century England*, Brighton: Harvester, 1985, pp. 19-46.
82. For South Wales, the classic account is Hwyel Francis and David Smith, *The Fed. A history of the South Wales miners in the twentieth century*, Lawrence & Wishart, 1980, ch. 1. Although the view that South Wales was synonymous with coal (p. 15) has been challenged, the contrast between the coalfield and an industry like furnishing is clear enough. For discussion of this issue, see Stefan Berger, 'Working-class culture and the labour movement in the South Wales and the Ruhr coalfields, 1850-2000: a comparison, *Llafur*, 8, 2, 2001, pp. 5-40; and the further contributions by Berger, Mike Lieven, Nina Fishman and Joe England in *Llafur*, 8, 3, 2002, pp. 89-139.
83. See the entry by Helen Corr and John Saville in William Knox, ed., *Scottish Labour Leaders 1918-1939. A biographical dictionary*, Edinburgh: Mainstream, 1984, pp. 121-6.
84. See the entry on O'Grady by David Martin in Joyce M. Bellamy and John Saville, eds, *Dictionary of Labour Biography. Volume II*, Macmillan, 1974, pp. 286-9; and for the Bristol Socialist Society/SDF, H.W. Lee and E. Archbold, *Social Democracy in Britain. Fifty years of the socialist movement*, SDF, 1935, pp. 92-3.

85. NAFTA *Monthly Report*, January 1911, pp. 8-9 and September 1911, pp. 14-15.
86. For biographical details see Kevin Morgan, 'Class cohesion and trade-union internationalism: Fred Bramley, the British TUC and the Anglo-Russian Advisory Council', *International Review of Social History*, forthcoming.
87. *Labour Woman*, 1 November 1925, cutting in TUC archives 292/21.12/3.
88. NAFTA *Annual Report and Balance Sheet*, 1911, p. 13. For Hardie, see Morris, 'Labour or socialism', pp. 351-2.
89. NAFTA *Monthly Report*, March 1912, pp. 9-10.
90. NAFTA *Monthly Report*, January 1913, p. 13.
91. For the former see the NAFTA leaflet 'To all workers in the woodworking and furniture industry' reproduced NAFTA *Monthly Report*, December 1911, pp. 2-3.
92. Price, *Masters and Men*, pp. 252-3, also pp. 232-3.
93. For disputes with the building trades, see NAFTA *Monthly Report*, May 1923, pp. 9, 17-18; December 1923, p. 8; January 1924, p. 16.
94. NAFTA *Monthly Report*, February 1913, p. 14.
95. NAFTA *Monthly Report*, September 1910, p. 11.
96. NAFTA *Monthly Report*, June 1913, p. 18.
97. Purcell, 'The Furnishing Trades' spirited move', *Syndicalist and Amalgamation News*, February 1913; also Arthur Marsh and Victoria Ryan, *Historical Directory of Trade Unions*, vol. 3, Aldershot: Gower, 1987.
98. NAFTA *Monthly Report*, August 1915, p. 13-14. In the furnishing trades' centre of High Wycombe, NAFTA's preponderance within the trades council was to see the establishment of a separate strike committee by the Railwaymen in 1926; see Raymond Postgate, Ellen Wilkinson and J.F. Horrabin, *A Workers' History of the Great Strike*, Plebs League, 1927, p. 45.
99. See Bramley, 'Trade unionism and the craftsman', *Socialist Review*, October 1922, pp. 163-9; and the discussion in *Bolshevism and the British Left*, II, pp. 103-4.
100. NAFTA *Monthly Report*, February 1911, pp. 12-17 (re Calico Printing Association) and January 1912, p. 13 (re Electrical Contractors' Association).
101. *Accrington Observer and Times*, 5 September 1911.
102. NAFTA *Monthly Report*, September 1911, p. 11; *Accrington Observer and Times*, 5 September 1911.
103. Purcell in NAFTA *Monthly Report*, March 1914.
104. See NAFTA *Monthly Report*, August 1911, p. 11 for the trades councils' role in the Riley's dispute.
105. NAFTA *Monthly Report*, July 1915, pp. 15-16.
106. Bramley, *Co-operative News*, 16 July 1921 and *Why Trade Unionists should be Co-operators*, Manchester: Co-operative Union, 1924.
107. Price, 'Contextualising', p. 271.
108. NAFTA *Monthly Report*, April 1913, p. 13. For Foster's advocacy of 'race suicide', see Ford and Foster, *Syndicalism*, pp. 17-18.
109. NAFTA *Monthly Report*, September 1910, p. 11 and June 1916, pp. 16-17. This did not preclude a prioritisation of the interests of existing

Syndicalism, internationalism and the furnishing trades 59

male members in particular cases (see e.g. *Monthly Report*, July 1918, pp. 10-11).
110. NAFTA *Monthly Report*, January 1914, 12-15 and 17-18, February 1914, 9-10 and 14-15.
111. NAFTA *Monthly Report*, September 1913, pp. 16-17.
112. For a characteristic case brought at the expense and instigation of E.J. Riley's, see *Accrington Observer and Times*, 5 August 1911; also Purcell's remarks, NAFTA *Monthly Report*, September 1911, pp. 10-11.
113. NAFTA *Monthly Report*, September 1911, p. 13; *Manchester Guardian*, 13 September 1911.
114. *Manchester Guardian*, 12 January 1911.
115. NAFTA *Monthly Report*, August 1911, p. 11 and September 1912, pp. 12-13.
116. NAFTA *Monthly Report*, February 1914, p. 9.
117. NAFTA *Monthly Report*, February 1914, pp. 14-15.
118. NAFTA *Monthly Report*, February 1910, pp. 8-10.
119. NAFTA *Monthly Report*, July 1911, p. 14.
120. Discussion class, Dowry Picturedrome, *Accrington Observer and Times*, 3 October 1911.
121. NAFTA *Monthly Report*, September 1914, p. 17,
122. NAFTA *Monthly Report*, January 1919, p. 13.
123. See his letter in the *Manchester Guardian*, 7 October 1930.
124. *Accrington Observer and Times*, 3 October 1911.
125. NAFTA *Monthly Report*, August 1913, p. 12.
126. NAFTA *Monthly Report*, March 1912, pp. 9-10.
127. NAFTA EC minutes, 27 August, 3 September and 12 November 1914.
128. Details can be found in Purcell's reports in the NAFTA *Monthly Report* July-September 1919. The provisional terms of settlement were published in the October 1919 issues, pp. 18-21.
129. NAFTA *Monthly Report*, May 1919, pp. 15-16.
130. See 'Executive Committee and lockout', NAFTA *Monthly Journal*, December 1919, pp. 19-21.
131. NAFTA *Monthly Report*, October 1919, pp. 11-15.
132. NAFTA *Monthly Report*, March 1920, p. 16; Reid, *Furniture Makers*, pp. 102-3.
133. NAFTA *Monthly Report*, March 1919, p. 13.
134. NAFTA *Monthly Report*, December 1919, p. 15.
135. NAFTA *Monthly Report*, December 1919, p. 16.
136. See however Reid, *Furniture Makers*, pp. 84.
137. 57th *TUC Report*, 1925, p. 511.
138. Price, *Masters*, p. 252.
139. NAFTA *Monthly Report*, April 1918, p. 17, May 1918, p. 2, and June 1918, pp. 8-9; also March 1919, p. 17 for the vote in support of a conciliation board and June 1919, pp. 15-16 for Purcell's comments.
140. 56th *TUC Report*, 1924, p. 68.
141. *Manchester Guardian*, 25 August 1919.
142. *Russia. The official report of the British trades union delegation to Russia and Caucasia Nov. and Dec. 1924*, TUC, 1925, p. ix.
143. See NAFTA *Monthly Report*, November 1920, pp. 18-21 for Purcell and the North-East Lancashire Furnishing Trades Joint Council.

144. NAFTA *Monthly Report*, December 1912, pp. 9, 12.
145. NAFTA *Monthly Report*, August 1919, p. 11; September 1912, p. 13; December 1920, pp. 19-20.
146. See R. Page Arnot, *The Miners: Years of Struggle. A history of the Miners' Federation of Great Britain (from 1910 onwards)*, Allen & Unwin, 1953, p. 377.
147. Calhoun, *United Front*, pp. 54-5 and passim.
148. See ch. 4:1 below.
149. Bramley, NAFTA *Monthly Report*, June 1913, p. 9.
150. Bramley, NAFTA *Monthly Report*, September 1916, p. 11, and October 1916, p. 12. For the earlier period, see Gareth Stedman Jones, *Outcast London. A study in the relationship between classes in Victorian society*, Penguin edn, 1984, ch. 1, pp. 106-9.
151. Susan Milner, *The Dilemmas of Internationalism. French syndicalism and the international labour movement 1900-1914*, Oxford: Berg, 1990, p. 29.
152. Lewis L. Lorwin, *Labor and Internationalism*, New York: Macmillans, 1929, pp. 31, 34.
153. NAFTA *Monthly Report*, December 1913, 11-14,
154. NAFTA *Monthly Report*, January 1914, pp. 12-15 and 17-18; February 1914, 9-10 and 14-15.
155. NAFTA *Monthly Report*, May 1919, p. 14, December 1919, p. 15; also e.g. May 1923, p. 18.
156. Figures extrapolated from David Feldman, *Englishmen and Jews. Social relations and political culture 1840-1914*, New Haven & London: Yale University Press, 1994, pp. 157, 163.
157. Regarding Terence MacSwiney, the Mayor of Cork on hunger strike in Brixton gaol, he wrote to Lloyd George as 'the head and fount of a barbarity' and warned that should MacSwiney die 'no rapprochement between we Irishmen and Englishmen whether in England, Scotland or Wales is possible'; Lloyd George papers F42/3/3, O'Grady to Lloyd George, 27 August 1920.
158. Labour Party conference *Report*, June 1918, pp. 69-70; Joseph Buckman, *Immigration in the Class Struggle. The Jewish immigrant in Leeds 1880-1914*, Manchester: MUP, 1983, p. 167; T. Woodhouse, 'The working class' in Derek Fraser, ed., *A History of Modern Leeds*, Manchester: MUP, 1980, p. 373; Peter Dahle Colbenson, 'British socialism and anti-semitism, 1884-1914', Georgia State University: PhD, 1977, pp. 433-4. In a parliamentary question in 1912, O'Grady urged that the Aliens Act be 'impartially administered' and no exemptions made for 'cheap' (and, in the instance he cited, Jewish) labour (46 Hansard fifth series, 30 December 1912, cols 53-4).
159. NAFTA *Monthly Report*, May 1913, pp. 9-10.
160. *Salford Reporter*, 8 January 1910.
161. NAFTA *Monthly Report*, June 1913, p. 11.
162. NAFTA *Monthly Report*, October 1912, p. 9.
163. NAFTA *Monthly Report*, May 1912, p. 15; also June 1912, p. 2 for Gossip's similar views.
164. Henry Srebrnik, *London Jews and British Communism 1935-1945*, Valentine Mitchell, 1995, pp. 22-3.
165. 'That many of their race are totally unreliable and erratic in their observance of, and adherence to, working-class interests, is quite beyond

dispute', he wrote with stern impartiality, 'but what applies to them, also, I think, can be show to apply with equal strength to our race or to other nationalities'; NAFTA *Monthly Report*, November 1914, p. 12, December 1914, p. 12, March 1915, p. 15.
166. NAFTA *Monthly Report*, September 1913, pp. 16-17.
167. *Manchester Guardian*, 1 December 1919; NA CAB 24/194 CP 2089, RRO 11 November 1920.
168. NAFTA *Monthly Report*, October 1913, p. 16.
169. NAFTA *Monthly Report*, November 1918, p. 14.
170. NAFTA *Monthly Report*, March 1918, pp. 13-15; June 1918, p. 16; August 1918, p. 15.
171. NAFTA *Monthly Report*, March 1919, pp. 12.
172. NAFTA *Monthly Report*, December 1920, pp. 19-20.
173. NAFTA *Monthly Report*, April 1918, pp. 10-11.
174. Emmet O'Connor, '"Sentries of British imperialism?" The question of British-based unions in Ireland', *Socialist History*, 29, 2006, pp. 1-19.
175. NAFTA *Monthly Report*, December 1920, pp. 19-20.
176. NAFTA EC minutes, 19 November 1914, also 20 May 1915. The concern in this case was with an anti-trade union firm in Colwick, Notts.
177. NAFTA *Monthly Report*, May 1918, p. 13.
178. Jolyon Howorth. 'French workers and German workers: the impossibility of internationalism 1900-1914', *European History Quarterly*, 15, 1, 1985, pp. 71-97.
179. NAFTA *Monthly Report*, July 1913, pp. 15-17.
180. Lovett, addresses 'to the Working Classes of France' (1844) and 'to the French' (1848) in his *Life and Struggles*, pp. 251, 275.
181. As for example in Christine Collette, *The International Faith. Labour's attitudes to European socialism 1918-1939*, Aldershot: Ashgate, 1998. While excluding both world wars Collette offers the unfathomable explanation (p. 4) that: 'Against the fact that workers fought against each other … must be posed their lack of knowledge of modern welfare and invidious familiarity with domestic poverty'.
182. See Lewis L. Lorwin and Jean A. Flexner, 'The International Union of Woodworkers', *American Federationist*, July 1926, pp. 846-52.
183. Reid, *Furniture Makers*, p. 69.
184. Ross McKibbin, *The Evolution of the Labour Party, 1910-1924*, Oxford: OUP, 1983 edn, p. 90.
185. See e.g. NAFTA *Monthly Report*, August 1914, p. 2; September 1914, p. 2; November 1914, p. 2; April 1916, pp. 2-3; also Gossip's introduction to NAFTA *Annual Report and Balance Sheet*, 1916, pp. 8-9.
186. NAFTA *Monthly Report*, November 1914, p. 6, also February 1915, p. 7. At the end of the war NAFTA members voted that wartime internees be accorded full membership rights, like returning service personnel; but the majority of 1650 : 1307 was a relatively narrow one (NAFTA *Monthly Report*, October 1919, pp. 22-3 and November 1919, p. 26).
187. NAFTA *Monthly Report*, January 1915, p. 14.
188. 'Manifesto to the members of the National Amalgamated Furnishing Trades Association', NAFTA *Monthly Report*, March 1915, pp. 27-30.
189. NAFTA *Monthly Report*, May 1915, p. 2.
190. David Blaazer, *The Popular Front and the Progressive Tradition. Socialists,*

Liberals and the quest for unity, 1884-1939, Cambridge: CUP, 1992, p. 22. The best history remains Marvin Swartz, *The Union of Democratic Control in British Politics during the First World War*, Oxford: OUP, 1971.
191. BWD, 8 April 1916*; see also Morgan, 'Class cohesion' for further details.
192. Fred Bramley, *Class Cohesion versus Spurious Patriotism. A straight talk to British workers*, Manchester: National Labour Press, n.d. but 1915.
193. GFTU 16th general council meeting *Report*, pp. 22, 24, contributions of R.W. Mann (Coopers) and James Bell (Ironfounders).
194. GFTU 16th general council meeting *Report*, 1915, pp. 18-20, contribution of Bramley.
195. NAFTA *Monthly Report*, June 1917, pp. 18-19.
196. *The Labour Who's Who 1924*, Labour Publishing Co, 1924, p.126.
197. Georges Fischer, *Le parti travailliste et la décolonisation de l'Inde*, Paris: François Maspero, 1966, p. 49.
198. 190 Hansard fourth series, 4 June 1908, cols 211-15.
199. W.T. Stead, 'The Labour Party and the books that helped to make it', *Review of Reviews*, June 1906, p. 578; E.D. Steele, 'Imperialism and Leeds politics, c. 1850-1914' in Fraser, *History of Modern Leeds*, p. 344.
200. NAFTA *Monthly Report*, May 1916, pp. 18-19.
201. NAFTA *Monthly Report*, July 1916, p. 18.
202. See ch. 8 below.
203. GFTU 18th general council meeting *Report*, 1917, pp. 34-6.
204. NAFTA *Monthly Report*, August 1917, p. 14.
205. *Manchester Guardian*, 5 and 8 August 1914.
206. NAFTA *Monthly Report*, September 1914, pp. 18-19.
207. NAFTA *Monthly Report*, July 1915, pp. 2, 13.
208. NAFTA *Monthly Report*, October 1914, p. 15.
209. *British Labour Delegation to Russia, 1920: report*, TUC and Labour Party, 1920, pp. 116-17.
210. E.g. in NAFTA *Monthly Report*, January 1916, pp. 14-15.
211. NAFTA *Monthly Report*, August 1918, pp. 2-3.
212. Jennings, *Syndicalism in France*, p. 226.
213. NAFTA *Monthly Report*, July 1917, p. 2.
214. *Manchester Guardian*, 7 May 1917.
215. NAFTA *Monthly Report*, February 1918, p. 5.
216. NAFTA *Monthly Report*, September 1919, pp. 17-18; IFTU *Press Reports*, 156, April 1922.
217. *Manchester Guardian*, 7 May 1917.
218. Comparing 1919-21 with 1910-14, both the average and peak figures for days lost in stoppages were considerably higher; see figures in Hugh Armstrong Clegg, *A History of British Trade Unions since 1889. Volume 2: 1911-1933*, Oxford: OUP, 1985, p. 568.
219. NAFTA Monthly Report, June 1919, p. 8; James Klugmann, *History of the Communist Party of Great Britain. Volume one: formation and early years 1919-1924*, Lawrence & Wishart, 1967, p. 79.
220. NAFTA *Monthly Report*, May 1920, p. 13.
221. *Manchester Guardian*, 29 July 1920.
222. *Daily Herald*, 12 July 1920.
223. Sidney Webb to Beatrice Webb, 24 June 1925, in Norman Mackenzie, ed.,

The Letters of Sidney and Beatrice Webb, vol 3, Cambridge: CUP, 1978, p. 239.
224. Kevin Morgan and Andrew Flinn, entry on Hardy, *DLB* vol. 11, pp. 98-109.
225. Zinoviev at CI Fifth Congress cited L.J. Macfarlane, *The British Communist Party. Its origin and development until 1929*, MacGibbon & Kee, 1966, p. 142.

Chapter two

Roads to freedom in the 1920s

2.1 THE SWING OF THE PENDULUM

By 1921, the combative spirit on which syndicalism had thrived was weakening. 'Black Friday' – the collapse that April of the triple industrial alliance of miners, railwaymen and dockers – proved the signal for a general industrial retreat. As Purcell wrote to Mann a few weeks afterwards, 'I am up to my eyes in the vile business of urging the giving of ground in the shape of reduced wages and unfortunately there [is] a ready response'.[1] In the search for alternative ways forward G.D.H. Cole in the *New Statesman* discerned a 'swing of the pendulum' between industrial and political action.[2] A widely held notion at the time, the idea of such a swing was seemingly borne out in the few years that followed. The ebbing of militant industrialism was succeeded by a cluster of general elections, Sidney Webb's heralding of the inevitability of gradualness and the corroboration in 1924 of a first Labour government. Lasting less than a year, this was followed by a revival of direct action as the antidote to a flaccid and accommodating parliamentarism. Culminating in the 1926 General Strike and miners' lockout, this in turn gave way to a more emphatic reassertion of parliamentary ascendancy and a second Labour government in 1929-31. When this too collapsed in disarray, there was no corresponding prospect of an industrial upsurge. For some like the Webbs, the failing of the pendulum meant the turn to communism as *deus ex machina*.

Purcell at first glance epitomises the pendulum swing. For a time after Black Friday he diverted his energies into more political channels. Though he then swung back to union action, the failure of the General Strike proved the prelude to his permanent departure from the national scene in the late 1920s. Whatever its wider justification, at the level of the individual biography the idea of an oscillation between political and industrial action is nevertheless inadequate. For the dealer in ideas, dramatic transitions were possible without getting up from the typewriter. Beatrice Webb, who immediately took up Cole's pendulum metaphor, is an obvious example. In Cole's case, even more than the Webbs', a series of such transitions and recantations were accommodated within a relatively conventional professional career. For their immediate practitioners, on the other hand, politics and direct action did not just present strategic choices but were issues of leadership, recognition and entitlement. If syndicalists looked warily on politicians, and politicians warily back, it was because these represented alternative claims to the movement's direction and the social and professional basis on which it should rest. In any case, the simple categories of 'industrial' and 'political' concealed both persisting political ambitions on the part of trade unions and the diverse forms in which both political and industrial action could be envisaged.

Three years earlier, Bertrand Russell had employed the less mechanistic metaphor of roads to freedom, or workers' emancipation, in discussing the rival claims of socialism, anarchism and syndicalism.[3] In 1920, the year he travelled to Russia with Purcell, Russell extended the discussion to Bolshevism and its attempted realisation of the communist ideal.[4] The idea of different roads, down which one might either lead the way or else turn off, seems closer in spirit to the pegs on which Purcell looked to 'hang his advocacy'.[5] Purcell was at one with Mann in expressing indifference to terms like 'Socialist, Spartacist, Bolshevist or Syndicalist' as long as they signified the rejection of capitalism.[6] Already at the CPGB's founding congress he deprecated differences over 'mere phraseology' and urged 'the working-class itself to rally for the purpose of ... owning and controlling the means of production'.[7] He returned to the theme in the *Labour Monthly* contribution that so exasperated Dutt:

> Policies, programmes, platforms and what not have the knack of nosing forward, and shifting either sideways or to the rear a little or much, just according to the bleat of those behind or the blast of those in the front line of advocacy. ... I have been in at the drafting and distribution of millions of them, but never once did I believe they would do the thing the chief enthusiasts desired. My view has always been that I regarded this literature attack as an effort to get the working class to know itself.[8]

Bolshevism, in the form of the CPGB, was one of these platforms. Guild socialism, in the form of the Furniture and Furnishing Guild (FFG), was another. Parliamentary socialism, during Purcell's two stints as MP, was a third. Running concurrently with all of them was the TUC general council, which for a time was presented as legatee to the syndicalist agitations of the previous decade. There was therefore no simple progression from one road to another. For simplicity's sake, however, the following sections describe each of these key political commitments of the 1920s in turn.

Purcell's innocent phrase, the working class itself, conveys a certain consistency of outlook underlying these diverse forms of activity. At the same time it obscures a more basic shift in the conditions on which they were performed. For Purcell, it implied a continuing orientation to the labour movement structures through which the working class was animated, and a belief that the movement's raison d'être was precisely this ethos and practice of self-representation. Inasmuch as this was exercised by and through the trade unions, Labour's emergence as a national political force offered greater opportunities for political intervention than ever before or since. With proliferating functions of representation, publicity and research, Purcell had a direct hand in all of them: as union-sponsored MP, nominal editor of a short-lived journal and three times a TUC signatory to international fact-finding reports. From *Hansard* to the flourishing left-wing press, the wider documentation of his views is suggestive in itself of the new public profile of the trade unionist-politician.

Nevertheless, Labour's coming of age turned out in this respect to have been its swansong. Even into the 1930s, as Ben Pimlott observed, the labour movement remained 'a network of industrial, social and cultural organisations, with the "political wing" as merely one feature'.[9] Even so, the establishment by this time of a modus vivendi between party and unions meant a far clearer sense of hierarchy, function and prerogative. Proliferating functions came to mean specialisation and professionalisation. Not infrequently this also meant the recognition of traditional forms of qualification embodying class and educational privilege. Already in the 1920s Purcell depended on editorial professionals for his magazine *Trade Union Unity*. He also relied on the reputed business skills of Samuel Hobson for the Furnishing Guild and on former career professionals from the military or diplomatic service for Labour's Russian delegations. Allegations quickly surfaced that theirs was in fact the controlling hand, and Purcell little more than a figurehead. As yet the role of such figures was nevertheless accommodated within the labour movement's traditional authority structures through the Webbian notion of 'clerks' or 'civil servants'. In any case their contribution was largely ad hoc and lacked the constraining solidity of a formal bureaucratic apparatus. For a few years at least, Purcell's career showed what room for manoeuvre there was between the Labour and communist parties, and what moral and material resources were to be derived from the rivalry between them. In retrospect it proved barely a moment, and his falling was as meteor-like as his sudden appearance on the national stage.

2.2 NON-PARTY COMMUNISM

In the spring of 1920 the British Socialist Party, successor to the SDF, set out its philosophy of political action within the context of the newly established Comintern. 'The British working class will move – have no fear of that', it insisted:

But it will move through its own institutions and impelled by the accumulated experience of its own historic past ... For ourselves, we shall continue to be with the mass of the workers wherever they are – even in the Labour Party, helping them in their struggles, pointing out their mistakes, opposing the influence of their opportunist leaders and seeking always to inspire them with our communist ideals.[10]

Numerically at least, the BSP provided the dominant component within the CPGB on its foundation a few weeks later. Its ambition, to remain true at once to Labour institutions and to communist ideals, was to prove an impossible balancing act. Nevertheless, Purcell at first found it plausible enough, not only to have joined the CPGB but to have moved the resolution that brought the party into being.

Other trade unionists drawn this way included Cook, Robert Williams and the syndicalist Jack Tanner. None, however, succeeded in combining union office with communist party discipline. If Mann proved a communist catch, it was possible only because of his retirement from union responsibilities. If Pollitt proved another, it was at the cost, in practice, of renouncing such ambitions. If Gossip remained the union leader closest to the CPGB, it was because he never took the step of actually joining the party. Within two years of its foundation, all of the others, including Purcell, were once more outside the party's ranks. Not until the years of the popular front was a British communist again to hold prominent union office.[11]

Potential difficulties were discernible from the start. Representing the South Salford BSP at the CPGB's foundation congress, Purcell moved the party's establishment on the basis of Soviets or workers' councils and the dictatorship of the proletariat. Already, however, he described the party as the movement's 'guide' rather than its leader; not 'prodding and pinpricking the working-class' but recognising the 'hard concrete facts of industrial organisation'.[12] For a time he appeared on communist platforms, and with Williams beside him put the case for a 'strongly organised Communist Party'.[13] One may doubt that he ever intended being strongly organised by it. In April 1921, Williams became the CPGB's first prominent expellee on account of his role in Black Friday. Cook left, or was expelled, shortly afterwards, jibbing at the outside direction of a 'small clique'.[14] For Purcell, their senior by a decade, the idea of being held to account by industrial neophytes was more implausible still. According to a list of 'renegades' in the Comintern archives, he 'ceased to take active part in [the] Party and finally dropped out' – also, according to this source, in 1921.[15] Still in February 1922 he 'fired up' and announced he had a party card when the presence of a communist translator was challenged at a conference of socialist parties in Frankfurt.[16] One wonders whether the card was still paid up. The incompatibility of the new party disciplines with the holding of high union office was in any case settled later that year by the CPGB's endorsement of the famous Dutt-Pollitt organisation report, with its central rationale of 'leading and concentrating the members' activities the whole time'.[17]

To maintain contact with such figures without compromising internal discipline, the Comintern quickly learnt the value of so-called front organisations. The first and arguably most important of these was the Red International of Labour Unions (RILU), also known as the Profintern.[18] Purcell himself played some part in its launching. While in Russia with the British Labour delegation in May-June 1920, he and Williams joined in discussions with Russian and Italian trade unionists regarding such an initiative, envisaged by the Russians as a mere industrial section of the Comintern. Alexander Losovsky, secretary of key Russian unions in the period of war communism, was to be the dominant figure in the Profintern throughout its sixteen-year existence. His position at this stage was that the Comintern itself was 'a fighting revolutionary class centre ... accessible to all proletarian, political, trade union and co-operative organisations', and that a separate trade-union international was at best a dispersal of forces and at worst a 'bad edition of the Second International'.[19]

Despite his background in revolutionary syndicalism, Losovsky's career was to be one of repeated collisions with western trade-union conceptions, including the deep-rooted syndicalist suspicion of party ties. When Zinoviev on 16 June announced a new 'Red Industrial International' this therefore had the appearance of a significant concession on the Bolsheviks' part. The Italians still had concerns about the proposed manifesto, and on returning to Britain with discussions still ongoing, Purcell and Williams were said to have 'given their names to any agreement that might be arrived at' in their absence.[20] Already the resolution of 'representatives of Russian, English and Italian labour organizations assembled under the auspices of the Executive Committee of the Communist International' stated that the proposed 'militant international committee' of trade unionists would act 'in accordance' with the Comintern.[21] Williams in any case had no hesitation on this score. Although a member of the Labour Party executive, who was due to attend the Geneva congress of the Second International, he announced on his return that he intended working instead towards the extension of the Third.[22]

In later years, the episode was resurrected both by supporters of the Profintern and by critics of Purcell who saw such associations as deeply compromising. There is little evidence, however, that Purcell took the commitment any further. When a British bureau of the RILU was established under Mann's chairmanship in early 1921, Purcell apparently declined to move the resolutions at its first London conference.[23] Attempts through Mann to involve him in an emergency conference on the German crisis in 1923 again proved unavailing.[24] In August 1924, the more ambitious National Minority Movement

(NMM) was formed as successor body to the bureau. Mann, who as chairman once more provided a self-conscious claim to continuity, described the movement as 'exactly analogous' with the syndicalism of the ISEL.[25] When later that year Purcell reaffirmed his support for the Soviets as head of the TUC's Russian delegation, hopes were revived of an 'organic connection' with the delegates on their return.[26] Pollitt, the NMM's secretary, nevertheless recalled the 'bitter experience' of promises made in Moscow and promptly forgotten, and once more Purcell could not be persuaded to appear on a Minority Movement platform. After further unavailing interviews, Pollitt concluded with some acerbity that it was 'one thing to be revolutionary in Soviet Russia and another thing to be openly identified with the revolutionary movement in England'.[27]

There was greater consistency in Purcell's stance than Pollitt appreciated. The guiding precept of his career, and the explanation of much within it that might otherwise be inexplicable, was the pursuit of working-class unity as expressed through its recognised institutions. The mineworker Nat Watkins, also active in the Minority Movement, was a figure more of Purcell's own generation. Though in one sense echoing Pollitt, Watkins also registered the pressures to which Purcell and those around him conformed in describing them as 'quite another thing when they come back here amongst friends of their own kidney'.[28] Critics of the TUC's laxity towards communism ascribed it to the lack of any serious internal communist challenge. From a TUC perspective, on the other hand, it was by involving the 'militant section' in their 'share in the work of the movement' that the possibilities of splitting and disorganisation had been successfully headed off.[29] On this basis it seemed quite plausible to embrace the Russian unions, and the achievements of the Russian revolution, while resisting any tendency to divide the British labour movement. One of the premises of the TUC's understanding with the Russians was that they were the only major trade-union movements enjoying 'full national unity', undisturbed by religious or political cleavages.[30] Repeatedly Purcell contrasted their undivided nature with the 'almost indescribable' rivalries which elsewhere split the unions into as many as (he claimed) six contending sections.[31] Just the same moral applied internationally, and when Purcell defended his communist attachments in Frankfurt, he also upheld the perspective of a 'great united working class international' against 'internecine squabbling'.[32] To be 'revolutionary' in Russia but not necessarily in Britain was the logic of unity as he conceived of it.

It is sometimes suggested that British Labour was hostile to communism in both its Russian and British manifestations.[33] Alternatively, its singularity is seen to lie in its dissociation of the Russians from the ineffectual nuisance of home-grown Bolshevism.[34] Purcell's approach was more discriminating. Within Britain, he was certainly hostile to any activity seen as threatening the labour movement's 'institutions and ... accumulated experience'. Equally, and according to the same logic of unity, he had no intrinsic objection to communists performing roles which respected these. When Bromley, Cook and Hicks sent fraternal greetings to the CPGB's 1924 party congress, Purcell for some reason was not among them.[35] As Mann observed of his wariness of the Minority Movement, he was 'anxious to carry the General Council along with him and I expect he feels the closer he is connected with us the less likely he is to carry the majority along with him at present'.[36] His support for the twelve communist leaders convicted in 1925 again demonstrated this basic ambivalence. Purcell readily joined a Free Speech Defence and Maintenance Committee and visited Pollitt in Wandsworth prison. At public rallies he revived his caustic assessment of a politically motivated legal process, and he defended the communists as part of a 'great united front' against the capitalist order.[37] Though initiated as a 'Fund' of the communist-sponsored International Class War Prisoners' Aid (ICWPA), the Free Speech committee was nevertheless reconstituted as an independent body sharing only a secretary with its progenitor, and according to communist reports it enjoyed a 'somewhat delicate' relationship with it.[38]

Communists were valued most of all as labour movement clerks, or in roles in which the official movement was deficient. The Labour Research Department (LRD) epitomised such a role, and in April 1925 there was launched from its offices a monthly journal, *Trade Union Unity*, under the nominal direction of Purcell, Hicks and the Dutchman Edo Fimmen.[39] When 'people associated with the left wing movement in the trade unions' had first pressed the Russians for assistance with such a venture, the CPGB had expressed strong opposition unless a party member was put in charge.[40] In a sense, this is what transpired: the journal assumed the specialised character of an 'international journal to promote unity', and its editor, 'in fact if not in name', was the Cambridge-educated Allen Hutt, who also worked in TASS's London office and who in Dutt's absence put together the *Labour Monthly*.[41] The frequent inclusion of communist contributors was hardly concealed by their use of union affiliations.[42] Nevertheless, it was Purcell who wrote (or signed) the main editorial and who secured the co-operation of his TUC colleagues, without whose regular input the journal would scarcely have merited its Russian subsidy. Though it was originally envisaged as an LRD supplement, and for five issues was freely distributed from the LRD offices, *Trade Union Unity* was therefore like the Free Speech committee in assuming an independent status.[43] As if resignedly, Hutt described himself as its editorial 'factotum'.[44]

This was indeed a characteristic arrangement at this time. When the then TUC chairman Alonzo Swales needed a speech for the first Commonwealth Labour Conference, he approached the LRD secretary Arnot, who in turn approached the CPGB's representative in Moscow.[45] A.J. Cook was widely known to enjoy similar support, in particular that of his 'CP private secretary' Glyn Evans.[46] Purcell doubtless drew on similar forms of assistance, though possibly with his usual sense of caution. His most durable relationship was with the Irishman W.P. Coates, a sometime BSPer and union activist who was secretary of the original Hands Off Russia committee and of its successor the Anglo-Russian Parliamentary Committee, both of which were chaired by Purcell. Already at the CPGB's founding congress, Coates had expressed a strong commitment to work within the Labour Party.[47] According to his wife and collaborator Zelda Kahan Coates, once a well-known figure on the BSP's internationalist wing, the couple by 1925 were actually Labour Party members, considering that 'a socialist party without the masses behind it is doomed to work ineffectually'.[48] Whatever his party status, it was Coates who, according to the communist defector Newbold, was entrusted with 'the Chesham House subsidy' once the Soviet embassy was re-established there in 1924. Again according to Newbold, Coates used it to grease those members of his committee who could be found 'washing necks' in the smoke room of the House of Commons.[49]

As Pollitt certainly appreciated, it was not only from the British side that there was a tendency to bypass 'the revolutionary movement in England'. As initially projected as a rationale for the Minority Movement, Mikhail Borodin's conception of union leaders as banners deserving 'persistent advertisement' was strongly resisted by Pollitt and Dutt.[50] When Purcell as congress chairman set the tone for the 1924 TUC, the fraternal delegation from the Russian unions was well-contented with the ovation it received. Petrovsky, Borodin's successor as Comintern representative, nevertheless commented privately on the 'treachery' of the lefts, and the *Workers' Weekly* even used Purcell's address to document their well-intentioned 'bankruptcy'.[51] The Russian union leader Mikhail Tomsky assured Purcell that the CPGB were just 'babes'.[52] Not only did Purcell and his colleagues decline to attend a Minority Movement conference on returning from Russia at the end of 1924. So, it was said, did any representative of the Russian unions, for fear of offending them.[53] When some months later Herbert Morrison attended a 'highly respectable' Chesham House reception on the anniversary of the revolution, the courses of food were plentiful and 'proletarian garb' little in evidence: 'I had great difficulty in finding any – I am not sure that I did find any – of the more working class leaders of British Communism present.'[54] Willie Gallacher, whose absence on this occasion one may perhaps infer, complained around this time that nobody ever knew what Coates was up to and that if there were 'many more Party members who give such little thought to the Party we would very soon be without a Party altogether'.[55] Between the Comintern, the Profintern, the Russian unions and the Soviet embassy, these very different ways of identifying with the Russian revolution help explain both the scope of the phenomenon and its politically ambiguous character. The CPGB may have held the Comintern franchise, but attempts by some historians to project the Russian connection onto this alone lack any real plausibility.

Purcell's commitment to the 'institutions ... [and] accumulated experience' of the British working class meant that association with the communists was possible only to the extent that they also respected these. In the spring of 1925 he willingly supported the new *Sunday Worker*, which disclaimed any pretensions as an official 'Left Wing' organ and described the left as Lansbury might have, as unofficial and heterodox by its very nature.[56] When the communists nevertheless proceeded towards a formally constituted National Left Wing Movement, rather after the fashion of the Minority Movement, Purcell's opposition was absolute:

> It was he who, from three accounts ... made the most savage and vindictive attack on the Party; he said that this could not stop at a resolution, they would have to go on to organisation, and he and Hicks could not countenance any split in the Labour Party, this is the sort of thing that has disrupted the Continental movement, the Communists could do nothing but disrupt and make trouble, etc.[57]

It was only after the General Strike that Purcell, like Lansbury, broke off significant association with communists in Britain. Insofar as they functioned as a repackaged BSP, he had recognised their contribution as a necessary element of the 'working-class mosaic'. The communists after 1926, however, had greater ambitions than this. Purcell took his stand with Labour's own institutions – at what cost to his own political effectiveness remained to be seen.

2.3 GUILD SOCIALIST

As Purcell was making his exit from the CPGB, the party itself was seeking to systematise its controls over the broader range of communist activities. Some organisations, like the LRD, became the focus of communist fraction work. Others were effectively abandoned. Perhaps the most prominent of these was the National Guilds League (NGL), which, as Leslie Macfarlane observed, the CPGB 'quietly dropped' over the winter of 1921-2 – though not so quietly as to prevent William Mellor from delivering an autopsy in the *Labour Monthly*.[58] Individual communists remained active in guilds circles, including the *Labour Monthly*'s own secretary and business manager Joan Beauchamp.[59] Mellor even suggested that S.G. Hobson, the founder of guild socialism, 'apart from his practical activities as an exponent of the Building Guild, is a Communist'.[60] Despite the continuing room for manoeuvre, Purcell's brief involvement with the guilds is indicative of a fluidity of association and forms of activity which party disciplines were beginning to undermine. There is nothing to suggest a direct link between his involvement with the guilds and his departure from the communist party. They did however take place almost simultaneously.

As a body of ideas, guild socialism can be traced from Hobson's essays on *National Guilds*, published in 1912-13.[61] As a movement it can be traced from the NGL's foundation in 1915. Subsequently it has become synonymous with Cole, its most lucid expositor, whose advocacy and relinquishment of the guild idea represented his own cerebral pendulum swing between workers' self-government and collectivism.[62] Cole, however, had little direct contact with provincial proletarianism and the likes of Purcell. For these, the more immediate public face of guild socialism bore Hobson's features, not so much as its intellectual progenitor as through his ill-fated attempt to put into practice the guild ideal and secure it organisationally within the labour movement. Hobson's qualifications for such an enterprise were two. As a travelling lecturer, journalist and parliamentary candidate, variously active in the ILP, Labour Church, Fabian Society and socialist representation committees, he had a wealth of labour movement contacts and had shared a Manchester platform with Purcell as far back as 1905.[63] More distinctively, he also had extensive if somewhat questionable business experience that may or may not have merited the sobriquet Soapy Sam.

Once more in Manchester as a government demobilisation officer, Hobson was quick to see the possibilities of the post-war Addison housing act and the direct subsidies to builders that were introduced at the end of 1919.[64] Among his union contacts was Dick Coppock, the Manchester-based organiser of the Operative Bricklayers who a decade earlier had been among the delegates at the founding conference of the ISEL. In January 1920 the collaboration between Hobson and Coppock saw the establishment of a Manchester Building Guild.[65] Seven months later its first housing contracts were secured, and the following June Hobson arranged its merger with its London counterpart to produce what was grandly described as the 'first National Building Guild in the history of the world', with offices in Upper Brook Street, Manchester.[66] Initially Hobson had enjoyed the assistance of sympathetic contacts at the new Ministry of Health. However, the national guild was confronted from the start with a de facto government embargo on further guild contracts on any other than an undercutting 'maximum sum' basis.[67] One response was to seek to raise a loan with which to negotiate the more difficult times ahead. Another was to extend the movement into other industries. The Furniture and Furnishing Guild (FFG), with Purcell as its secretary, was the result.

Immediately Hobson began canvassing support for a Building Guild, Purcell had become involved. In December 1919 he presided over a Manchester meeting of the NGL that was well attended by union representatives.[68] His first intimation of a possible furniture guild followed swiftly on the formation of the Manchester Building Guild the following month.[69] It nevertheless took the ebbing away of strike activity for this to become the focus for his activities; indeed, the decision to form the Furnishing Guild was taken just a fortnight after Black Friday.[70] Some weeks later a Trades Union Guild Council was launched in Manchester with the aim of reaching beyond the building industry and establishing the guilds at the heart of the organised labour movement. Its founding premise, the *Manchester Guardian* reported, was that 'in a season of barren wage disputes conventional trade unionism may be led to a knowledge of its limitations', and thus more readily embrace a vision of the promised land where the wage contract was unknown.[71] The Furniture Guild, having commenced work in October, was established as a limited company in February 1922, sharing offices with the Building Guild and operating a workshop rented from the AEU in nearby Plymouth Grove. The following spring a National Guilds Council was established on Hobson's motion, as an umbrella organisation for both working guilds and agitational bodies like the NGL. Several industries were represented, some by leading officers. Among them were the Tailor and Garment Workers' secretary, Andrew Conley, and the editor of the Post Office Workers' journal, George Middleton. However, with the Bricklayers' secretary George Hicks taking the chair, and Purcell and Coppock supporting Hobson's resolution, the unions most conspicuously represented were the building and furnishing trades.[72]

The two industries had long been closely associated and within the TUC were combined in a trade group also including the other woodworking trades. This certainly accorded with NAFTA's priorities, which in the immediate post-war period included the application to the furnishing trades of building trades agreements, and recognition by appropriate boards and associations on both the workers' and employers' side.[73] Though relations between NAFTA and the Building Trades' federation were never straightforward, both Coppock and Hicks shared Purcell's syndicalist background and his readiness to associate with disparate left-wing movements, including the communists.[74] Furnishing workers also shared with the building trades the late Victorian rediscovery of the ideal craftsman, representing both aspiration for fulfilment in work and indictment of the shoddiness and deceit of modern commercial practice. Even O'Grady had reported effusively on an 'Arts and Crafts Exhibition' of hand-produced work by trade unionists, including a bedroom suite made by NAFTA members in their spare time.[75] Purcell employed such notions in a more combative and instrumental way. During the 1919 lockout he excoriated the 'lying and filthy dogs' who dominated the employers' association and who were 'daily fleecing the public with furniture rubbish', including bogus oak and mahogany and the 'great Jacobean and "rub off" furniture swindle'.[76] One can only imagine the reaction to this of O'Grady, who 'for many years earned his living as a maker of "antique" furniture'.[77] But furnishing workers, like the building trades, employed a discourse of the 'public' or consumer's interest in avoiding shoddy and undercutting through the recognition of established skills, materials and conditions of employment.[78] Through his involvement in tenants' activities, Purcell also drew on this from a consumers' perspective, urging low-density building with full amenities against the 'mean little hutches' and tenements by which today's workers were fobbed off with tomorrow's slums.[79]

The disparate features of Purcell's socialism are easier to understand within such a context. Challenged about his absorption in the guild's work, he cited the commitment in NAFTA's rule book to 'the complete control of industry by those who work in it'. Instead of the 'zig-zag' movement of industrial advance and retreat, the guild offered training in the administrative skills the unions would require in assuming that control and the harnessing of energy and enthusiasm to a higher conception of production. Possibly it may therefore be seen as a distinctly industrial response to the pendulum swing. Its claims were reminiscent of the justifications offered for earlier endeavours in co-production, like the Christian Socialists', but with a distinctive emphasis on what in Germany would have been called quality work. As Purcell put it, workers exposed to the 'fine school and workroom of industrial experience' came to see that 'tricks worked off in industry and today known as good and profitable business' were incompatible with any higher social purpose.[80] As far as possible, consumers would be provided with the best that the guild could manufacture, 'even if the quantity is at the moment less than their needs demand'.[81] The quality of the work was widely commented upon, and was demonstrated at Manchester's May Day rally by its being displayed side by side with that of private manufacturers.[82]

Purcell conceded that the 'shoddy and deceptive' would be fully cast aside only as the guild outgrew its dependence on the industry's established structures. Unlike the earlier arts-and-craft guilds, it proposed making 'only useful household furniture' on what effectively would have been a mass scale corresponding to the projected public housing programme. A cheaper as well as better article than the capitalist's, it was to undercut it by as much as half – perhaps, it was briefly suggested, through the importation of Soviet timber on 'very advantageous terms'. The synthesis of modernism and the labour movement was a continental European phenomenon, and the guild's published catalogue shows little distinctiveness in design terms from ordinary commercial production.[83] The vision held out was nevertheless a heady one: 'That all those people between the actual *User* and the *Producer* shall be eliminated, ultimately giving to the Workers *complete control of the Industry* to exploit it for *Use* as against *Profit*.'[84]

As a business proposition, the guild was nevertheless doomed from the start.[85] By the time of its launch, the guilds movement as a whole was mired in the financial difficulties that were to lead to its collapse. Hobson, through the Building Guild, found £1000 with which to launch the Furnishing Guild; this, however, was a far cry from the larger sums he had urged the unions to divert from the pursuit of unwinnable strikes.[86] Undercapitalised from the start, the guild after thirteen weeks still boasted thirty workers and a full order book.[87] Purcell himself was effectively full-time secretary, and temporary arrangements were made for the payment of his NAFTA salary by the guilds themselves.[88] Working branches were also set up in other localities, although the Manchester guild absorbed most of the funding raised within NAFTA and a London section nominally attached to it claimed to have had no help or recognition despite persistent representations.[89]

Very likely this contributed to the waning enthusiasm of the union's members and executive alike. A 'Furnishing Guild Million Pennies Stamp' did not produce a million pennies.[90] A requested loan of ten thousand pounds did not materialise.[91] A 'National Guild Building Society', envisaging 100,000 weekly subscriptions for furnished homes to be allotted by ballot, would have taken a hundred years to provide them at the projected rate of completion.[92] With the rejection in a NAFTA members' ballot of a further financial appeal, a winding-up order was issued at the beginning of 1923. At the second National Guild Conference in December 1922, Hobson insisted that Purcell was doing his utmost to rescue the guild from collapse. Purcell himself, however, neither attended nor submitted a report, and the representative of the London guild complained that he had never succeeded in making contact with him.[93] In its year of existence, the guild had actually carried out some £8000 worth of orders.[94] In the ballot for the National Guilds Council Purcell nevertheless came only eleventh, behind less well-known trade unionists like Middleton and the communist Sam Elsbury.[95] Though this was still enough to secure him a seat on the council, Purcell appears never to have attended.[96]

It was characteristic of him to offer so little reflection on what had gone wrong. At best, he put it down to external contingencies and lack of finance.[97] At worst he all but disclaimed responsibility.[98] More modest schemes proved more durable. The London guild maintained its operations for at least a few months longer; and a Piano Workers' Guild, initially established on a voluntary basis, could five years later boast a hundred guildsmen and eight full-time workers manufacturing 'High Grade Pianos ... under Workers' Control'.[99] Probably Purcell did not sufficiently esteem such pockets of achievement. He was, as we shall see, among the advocates of the demonstration strike as a form of declamation by the deed and a means of soldering workers' solidarity. His promotion of the guild may similarly be regarded as a form of demonstration, education or even agit-prop. What it offered was less a way out of capitalism than an expression of alternative production values and social relationships. Symptomatically, Purcell's first report as secretary described the guild's work as if already half-accomplished. Released from a profit-making environment, its workers had exhibited higher skill, greater craftsmanship, cleaner and brighter types of production and a 'keener perception of solidarity' among the varying departments of production.[100] Though its high standards of work appear to have contributed to the guild's demise, Purcell nevertheless saw them as 'a good piece of Guild propaganda'.[101]

There were some longer-term effects on Purcell's political outlook. Hobson's weekly wage of £15, almost double even Purcell's, perhaps confirms the attachment of socialists from professional backgrounds to differential forms of remuneration.[102] It was nevertheless to their underestimation of the role of clerical and administrative skills that Hobson partly attributed the guilds' difficulties. They had started, he admitted, by seeking 'to carry democratic principles to the fullest extent' of workers' self-government, 'with an absolute minimum of technical assistance'. Having considered and rejected the idea of a strong technical staff overriding local initiative, the lesson they had learnt was that local autonomy had to be modified and technical administration 'stiffen[ed] up'.[103] It is difficult to miss the parallel between this and the larger experiment of Bolshevism itself. 'Our greatest mistake was to undervalue the importance of the technician', Lenin had told the British delegates in Russia in 1920.[104] Conceivably there were also similar reflections regarding labour discipline, overmanning and slack time-keeping; and one can perhaps imagine the Bolshevik response to the Stockton building guild which granted itself a week's holiday to attend a race meeting.[105] Though Purcell gave little indication of his own conclusions from the episode, he had regarded as one of the guild's central objects that of having 'trained and educated, even if ever so elementarily, a vast body of their own administrators, who will the more readily be able to operate for the true industrial requirements of a workers' community'.[106] These were sentiments which he was later to echo almost word for word, but in the context of the nationalisation of the mines.[107] Perhaps this small-scale failure of workers' self-government made him more responsive to the 'productivist' reading of workers' control which in Soviet Russia supplanted more radical and democratic readings.[108]

There was perhaps one other lesson. Hobson had no doubt that changing attitudes within the Ministry of Health played a major part in the National Building Guild's troubles. By implication, a friendlier administration meant a greater chance of success for such ventures.

The Soviets themselves were to be approached to deal preferentially with the guilds. Within Britain too, the formation of a Labour government in 1924 encouraged renewed hopes of government support for such initiatives.[109] Collectivism and self-government might be constructed as alternatives; but as, at the time of writing, a neo-liberal 'big society' project wrecks a multitude of grassroots, non-statist activities, it is easier to see that these were anything but mutually exclusive. During the whole period of his involvement with the CPGB and the Furnishing Guild, Purcell, in any case, already headed the list of NAFTA parliamentary candidates and nurtured expectations of a parliamentary career. In the end, this proved hardly more enduring than his attachment to the communist party or the guilds. But his activities as an MP did play their part in Purcell's international notoriety; and they offer insight into the dilemmas of labour representation at a crucial moment of transition.

2.4 PARLIAMENTARY SOCIALIST

Purcell twice served as a member of parliament – for Coventry in 1923-4 and for the Forest of Dean in 1925-9. Nevertheless, as W.P. Coates rightly observed after his death, 'parliamentary work was not his forte and certainly not to his liking'.[110] For an activist of syndicalist disposition, this was the least one would have expected. As generally understood, syndicalism signified not just aversion to but the outright rejection of political ambitions and pursuit of elected office. W.Z. Foster in the States denied the very existence of a 'so-called political "field"', and made much of the 'horde of doctors, lawyers, preachers and other non working-class elements universally infesting and controlling the Socialist Party'.[111] In France, where syndicalism as anti-politics was originally strongest, there was a marked preponderance of such elements within the socialist movement, whom the CGT defied with the watchword *Le syndicat suffit à tout!* The precepts of the new syndicalist international established in 1922 were unambiguous: 'Revolutionary syndicalism repudiates all parliamentary activity and all collaboration in legislative bodies.'[112]

In Britain, there was a far more ambivalent attitude. Initially the predominant form of labour representation was that of direct sponsorship of candidates by the very unions in which the syndicalists aimed at boring from within. Keir Hardie himself expressed pride in the PLP's exclusively plebeian composition.[113] IFTU as late as 1924 cited the high political representation of union officials as a distinctive, often misunderstood feature of British Labour politics.[114] At the 1913 international syndicalist congress the London building worker Jack Wills was removed as co-president on the discovery that he served not as MP but as a mere borough councillor.[115] Tom Mann's *Syndicalist*, on the other hand, had no fundamental objection to such activities; it urged the positive value of a 'group of revolutionary Socialists in Parliament' and welcomed the middle-class politician Lansbury as the ISEL's first applicant for membership.[116]

Purcell in embracing syndicalism had decried over-dependence on political action, and in 1913 he had stood down at the end of his second stint as a Salford councillor. Even so, the adjustment of his personal priorities did not imply the outright repudiation of such roles. When the emergent CPGB divided over the issue, Purcell was among those supporting parliamentary activity as 'a valuable means of propaganda and agitation', though not of achieving socialism.[117] Three months earlier he had replaced O'Grady as one of NAFTA's parliamentary candidates.[118] Briefly he is said to have been adopted as a communist parliamentary candidate in Salford.[119] Unavailingly he contested the idea of such candidates' exclusive obligation to their party mandate.[120] As a Labour candidate too, his loyalty to party was subsumed within a more complex notion of representation in which elements of trade, class, constituency and faction all played a part.

His first commitment was to the sponsoring union without which he could hardly have reached parliament at all. Within the early PLP, the initial preponderance of union officials encouraged expectations that relevant business would be handled on a 'trade basis', exemplified by the strong collective identity of the Miners' MPs. As he negotiated the transition from interest group to national party, MacDonald's rejection of this principle provoked considerable discontent. In making his first appointments as a Labour premier he aroused particular concern by entrusting the Mines Department to the Clydesider Shinwell, who had no connection with the industry. Especially indignant was the Lanarkshire Miners' leader Duncan Graham, the sort of MP that MacDonald despised, who spoke out forcefully on such sectional issues and otherwise hardly at all.[121]

NAFTA was a different sort of case. There was no state department or overriding trade interest demanding parliamentary expression, nor any possibility of NAFTA exercising a significant numerical weight within the PLP. In this sphere too, weakness as a sectional actor therefore encouraged a more inclusive conception of representation, and the contesting of MacDonald's ideal of the professional politician in the name of organised labour as a whole. In more general terms than that of the mines (or mines department) for the miners, Purcell thus bemoaned the inadequate representation in Macdonald's government of 'fully fledged Trade Unionists and really well tried working-class representatives'.[122] Following the uneasy passage of an Agricultural Wages Bill, he also urged that trade unionists would do a better job than 'some of our associates in the political Labour Movement' like the ex-Liberal agriculture minister Noel Buxton.[123] There was, however, no suggestion of trade representation. One reaction to the government was the formation of a 'Trade Union Group' of MPs, whose secretary was the Miners' MP Mardy Jones.[124] Another was a revival of the idea of a 'trade union' labour party, but with a syndicalistic flavour displacing the earlier rejection of the politician-as-socialist.[125] A third, to be considered more fully in due course, was a reassertion of the TUC's independence of the Labour Party. Among the earliest expressions of this approach, not perhaps fortuitously, was the launching of a campaign among agricultural workers in which the TUC declined to involve the Labour Party.[126]

In the case of the building and woodworking trades there was even a degree of progressive alienation from the Labour Party. When Labour made its first substantial parliamentary breakthrough in 1906, these trades had provided three of its fifty parliamentary candidates, and in 1910 the figure was six out of ninety-one.[127] By 1945, as Labour's challenge extended to virtually every constituency in the country, the figure had actually fallen back to five. With the enforcement of 'contracting in' to the Labour Party under the 1927 Trades Disputes Act, affiliation rates were also lowest in the craft unions; and out of forty unions surveyed by Cole in 1945-6, NAFTA's rate of affiliation was lowest but one.[128] Such diffidence was the more remarkable in the case of the building unions, given their strong producer interest in the politics of housing and the progressive marginalisation of their role in determining Labour's own housing policy.[129]

This has been construed as half-heartedness towards labour representation, as indifference born of relative affluence, or even as a mark of patriotism.[130] As in the case of a trade-union Labour Party, it is true that the radical and not-so-radical variants of such an attitude can be difficult to separate. In NAFTA's case, it is nevertheless clear that scepticism regarding Labour's political machinery did not reflect an acquiescence in Liberal hegemony. NAFTA's socialist commitment not only predated the development of a more managed party organisation; it also proved obstinately resistant to it. Support for the Labour Party's excluded communist elements was a tangible expression of this. Rules regarding the eligibility of delegates might be resisted at local level.[131] When Pollitt in 1930 fought a credible by-election campaign in Whitechapel, he acknowledged 'substantial backing' from the political funds of local NAFTA organisations.[132] NAFTA by this time was the sole union in which communists could seriously discuss using the political levy, not for but against the Labour Party.[133] A decade later, Purcell's successor as its parliamentary secretary openly supported the communist-sponsored People's Convention during the period of the Nazi-Soviet pact.[134]

Sponsorship by the union may have signified relatively little in terms of trade lobbying. It did, however, mean reflecting the wider values and policy positions of the union where these could be expressed in parliamentary terms. O'Grady's refusal to do so in respect of the war had been met with a new provision for the annual re-election of the union's parliamentary nominees.[135] Refusing nomination on these terms, O'Grady retained his parliamentary seat but obtained the endorsement of the Dock, Wharf, Riverside and General Workers – a warning once more against assumptions of a homogenised trade-union interest.[136] NAFTA's lack of a delegate conference made for somewhat ad hoc forms of accountability. Nevertheless, Purcell as the union's sole parliamentary representative of the 1920s was expected to provide a continuous account of his activities in the NAFTA *Monthly Report*.

Constituency provided a second basis of representation, but again in ways reflecting the specificities of trade and membership density. For groups like the miners or textile workers, geographical concentrations of membership could make for a formidable constituency presence and a virtual sense of ownership of the Labour nomination. Small and geographically dispersed, NAFTA had no such claim to any parliamentary constituency. O'Grady had represented a Leeds division; Purcell was interviewed or adopted in Bath, Stockport, Bristol North and doubtless other constituencies before contesting Coventry in the December 1923 election.[137] A city of migrants and many trades, mostly involving metalworking, Coventry since the war had enjoyed a succession of militant outside candidates. Curiously, all of them – Wallhead, Williams and now Purcell – were members of Labour's first Russian delegation in 1920. In one sense, the incoming trade-unionist candidate may doubtless be regarded as a 'carpet-bagger' to whom the issue of locality was secondary.[138] Unlike the middle-class candidate, however, Purcell brought with him notions of delegacy and accountability that helped shape his conception of the role of constituency representative. Already within the CPGB he had moved an amendment to a resolution that denied its candidates any local electoral mandate, proposing that a party mandate should be held 'as well as', not in place of, that of the particular constituency concerned.[139] There was no reason why that should not also apply to the Labour Party.

As post-war boom gave way to slump, the discharging of unattached young men from Coventry's workshops introduced a militant, almost insurrectionary note into local labour politics, exemplified by communist activities among the unemployed. The authorities urged the need for counter-propaganda, and a popular local preacher, J.R. Armitage, attracted weekly crowds through rhapsodies to Mussolini and diatribes against Bolshevism and Jews.[140] Purcell might have been in his element here, and the local communist organiser rubbed his hands at the thought of reducing his overfed Conservative opponent to a 'grease spot'.[141] Militancy by this time was ebbing, however, and Purcell's election campaign was a model of restraint. Even opponents commended his eschewal of 'extreme views' and repudiation of rowdyism.[142] Supporting speakers ranged from the communists on the left to the Countess of Warwick and the ultra-moderate miners' leader Frank Hodges.[143] Purcell's agent, finding his oratory a little too fervent for his 'Sunday school training', ordered counterbalancing posters emphasising themes of altruism and moral responsibility.[144] But in reality Purcell's own address was of a timelessly melioristic character that was not to be diverted from Labour's own core objectives. When he had first stood for parliament in Salford in 1910, the peers versus the people had threatened to obscure this basic issue. Now it was free trade versus protection, and Purcell showed his disregard for both sets of alternatives by simply paraphrasing his Salford address – albeit that the vision of an 'England of the people' had now become 'an England of the Workers'.[145] Offered the endorsement of the industrialist and former mayor Siegfried Bettmann, an ILP supporter but fervent free trader, Purcell did not disdain it.[146] Nevertheless, his slogan of 1910 ('Hungry Men, Women and Children a million times more important than the House of Lords, Protection, or Free Trade') had been barely modified in fourteen years ('Thousands of hungry men and women are more important than Tariff Reform or Free Trade').[147]

In a tight three-party contest, Purcell scraped in with the lowest share of the vote of any successful Labour candidate. MacDonald as his leader held that an MP's first responsibility was to attend to the parliamentary business for which he had been elected.[148] Gossip on similar grounds had in 1918 declined a NAFTA parliamentary nomination as impossible to combine with union office and tending to unacceptable levels of absenteeism from the House.[149] It was a position Gossip consistently upheld, reminding those inclined to prioritise other commitments that ordinary trade unionists had 'worked hard and paid from their wages considerable sums' to get them into parliament.[150]

Purcell, whom Gossip must surely have had in mind, nevertheless made no secret of the greater significance that he attached to his TUC responsibilities.[151] This was quickly reinforced by his scepticism and frustration on encountering at first hand how parliament conducted itself. In this he was not alone. On the basis of the modernised procedures and facilities of a municipality like Manchester, the Liberal Ernest Simon condemned the dysfunctionality of the national legislature.[152] From a background in the suffrage movement, Dorothy Jewson scorned the obsession with ceremonial and theatre as inimical to any real sense of purpose.[153] Even MacDonald had until lately shown a penetrating insight into how, by these means, the imposition of a 'novitiate upon the elected ones' served to impress upon them 'the manner and the mind of the governing priesthood'.[154]

Purcell, with his trade-union background, observed the proceedings with an anthropologist's eye for cultic practices. 'All the processions to and from the House of Lords are childish in the extreme and the foolish proceeding of listening to someone reading aloud what others have written belongs to a past age', he wrote of the King's Speech. The 'parade of pomp and jewels' was similarly a 'frightful and disgusting mockery', and, in defiance of its Bagehotian rationale, both the 'show part' and the 'business part' impressed him only in a 'very depressing way'.[155] Through his role in the TUC Purcell several times led deputations to Labour ministers, and he could hardly have failed to note the greater attention these were accorded than was the backbench MP.[156] In Dutt's *Labour Monthly* symposium he suggested that if parliament had any role under the new industrial order it would be as 'new place … for co-ordinating the industrial structure'.[157] In the meantime, he warned that even its swarming with workers' representatives would only provoke the certain obstruction of the 'vast mass of black reaction' that dominated Britain's state machinery. 'It is this phase of our Governmental make-up which causes so many of our thoughtful adherents to despair of Parliament ever becoming a potential factor in great working-class changes for the better.'[158]

Purcell treated with greater respect his relationship with his constituents. Only after the Second World War was a modern conception of constituency representation generally adopted in Britain. In this period, even visiting their constituencies was for many MPs a somewhat negligible consideration.[159] Purcell, on the other hand, had acquired a motor-bike that allowed him to reconcile commitments in Coventry and London with the dash of a latterday Dick Turpin.[160] His principal innovation was the holding of open report-back meetings whose purpose, according to a local newspaper, was to review the week's parliamentary business and justify the way he had voted.[161]

In such an environment, Purcell slipped easily into an us-and-them idiom of plebeian wonderment and derision. Speeches of an hour dealt with matters so trivial 'that a Trade Unionist would have dealt with it in two minutes'. Discussion of the 'marking of eggs' was conducted as if none could take part who had not been at Oxford or Cambridge. Procedures and regulations were a century behind the times and for the energetic new arrival the Commons seemed 'about the laziest place that could be found on the face of the earth':

> Only about one ninetieth of the speeches, or perhaps a little less, were of any value at all, and … the work accomplished by many Labour members of the city, borough and urban district councils by far exceeded in absolute results the usefulness got out of the House of Commons when the amount of talking was compared. When a statement was made members kept getting up either to confirm or deny it, which was not a very useful occupation. Many of the members had gone there to make careers for themselves … but this made things difficult for anybody entering the House of Commons who was used to constant movement and anxious for progress to be made.[162]

Chairing the Hull TUC that year, Purcell returned to the issue and ascribed the TUC's 'workmanlike' conduct of business to its delegates having come to do a job and not simply to talk.[163] The TUC's spirit of 'Go at it and get it done with' was also remarked upon by the American observer Scott Nearing:

> A business-like air pervades ... There is no oratory. The mover of a resolution has ten minutes; the seconder has seven minutes; speakers who can get the floor have five minutes each. Delegates speak to the point ... [and] receive careful attention as long as they have anything to contribute. The moment their fund of material has run out they are invited from all over the hall to 'Sit down!' .... There is a great deal of sharp repartee, much laughter, some banter, a very little recrimination, and an almost complete absence of personalities ... [and] little appeal to parliamentary procedure. Discussion continues until the delegates feel that the problem has been fully stated, whereupon they begin to shout: 'Agreed! Agreed!' or 'Vote! Vote!'[164]

In his disdain for parliamentary conventions Purcell had a good deal in common with the Webbs, for whom it also derived in part from local government and trade-union practice.[165] It could be that the undistinguished parliamentary careers of so many trade unionists did not necessarily represent innate incapacity – unless perhaps it was parliament's incapacity to modernise its own procedures. On the other hand, impatience with simply confirming and denying things may also explain why so little was found wanting, by the Webbs as well as Purcell, in the similarly expeditious but less good-natured methods of the Soviets.

The issue of party or constituency was posed directly for Purcell by Philip Snowden's first ever Labour budget. The sole distinguishing feature of the budget, even according to Snowden's own estimation, was the repeal of the wartime McKenna duties on imported 'luxury' goods.[166] Though Purcell in the election had expressed so little interest in such matters, he had a union interest in the piano trade and a constituency one in the motor trade, both of which benefited from the duties, with the motor industry becoming the focus of the debate. 'If anyone does not believe in the McKenna Duties', said Tory leader Baldwin, 'let them go and fight Coventry'.[167] Manufacturers in the city not only campaigned vociferously against repeal, but also organised Soviet-style workers' consultations producing majorities of hundreds to one in their support.[168] Both Purcell and his defeated Liberal opponent took the line of least resistance on the issue, and in his maiden speech Purcell supported a Tory amendment to retain the duties, though he abstained in the subsequent vote.[169] He even took the platform at the Coventry Drill Hall when a sort of ad hoc producers' alliance was mobilised in the interest of industrial protectionism.[170]

Two features of Purcell's argument may be noted. First, that he described himself as accountable, not so much to his constituents as a body, as to the 'union men of Coventry', whose virtual delegate he purported to be, and whom he had consulted through the 'presidents, secretaries, treasurers, shop stewards or check stewards of their particular branches'.[171] This was to be echoed in the markedly trade-union flavour of his subsequent election campaign, which featured many of his TUC colleagues, and which was introduced with the remark that any trade unionist failing to support him was a blackleg.[172] Purcell further presented protectionism, not as a necessary retreat from internationalist principle, but as if as a means towards the same ends. Whenever workers achieved conditions capable of being undermined, he told the Commons, 'we would indeed be fools if, under a better social order, we allowed anybody else to interfere with that standard and with those conditions. ... We would say, "You cannot come in under any circumstances".'[173] This basic tension and anomaly will need to be revisited in the context of Purcell's trade-union internationalism.

Whatever the concessions to expediency, they were to no avail. By the time the government fell in October 1924, Purcell had gained notoriety for his role in support of the controversial Russian treaties, as will be described in the following chapter. The specific issue over which the government fell was the withdrawal of the intended prosecution of the *Workers' Weekly* editor J.R. Campbell, and Purcell, along with Lansbury and the ILPer Maxton, was among those whom the communists cited as having helped secure this withdrawal.[174] Liberals in Coventry made much of the Russian issue, and Armitage, rousing two thousand Tories to frenzied patriotic anthems, described the city as one of the world's great centres of communist intrigue.[175] Local reports nevertheless suggest that the Conservative campaign focused more on the issue of the McKenna duties. Assisted by an enormous motor flotilla on a polling day of intermittent downpours, this secured a comfortable victory, while Purcell, against national trends, saw a slight fall in the Labour share of the vote.[176] At the declaration of the poll, he shook hands with the Tory but signally failed to extend the same courtesy to his Liberal opponent.[177]

Though Labour lost the election, this was primarily because the Liberal vote collapsed, to the advantage of the Conservatives. That Labour's own share of the national vote increased suggests that Russia, even in 1924, was not necessarily the liability with Labour's core constituency that some imagined. It certainly did not prevent Purcell achieving a famous by-election victory in the Forest of Dean the following June. Compared to Coventry's political and demographic volatility, the Forest of Dean had the more stable characteristics of a mining constituency, on which Labour's hold even in 1931 was shaken only by a National Labour candidate. Its MP since the war had been James Wignall, a TGWU-sponsored candidate of moderate views and nonconformist faith, and with Labour's setback in the general election there was no shortage of possible successors following Wignall's death. A strong preference having been expressed for a national figure, the first choice, Margaret Bondfield, encountered local resistance to the running of a woman candidate, supposedly in deference to Wignall's views in the matter.[178] The second choice, Oswald Mosley, was then selected and endorsed by Labour's NEC, but withdrew at the request of his prospective Birmingham constituency.[179] Purcell was thus the third choice, adopted amidst some commotion in the presence of Labour's national secretary Arthur Henderson. Despite his initial backing for Bondfield, Henderson actively assisted Purcell's campaign, whereas MacDonald as party leader occasioned much adverse comment by declining to provide even the customary leader's declaration of support.[180] In the Forest of Dean campaign there was again a strong TUC presence, and Henderson was doubtless concerned not to aggravate the currently fraught relationship between the Labour Party and the unions.[181] Even as it was, Ernest Bevin's disgruntlement at the loss of a previously TGWU-sponsored seat may well have contributed to his dalliance for a while with the idea of an independent trade-union party.[182]

Uncertainty as to the candidate made it difficult for Labour's opponents to know how to counter its appeal. Initially seeking to target the patrician Mosley, the Liberals put up a Baptist lay preacher who had worked at the coalface all his life. Even the Conservatives invited in one of their very few MPs to boast any sort of union background.[183] Once Purcell was in the ring, the overwhelming focus of both campaigns shifted to his alleged extremism, both political and religious.[184] Amidst extensive national press interest, Purcell played up to the image and told the *Sunday Worker* how audiences seemed hungry for his cries against war and capitalism – the more his enemies lied, 'the more I hammered them'.[185] He had strong support from the Forest of Dean Miners' Association (FDMA), which, like NAFTA, was a small, militant union that regularly supported communist causes, and whose agent Jack Williams was associated with the Miners' Minority Movement.[186] Polling Labour's largest ever vote in the constituency, Purcell's victory was described by Labour's national agent as one of the party's most satisfactory results for some time.[187] Possibly in response to the Bondfield affair, the equality of the sexes had been emphasised in Purcell's campaign, and at the declaration of the poll the number of women among his supporters was particularly remarked upon.[188]

Half a century earlier, the Forest of Dean miners' leader Timothy Mountjoy, who was also a Baptist preacher, had urged that a working man could 'never be truly represented except by a working man'. This did not a necessarily mean a worker of the same trade, and it was the building worker George Howell whom Mountjoy and his colleagues approached as possible candidate. Shorn of its labourist-syndicalist trappings, this is a conception of labour representation that can be traced across the decades and had its final flowering in the 1920s. 'Is it not an outrage on justice', said Mountjoy, 'that the least useful class of all should have a representative in Parliament for every family, while the most useful class, which produces all the wealth, should not have one representative for a million families?' 'I go to the House of Commons to represent the working classes', Purcell similarly stated after his election victory. 'It is our class that requires more and more representation.'[189] Though it long predated socialism, this idea of labour representation continued to provide a distinctive accent within it. In Coventry Purcell even conceded there might be good men among the Tories; perhaps, he once confided to Walter Citrine, even Churchill was among them.[190] In the Forest of Dean he paid particular tribute to his well-born Liberal predecessor Sir Charles Dilke, whose radical and trade-union sympathies were so highly regarded within the labour movement.[191] Good government, even in such hands, was nevertheless 'not the equal nor could be the substitute of representative government. It was the Labour Party that gave the workers, whether manual or by brain, the chance of determining their own destiny.'[192] Bramley, in the same way, while warmly approving Dilke's achievements, pointedly commended his refusal to accept a position in the early ILP, on grounds that 'Labour should find its leaders in its own ranks ... a view that the present generation of Trade Unionists will heartily endorse'.[193] Workers 'by brain' were now acknowledged; but the Hardie myth to this extent remained intact.[194]

Purcell was both a wantonly negligent MP and an exemplary one. With the novel experience of a safe Conservative majority, there was a widespread view in Labour circles that parliament risked expiring of 'inanition'.[195] Purcell was openly scornful of the 'constant crawling in and out of division lobbies', generally on the 'most trifling subjects', both as a futility in itself and as a distraction from more pressing issues.[196] In his chairman's address at the Scarborough TUC in 1925, Alonzo Swales cited basic parliamentary arithmetic to show that MPs could best advance their cause by 'incessant propaganda' outside of the House of Commons.[197] It is commonly said that the position of trade-union MPs was becoming a form of superannuation.[198] In Purcell's case, on the other hand, his parliamentary salary was a sort of subvention allowing him to take on the responsibilities within the wider industrial movement that he saw as the real key to his political effectiveness.

He was exemplary, however, in his regard for his constituency. Unlike a middle-class carpet-bagger like Sidney Webb, he took the view that he ought to live in the constituency that he represented. No other member had found it necessary or convenient to do so, Williams reported. 'He would be in close touch at all times with the people he represented. (Applause.)' Though she is rarely mentioned in any other context, Purcell's wife also impressed in this respect, as an 'ordinary working class woman' who settled among her husband's constituents.[199] There could be no greater contrast than with the somewhat patronising communications which Beatrice Webb addressed to Seaham women from her Westminster home. Even the local newspaper commended the informed and educative way that Purcell, as his internationalism became ever more pronounced, addressed constituency audiences on issues like Mosul and Mexico.[200]

Uncommon even in Purcell's time, the distinctiveness of such a conception of representation was eventually to be lost sight of. As Labour swept to power in 1945, the hopes of the 1920s seemed in many respects to be fulfilled. 'They voted Labour because they felt that Labour meant *themselves*, and people like them', wrote Richard Crossman, a successor to Purcell as Labour MP in Coventry. 'For the first time the working class was not afraid of being run by themselves...' An Oxford don himself, Crossman was not unaware of the ambiguity of such a claim, and of the 'gulf' that existed between Westminster and Coventry. Vividly he evoked his 'entirely new absorbing life in the House, and very remote – those eager faces crowding round the loudspeaker, and those voices ... "Dick, when you get there will you be sure not to forget us."' Pursuing the issue with his parliamentary colleagues, Crossman could detect little interest in the idea of 'organized information' such as Purcell had used to keep in touch his constituents. 'Strange how politicians like *personal* publicity and fight shy of information sessions. ... Or rather they love talking freely inside the "closed circle", and making speeches outside it. And their speeches are very different from their talk.'[201]

Purcell's speeches were not so different from his talk. Labour's trade unionist representation was certainly circumscribed in its own ways, both occupationally and in respect of gender. Nevertheless, an MP like Purcell embodied at least the aspiration to a more socially representative form of government, and he did talk to constituents as if the closed circle might have included them, or else the arcane rituals that excluded them kept him out too. Within his lifetime, both Coventry and the Forest of Dean were reclaimed by gentleman Labour candidates of Liberal proclivities and social pedigree.[202] In Coventry by 1945, the displacement of the 'horny hands of toil' by clerical and professional workers was also evident at municipal level.[203] Even union nominees began to look more like professional politicians, and increasingly over time they at least demonstrated a professional commitment to their responsibilities. The weakness of any enduring conception of self-representation has nevertheless remained an enduring failing of British democracy. Purcell, as we shall see, made what was effectively an unforced withdrawal from parliament in 1929, and this was symptomatic of the weakness in the end of the challenge to parliamentary mores. In social though not in gender terms, the trade unionists of Purcell's generation did nevertheless do more than anybody else to address these deficiencies.

2.5 ALL POWER TO THE GENERAL COUNCIL?

Hyndman believed that Tom Mann would have been a still more formidable leader had 'his mind ... been capable of continuous action along one definite line'.[204] This was the perspective of the emerging party career, identified with a single institution, even if Hyndman's SDF was not a particularly successful one. Mann's longevity, conversely, represented adaptability as the key to effectiveness, employing whatever organisational channels were most readily available. With his philosophy of the good-looking peg, Purcell likewise made no special virtue of continuity on a single definite line. In this again, he appears a figure influenced far more by Mann and syndicalism than by Hyndman and orthodox social democracy.

The resemblance, even so, was partial and in some respects superficial. Until he found a resting place among the communists, and to some extent even then, Mann always retained the mindset of the freelance agitator. Even his union, the Engineers, provided only intermittent focus; and while standing three times for the post of general secretary, he did so at long intervals and on the basis of credentials earned almost anywhere but in its service. Tied to office in neither the physical nor the institutional sense, Mann's several sojourns overseas encapsulate the peripatetic quality of his socialism.

Purcell's attachments, by contrast, must at every stage be located within the secure institutional framework of a labour movement career and a stability of position mirrored domestically by small-scale address changes within Manchester's working-class suburbs.[205] Mercurial as he seemed, Purcell knew the value of this union base. As a communist he defended the position of union-sponsored parliamentary candidates. As the Building Guild took shape, he advised Coppock not to abandon union office for such a venture; and though Purcell for a period worked full-time for the Furniture Guild, he arranged a sort of secondment from NAFTA while he did so.[206] On entering parliament, he insisted on remaining a paid union officer, and as NAFTA's 'parliamentary secretary' received a further subvention equivalent to half his parliamentary salary. When this was reduced to £25 a year after he lost his Coventry seat in 1924, he wrote to Bramley that it looked like pushing him 'to the Beach' – in other words, getting his cards.[207] Even such an honorarium nevertheless secured his continuing eligibility for the TUC general council.

This indeed was a basic consideration. Purcell's was the syndicalism of the union officer, but of a distinctive type. Unlike the miner Cook or the engineer Tanner, he could not have aspired to a wider influence merely through his union. Ambivalence about conventional politics did not therefore take the sectional form of an accentuated group identity like that of the miners or dockers. Instead, Purcell found a vehicle in the broader trade-union interest that was identified locally with the trades councils and nationally with the TUC. In the period of Purcell's involvement, these bodies aspired to a quasi-political authority, removed from the immediate pursuit of trade interests but deriving their legitimacy from the workers as producers. Assuming roles of industrial co-ordination and political advocacy, their field of competency was subject to three competing claims. One was that of the unions from which they drew their authority, but which nevertheless remained jealous of their individual prerogatives. A second was that of the emerging Labour Party and its claim to represent the movement's sole or pre-eminent political voice. A third, potentially, was that between the trades councils and TUC themselves, as co-ordinating bodies at national and local level. By the end of the 1920s, these tensions had to some extent been resolved. Separate spheres of industrial and political competency were becoming more clearly demarcated, in each case subjected to more formalised systems of control and the restriction of local autonomy. The scope for a career like Purcell's was thereby reduced if not actually eradicated. The role of the communistic union leader has had its counterparts in subsequent periods of trade-union history. Never again, however, was such prominence achievable on so slender an industrial basis, through the affirmation of the unions' collective interests by a mere French polisher.

Framing Purcell's career at both ends were the trades councils. From his earliest days in Manchester he was a branch delegate and executive member of the Manchester and Salford Trades Council (MSTC), serving as its chairman (1905-7, 1917-19, 1922), its vice-chairman (1914-17), and as a delegate to the Lancashire and Cheshire Federation of Trades Councils.[208] Syndicalism in this instance provided a rationale and reinforcement for activities to which he was already committed. There was a heavy trades council representation at the ISEL conferences, and Bowman drew on the French example of the *bourses du travail* in urging a National Federation of Trades Councils as Labour's 'natural discussion ground ... in its general interests' and an affirmation of class over craft.[209] As envisaged by both Bowman and Mann, the trades councils would displace municipal authorities as 'the Industrial Councils of tomorrow'.[210] In the meantime, given the rudimentary state of Labour's electoral organisation, except as provided by the unions themselves, trades councils claimed a role in the representation of labour interests going beyond simply industrial matters. In Manchester and Salford, it was the trades council which in 1902 took the initiative in the establishment of a local Labour Representation Committee, with Purcell in due course as one of its five trades council delegates. As yet, the city had no divisional labour parties and the MSTC remained jealous of its own prerogatives, whether in the nomination of candidates, affiliation to the national Labour Party or the local representation of labour interests.[211] During the war years, its role was further enhanced by the electoral truce, and Purcell's activities ranged from helping to form a tenants' defence league to representing labour on the Manchester section of the National Committee for Combating Venereal Disease.[212]

Even into the 1920s Purcell described the trades councils as a basis for the one big movement of the workers. In Dutt's *Labour Monthly* symposium he wrote of 'the inclusion of administrative, technical, manual and mental workers inside the industrial organisation; the organisation of the Trades Councils ... into integral parts of the National Industrial Union, the direct connection everywhere of the finger tips to the head'.[213] Purcell chaired a committee of the TUC and the trades councils aimed at formalising their relations, and in the notion of the trades councils functioning as the TUC's local 'correspondents' there remained an echo of the idea of labour's discussion ground.[214] By this time, however, it was the general council itself that provided the primary focus for Purcell's ambitions. If the general council as co-ordinating 'head' represented the logic of the general staff now realised at a national level, the downgrading of the trades councils to its fingertips or correspondents implied subordination and in due course the stifling of local initiative and grassroots militancy.[215] For the time being, however, this was obscured by the TUC's appearance of combativity, of which Purcell was the virtual personification. Already during the 1922 engineering lockout he had headed off calls for a local council of action by referring to the greater potential effectiveness of the general council.[216] Despite its disparate manifestations, his career as a significant public figure started and finished with his membership of the general council.

Purcell had first attended the TUC in 1917, replacing Bramley as NAFTA delegate on the latter's appointment as TUC assistant secretary. Two years later he began a nine-year stint on what was then still the TUC's parliamentary committee, and a body hardly more effective than when the Webbs in the 1890s had described its powers as 'absurdly inadequate'.[217] In 1921, however, the general council took its place as an 'actively functioning organ' empowered to act upon its own initiative.[218] Even as its assistant secretary, Bramley was identified with this more active role. Unlike the secretary, C.W. Bowerman, he was undistracted by parliamentary responsibilities, and on succeeding Bowerman in 1923 he accepted the condition that he relinquish any parliamentary ambitions of his own. Already as assistant secretary he made claim to 'freedom of initiative and some power to take action in matters of detail'.[219] He could not, however, take things further than commanded support within the general council itself. If in 1924-5 he had the opportunity for some extraordinary initiatives in policy, it was because he had willing collaborators among the other leading actors on the general council.

Despite his union's lack of leverage, Purcell was perhaps the most important of these. In theory the general council had been provided with a rationalised basis of representation to match its heightened authority. Seventeen trade groups were established; and where the parliamentary committee had functioned as an undifferentiated general body, these were now represented on the general council according to a rough proportionality. Among other things, this was meant to put an end to the 'vicious principle of bartering and bargaining' which had produced anomalies like the exclusion of miners' representatives in 1919.[220] Even so, the continuing practice of election by the whole congress meant the tempering of the representative principle wherever there were competing nominations to the general council. Justified as offsetting the direct nominating powers of the larger unions, the system allowed Purcell an uninterrupted tenure as one of two representatives of the building, woodworking and furnishing trades. Like the Building Trades' secretary Hicks, he received some five times the congress vote of the Woodworkers' Society nominee, even though the Woodworkers' membership was greater than that of both their unions combined.[221]

The common impression that the general council comprised 'the established leaders of the main trade unions' is therefore not quite accurate.[222] Nor indeed did such figures automatically assume positions of pre-eminence. Unencumbered by the heavier union commitments, someone like Purcell was able to take on major TUC responsibilities for which longevity, translating into a sort of seniority, seemed a sort of credential. While TUC chairman in 1924, he also sat on the Disputes Committee, the Indian Affairs Committee and the committee for the metal and building trades, as well as chairing the National Joint Council with the Labour Party and the Joint International Committee. Crucially, both as chairman and as vice-chairman in 1924-5, Purcell also chaired the TUC's international committee. Not surprisingly, there was some concern to establish a more equal distribution of responsibilities.[223] Nevertheless, as Purcell now took on the further responsibility of IFTU president, he more and more began to function as a TUC full-timer. Indeed, though while out of parliament in 1924-5 he was reportedly working at his trade, the payment of general council fees and expenses still allowed him to meet heavy commitments as the TUC's vice-chairman.[224]

If nothing else, officers from the smaller unions were above suspicion of pushing significant sectional interests. They thus provided successive TUC secretaries, and in securing the position in 1923 Bramley defeated candidates from several of the larger unions.[225] Another contributory factor was that the more powerful unions in several cases treated the general council as a distinctly second-level responsibility. Among them was the numerically and strategically crucial Transport and General Workers' Union (TGWU), founded in 1922 and led by Ernest Bevin. If illustration were needed of the general council's initially haphazard composition, it is that Bevin as yet ceded the transport group nomination to veteran figures like Tillett – 'an old fuddler' according to Bevin – and Harry Gosling.[226]

Given the relatively fluid and ecumenical basis of trade-union politics, there was never any formal left slate or programme. There was, on the other hand, the shared formative experience of a movement strong in collective ethos and weak in collective disciplines, and providing an assortment of causes and credentials in place of a party card. Tillett, for example, was a steadfast associate of Purcell, speaking for him often in the Forest of Dean and commending his 'proletariat sense' in whatever consistent meaning the erratic Tillett attached to the phrase.[227] Overshadowed by Bevin domestically, in this final phase of his career Tillett also resumed his earlier international interests, taking part in the Russian delegation, missing the one to India only through ill health, and raising funds in the USA during the 1926 miners' lockout.[228] Especially close to Purcell over a number of years was Hicks. Both had combined union office with a syndicalist rhetoric; both drew from marxism a legitimation of industrial struggle that precluded any sense of responsibility for the ruling capitalist order without generating much idea of how to bring it to an end. Though never a CPGB member, Hicks shared Purcell's disposition towards unofficial or communist-sponsored movements like the LRD, the ICWPA and what Rodney Barker has called the educational syndicalism of the labour colleges' movement.[229] Both were also steadfast supporter of the Soviets, and their close relations were cemented by Hicks's nominal co-editing of *Trade Union Unity* in 1925-6. Between them, they represented their trade group continuously on the general council until Purcell's departure in 1928.

With the temporary ascendancy of its left-wing elements, attempts to order the TUC's relations with the Labour Party according to relatively formalised if unwritten lines of demarcation left room for uncertainty and even tension.[230] From neighbouring offices in Eccleston Square, joint Labour-TUC departments had been established for research, legal advice, publicity and international affairs. In 1922 there also appeared under their joint auspices a monthly *Labour Magazine*, conceived as 'frankly and avowedly the official monthly journal of the Labour Movement'.[231] On the other hand, there was no cross-representation between the general council and the Labour executive, nor any requirement on the parliamentary leadership to attend to the demands of the TUC or its constituent unions. In 1923 the Labour Party urged that the two bodies' annual conferences be held in the same town consecutively and thus effect 'a more satisfactory arrangement for the Agendas for discussion upon purely industrial and purely political subjects'.[232] Not only was the proposal resisted, but the following January members of the general council entering MacDonald's government were required to vacate their seats. With Bramley now installed as full-time secretary, the TUC was beginning to show a new assertiveness regarding its need for a separate political voice.

The experience of the MacDonald government could hardly fail to reinforce this tendency. While necessarily intervening in 'industrial' subjects, it studiedly refused any special rights to consultation on the unions' part. By the eighth month of the government, Purcell was successfully moving that the TUC decline to co-operate with a Board of Trade committee on whose composition it had not been properly consulted, while Bramley had failed to secure even a single meeting with MacDonald.[233] With the exception of the Wheatley housing reforms, which were drawn up with the involvement of the building industry, Purcell gave the government's record a decidedly lukewarm reception at the 1924 TUC and emphasised that a 'well-disciplined industrial organisation' remained the principal weapon of the workers.[234] Bramley on similar grounds proposed the TUC's recovery of its 'distinctly separate' identity and public profile. 'We have had no trade union literature, no trade union publicity, no trade union voice in the public press or elsewhere on the initiative of our Joint Departments', he complained. 'The Labour Party cannot have it both ways. If when in office we are to be detached from the Labour Movement we cannot be treated as an integral part of that movement when Labour is out of office.'[235] In this spirit the TUC declined to involve the Labour Party in activities addressed to the rural areas and the issue of unemployment, and at the following year's TUC voted to assume complete control of its own research, publicity and international departments.[236]

The most dramatic example of this unwillingness simply to defer to the Labour Party was in respect of international affairs. Bramley's appointment as assistant secretary had coincided with a qualitative expansion of the TUC's international activities, symbolised by the establishment of an international department and the *International Trades Union Review*. It was also under Bramley's impetus that the TUC assumed the functions of international representation that had hitherto been exercised mainly by the smaller and less inclusive GFTU. [237] One result was that the TUC took over from the GFTU the British prerogative of nominating the IFTU president. The first such nominee, replacing the GFTU general secretary W.A. Appleton, was J.H. Thomas; the second, succeeding Thomas after his entry into the MacDonald government, was Purcell himself. From the tiny pool of NAFTA activists, Bramley and Purcell had emerged to enjoy what briefly was a directing role for a movement four-and-a-half million strong.

What could not have been anticipated was how their spirit of independence would above all be demonstrated in respect of Russia. In 1920 the TUC played its part in a general labour movement delegation to the new workers' Russia. It also accepted the idea of a joint international committee that would service the Labour Party on 'political' questions and the TUC on 'industrial' ones, thus implicitly circumscribing the political role of the latter.[238] Four years later, on the other hand, it organised its own Russian delegation, passing over the possible participation of the ILP. This could only be taken as a statement of intent given that relations with Russia had latterly been the most sensitive and contentious area of Labour Party policy. That the delegation also undertook to investigate the Zinoviev letter, whose handling had so glaringly called MacDonald's judgement into question, merely underlined the apparent challenge to his authority. In subsequently urging the need for the TUC to control its own publicity, Bramley specifically cited the example of its Russian delegation.[239] As the TUC then revived its independent publications, two of the first five pamphlets, along with delegation report itself, dealt with Russian matters.[240] It was as if Bolshevism were in some distinctive way a peculiarly trade-union issue. As Tillett put it, while other European trade-union movements had 'largely surrendered industrial identity to political action', the British movement alone stood 'four-square to all its obligations or enmities ... retaining relentlessly a firm grip on economic, wage and trade union action apart from politics and politicians'.[241]

Purcell and Bramley were respectively chairman and secretary of the Russian delegation. They were also the only common denominator between the delegation itself, the twelve-strong contingent at the subsequent Anglo-Russian trade-union conference, and the five-member commission which then approved a joint advisory council of the British and Russian unions, or ARJAC.[242] On being elected to the TUC's parliamentary committee in 1916, Bramley had observed that 'a representative of a small union, though pleading from sometimes an unpopular cause, can depend on the tolerant support of Congress, provided on Trade Union matters responsibilities are faced and duties done'.[243] On meeting this condition, he and Purcell were entrusted for a time with key offices which they used to project onto Russia the internationalist precepts they had learnt within the Furnishing Trades. It is to this development that we now turn.

NOTES

1. Torr papers CP/Ind/Torr/8/3, Purcell to Mann, 2 June 1921.
2. A.W. Wright, *G.D.H. Cole and Socialist Democracy*, Oxford: OUP, 1979, p. 138.
3. Bertrand Russell, *Roads to Freedom: socialism, anarchism and syndicalism*, Allen & Unwin, 1918.
4. Russell, *The Practice and Theory of Bolshevism*, Allen & Unwin, 1920.
5. See ch. 1 above.
6. Chushichi Tsuzuki, *Tom Mann, 1856-1941. The challenges of Labour*, Oxford: OUP, 1991, p 193.

7. Communist Unity Convention, *Official Report*, CPGB, 1920, p. 7.
8. Purcell, 'Towards a new policy: V', *Labour Monthly*, May 1924, pp. 268-9.
9. Ben Pimlott, *Labour and the Left in the 1930s*, Allen & Unwin, 1986 edn, p. xi.
10. RGASPI 495/1006, BSP executive committee to ECCI Amsterdam subbureau, 6 May 1920.
11. For Mann see *Bolshevism and the British Left*, I, pp. 219-23; for Pollitt, Kevin Morgan, *Harry Pollitt*, Manchester: MUP, 1993, ch. 2; for Tanner, the entry by Nina Fishman in *DLB* XI, pp. 274-83.
12. Communist Unity Convention, pp. 6-7.
13. *Communist*, 25 November 1920, report of meeting at Hackney addressed by Williams and Purcell.
14. NA CAB 24/126 CP 3179 RRO 28 July 1921, 24/128 CP 3333 RRO 24 September 1921. The CPGB version was always that Cook had been expelled; see RGASPI 495/100/42, 'Renegades of the Communist Party of Great Britain', n.d., c. 1926-7.
15. 'Renegades of the Communist Party of Great Britain'. The reliability of the source is questionable, and Purcell's first name is given as Harry.
16. RGASPI 495/100/94, unnamed correspondent to W.N. Ewer, 28 February 1922.
17. For a discussion see Morgan, *Harry Pollitt*, Manchester: MUP, 1993, pp. 26-31.
18. For the Profintern see Reiner Tosstorff, *Profintern. Die Rote Gewerkschaftsinternationale 1920-1937*, Paderborn: Schoeningh, 2004. An English translation is due to appear in 2014.
19. Reproduced in *Trade Unions in Soviet Russia. A collection of Russian trade union documents compiled by the ILP Information Committee and the International Section of the Labour Research Department*, LRD/ILP Information Committee, 1920, p. 44.
20. Tanner papers 6/2, 'A brief summary of discussions & negotiations re Industrial Red Inter.', c. July 1920. The discussions summarised took place between 16 and 30 June; see also Morton H. Cowden, *Russian Bolshevism and British Labor 1917-1921*, New York: Columbia University Press, 1984, pp. 90-1.
21. Also in Tanner papers 6/2.
22. *Daily Herald*, 15 July 1920.
23. Tanner papers 6/2, circular of Provisional International Council of Trade and Industrial Unions (British Bureau), London division council (secretary: Pollitt; chairman: Mann), April 1921.
24. NA CAB 24/162 CP 422 RRO 18 October 1923. A communist motion on the subject at the MSTC was carried against Purcell's express recommendation; see *Manchester Guardian*, 18 October 1923 and (without mention of Purcell's contribution) *Workers' Weekly*, 26 October 1923.
25. *Sunday Worker*, 12 July 1925.
26. CPGB party council meeting, 20 November 1924, reported *Workers' Weekly*, 5 December 1924; see also *Workers' Weekly*, 12 December 1924.
27. RGASPI 495/100/168, Pollitt, 'Organisation of the left wing', c. November 1924; Pollitt, report on Russian trade union congress, *Workers' Weekly*, 5 December 1924; RGASPI 534/7/24, Pollitt to Andrés Nin, 31 December 1924.

28. RGASPI 534/7/32, Watkins to Losovsky, 5 March 1926.
29. *Report of the Proceedings of the Forty-Fourth Annual Convention of the American Federation of Labour*, 17-25 November 1924, pp. 156-7, contribution of Swales.
30. Purcell, 'The burning question of international unity', *Labour Monthly*, September 1925, pp. 526-7.
31. *Lansbury's Labour Weekly*, 7 March 1925.
32. NAFTA *Monthly Report*, March 1922, p. 18.
33. Andrew Thorpe, 'Stalinism and British politics', *History*, 83, 1998, pp. 608-27.
34. E.g. Hugh Armstrong Clegg, *A History of British Trade Unions since 1889. Volume 2: 1911-1933*, Oxford: OUP, 1985, p. 363.
35. NA 30/69/220 RRO 29 May 1924.
36. RGASPI 534/7/24, Mann to Losovsky, 23 December 1924.
37. *Lansbury's Labour Weekly*, 5 December 1925; James Klugmann, *History of the Communist Party of Great Britain. Volume two: the General Strike 1925-1926*, Lawrence & Wishart, 1969, pp. 81-2; LHASC CP/Ind/Hann/1/12, programme for 'Great United Demonstration', 7 March 1926; NAFTA *Monthly Report*, January 1926, pp. 23-4; Watkins to Losovsky, 5 March 1926.
38. RGASPI 539/3/294, Bob Stewart to MOPR EC, 11 December 1925
39. For Fimmen see ch. 4 below.
40. RGASPI 495/100/171, Inkpin to CPGB PB to Zinoviev 9 October 1924. It would appear that S.G. Hobson's production *The Left Wing*, of which only one issue appeared was the first manifestation of this project; see *Bolshevism and the British Left*, I, pp. 116-17.
41. RGASPI 495/100/176, letter from unnamed correspondent, 3 November, forwarded A. Valenius, Moscow, 6 November 1924; Hutt papers CP/Ind/Hutt/1/2, Hutt to 'Karl August', 29 December 1925; MacDonald papers (NA) 30/69 1171, Walton Newbold to MacDonald, 2 June 1926 .
42. Even Tom Bell, the CPGB's head of agit-prop, contributed as 'sometime President of the Amalgamated Ironmoulders of Scotland'.
43. LRD minutes, 12 March and 2 April 1925, also 'Unity an appeal', printed circular, March 1925. A subscription basis was introduced with the September 1925 issue.
44. Hutt papers CP/Ind/Hutt/1/2, Hutt to Joanny Berlioz, 2 April 1925.
45. RGASPI 495/100/227, undated letter c. 1925 to Albert Inkpin.
46. The characterisation is Newbold's: MacDonald papers (NA) 30/69 1172, Newbold to MacDonald, 19 July 1927.
47. Communist Unity Convention, pp. 44-5.
48. GARF 5451/13a/55/37, biography of Zelda Kahan Coates, 1925.
49. Newbold to MacDonald, 19 July 1927.
50. RGASPI 495/100/96, typescript report on work of the RILU British bureau, n.d., c. July 1923?; Morgan, *Harry Pollitt*, ch. 2.
51. RGASPI 495/1/140, Petrovsky to Manuilsky, n.d. but September 1924 (translation from Russian courtesy Francis King); *Workers' Weekly*, 5 and 12 September 1924; for the Hull TUC see also ch. 4 below.
52. Newbold to MacDonald, 19 July 1927.
53. Jan Oudegeest, 'Amsterdam – London – Moscow', IFTU *Press Reports*, 14 April 1925.

54. MacDonald papers (NA) 30/69 1170, Morrison to MacDonald, 12 November 1925.
55. RGASPI 495/100/243, Inkpin to Brown, 17 June 1925 enclosing Gallacher to Bennett 17 June 1925.
56. 'The "Left Wing" and the Sunday Worker', *Sunday Worker*, 15 March 1925; prospectus for Campaign Committee, *Sunday Worker*, 17 and 24 May 1925.
57. RGASPI 495/100/245, unnamed correspondent to 'Max' (Petrovsky), 29 December 1925; also 495/100/303 for Petrovsky's information report, stamped 21 January 1926 and 534/7/32, 'Black' to Losovsky, 1 January 1926; *Sunday Worker*, 20 December 1925 and 10 January 1926 (Winifred Horrabin's account); *Manchester Guardian*, 21 December 1925.
58. L.J. Macfarlane, *The British Communist Party. Its origin and development until 1929*, MacGibbon & Kee, 1966, p. 36; Mellor, 'A critique of guild socialism', *Labour Monthly*, November 1921, pp. 397-404.
59. Bedford papers M/8, second National Guild Conference, 9 December 1922, report and related papers. For Beauchamp see the entry by Raymond Challinor and John Saville in *DLB* X, pp. 19-22. Other communists with a more durable involvement in the guilds included Beauchamp's husband, the lawyer W.H. Thompson, Sam Elsbury of the National Tailoring and Clothing Guild and the sometime Christian socialist and Trotskyist, Stuart Purkis.
60. Mellor, 'Critique', p. 399.
61. For Hobson and guild socialism, see Kevin Morgan, 'British guild socialists and the exemplar of the Panama Canal', *History of Political Thought*, 28, 2007, pp. 120-57.
62. See *Bolshevism and the British Left*, II, ch. 8.
63. *Manchester Guardian*, 3 July 1905.
64. The best account remains Mark Swenarton, *Homes Fit for Heroes. The architecture and planning of early state housing in Britain*, Heinemann, 1981.
65. See Frank Matthews, 'The building guilds' in Asa Briggs and John Saville, eds, *Essays in Labour History 1886-1923*, Macmillan, 1971, pp. 284-331.
66. Matthews, 'The building guilds', pp. 308-9.
67. See Hobson's report to third National Building Guild conference, *Manchester Guardian*, 14 August 1922.
68. *Manchester Guardian*, 8 December 1919.
69. *Manchester Guardian*, 22 March 1920.
70. *Manchester Guardian*, 30 April 1921.
71. *Manchester Guardian*, 13 June 1921.
72. Bedford papers M/11, circular for National Guild Conference, 29-30 April 1922.
73. See Gossip's observations, *Monthly Report*, October 1919, pp. 18-21. Local practice varied widely; for example, in the same issue (p. 10) the union's regional organiser described how in Reading the employers were members of the building employers' association but NAFTA was not eligible for affiliation to the Bulding Trade Conciliation Board.
74. There is an entry on Coppock by John Saville in *DLB* III, pp. 49-52.
75. NAFTA *Monthly Report*, October 1910, p. 9.

76. NAFTA *Monthly Report*, August 1919, p. 11; see also *Manchester Guardian*, 18 September 1919.
77. *Daily Express*, 5 April 1925.
78. See Kevin Morgan, 'The problem of the epoch? Labour and housing, 1918-1951', *Twentieth Century British History*, 16, 3, 2005, pp. 227-55.
79. *Manchester Guardian*, 1 August 1917, 8 November 1919; NAFTA *Monthly Report*, December 1918; Federation of Lancashire and Cheshire Trades Councils, conference on housing, reported *Manchester Guardian*, 9 April 1923; see also NAFTA's resolution to the National Labour Housing Association, NAFTA *Monthly Report*, September 1924, p. 13.
80. NAFTA *Monthly Report*, April 1922, pp. 16-18.
81. Bedford papers M/15, Purcell, typescript report, 'The Furniture and Furnishing Guild Ltd', 24 February 1922.
82. *Manchester Guardian*, 22 March 1920, 30 April, 13 June, 12 August and 17 October 1921, 6 May 1922.
83. There is a copy in TUC archives 292/9.2/6.
84. TUC archives 292/9.2/6, FFG manifesto, 21 September 1921.
85. See the summary of the assistant official receiver, *Manchester Guardian*, 9 March 1923.
86. S.G. Hobson, *Pilgrim to the Left. Memoirs of a modern revolutionist*, Edward Arnold, 1938, p. 246; *Manchester Guardian*, 9 March 1923.
87. NAFTA *Monthly Report*, February 1922, pp. 26-8.
88. NAFTA *Monthly Report*, June 1922, p. 16.
89. NAFTA *Monthly Report*, April 1922, p. 16; June 1922, p. 20; November 1922, p. 9; Bedford papers M/15, note of conversation with G. Kempton, London Furnishing Guild, 19 February 1923.
90. FFG manifesto, 21 September 1921.
91. NAFTA *Monthly Report*, June 1922, p. 20.
92. *Manchester Guardian*, 14 August 1922; NAFTA *Monthly Report*, October 1922, pp. 23-4.
93. Second National Guild Conference, 9 December 1922, contribution of G. Kempton.
94. NAFTA *Monthly Report*, December 1922, pp. 6-7; March 1923, p. 10; *Manchester Guardian*, 9 and 11 January 1923.
95. Second National Guild Conference.
96. Bedford papers, National Guilds Council building guild sub-committee minutes.
97. *Manchester Guardian*, 15 December 1922.
98. At least with the passage of time; see *Dean Forest Mercury*, 21 October 1927.
99. Bedford papers M/15, H.C. Davies, secretary, Piano Workers' Guild, to unnamed correspondent, 25 May 1924; *Lansbury's Labour Weekly*, 11 April 1925 (advertisement); Lansbury, 'Workers' pianos', *Lansbury's Labour Weekly*, 4 June 1927; TUC archives, 292/9.2/6, Davies to Citrine, 28 March 1928.
100. Purcell, 'The Furniture and Furnishing Guild Ltd'.
101. Purcell, 'The Furniture and Furnishing Guild Ltd'; see also Bedford papers M11, letter to Cuthbert Johnson, 27 August 1922: 'The Guilds are extremely keen on quality of workmanship, and the Furniture Guilds ... have found that this somewhat prejudices them with new customers who

(naturally enough) compare their tenders with the prices asked for the usual commercial shoddy'.
102. See *Bolshevism and the British Left*, II, ch. 6.
103. Second National Guild Conference, contribution of Hobson. In attempting to establish the National Guild Building Society, Hobson was to recognise the desirability 'from a functional point of view' of having 'trained business men' of guild sympathies on the board; see Bedford papers M/11, Hobson to J.H. Marriott, 24 March 1923.
104. Margaret Bondfield, *A Life's Work*, Hutchinson, n.d., p. 200, diary entry for 26 May 1920.
105. Second National Guild Conference, contribution of Hobson.
106. NAFTA *Monthy Report*, April 1922, pp. 16-18.
107. *Dean Forest Mercury*, 3 July 1925.
108. For the Soviet parallel, see William J. Chase, *Workers, Society, and the Soviet State. Labor and life in Moscow 1918-1929*, Urbana & Chicago: University of Illinois Press, 1987, pp. 38-43.
109. Bedford papers, M/9, memorandum to Tom Shaw, Minister of Labour, n.d. but early 1924.
110. Anglo-Russian Parliamentary Committee *News Bulletin*, 4 January 1936.
111. Earl C. Ford and William Z. Foster, *Syndicalism* (1912), Chicago: Charles H. Kerr, 1990 edn, ed. James R. Barrett, pp. 23, 26.
112. See the discussion in Wayne Thorpe, *'The Workers Themselves'. Revolutionary syndicalism and international labour, 1913-1923*, Dordrecht: Kluwer Academic Publishers, 1989, pp. 18-20, 323.
113. See *Bolshevism and the British Left*, I, ch. 5.
114. IFTU *Press Reports*, 20 November 1924.
115. Thorpe, *'The Workers Themselves'*, pp. 73-4.
116. 'What is syndicalism? Is it the future creed of labour?', *Syndicalist*, March-April 1912; editorial, *Syndicalist*, July 1912.
117. See Communist Unity Convention, pp. 9 and 29. The word 'valuable' was removed in the final resolution as a concession to anti-parliamentarians.
118. NAFTA *Monthly Report*, February 1920.
119. 'Renegades of the Communist Party of Great Britain'.
120. Communist Unity Convention, p. 27.
121. MacDonald papers 30/69/1168, Graham to MacDonald, 25 January 1924; also the entry on Graham by John Saville and Joyce Bellamy in William Knox, ed., *Scottish Labour Leaders 1918-1939. A biographical dictionary*, Edinburgh: Mainstream, 1984, pp. 127-8. For MacDonald's concerns with trade representation, see for example his *A Policy for the Labour Party*, Leonard Parsons, 1920, pp. 31-2.
122. NAFTA *Monthly Report*, February 1924.
123. NAFTA *Monthly Report*, August 1924, pp. 22-3.
124. MacDonald papers (NA) 30/69/1168, Mardy Jones to MacDonald, 28 May 1924.
125. See 'John Ball', 'What is wrong with us?', *Lansbury's Labour Weekly*, 28 March 1925 and Tanner's 'hearty endorsement' the following week; also Sidney Webb to Beatrice Webb, 29 September 1925 in Norman Mackenzie, ed., *The Letters of Sidney and Beatrice Webb*, vol. 3, Cambridge: CUP, 1978, p. 249.
126. 56th TUC *Report*, 1924, pp. 430-3; 57th TUC *Report*, 1925, p. 240; also

Clare Griffiths, *Labour and the Countryside. The politics of rural Britain 1918-1939*, Oxford: OUP, 2007, pp. 114-17.
127. Details in Frank Bealey and Henry Pelling, *Labour and Politics 1900-1906. A history of the Labour Representation Committee*, Macmillan, 1958, pp. 290-2; Duncan Tanner, *Political Change and the Labour Party 1900-1918*, Cambridge: CUP, 1990, p. 328.
128. G.D.H. Cole, *A History of the Labour Party from 1914*, Routledge & Kegan Paul, 1948, pp. 482-4; Cole, *British Trade Unionism Today. A survey*, Gollancz, 1939, pp. 214-15.
129. See Morgan, 'The problem of the epoch?'.
130. Tanner, *Political Change*, pp. 324, 401, 403.
131. York DLP executive committee minutes, 11 October 1922.
132. Pollitt, 'The communist party and the Whitechapel by-election', *Labour Monthly*, January 1931, p. 33. In the subsequent general election, a contribution of £4 from NAFTA's East London United branch is noted in Pollitt's *Communist Election Special* (LHASC CP/Ind/Poll/10/2).
133. RGASPI 495/100/480, report on options for the political levy by F. Wagner.
134. This was F.E. Sweetman, prospective parliamentary candidate for Chatham; see 'The policy of coalition has failed', *World News and Views*, 31 May 1941, p. 347.
135. NAFTA *Monthly Report*, April 1919, p. 18.
136. NAFTA *Monthly Report*, February 1920, pp. 16-18.
137. NAFTA *Monthly Report*, October 1920, p. 27; Stockport Trades Council and Labour Party minutes, 22 October 1922.
138. The view of Jon Lawrence, *Speaking for the People. Party, language and popular politics in England, 1867-1914*, Cambridge: CUP, 1998, pp. 229-36.
139. Communist Unity Convention, pp. 9, 27,
140. For lurid examples see *Coventry Herald*, 19-20 January and 27-8 April 1923. See also See Frank Carr, 'Municipal socialism. Labour's rise to power' in Bill Lancaster and Tony Mason, eds, *Life and Labour in a Twentieth Century City: the experience of Coventry*, Coventry: Cryfield Press, n.d., pp. 183-94.
141. NA CAB 24 RRO December 1923.
142. *Coventry Herald*, 23-24 November, 7-8 and 14-15 December 1923.
143. NAFTA *Monthly Report*, January 1924, pp. 16-17.
144. George Hodgkinson, *Sent to Coventry*, Robert Maxwell, 1970, p. 81.
145. NAFTA *Monthly Report*, December 1923, pp. 20-1; Purcell, West Salford election address, January 1910, WCML.
146. Siegfried Bettman, 'Struggling: the autobiography of S. Bettman', Coventry City Record Office 1417/1, p. 731; *Coventry Herald*, 7-8 December 1923.
147. Purcell, West Salford election address; Hodgkinson, *Sent to Coventry*, p. 81.
148. See e.g. MacDonald papers (NA) 30/69 1771, MacDonald to J.E. Walton, 13 July 1926.
149. NAFTA *Monthly Report*, May 1918, EC business. O'Grady had similarly resigned as a union organiser on the introduction of parliamentary salaries in 1911.
150. NAFTA *Monthly Report*, April 1926, pp. 2-3.
151. NAFTA *Monthly Report*, February 1924, pp.20-1 and March 1924, p. 10.

152. Mary Stocks, *Ernest Simon of Manchester*, Manchester: MUP, 1963, pp. 71-2, 86.
153. Jewson, 'What a woman Labour MP thinks of the House', *Labour Magazine*, February 1924, p. 447.
154. MacDonald, *Policy*, pp. 100-2.
155. NAFTA *Monthly Report*, February 1924.
156. See 56th TUC *Report* 1924, pp. 85-125.
157. Purcell, 'Towards a new policy: V', p. 270.
158. NADRA *Monthly Report*, April 1925, pp. 21-2.
159. See Greg Power, *Representatives of the People? The constituency role of MPs*, Fabian Society, 1998.
160. T.J. Williams, 'Labour in the playing fields', *Labour Magazine*, June 1924, p. 67.
161. 'Mr Purcell's Weekly Address', *Coventry Herald*, 14-15 March 1924.
162. *Coventry Herald*, 22-23 February 1924, 14-15 March 1924, 21-22 March 1924; also NAFTA *Monthly Report*, April 1925, p. 21.
163. 56th TUC *Report* 1924, p. 498.
164. Scott Nearing, *British Labor Bids for Power. The historic Scarborough conference of the Trades Union Congress*, New York: Social Science Publishers, 1925, p. 18.
165. See *Bolshevism and the British Left*, II, pp. 106-7
166. Philip Snowden, *An Autobiography. Volume two: 1919-1934*, Nicholson & Watson, 1934, pp. 638-59.
167. Baldwin cited Noel-Baker papers, Nbkr 1/42, Coventry Labour Party, 27th annual report, 1929.
168. See for example *Coventry Herald*, 25-26 April and 2-3 and 9-10 May 1924.
169. NAFTA *Monthly Report*, June 1924, pp. 22-3. In declining to join with the 'anti-Labour attack' Purcell had no doubt came under pressure not to do so.
170. *Coventry Herald*, 2-3 May 1924.
171. 173 Hansard fifth series, 13 May 1924, cols 1239-44.
172. Speech of G. Morris of Coventry Labour Party at Purcell's adoption meeting (*Coventry Herald*, 17-18 October 1924). Speakers in Purcell's support included Cramp, Swales, Hicks, Quaile, Varley (all general council members) as well as Bramley, Gossip, Coppock and Bevin.
173. 173 Hansard fifth series, 13 May 1924, cols 1239-44.
174. NA 30/69/220 RRO 21 August 1924 citing CPGB press statements, 13 and 16 August 1924.
175. *Coventry Herald*, 24-25 October and 31October-1 November 1924.
176. NAFTA *Monthly Report*, November 1924, pp. 26-7.
177. *Coventry Herald*, 31October-1 November 1924, also 4-5 April and 17-18 October 1924 for similar disparagement of the Liberals.
178. *Gloucester Citizen*, 16 and 18 June 1925; Labour Party NEC minutes, national agent's by-election report, 24 June 1925; Sidney Webb to Beatrice Webb, 24 June 1925 in Mackenzie, *Letters of Sidney and Beatrice Webb*, vol. 3, p. 239.
179. Labour Party NEC minutes, 24 June 1925. In recording these facts as a sort of accolade to Mosley, Robert Skidelsky, *Oswald Mosley*, Macmillan, 1981 edn, p. 157, does not mention the nature of the objection to

Bondfield's candidacy, and compounds this by his slighting references to the jealousy of Mosley's rivals.
180. IISH SAI 1663, Henderson to Tom Shaw, 24 June 1925.; MacDonald papers 30/69 1170, Hamilton Fyfe to MacDonald, 17 July 1925; Ellen Wilkinson, *Lansbury's Labour Weekly*, 25 July 1925; Labour national agent's by-election report, 24 June 1925. In other circumstances MacDonald fully accepted that 'the duty of the Leader of the Opposition is to send a letter to every candidate' (MacDonald papers 30/69 1172, MacDonald to Mrs Mears, *Daily Herald* editorial secretary, 1 April 1927).
181. TUC archives 292/20/9, TUC general council minutes, 10 July 1925; Lansbury in *Lansbury's Labour Weekly*, 25 July 1925. Visiting general council members included Swales, Tillett and Smillie.
182. MacDonald papers 30/69 1172, Bevin to MacDonald, 3 December 1927; Sidney Webb to Beatrice Webb, 29 September 1925.
183. Extensive coverage of the campaign can be found in the *Dean Forest Mercury* and the *Gloucester Citizen*.
184. See in particular 'Labour and the Churches', *Dean Forest Mercury*, 17 July 1925.
185. *Sunday Worker*, 19 July 1925.
186. National Minority Movement, *Report of Second Annual Conference*, NMM, August 1925; *Workers' Weekly*, 17 October 1924.
187. Labour Party NEC minutes, national agent's by-election report, 28 June 1925.
188. Speeches by Williams and Mrs Fawcett, Labour national women's organiser, *Dean Forest Mercury*, 3 July 1925, and by Purcell, *Dean Forest Mercury*, 17 July 1925.
189. Ralph Anstis, *Four Personalities from the Forest of Dean*, Coleford: Albion House, 1996, p. 152; *Dean Forest Mercury*, 17 July 1925.
190. *Coventry Herald*, 24-5 October 1924; Citrine papers 1/7, copy diary entry 4 August 1925.
191. *Dean Forest Mercury*, 3 July 1925 and 5 February 1926.
192. *Coventry Herald*, 24-5 October 1924.
193. Bramley, 'Dilke, a defender of the people', *Labour Magazine*, April 1925, p. 551.
194. See *Bolshevism and the British Left*, I, ch. 5.
195. TGWU *Record*, June 1925, p. 241; Ellen Wilkinson, *Lanbury's Labour Weekly*, 27 March 1926.
196. NAFTA *Monthly Report*, January 1926, p. 22.
197. 57th TUC *Report*, 1925, pp. 66-7.
198. E.g. Clegg, *History*, p. 356.,
199. *Dean Forest Mercury*, 4 September and 4 December 1925; NAFTA *Monthly Report*, October 1925, p. 9.
200. *Dean Forest Mercury*, 5 February 1926.
201. Crossman papers 154/3/AU/1/127-8, notes 2 August 1945.
202. Respectively Philip Noel Baker and Morgan Philips Price, see *Bolshevism and the British Left*, I, pp. 158-9, 166-8.
203. John A. Yates, *Pioneers to Power: the story of the working people of Coventry*, Coventry Labour Party, 1950, p. 20.
204. Henry Mayers Hyndman, *Further Reminiscences*, Macmillan, 1912, p. 463.

205. Purcell is recorded as living at Brook Terrace, Davyhulme in 1916; at Talbot Road, Davyhulme in 1925; and at Kendall Road, Crumpsall in 1929 and until his death.
206. Hobson, *Pilgrim to the Left*, p. 220; NAFTA *Monthly Report*, June 1922, p. 16.
207. Bramley papers box 1, Purcell to Bramley, 22 December 1924.
208. The *DLB* entry by David Martin provides basic career details.
209. Clinton, *Trade Union Rank and File*, pp. 84-7.
210. Clinton, *Trade Union Rank and File*, pp. 85, 87.
211. Tanner, *Political Change*, p. 145; L.A. Bather, 'A history of the Manchester and Salford Trades Council', Manchester: M Phil, 1956, pp. 161-71; Clinton, *Trade Union Rank and File*, p. 51.
212. *Manchester Guardian*, 1 and 2 August 1917.
213. Purcell, 'Towards a new policy: V', p. 270.
214. TUC *Report*, 1924, pp. 180-2.
215. As argued in Clinton, *Trade Union Rank and File*.
216. *Manchester Guardian*, 20 April 1922.
217. Sidney and Beatrice Webb, *The History of Trade Unionism*, Longmans, Green & Co, 1894, p. 472.
218. *The General Council of the Trades Union Congress. Its powers, functions and work*, pref. A.B. Swales, TUC General Council, n.d. but 1925, p. 4.
219. TUC archives 292/28/1, 'Office development. Supplementary statement by F. Bramley', n.d., c. 1918.
220. Clegg, *History*, pp. 308-9
221. See the discussion and voting figures in 56th TUC *Report*, September 1924, pp. 333-4 and 489-93. Understandably, the ASW was seeking to have the method of election changed.
222. Margaret Morris, *The General Strike*, Harmondsworth: Penguin, 1976, p. 171.
223. See TUC archives 292/28/1, 'Functions of committees. Interim report', July 1925.
224. For example, he served on the majority of the TUC's government deputations in that period; see *Sunday Worker*, 28 June and 5 July 1925 for reports that he was working at his trade and Clegg, *History*, p. 451 for the general council's financial arrangements.
225. TUC archives 292/21.12/1, Bramley biographical file.
226. Cited Robert Taylor, 'Citrine's unexpurgated diaries, 1925-26: the mining crisis and the national strike', *Historical Studies in Industrial Relations*, 20, 2005, p.77.
227. *Dean Forest Mercury*, 2 March 1928.
228. NTWF archives 159/3/C/188, Edo Fimmen to Robert Williams, 17 February 1922 for Tillett's renewed interest 'in the International'. Tillett had played some part in the early years of the ITF and was briefly its secretary and president.
229. Rodney Barker, *Education and Politics 1900-1951. A study of the Labour Party*, Oxford: OUP, 1972, ch. 7. Purcell differed from Bramley in this, and when in 1924 the more respectable Workers' Educational Association elected Bramley as its president, the more proletarian National Council of Labour Colleges followed by electing Purcell to the same position (*Manchester Guardian*, 12 May and 14 September 1925).

230. On this theme see Lewis Minkin, *The Contentious Alliance. Trade unions and the Labour Party*, Edinburgh: Edinburgh University Press, 1991, ch. 2. The use of Minkin's idea of 'rules' in relation to the CPGB is discussed in *Bolshevism and the British Left*, I, pp. 41-3.
231. *Labour Magazine*, May 1922, p. 24
232. TUC archives 292/20/8, TUC general council/Labour Party NEC joint minutes, 27 September and 31 October 1923.
233. TUC archives 292/20/9, TUC general council minutes, 24 September 1924, 292/28/1, 'Mr Bramley's points re joint departments', n.d. but 1925.
234. 56th TUC *Report*, 1924, pp. 66-8.
235. 'Mr Bramley's points'.
236. 57th TUC *Report*, pp. 84-5, 356-69.
237. Marjorie Nicholson, *The TUC Overseas. The roots of policy*, Allen & Unwin, 1984, pp. 21-3; TUC archives 292/28/1, 'International Bureau', memo by Bramley presented TUC parliamentary committee office committee, 16 May 1919.
238. Christine Collette, *The International Faith. Labour's attitudes to European socialism 1918-1939*, Aldershot: Ashgate, 1998, p. 49.
239. TUC archives 292/28/1, 'Mr Bramley's points re joint departments', n.d. but 1925.
240. For details see 57th TUC *Report*, p. 324.
241. Ben Tillett, *Some Russian Impressions*, LRD, 1925, p. 19.
242. Daniel F. Calhoun, *The United Front. The TUC and the Russians 1923-1928*, Cambridge: CUP, 1976, pp. 54-5.
243. NAFTA *Monthly Report*, October 1916, p. 18.

Chapter three

Labour's Russian delegations

3.1 INSULAR INTERNATIONALISTS

A communist correspondent provides a snapshot of British delegates at an international socialist gathering in Frankfurt in February 1922. The trade unionists were the best of them, and Purcell even had a 'real revolutionary temper'. None, however, was a match for the 'intellectual Socialists of the continental type'; unless it was Tom Shaw, secretary of the International Textile Workers, who was a 'real John Bull against whose stodginess they had to pull up'. Industrious and prolific in speech and resolutions, the French and Belgian social democrats were 'in debate head and shoulders above everybody else'. The sometime German communist Paul Levi took a 'really revolutionary, class-conscious attitude', and when they were 'not in the pub or splitting ILP hairs' the British broadly sided with him. Shaw alone of them, however, was not 'either dilettante or "out for a spree"'. 'Tillett talked very red, but during critical moments he was generally to be found with Purcell swilling lager beer in a pub over the way.'[1]

One might almost describe it as a typical encounter. For the better part of two centuries, the relations of the British with their fellow Europeans had been a matter of paradox, bewilderment and satire. The dilation of the labour movement into international affairs simply added to the stock of incongruities. Studies of labour internationalism usually portray British trade unionists as preferring even to take their beer among themselves. 'The insular position of Britain has always given the British working-class movement a peculiar national stamp', wrote the Russian marxist G.M. Stekloff in the 1920s. It was consequently on the continent, where the workers of different countries were more closely interconnected, that international sentiment 'developed earlier and had a more concrete character'.[2] The US labour economist Lewis L. Lorwin also observed that the British workman 'did not travel', except within the empire, and that 'foreign workers' had no important role in Britain itself. Even the appreciation of international competition was constrained by 'psychologic' factors of insular mentality, linguistic ineptitude and 'sense of superiority in representing the oldest trade union country in the world'.[3] Tillett, when not talking red, was the epitome of this attitude, as when some thirty years earlier he gratuitously impugned the 'hare-brained chatterers and magpies of Continental revolutionists' at the founding conference of the ILP.[4]

Later accounts support this impression. Stephen Howe describes the inter-war TUC as 'almost wholly parochial', and the unions as the section of the labour movement least interested in international questions.[5] Douglas Newton reached a similar conclusion on the basis of a detailed study of the pre-1914 period.[6] Clegg's biographical profiles simply omitted international affiliations and responsibilities as if extraneous to the unions' history.[7] Ross Martin mentions but does not describe the TUC's 'burgeoning international aspirations' post-1918, and neither Russian delegations nor Purcell fit into his conception of the TUC's history.[8] Britain may have been the oldest trade-union country, but the TUC's participation in IFTU was belated, and Shaw's International Textile Workers' Federation was one of only two of the nearly thirty international trade secretariats that were based in Britain. Internationalists within Britain were uncomfortably aware of the contrast. The ILPer Ernest Hunter, returning from international festivities in Belgium in 1924, thought London by comparison 'a veritable Arctic region in its treatment of allies and friends'.[9] Comparing international strike support, Purcell himself conceded that the British had not 'developed so much the idea of internationalism as they have on the Continent. We have the Channel between us, while they have simply an ordinary border or railway to separate them ...'[10]

Proverbial truths nevertheless leave something unexplained. Even Stekloff and Lorwin recorded, not just the assumed fact of British insularity, but how it was that on British soil and among British workers the idea of an international labour organisation first took root. Lorwin described William Lovett as the 'first working man of modern times with an international outlook'.[11] Stekloff cited Theodore Rothstein: 'it was precisely in England that the proletariat did not merely develop the keenest sense of its solidarity with its foreign brethren, but also became aware how essential to success in the struggle with bourgeois society was a co-ordination of effort based upon this solidarity'.[12] Purcell himself described Britain as 'the registered birthplace of the Workers' International'.[13]

The Channel, as the sometime exile Rothstein knew, was not just a barrier but a conduit and a cushion. On the one hand, Britain's relative prosperity and legal security attracted economic and political migrants, and turned London into 'a minor "International" in its own right'.[14] At the same time, the cushion of a liberal political order allowed the development of a labour movement presence that seemed both financially and politically indispensable to a viable international organisation. Founded in 1864, the First International had already shown the possibilities of co-operation between an adoptive Londoner like Marx and Victorian trade-unionists of the John Bull type. Thirty years later Purcell had seen how most of the delegations of the International again favoured the location of its secretariat in Britain.[15] The International Co-operative Alliance already had a London headquarters and a British-dominated executive.[16] Even syndicalists responded to the call of the virtually non-existent ISEL by holding their first international conference in London.[17] International conditions between the wars, from political repression to the depreciation of the mark, conspired to reinforce the relative weight of the British contribution. Writing in the 1920s, when the Second International had also been re-established on British soil, the Bolshevik Stekloff would not have failed to note that the peculiarity of British insularity was its international scope.

Such seeming inconsistency may in part be explained by the ambiguity of the notion of internationalism itself. While one must recognise the contemporary currency of phrases like 'the international faith', latterly invoked by Christine Collette, in some ways they are likelier to confuse issues than illuminate them. Certainly, the claim that this faith infused the British labour movement at every level would have astonished Purcell, in his efforts to promote this desirable condition, or Ernest Hunter, who tartly observed that 'money and delegates do not make up for a genuine interest on the part of the masses'.[18] Lorwin, for whom internationalism signified the pursuit of mutual interest and goodwill as opposed to war and conflict, identified the five distinct varieties of humanitarian, pacifist, commercial, social-reformist and social-revolutionary internationalism.[19] These can certainly be identified with different end goals conceived in the spirit of internationalism. Pending their achievement, however, the projection of these aspirations within and upon diverse parties, regimes and systems of government proved a fruitful source of partisan and even inter-state conflict into which, as a result, internationalists themselves were reluctantly drawn.

Socialism in particular, whether reformist or revolutionary, was a philosophy of advancement through social conflict, and of resistance to social retrogression, whose diverse expressions generated rivalry, solidarity, tension and sometimes all-out war. Just as economic boycotts were directed at particular employers, so sundry sanctions might be directed at particular states, not in any purely national spirit, but on grounds of common interests cutting across national boundaries, but unevenly secured within them. In the same way, though working-class internationalism might have no national centre, the achievement of a purported workers' state after 1917 attracted a vehement partisan allegiance for what it represented in social rather than national terms.[20] What Eric Hobsbawm refers to as the oppositionist stance hitherto adopted by labour movements was likewise tempered by a variegated experience that extended from labour governments and legal codes on the one hand to intensified persecution on the other.[21] As the dilemma of a transnational anti-fascism was above all to demonstrate, what internationalism represented between the wars was not just a matter of faith but a moral and political conundrum.

Where Lorwin characterised internationalism as an ideal, a policy or a method, it could equally be regarded as a field of engagement into which diverse priorities and points of perspective introduced the elements of discord and dissension that were so much a feature of internationalism in practice. In Britain, E.D. Morel was the most distinguished of the Liberal internationalists who threw in their lot with the post-1914 labour movement. Morel was the moving force behind the Union of Democratic Control (UDC), from 1914 the primary vehicle of this form of internationalism, and the initiator in 1919 of the monthly *Foreign Affairs*, which expressly addressed itself to a Labour readership.[22] 'Foreign affairs', according to Morel's definition, signified conditions prevailing in other countries '*as they affect and as they are linked up with conditions in our own country*'.[23] While this might seem an unduly restricted conception of the international, it seemingly justified Morel's contention that these were matters of the most immediate trade-union concern – particularly in a country as dependent on international trade as Britain.

At the time of his death in 1924, Morel was collaborating closely with Purcell, who repeatedly advanced a similar line of argument:

> The workers in this country, in particular – because Britain is such a great international capitalist power; because our employing class has such world-wide interests; because our seamen, skilled workers, higher technicians, go to every country; and because, at every turn, our destinies are so intimately interwoven, in a basic, economic manner, with the destinies of the workers of other countries – have every reason to view matters in an international sense, and from a world standpoint.[24]

What this recognition implied politically was far from clear. 'Worldwide interests' could also give rise to the internationalising discourses of globalisation: already Stekloff cited the notion of a 'Golden International' put forward by the German social conservative Rudolf Meyer, while Lorwin's 'commercial' internationalism could be traced back at least a century.[25] Similarly in political terms, as Labour displaced the Liberals as a party of government, the empire had either to be maintained or to be dismantled. It could not, however, simply be disregarded, at least by Labour's political class. Working-class internationalism was thus only one variety of internationalism, indeed may itself be regarded as a portmanteau category containing the distinct but interdependent notions of labour and socialist internationalism. Labour internationalism, for present purposes, may be characterised as a mutualist or solidaristic approach to 'foreign affairs' in respect of trading and inter-state relations, on the assumption of a common interest as expressed in and measured by the organisation of labour itself. Purcell's internationalism may be defined more specifically as a left-wing variant of this labour internationalism, or perhaps as the projection of socialist internationalism through established trade-union structures as another variation on the theme of boring from within.

As Susan Milner has observed, labour internationalism has received far less attention than socialist internationalism and there is not even consensus as to the conditions which favoured its development.[26] Douglas Newton's account, premised on the strong commitment to internationalism of the pre-1914 German labour movement, offers the almost post-materialist argument that internationalism took root where workers felt assured of their long-term future and had no fear of foreign competitors.[27] It is certainly true that the better developed the organisation nationally, the better equipped it was to support the extension of such organisation internationally. It is also true that this involved considerable transaction costs and that the movements best able to support these might find their commitment cemented by the influence they thereby wielded, or felt they ought to wield. In the British movement's greater commitment to IFTU in the inter-war period, a clear motivation was concern to assume the prerogatives to which it felt its financial commitments entitled it.

A more influential model of trade-union internationalism, influentially expounded by John Logue, posits an inverse correlation with the degree of integration into national political systems, so that 'the stronger the national trade union movement, the less likely it is to be internationalistic'.[28] This would be consistent with the view that the 1940s marked the end of a 'classical age' of working-class internationalism, and the embedding of strong national labour organisations in the countries in which this internationalism had classically been expressed.[29] By these criteria, British unions of the later nineteenth century might have lacked the stimulus to a more thoroughgoing internationalism to the extent that they enjoyed a basic minimum of recognition and acceptance. While this may have remained the case, the loss of Britain's dominant trading position meant a new sense of exposure to what Logue calls 'foreign variables', particularly in the decades around the First World War. Internationalism here offers a further perspective on the pendulum notion, as a diminished sense of industrial self-sufficiency encouraged ventures beyond the unions' 'primary' functions, internationally as well as domestically. By 1914, issues of both parliamentary and international representation intruded on the TUC's affairs in a way that had not been the case a quarter of a century earlier.

The weakness of Logue's approach is its dismissal of ideology and excessive reliance on a short-term rational self-interest model. There is little recognition of the impact of events like the First World War, which certainly impinged on the self-interest of unions and union members, and which showed a capacity for diverse responses, nationalist more often than internationalist, that are incomprehensible in terms simply of rational calculation. There is similarly little appreciation of the shaping of internationalism as a set of values and arguments to which key cohorts of activists might be more than instrumentally committed.

There is even a basic incongruity in Logue's stress on the dominant role of elites while representing their activities as the 'rational collective action' of the larger group. Without considering the character of these elites, Logue circumvented the problem by trivialising 'parasitic elite internationalism' as a form of rational self-interest in the form of lager imbibing and junketings.[30] One should certainly not discount what the Webbs would have called the expansion of personality through foreign travel. In Jeffrey Harrod's work on the post-war period this emerged as a significant recompense.[31] Even in Purcell's day it included hotel bookings, out-of-pocket expenses, first-class travel, at least when he went to India, and occasional air transport even within Europe.[32] On the other hand, the Dutchman Edo Fimmen, secretary of the International Transportworkers' Federation (ITF) and a collaborator of Purcell, pointed out in 1922 that work in connection with the ITF had been carried out exclusively 'in the "spare hours" of a man who for years past has not known what spare hours mean'. Foreign travel in Fimmen's case meant late shifts to free up the time to make it possible and outstanding paperwork to be dealt with in transit.[33] Internationally as previously at national level, even administrators could hardly be regarded as the 'creatures' of organisational structures that were still in the process of formation.[34]

With all its limitations, the strength of Logue's approach was that it did acknowledge the specificities of a form of labour internationalism rooted in the economic objects of trade unions. This basic insight has been convincingly developed by Milner to help explain variation both internationally and between different industrial sectors over time. Milner's focus, like Newton's, is on the pre-1914 period, where she identifies a weakening of labour internationalism with the growth of stronger national organisations less reliant on the compensatory function it performed.[35] Nevertheless, the suggested link between internationalist activity and exposure to international forms of competition has obvious relevance for the inter-war years. It would certainly have made sense to Purcell, who looked to the impact of Britain's intractable 'million unemployed problem' for an upsurge in internationalist sentiment.[36]

Trade-union internationalism may thus, according to Logue, be understood as a response to the input of foreign variables into the unions' domestic environment.[37] It was not however the only such response, and an international sense of interest and agency did not always equate to universalist or solidaristic values. The Webbs in *Industrial Democracy* had suggested that there were ultimately only two expedients available to trade unionists in the defence of their interests: the Device of the Common Rule and the Device of Restriction of Numbers.[38] There was no absolute dividing line between these, and competition from unorganised labour could give rise to restrictionist impulses precisely in the name of some common rule or standard. Across national boundaries as within them, there was therefore no watertight division between labour internationalism and labour protectionism as possible responses to more exploitative or otherwise cost-effective forms of production. Hobsbawm rightly referred to the multidimensionality of the trade unionist, who was never only a trade unionist, and thus registered the influence in these matters of other such dimensions as ethnicity or gender. On the other hand, the intrusion of a protectionist or exclusionary impulse was not simply the effect of external force, but arguably was implicit in the repertoire of 'spontaneous' trade-union practices.[39]

Protectionism, in its various guises, was thus also an acknowledgement of foreign affairs as these 'linked up with' domestic conditions. Morel has rightly earned notoriety for his obsessional attacks on the use of black troops in the Ruhr. Appearing in Lansbury's *Herald* and other labour papers, these were certainly symptomatic of attitudes more widely held.[40] There were however important distinctions. Purcell in 1917 had also moved a trades council resolution opposing the importation of 'coloured' building labourers 'both from the economic and the moral standpoint'.[41] Bramley had cited the same issue in arguing against Labour's continued participation in the wartime coalition.[42] There is nevertheless little sign in their public statements of the moral and sexual anxieties alluded to in the trades council resolution and abundantly attested in Morel's later writings. On the one hand, the introduction of Belgian refugees into the furnishing trades had previously given rise to similar objections without any such moralistic overtones.[43] On the other hand, NAFTA took a strong line against branches or individual members seeking the victimisation of German or other union members on grounds of nationality.[44] The primary object of a union, said Bramley, was control of the labour supply.[45] This could be directly, or through regulating the distribution of the goods and services in which this labour was expressed. The tension between these strands would resurface throughout Purcell's career, and he was later to describe himself as both an internationalist and a nationalist. Like the Webbian concerns with the rise and fall of civilisations, even his nationalism was not, however, fundamentally an issue of race. For both Purcell and later the Webbs, the Chinese provided the example of threat transformed into inspiration, according to conceptions of social development that were neither innate nor immutable.[46]

The labour internationalism of a body like NAFTA could be accommodated within the pluralistic ethos of the labour movement.

Bramley after all was elected a full-time officer of the generally prowar TUC in 1917. What did provoke dissension was the encroachment of such figures onto wider spheres of national and international positioning and decision-making. Of all the fields of labour politics, international exchange seemed most to lend itself to specialisation of function. Within Britain, defecting Liberal internationalists brought cultural resources that could include language skills and more cosmopolitan experiences of education, travel or employment. Coinciding with a period of trade-union assertiveness, their adhesion to the cause of labour gave rise to unlikely alliances, like that between Purcell and Morel, as well as to antagonisms. Through the anomaly of direct tradeunion representation, the British were unusual in being represented by manual workers at international socialist congresses. Here they found that the construction of national difference was just as much a matter of social class as reproduced in national stereotypes. If 'intellectual socialists of the continental type' shuddered at the intrusion of British working men, their liberal condescension would certainly have extended to many of their own compatriots had they succeeded in attending such occasions. Camille Huysmans, a Belgian delegate at Frankfurt, was a university professor, educated for the priesthood, and bearing all the marks of 'bourgeois culture and refinement'. Beatrice Webb described how London audiences marvelled at his polylingual wit and eloquence, while Huysmans in turn felt nothing but scorn for the brutishness, stupidity and lethargy of the union officers at the head the British labour movement.[47] The Channel was less the barrier here than the instinct which Bramley might have described as class cohesion. After all, on a Labour delegation in Paris in 1918, it was Beatrice herself who described the union members as '"cripples"', except in their voracious appetites, and commented on the gulf between them and 'neurotic intellectuals' like MacDonald.[48]

Even within the milieu of trade-union internationalism there were issues. At the beginning of the war, IFTU had relocated to Amsterdam under the secretaryship of the former railway worker Jan Oudegeest. From 1919 Oudegeest was assisted by his fellow Dutchman Edo Fimmen as joint general secretary. Functionaries from smaller or linguistically divided European nations contributed disproportionately to international organisation. As well as the language skills they possessed, there may be an analogy with the smaller unions that were readiest to look beyond their sectional interests and least capable of imposing these upon other sections of the movement. Oudegeest, even so, had been a German nominee, very close to the German union leader Legien, and with Fimmen in 1919 was regarded as a representative of the 'Germanic nations'.[49] In the longer term, this was less an issue of lingering wartime animosities than of the deeper cleavage between communism and social democracy which quickly overshadowed them. Fimmen's evolution towards the left meant his exclusion from office at the Germans' behest in 1923. Oudegeest, on the other hand, typified a sort of career internationalism which stood for the clear political alignment of the unions with the interlocking structures of European social democracy – so that Oudegeest was able to assume the chairmanship of the Dutch SDAP when displaced from his IFTU functions in 1927. It was a common criticism, voiced among others by Purcell, that IFTU in the 1920s functioned as a virtual instrument or client organisation of the German SPD.[50]

Had the TUC returned to its former isolation, as did its American counterpart the AFL, a good deal of acrimony might have been avoided. This however was unthinkable. British Labour was at once crucial to any viable alternative to the Moscow internationals, and the trojan horse that sought accommodation with them. On the strength of its affiliation fees alone it had a claim to high international office. It nevertheless lacked experienced functionaries possessing administratively indispensable language skills. A characteristic pattern was thus established involving a Briton as figurehead and a secretariat supplied by Germany or the low countries. This was not necessarily a recipe for discord. A secretary like Fimmen shared the disaffection with political social democracy. A figurehead like J.H. Thomas, IFTU's president from 1920, ceded nothing to the continentals in anti-communism. But between Oudegeest and Purcell, when the latter succeeded Thomas in 1924, there was nevertheless a perfect mismatch.

At the root of this mismatch was Russia. For the British labour activist, Russia had always been a focus of internationalism. Trades council minute books were 'littered' with denunciations of Tsarism, often, Newton suggests, as their sole excursions into foreign policy.[51] For Purcell's trades council in Manchester only the direct British involvement in the South African war seems to have attracted a comparable interest.[52] Following the massacre of unarmed Russian demonstrators on 'Bloody Sunday, 1905, Purcell was among the speakers addressing a 'great international meeting' of protest chaired by Mrs Pankhurst.[53] Challenging the royal visit to Russia two years later, NAFTA's MP O'Grady again raised the spectre of Bloody Sunday. Seventeen years later, the frontispiece to the TUC's Russian delegation report depicted the same events to stir the reader with the dark historical legacy from which the Bolsheviks were seeking to extricate their country. It was nevertheless far from clear to many that the logic of internationalism was to uphold the Bolshevik regime. The arbitrary arrests and denial of basic freedoms that had so disturbed O'Grady could equally be alleged against the revolution itself. This indeed was a point which from its launching in 1920-1 was continuously urged against the new 'red international' of labour unions by the rival IFTU. The unity of internationalism's oppositional phase had broken down. Social democrats resisted the unions' subordination to the Bolsheviks' political ambitions.[54] But equally, dissenters like Purcell complained that IFTU itself was subservient to social-democratic politicians who in certain cases were even implicated in coalitions with the bourgeois parties. Whatever internationalism signified, the workers of all countries were not united.

Why they divided as they did is another matter. In a wider European survey, Bruno Naarden has proposed that revolution in the east provided socialists in the west with a safety valve and compensation for their own sense of impotence.[55] It is nevertheless unclear why in Britain of all countries this need should have been so keenly felt. With the travails of the second Labour government, and its eventual collapse in 1931, the sense of a political impasse contributed significantly to a new wave of interest in Soviet Russia in the 1930s. It is far less clear why this should have been the motivation of those who had earlier promulgated the inevitability of gradualness, or else, like Purcell, taken issue with the premise of gradualness rather than the inevitability of the coming social change. The incongruity was often noted of what Oudegeest described as 'the peculiar form of radicalism which has so suddenly developed among the British trade unions'.[56] Trotsky suggested that it was a form of left-wing cover to head off the rising discontent of ordinary workers.[57] But that too begged the question of why alone in Britain.

There were, however, precedents. Milner notes how in an earlier period British unions' aversion to the political direction of the socialists made for a sort of common cause with the syndicalists of the CGT.[58] At the international trade-union congress of 1888 'shouts of laughter' were reported as British trade unionists supported an anti-political resolution of the anarchist Tortelier, who for years had proclaimed his sole belief in dynamite and insurrection.[59] Anarchism in the age of the *attentat* was certainly no less controversial than Bolshevism. Eight years later, Hardie and Mann were nevertheless undeterred by Tortellier's presence among the anarchist delegates whom once again they wished to embrace within the International.[60] Indeed, after the intervening Zurich international congress of 1893 the Dutch anarchist communist Christian Cornelissen anticipated a possible split between the syndicalists, anarchists and 'trade unionists on the English model' on the one hand, and unions adhering to social democracy on the other.[61]

IFTU's prehistory has been described as one divided at its core between a syndicalist concept of trade unionism identified with the French and a social-democratic one identified with the Germans.[62] Against the common threat of communism, these erstwhile antagonists for the most part drew together. It was the British, rather, who for the time being embodied a strain of trade-union independence which might be traced back to syndicalism, or equally to the 'British model' that had had them clutching their sides in the 1880s.[63] Extended to the beneficiaries of insurrection, as previously to its most energetic proponents, the instinct of independence was not of course confined to Britain. Nowhere else, however, was a relatively pluralistic culture so combined with an ethos of unity as to allow it such free expression through official channels. The anomaly was encapsulated by the Labour delegations to Russia in 1920 and 1924. Purcell, and Purcell alone, was a delegate on both occasions.

3.2 RUSSIA 1920

With the easing of the international blockade during 1919, the traffic of British visitors to the new Soviet Russia began to develop. Two years later the Frenchman André Morizet cited six examples of external commentaries on Bolshevism. All of them were British, and all of them the work of independent travellers of one sort or another.[64] Individual trade unionists had neither the time nor the resources for such activities. Internationalists they may have been, but by the fifth and sixth decades of their lives neither Bramley nor Purcell appears to have set foot outside the British Isles. The organisation of a representative Labour delegation to Russia in the spring of 1920 therefore linked the incursion of the democracy into the class-bound preserve of foreign affairs with the radical appeal of the new workers' Russia. This connection was to resonate for years to come, both for trade-union internationalists and for some within the UDC tradition. It also registered on an international scale. Worsening relations between Amsterdam and Moscow meant that a suggested IFTU delegation was never feasible, nor would IFTU's continental affiliates have proceeded independently. As the only such venture of comparable standing, the British party that arrived in Petrograd in mid-May 1920 advanced a sort of claim to act as interpreter and interlocutor of the Russians in the west.

While the delegation was away, IFTU proposed to the TUC that it be consulted about such initiatives 'in order that a United Report could be made'. This suggestion, the TUC minute drily records, 'was noted'.[65] Even disregarding such external pressures, a united report at this stage was scarcely within the capacity of the British movement itself. In character and composition the delegation of 1920 epitomised the makeshift character of its current organisation, and in rough-and-ready fashion reflected the range and incoherence of labour opinion on Russia and its expression through diverse media and political networks.[66] The party's immediate origins lay in a TUC resolution of December 1919, and Purcell joined the party as a TUC delegate along with Margaret Bondfield, then of the National Federation of Women Workers, and Herbert Skinner of the Typographical Association. The extension of the invitation to the Labour Party led to its nomination of three further union officials, Ben Turner, Tom Shaw and Robert Williams, along with the ILPer Ethel Snowden. There were also two secretaries, Charles Roden Buxton and Leslie Haden Guest, both of them drawn from Labour's recent influx of middle-class parliamentary candidates. Buxton was a former Liberal who as the delegation's one Russian speaker acted as interpreter. Haden Guest was a medical practitioner, theosophist and London county councillor, whose fluent French also assisted with Russian interlocutors. Neither was disposed to play a merely ancillary role. The services of a Russian anti-Bolshevik trade unionist, at the suggestion of the Hyndmanite National Socialist Party (NSP), were declined.[67]

Accompanying the party were two ILP delegates, Dick Wallhead and Clifford Allen, who reported separately and who at this stage were much impressed with Bolshevism. 'That idiot Bertrand Russell', as the Soviet foreign minister Chicherin called him, came along in some unspecified personal capacity.[68] As if this were not variety enough, they were later joined for parts of the trip by a Labour defector from the diplomatic service, George Young; a journalist from the Liberal *Daily News*, Walter Meakin; and two revolutionary shop stewards, Jack Tanner and Dick Beech, who had travelled out illegally for the second Comintern congress and scorned those proceeding by the grace of capitalist passports.[69] Within this cross-section of labour opinion, Purcell and Robert Williams constituted a declared pro-Bolshevik left, though hardly yet a faction. Indeed, when the party divided to cover different subjects Purcell often travelled with Bondfield, who with Turner and Skinner represented a mainstream trade-union view sympathetic to the Soviets.[70] Shaw, on the other hand, was more sceptical, and his fluency in French and German gave him the chance to sound out educated Russians without the need for interpreters.

If the British were learning how to organise foreign delegations, the Bolsheviks were learning how to handle them. The heterogeneous composition of this earliest such party merely compounded the dilemma. Lenin's instinct was to expose them as social traitors and thus undercut the impact of their '*inevitable* Menshevik speeches' once back in Britain.[71] It is unclear whether he feared more their hostility to the regime or the cultivation of a spurious legitimacy through identification with it. Either way, such a counsel took little account of the efforts being made to establish better relations with the western powers, currently focused on the Russian trade delegation in London. Leonid Krasin, the delegation's leader, was unequivocally a partisan of such an accommodation. In Moscow, the case for greater finesse was put by the acting Comintern secretary Karl Radek. Chicherin too, a sometime Menshevik, adoptive Londoner and BSP member, recognised that there were 'first-rate, high-calibre minds' among the visitors.[72] Following discussions with Radek and Chicherin, Lenin agreed that 'leftist and rightist' elements should be differentiated, and if possible turned against each other.[73]

The tension between these approaches persisted during their visit and for some years thereafter. Bukharin, at this point one of the Bolsheviks' intransigents, launched a 'bruising attack' on the delegates; Losovsky, future head of the Profintern, set the tone for a series of denunciations of their half-hearted campaign against anti-Soviet intervention.[74] On the other hand, the 'political commission for the reception of the British guests' comprised the more accommodating figures of Radek, Lev Kamenev, and the head of the Russian unions Mikhail Tomsky.[75] Tomsky in particular would prove a key point of contact for British trade unionists. A printer by trade, aged forty in 1920, he boasted an early grounding in industrial struggles and invariably impressed trade-union interlocutors as speaking the same language as they did.[76] A thumbnail sketch from 1922, the year he joined the Russian politbureau, depicted him as a lifelong labour organiser who in spite of his official position and responsibilities had 'remained a worker – unpretentious, sympathetic, accessible, and loved by the workers as a fellow-worker'.[77] Williams had 'many intimate conversations' with Tomsky while in Russia, and one may be sure that Purcell was not excluded from such contact.[78] Tomsky not only spoke Bolshevik in a way the British trade unionist could understand. He apparently valued the connection as one abetting the unions' independent role in Russia itself. When the connection with Purcell was re-established in 1924, it was to prove a fateful one, and perhaps in due course for Tomsky even a fatal one.

Discussion of the delegation has tended to portray it as an exercise in manipulation, whether willingly or unwittingly undergone. Some of the commentary is asinine. Orlando Figes thus describes Ethel Snowden's reaction to learning that a monthly wage paid for only three days' food: 'Oh! how clever and frugal of the workers to live without any food for the other twenty-seven days of the month.'[79] Whoever was the useful idiot here, there is no hint of such a sentiment in Snowden's contemporary account, and its opening chapter, 'A starving people', offers no concealment of the scale of human suffering.[80] Conveyed in a special train and attended by guards of honour, the guests were extravagantly feted and banqueted, as if, said Russell, they were on a royal progress.[81] Even Trotsky, to his subsequent regret, took his bows with them in a Moscow theatre box.[82] Williams was received with rapture whenever he hailed the revolution in his 'execrable' smattering of Russian.[83] Turner, the delegation's chairman, took most of this at face value and was entirely won over.[84]

Nevertheless, the anarchist Alexander Berkman noted how the constant round of festivities began to pall on some at least of the delegates. Moreover, though they perfectly understood that they were fed far better than the native population, Russia was a ravaged country and the luxury which was 'heaped' upon them would not have been so regarded by British standards.[85] All the delegates were said to suffer from the 'lack of English food and drink', Allen fell seriously ill, and Purcell conceded that his view of Soviet institutions 'rose or fell according to the effect of Soviet bread on my digestion'.[86] He also acknowledged the assistance of NAFTA's Manchester Hebrew branch with 'advice as to certain branches of the commissariat'; an admission of the problems of food supply that may be contrasted with Bernard Shaw's later boast that he might as well have left his provisions behind him in Poland.[87] There was also prohibition, apparently relaxed for the delegates. Williams on his return described this as regenerative in its effects and an essential feature of any revolutionary transition, though Purcell's verdict is likely to have been a good deal more tentative.[88] The overall impression was of desperate economic hardship, primarily ascribed to the Allied blockade, and it was this which four years later provided Purcell with the lowest possible yardstick by which to measure the regime's subsequent progress.[89]

The Bolsheviks' desire to impress was counterbalanced by the desire to contain. Snowden expressed a grudging admiration for how 'our clever hosts contrived to place us under a very real and lasting obligation by their generous regard for our physical welfare … and at the same time to extract from us for their own purposes the last ounce of propaganda usefulness'.[90] Like other delegates, she was not so impressed with the surveillance continuously exercised, and Berkman noted their dissatisfaction with the barrier set up around them by the *propusk* system.[91] 'Arrange for *reliable* interpreters, who should take turns, in order to be *inseparable* from the "guests"', Lenin had directed.[92] Co-operative officials declined to meet delegates for fear of the Cheka, and cases were subsequently reported of individuals persecuted for illicitly passing on information.[93] In Guest's view this amounted to 'an almost universal and all-pervading system of espionage', while Chicherin in turn described Guest as 'nothing but a spy'.[94] Though only Guest had such openly hostile relations with his hosts, he was not alone in failing to see the sense in alienating those who came as friends.[95]

With a society in upheaval, conflicting signals from their hosts, a general lack of Russian and diverse political starting points, the scope for any common verdict hardly extended beyond the pernicious effects of outside interference.[96] Instead, the device was employed of addressing a range of more contentious issues through individually signed appendices amounting to twice the length of the delegates' collective report. There was no restriction, moreover, as to the wider dissemination of personal findings. Snowden, whom Klishko of the trade delegation described as foaming at the mouth, had recourse to the lucrative commercial market for first-hand accounts.[97] Buxton's *In a Russian Village* was published by the Labour Publishing Company albeit two years later. Russell, whom Klishko described as antagonistic but 'behaving decently', provided a more theoretical assessment, including one of the earliest presentations of Bolshevism as the rule of a new class and at the same time as a militant religion akin to Islam.[98] The latter point was also stressed by Guest in a series of damning assessments depicting Lenin as a 'Central Asiatic Mahomed' spreading materialism by fire and sword.[99] While Guest's views appeared in the *Times*, the *Fabian News* and the *Nineteenth Century*, Williams's effusions of pro-Bolshevism appeared both in the *Herald* and in pamphlets issued by the ITF and the infant CPGB. What Friedrich Adler later referred to as the hospitality of enemy publications extended in Britain to left and right alike.[100]

Not even Williams and Purcell managed a joint pamphlet. Though both at this point believed themselves communists, there were indeed clear differences of emphasis in the endorsements they extended the new regime. It is sometimes suggested that Bolshevism at this stage resembled a sort of enactment of Lenin's *State and Revolution*, in which ingenuously libertarian vision congenital rebels could reasonably vest their hopes until the shadow of Stalin descended.[101] It is a notably partial view in both senses of the word. Just as co-operators in 1920 were confronted with the statification of their movement, trade unionists had to reach a verdict on the militarisation of labour. Throughout the summer of 1920, the issue simmered in the British Labour press. Losovsky's brochure *The Trade Unions in Soviet Russia* was issued in English at the time of the delegation's visit and subsequently reproduced in full by the LRD and ILP.[102] In this way British readers were fully apprised of the principle of the unions' 'nationalisation', albeit with the ambiguous inflexion both of 'a necessary supplement and support of the proletarian dictatorship', which correctly implied a subsidiary role, but also of providing its 'fundamental basis'. Whichever the accent, the notion of trade-union independence was seen as a counter-revolutionary survival of capitalist social relations. No longer identified with the old bugbear of economism, a narrow trade-union consciousness represented a 'complete political philosophy' antagonistic to the Soviet state.[103]

Conflation of the backslider with the conscious traitor did not therefore begin in the Stalin era. According to the *Daily Herald*, Lenin not only announced the unions' transformation into 'State departments' but described grumbling and shirking as treason to the 'armed proletariat'.[104] As Berkman and Russell both noted, it was precisely this armed proletariat which greeted the delegates at every turn, while the plebs was kept 'carefully out of sight'.[105] There were also obvious parallels between the militarisation of labour and the wartime threat of industrial conscription which unions far more moderate than NAFTA had consistently opposed. Though Guest in his hostility to Bolshevism was especially critical of 'militarised' forms of work discipline, he could plausibly evoke in his support the syndicalist Tanner's advocacy of workers' control and its immediate dismissal by

Soviet officials.[106] While acknowledging the extreme conditions which prompted such desperate remedies, both Allen and Russell expressed justifiable forebodings as to their possible consolidation into an industrial autocracy.[107]

It was nevertheless Purcell and Williams who, with their obvious credentials, contributed the appendix to the report that dealt with industrial organisation.[108] Though in milder language than the Bolsheviks themselves, this again stressed the difference between the unions' functions under capitalism and their new constructive role as a 'social force' co-operating with the government. 'Compulsory labour service' was justified by the analogy between military and industrial forms of service, and the higher ends to which both were now being devoted. One view of socialism, recently expressed by Gossip, was that obligatory labour was the basis on which all societies depended, and that the Soviets were to be commended for extending this obligation to all.[109] With understandable delicacy, Purcell and Williams nevertheless referred to this, not as the militarisation of labour, but as its 'mobilisation or organisation'.

Perhaps they were not entirely at one on this. Exceptionally, a draft of this section survives which includes the assurance, omitted from the published version, that their investigations had established that there was 'no actual compulsion to labour whatsoever'.[110] Whoever's excision this was, Williams's endorsement of Soviet methods showed a positive relish for the reassertion of central authority. Most remarkably, though in Russia he had undertaken to 'counter all Guest's machinations', he now combined with him to produce an effusive account of 'Russian militarism and the new patriotism'.[111] Urging the benefits for public health of compulsory drill and semi-military gymnastic displays, Guest and Williams described these as conducive to 'a new virility ... [and] a new national pride and patriotism'. Williams in his separate pamphlets not only referred frankly to the militarisation of labour, a formulation which the delegation report avoided, but devoted the second of his four sections to the Soviet military organisation itself, and favourably compared its 'thoroughgoing efficiency' with the British War Office. He also applied to Bolshevism the notion of an aristocracy of ability, upheld by discipline and organisation: 'Discipline first of all to break down the capitalist system, and then strict military and industrial discipline in order to establish the Socialist or Communist State.'[112] Ironically, less than twelve months later Williams was almost the first British communist to fall foul of this discipline.

Compared to Williams, Purcell might have been a rock of consistency. The only detailed account of his Russia impressions appeared in the NAFTA *Monthly Report* and it was certainly written more in a spirit of solidarity than of arid factuality. A three-month repair job took five days to complete; literacy among building workers had quadrupled in two years; workshop conditions were already far superior to those in Britain.[113] Most importantly, Purcell accorded the unions' commanding role a prominence and centrality not found in other delegates' accounts. He claimed that more than any other delegate he had moved about independently, attending meetings of both unions and soviets.[114] In describing the unions' new administrative functions as a sort of realisation of workers' control, he did so, characteristically, from the union officer's perspective of control as exercised through institutions. The signing of his credentials by Tomsky as well as Kamenev appeared to him the evidence already of a sort of dual authority exercised at every level of society.

As much as any Fabian, Purcell was impressed by institutional forms of recognition. He illustrated these with an organogram in which the interdependency of unions and workers' state was graphically depicted and the role of the communist party effaced.[115] Williams stressed the obsolescence of traditional union functions and warned against 'Trade Union leadership becoming a vested interest under the existing regime and an adjunct for the maintenance of capitalist conditions'.[116] Purcell, on the other hand, described the unions as a 'controlling and authoritative part' of every government institution from the nationalised workshop upwards. 'You cannot enter an institution in Soviet Russia without rushing up against its representatives; you see its hand in everything, you see its power behind everything ... resolved upon retaining its dictatorship until it enters into the final phase of its own emancipation'.

Though such presentations were not exactly contradictory, the differences of emphasis are apparent. Ethel Snowden felt a sense of guilt towards the former owners of the Narishkin Palace in which the delegates were accommodated. Purcell, on the other hand, revelled in the workers' expropriation of such buildings. 'Standing out beneath the galleries', he wrote in wonderment of the central trade-union hall in Moscow, 'are 24 huge porcelain pillars, each not less than four feet in diameter ... and between each pair of pillars is a huge electrically-lighted chandelier, and in the galleries is a smaller one, then running round the frieze are over 2,000 candle-shaped electric lights'.[117] It was here, in the Hall of Columns, that sixteen years later the first of the Moscow show trials was to be held. Kamenev, who had signed Purcell's credentials, was one of the main defendants. Tomsky, the other signatory, committed suicide a few months later.

Even in 1920, proletarian discipline posed invidious choices. Along with Wallhead and Skinner, Purcell attended the famous meeting of the Moscow Printers' Union at which Victor Chernov, a leader of the Socialist Revolutionaries (SRs), made an impromptu appearance to excoriate barracks socialism. Though Chernov managed to slip away in the ensuing commotion, several Printers' leaders were arrested and the union was duly suppressed.[118] When four days later the delegation visited the Cheka, Purcell raised the issue of arrests that were said to be planned as soon as the delegates had left Russia.[119] Whatever discussions ensued, Purcell was never again to push such an issue. Subsequently he dismissed the Chernov meeting as an anti-Bolshevik stunt in which craftsmen opposed to the Bolshevik ideal of industrial unionism were willingly exploited by 'well-dressed intellectuals' with counter-revolutionary aims. 'It seems to me', Purcell wrote in the *Communist*, 'that *any* union which fosters counter-revolution must expect to be dealt with accordingly by the Revolutionary Government'.[120]

Purcell did not remain a communist, but nor did he deviate from this stance on the Russian revolution. His was a trade unionist's view of Russia, but one which from the start accepted that workers' power meant constraint in return for the delegation of that power. Unlike Williams, he does not appear to have been accorded a personal interview with Lenin. His most obvious counterpart and interlocutor, instead, was Tomsky. For a period in the early 1920s, Tomsky was to fall under something of a shadow. Indeed, when a Soviet trade-union delegation was invited to reciprocate the British visit, Tomsky was for some reason not included in the list of members.[121] Losovsky, who was to have headed the party, had a very different style of address. When the delegates were refused entry into Britain, he ridiculed the 'childish naivety and senile helplessness' of those unable to force such an issue, and described them as 'smitten with the blindness of a chicken'. He also wrote that the chief instruments of capitalist oppression were the workers' own organisations, industrial and political, which functioned as 'fortresses of capitalist politics' and continuously instilled their members' minds with poison.[122]

One can understand why Oudegeest and others were wary of Losovsky. Indeed, his relations even with communists in Britain were somewhat tempestuous. How different were the signals sent out by Tomsky when he re-emerged in 1922, after a spell of virtual banishment in Tashkent. With the coming of NEP and the turn to the united front, Tomsky was not slow to give the signal that he had been opposed to the militarisation of labour and had at every stage stood for the fullest possible autonomy for the unions.[123] Between 1920 and 1924 there were no direct contacts between the British and Russian unions. But with the arrival of a full Soviet diplomatic delegation in April 1924, there was now no place for Losovsky, while Tomsky was included as a point of contact with the unions. Greeting him as a 'true-hearted champion of the workers', it was thus that Tomsky made his reacquaintance with Purcell.[124]

3.3 'GETTING TOGETHER'

In the intervening period there had been a general hardening of divisions between communism and its rivals. The Communist International, to which Williams and Purcell had improvidently pledged allegiance, had been moulded and purified in the spirit of its twenty-one conditions of admission. The 'Red International' of communist-sponsored unions, or RILU, had been launched in 1921 as the Comintern's shadow in the industrial field. IFTU, having quickly abandoned any thought of its own Russian delegation, engaged with the Profintern, as RILU was also known, in a vituperative propaganda war in which the workers' conditions under Bolshevism figured centrally.[125] When communists after 1921 rediscovered the urge to unity, the realities of Bolshevik rule seemed to expose the hollowness of such rhetoric. In particular, attention focused on the suppression in 1921 of the Georgian Menshevik government, which had shortly before been visited by western socialists, and on the persecution of dissident socialists which reached a head with the SR show trial in 1922. Following the five-country Frankfurt conference at which Purcell swilled his lagers, a meeting of the communist and two non-communist internationals was arranged in Berlin in March 1922. Amidst venomous exchanges it merely confirmed that their differences were insuperable. The main practical outcome was the establishment of a reunited Labour and Socialist International (LSI) at Hamburg in May 1923, excluding only the communists, whose diverse provocations rendered other political differences for the time being entirely secondary.

There was little suggestion at this stage that the British would fall seriously out of step. When IFTU held an extraordinary congress in London in November 1920, only the Norwegian and Italian delegates failed to support a resolution condemning the attacks of the 'so-called Moscow Trade Union International'.[126] In June 1922 Labour conference delegates overwhelmingly condemned the Bolsheviks' treatment of political prisoners, urged by Sidney Webb, on grounds which he subsequently forgot, that Labour's bias was against such abuses of state power whatever the context.[127] The *Labour Magazine* ran a piece denouncing the SR 'show trial' by the Belgian social democrat Emile Vandervelde, and in general its coverage was fully as critical as Vandervelde's own.[128] The ILP, whose pro-communist faction had by now moved over to the CPGB, gave similar attention to Georgia's plight, including a special supplement to the *Socialist Review* and several contributions by Georgian Mensheviks.[129] MacDonald, who had visited Georgia with Vandervelde, was in March 1922 elected honorary president at a conference of the exiled Georgian Mensheviks, and at the Berlin conference of the three internationals voiced the anti-Bolshevik case with a cogency that on some other subjects eluded him.[130] It was at MacDonald's suggestion that the joint TUC-Labour Party international committee contributed financially to the cost of observers at the SR show trial.[131]

With MacDonald's election as Labour Party leader in November 1922, and Thomas adopting a similar stance as IFTU president,

London might have seemed as unambiguous an alternative to Moscow as Amsterdam. It was in London that the Second International had in November 1920 relocated its offices, with MacDonald, Henderson, Thomas and Shaw variously functioning as its leading officers. Though the Austrian Adler took over as full-time secretary with the LSI's establishment in May 1923, there seemed no political objection to the offices remaining in London. Stephen White concluded that British Labour, 'far from manifesting any sympathy for Bolshevism, was among its most determined and vigorous opponents on both the national and international arenas'.[132] Within barely a year, however, a clamour began to build up for the removal from London of the LSI offices, while IFTU meetings for a number of years were dominated by the divisions between the TUC and other major affiliates.[133] The issue, overwhelmingly, was sympathy with Bolshevism.

Such extreme volatility may in part be attributed to contingencies of leading personnel. At the same time, the British movement had never adopted anti-communism as an organising principle in the manner of European social democracy as a whole. In 1920 Beatrice Webb had noted with complacency the bewilderment of foreign guests at the welcome received by Krasin and Kamenev at the Fabian summer school. 'It was strange enough, they explained, to see Guild Socialists and members of the new English Communist Party on terms of intimate comradeship with Fabians, but to invite the official representatives of Lenin, who had expressly denounced all Fabians as traitors … was really carrying the principle of tolerance too far!'[134] It is difficult in such cases to separate the treatment of Bolshevik supporters in Britain and attitudes to Soviet Russia itself as a factor in the international labour movement. Even Thomas and Henderson, Beatrice observed on another occasion, showed the 'same sort of good-natured tolerance to the Bolshevik that they give to their own rebels'.[135] Relations were not always so equable, and some favoured a more categorical rejection, like Philip Snowden, who broke his connection with the ILP's *Labour Leader* over the issue.[136] Even so, in a period of bitter and even murderous divisions on the European left, the mildness of such antipathies in Britain was frequently remarked upon. Against the Comintern's twenty-one conditions, social-democratic parties had one at least which they defended just as fiercely, that communism itself was anathema. In failing to meet this condition, British Labour harboured significant dissenting minorities which it needed only a turn of the wheel to bring to the surface. When this occurred with the formation of the first Labour government, the most immediate effect was in attitudes to Soviet Russia.

The potential for future conflict had been clearly indicated the previous year. In May 1923 the Tory foreign secretary Curzon issued an 'ultimatum' to the Soviets which, in a tone of naked belligerency, bundled together issues of trading relations, international conspiracy and Soviet domestic oppression.[137] The Soviets' conciliatory response was personified by Krasin's reappearance in London, and in an atmosphere recalling the earlier Hands off Russia agitation he immediately re-established a good understanding with UDC-type parliamentarians.[138] Fortuitously, the LSI's founding conference was scheduled to take place in Hamburg as the crisis reached its height. As Labour Party leader, MacDonald felt obliged to attend to his parliamentary responsibilities as leader of the opposition. Would his presence at Hamburg have made much of a difference? In any event, in his absence the British delegation held that in such an atmosphere of international tension no pronouncement specifically against the Soviets was allowable. When the Menshevik Abramovich nevertheless moved such a resolution, they almost alone continued to uphold this position.[139]

Immediately the attempt began to explain the distinctiveness of the British position on Russia. A key issue often remarked upon was a pattern of party competition marked at once by the peripherality of the CPGB and the centrality of Labour's antagonism to the Conservatives. 'For the same reason that a strong Communist Party in France and Germany makes the French and German Social-Democratic parties the symbol of petty-bourgeois opportunism', wrote Philips Price from his continental vantage point, 'so the existence of a numerically small Communist Party in England causes the ILP to contain elements who are sincerely out to fight capitalist Imperialism ...'[140] Though this also served as rationalisation of Price's own transfer of allegiance from the CPGB to the ILP, it was indeed the ILP delegates, including Allen and H.N. Brailsford, who had taken the lead in Hamburg. The Mensheviks were sufficiently concerned that they considered initiating an English-language bulletin to be sent to the party's branches.[141] The British delegation in Hamburg nevertheless represented all sections of the political and industrial movement, and all accounts agreed on what Beatrice Webb, who was there for the Fabian Society, called its called 'singularly harmonious' character.[142] According to Abramovich's somewhat apocryphal account, it was Beatrice herself who opposed the inclusion within the international of groups like the Mensheviks 'fighting against a socialist government in their own country'.[143] The blanket anti-Bolshevism of Conservative Britain, and its extension to the Labour Party itself, forced even moderates and sceptics into acquiescence, at the risk of otherwise jeopardising Labour's still fragile cohesion.

With the LSI's establishment, the anomaly of the TUC's direct participation in such delegations was brought to an end. Within IFTU, it was nevertheless at precisely this moment that the issue of relations with the Russians became the focus of serious internal differences. Almost simultaneously with the Hamburg conference, Fimmen, on behalf of the International Transportworkers Federation, had convened a joint meeting with the Russian transport unions to discuss the issue of trade-union unity. Though Fimmen retained the confidence of the ITF, and that of Williams as its president, the adamantly anti-Profintern IFTU majority was still further provoked by the participation of Losovsky in the meeting.[144] With the German unions to the fore, Fimmen's position as one of IFTU's secretaries was fiercely challenged, and by November he was more or less forced into resigning his position.[145] Although Thomas as IFTU president made clear his disapproval of Fimmen, the majority of his TUC colleagues strongly disapproved of the treatment which Fimmen received.[146] The TUC in response sought not only to 'strengthen and safeguard' its own representation within IFTU but to commit the organisation to unity negotiations with the Russian unions, albeit to the explicit exclusion of Losovsky and the Profintern.[147] The result, according to IFTU's historian, was 'a Babel-like confusion', which in a sense it took some four years to clear up.[148] Fimmen, who unlike Purcell was a recent convert to the pro-Soviet view, was to provide him with an indispensable ally able to locate the issue of Russia within the wider context of international unity.

Within Britain, Purcell reached a similar understanding with the foremost representative of the UDC tradition in the shape of Morel. In forming his government, MacDonald had virtually invited such a combination against him. Like their trade-union colleagues, UDC radicals were both disillusioned and disencumbered by MacDonald's advancement only of the more compliant of their number. When MacDonald then antagonised both radical and trade-union internationalists by endorsing the Dawes plan for managed reparations, the ministers in question felt obliged to resign their membership of the UDC.[149] By himself combining the roles of premier and foreign secretary, MacDonald further reinforced Morel's sense of exclusion, in spite of warnings that he would prove a magnet for foreign-policy discontents.[150] A second such magnet was the arrival in April of a seven-strong Soviet delegation commissioned to carry through treaty negotiations with the British. Purcell's proposal that British trade unionists be represented in the negotiations was of course ignored.[151] Suggestions that O'Grady be sent as ambassador to Moscow had already been forgotten. There were, however, no reasonable grounds for preventing a trade-union component in the Russian delegation, and thus the first face-to-face contact between the Russian and British labour movements since 1920.

Head of the delegation was the Romanian Christian Rakovsky. Rakovsky was second only to Trotsky in the emerging Bolshevik opposition and it has plausibly been suggested that he was sent to London as Stalin's way of getting rid of him.[152] His aristocratic background and cosmopolitan culture also made for easy intercourse with foreign-policy specialists like Arthur Ponsonby, the Lib-turned-Lab under-secretary to whom MacDonald entrusted the negotiations.[153]

Tomsky's inclusion within the delegation was a sure sign that the Soviets were not content to rely on such channels. According to an intercepted letter summarised for MacDonald, the Comintern president Zinoviev urged the CPGB to contact Tomsky and prepare for mass demonstrations should the negotiations be interrupted.[154] Given the forgery of a similar communication just a few months later, one may reasonably question the document's authenticity.[155] In any case, it was with the TUC, not the communists, that Tomsky established a more important liaison. With Purcell presiding, a welcoming dinner was held at Frascati's restaurant in mid-May. Waspishly, the disaffected Walton Newbold likened Tomsky to a dove 'flitting around Eccleston Square cooing "I'm not Losovsky, I'm Tomsky!"' and 'being "so different" to an undercurrent of champagne & a banging of corks'. Tillett joined in with the *Internationale* and said that he felt young again. Tomsky, as we have seen, assured Purcell 'what babes' the CPGB were. Bramley, to Tomsky's evident satisfaction, proposed 'uninterrupted contact' with their fellow trade unionists in the Soviet delegation. 'You must not forget', Bramley assured them, 'that in our country at the present time the political administration is carried on by persons who are not the masters, but the servants of the trade union movement'.[156]

The opportunity to make effective this promise of assistance occurred with the breakdown of negotiations on 5 August. Already, following a two-month hiatus in the talks, it was through Morel and his 'group', including Lansbury, that Ponsonby had secured Rakovsky's return to London.[157] When talks now seemed to stall completely, it was Purcell and Morel who took on the role of intermediaries, assisted by Lansbury and Wallhead. After a Commons meeting chaired by Purcell, whose truculence Ponsonby noted, vigorous complaint was made of Foreign Office obstruction and Ponsonby's assent was secured to a draft acceptable to the Soviets.[158]

Morel had the contact with Ponsonby and Rakovsky, and the latter was effusive in his sympathies when Morel died unexpectedly a few weeks later.[159] It was Purcell, on the other hand, who had invited the Russians to make use of the general council in the event of such a rupture.[160] Though MacDonald was hardly the unions' servant, he was susceptible to union pressure and resented it. His special aversion to Purcell, which seems to date from this episode, was doubtless reinforced when the treaty helped bring the government down. The Bolshevik Kamenev depicted the intervention as a wielding of the 'big stick of the workers'.[161] Purcell himself described it as an exercise in direct action from above and a form of open diplomacy 'bound up with and promoted by the working classes'. 'When we found that the representatives of the Governments were falling out one or two working men went along and said to them, "You had better come to an agreement anyhow".'[162] As a mark of their understanding, he and

Morel issued a pamphlet urging ratification of the treaties under the auspices of Coates's Anglo-Russian Parliamentary Committee. MacDonald was not alone in feeling discomfited. Three weeks after Tomsky's welcoming dinner, Bramley had also intervened to prevent the closing of the door on the Russians at IFTU's triennial congress in Vienna. Supporting him was Fimmen for the ITF; strongly opposed were the Belgian Corneel Mertens and the head of the German union confederation Peter Grassmann.[163] Proceedings were concluded in orderly fashion: Purcell was confirmed as IFTU president, and Bramley joined the management committee. Oudegeest, however, had no intention of allowing Purcell any scope for initiative, while Tillett in his inimitable way expressed a deep-rooted British suspicion of the IFTU apparatus.[164]

Invited to address the Hull TUC in September, Tomsky was the first Bolshevik leader to speak in such a capacity at a western trade-union confederation. Preceding him, Oudegeest made no mention of the Russians but spelt out conditions of IFTU membership that made a rapprochement with them presently unthinkable. Translated by the communist Rothstein, Tomsky then played adroitly on his audience's sensibilities in describing himself as bored to the teeth with his diplomatic responsibilities and breathing freely once again as a trade unionist 'pure and simple' among his fellows. In published TUC proceedings, fraternal delegates were usually provided with a concluding 'cheers'. Oudegeest, who spoke in 'splendid English', on this occasion managed a second. Doubtless assisted by Bramley's enthusiastic editing, Tomsky nevertheless ran up six cheers, seven 'hear hears' and four laughters – for as Mme Tomsky observed the following year, British trade unionists were 'a very laughter-loving people'. Describing it as 'the greatest éclat ever known in a Labour conference', Newbold asked rhetorically: 'how long did those delegates stand and cheer the Russians?'[165]

Figuratively speaking, the answer was twenty-one months. A few weeks before the conference, Tomsky had invited the TUC to organise a delegation 'to establish permanent regular connections' with the Russian unions.[166] Despite its postponement because of the October general election, the Russians put back their own annual congress to make sure the British delegates could attend.[167] On 7 November, the seventh anniversary of the revolution, Purcell set off once more for Russia. He returned seven weeks later, a figure of international notoriety.

3.4 RUSSIA 1924

Compared with 1920, the delegation was conducted on lines of collective responsibility. Although the Russian invitation had extended to the ILP, the TUC, as already noted, had apparently taken the matter no further.[168] The main objects of the visit, as outlined by Bramley as the delegation's secretary, were to investigate Russian workers' rights of organisation and free expression. 'We want to know what relations the Russian trades unions sustain with the Soviet Government and whether the Russian workmen have the same elementary rights of combination as the workers of other countries.'[169] For Purcell as the delegation's chairman this was hardly a matter of any doubt. Returning to the Hall of Columns, within three days of the delegation's arrival he delivered to the Russian unions a eulogy of the revolution and an anticipation of similar developments in Britain.[170] A similar message to *Izvestia* was even dismissed as a forgery by the SPD paper *Vörwarts*.[171] Throughout the tour, one British official reported, it was Purcell who took the leading part 'and his speeches were certainly the most fiery'.[172] Another official gloomily minuted the further indecorum of 'the refuse of the incompetent or otherwise disgruntled workman ... [with] physical characteristics of a large frame, a large voice and a large thirst'.[173]

Even Purcell, however, was bound by tighter collective undertakings. With what his French counterpart Jouhaux described as 'a really English humour', Bramley was to defend the principle of individual delegation members having a 'certain degree of liberty' to express their views.[174] All were nevertheless bound by the agreement that they should not release material for publication pending the appearance of their collective findings.[175] On their returning to Britain, this embargo was confirmed by the general council pending publication of the full delegation report, which did not occur until the end of February. Invitations to address rallies of the *Herald* or Minority Movement were declined, and only Tillett of the delegates ever did publish a pamphlet of somewhat disordered personal impressions.[176]

One possible concern was the impetuosity of Purcell himself. Another must have been the wide range of opinion represented within the delegation. Apart from Bramley and Tillett, this comprised the phlegmatic Miners' president Herbert Smith; the more volatile Locomen's secretary John Bromley; the Shop Assistants' organiser John Turner, whose anarchist affiliations might have posed a particular constraint; and the taciturn Patternmaker Alan Findlay, who made it a point of union principle not to overwork the TUC's stenographers. Covering the gamut of trade-union opinion, these by their own account were men 'whose political tradition tended to make them critical of the Communist philosophy and policy'.[177] Most, according to the Foreign Office report, confined themselves 'to polite speeches and expressions of good will'.[178] Purcell, and to some extent Bramley and Tillett, were exceptions. But when the delegation duly published its report there were no appendices or minority statements.

The Bolshevik reception was also better co-ordinated. Though the one surviving letter of Purcell's tells us little, Bramley's letters to Citrine convey the exhilaration of a socialist activist on witnessing the ubiquity of symbols that had become inextricably associated with the vision of a new society. 'There is no doubt about the workers being in possession', as Bramley put it. 'The Red Flag predominates everywhere, and the Photos, huge examples of Lenin, Trotsky and others meet you everywhere. The flag flies on all the principal buildings and the Dictation of the Proletariat is complete.'[179] With exclusive use of two railway coaches, and a third containing armed guards added for the journey to the Caucasus, the delegation once more resembled a 'triumphal procession' marked by welcoming crowds.[180] Bramley afterwards admitted that the atmosphere was charged with such revolutionary fervour that he felt great nervousness whenever he made a speech – 'the excitement was irresistible, and the effect … was amazing in its reserve and restraint'.[181] Following Purcell at the ARTUC, he acknowledged differences of method but not of aim, and insisted that the 'sole possible means of putting an end to the misery of both body and soul is the seizure of complete rule of all the means of production by the workers'.[182]

Even so, awareness of 'restraint' helped to counteract it. The British official who met the delegates thought their response to the hospitality provided 'very sane' and open-eyed, and Bramley himself said that were 'trying to penetrate below the crust but find it very difficult'.[183] Purcell, who might certainly have tried harder, described the massive demonstrations, as Bramley did the images of Lenin, as the mark of a society in which the workers were in control.[184] Even so, the Russian unions sought less to overwhelm the visitors than to impress upon them what they had in common. Tellingly, when initially they rearranged their annual congress, a Comintern correspondent warned them not to be 'too lavish' in their honours. 'What might be very good for French, Italian and even German delegations might have the contrary effect upon the Britishers. Receive and treat them well, but do not let them get the impression that you attribute too much importance to their being in Russia.'[185]

Tomsky and his collaborators understood very well the advantages of modesty and demonstrating that they knew their trade.[186] Bramley could thus dismiss the usual caricature of wild-eyed revolutionaries with the image of 'a type of Trade Union leader as steady, as constructive, as logical, as clear and as well-informed as … you will find in any part of the world'.[187] In a perfectly judged farewell message to the delegates, the limitations as well as the achievements of the revolution were admitted, but the agency of 'our millions of workers and peasants' invoked to justify some lenity of judgement even in respect of possible failings.[188] More deeply impressed than by the crowds 'bubbling with excitement', Bramley wrote afterwards to the metalworkers' leader Melnichansky of how his thoughts kept going back to the 'useful little talks we had quietly in your own cabin during our tour', and the possibilities that these seemed to hold out of a more durable relationship.[189]

There were two enduring legacies of the delegation that ensured that it provided more than a momentary press sensation. The first was its published report, authoritative in appearance and comprising some 280 pages of text, maps, diagrams and photographs. The object was 'to reproduce the character of an official report', directly encroaching upon the traditional prerogatives of the state and political establishment.[190] Purcell himself described it as a 'first text-book ... showing how a Workers' Republic is rising, Phoenix like, from the ashes of the most despotic regime of history'.[191] While he did not hesitate to relay his purely external impressions of the Russians' frame of mind, it was obvious that neither he nor any of the other delegates could have produced such a document unassisted. The challenge to the Foreign Office view was therefore effected by a renewal of the connection with the UDC tradition in the shape of three sometime British officials who accompanied the delegation as advisers. A.R. McDonell, a former vice-consul and serving officer in the Caucasus, had left the Foreign Office only the previous year. Harold Grenfell, former member of the Petrograd naval mission, had since the revolution had a better established connection with the left and was an intimate of the Dutts.[192] These were responsible for the sections on social affairs and the army respectively, and their role must clearly have gone beyond 'editing and other technicalities'.[193] Nevertheless, it was the third adviser, George Young, who not only prepared the bulk of the report but was far and away the most widely advertised, politically significant and overweeningly contentious of the three.

The mugwumps in the Labour Party could have had no better representative.[194] An old Etonian and future baronet, Young was brother of a Tory minister, brother-in-law of a Liberal one, himself a Labour candidate, a professor of Portuguese literature, an examiner in Ottoman Law and an Admiralty cypher expert. He also had a 'lovely house and beautiful wife and brilliant children' – one trusts in no particular order – and a decoration 'for rescuing the Queen of Spain from a bomb'. This, at least, was according to *Lansbury's Labour Weekly*, apparently cross-pollinated with the *Tatler*.[195] Among these diverse accomplishments a career diplomat, Young had resigned in 1915, and joining the Labour Party and the UDC had been described by Philips Price in his communist phase as 'almost a fairy godmother'.[196] Unofficially attached to Labour's first Russian delegation, Young had reported to the ILP on the withering, not of the state, but of the soviets.[197] A member of Labour's Advisory Committee on International Questions (ACIQ), he had also proposed radical reforms of the foreign service including the politicisation of appointments.[198] MacDonald had shared much of this radical agenda, and Young in 1924 felt encouraged to apply for official reinstatement, only to discover that MacDonald had now determined against the 'straining' of Foreign Office conventions.[199] For Young, like Morel, the perfidious role of officials over the Zinoviev letter confirmed the folly of such a stance, as well as his own strong sense of personal pique.[200] Young was not remotely a figure of Morel's stature or reputation. But if, as rumoured, he was the 'U.D.C.' who published 'The diplomacy of Ramsay MacDonald' in the *Labour Monthly*, he was certainly capable of brilliantly acerbic commentary in a spirit that justified the nom de plume.[201] He also continued to push for political appointments to key Foreign Office and diplomatic positions, to be made with immediate effect where 'Labour', as in Russia, held power.[202] His view of Bolshevik Russia was, if anything, as a force for stability. Indeed, in the report he drafted for the delegation on the Zinoviev letter, he described the Comintern itself as tending to 'prevent local extremists from disturbing the peace' and proceed instead on moderate and constitutional lines.[203] Reviewing a volume of Tomsky's speeches, including that at the welcoming dinner at Frascati's, he celebrated the passing of foreign affairs 'from the secret methods and sinister motives of the old diplomacy into the hands of a new diplomacy of the peoples – by the peoples – for the peoples'. For this, he said, the people naturally employed their own union organisations, 'just as the old ruling class used their organisations, the Civil Services'.[204] Young, in moving from one to the other, did not thereby lose his sense of social caste. 'I am taking a Trades Union delegation out to Russia', he wrote to his fellow UDCer Charles Trevelyan as they departed, adding that he could hardly 'throw them over as they would be pretty helpless without someone to take their tickets and write their report.'[205]

The report itself was an exercise in historical extenuation. While the sixteen photogravure plates, like most of the chapters, illustrated diverse aspects of the new Russia, the opening image of Bloody Sunday provided a measure of what the Bolsheviks had had to confront and what they had so far achieved. Assimilating the revolution to the rhythms and values of the British labour movement, the TUC presented NEP as the achievement of stability on a new social basis following a necessary moment of reckoning.[206] Characterised as 'State Socialism' or 'State Capitalism', it was precisely this retreat from the 'height of communism' that allowed the normalisation of trade-union functions through the restoration of labour from a conscript to a commodity basis and the differentiation between functions of management and representation.[207]

In respect of Bramley's remit for the delegation, constraints as regards political freedom and the communists' political monopoly were readily conceded. Nevertheless, the moral and social status of labour and its organisations, 'so far from being undemocratic in the widest sense of the word', was seen as providing the individual worker with a greater scope for participation than a parliamentary or 'party' system.[208] The emergence of an opposition was anticipated, not through the external challenge to these arrangements, but through differentiation within the communist party itself.[209] Party rights, however, did not seem a major concern, and the restricted franchise and electoral system were described as comprehensible 'from the point of view of the British Trade Union arrangements', if less so from that of a parliamentary system.[210] The echoes of Fabianism and guild socialism are clear enough. Addressing the ARTUC, Bramley, in whom the Webbian influence was palpable, had outlined British labour's three-pronged attack on the capitalist system through its political, industrial and co-operative organisations.[211] There was therefore a clear Webbian accent in the report's postulation of a 'threefold democracy' or 'tripod' of soviets, trade unions and co-operatives.[212] Though in one sense this echoed the Webbs' *Constitution for a Socialist Commonwealth of Great Britain*, published four years earlier, in its particular application it may be seen as an anticipation of the Webbs' later belief that their multiform democracy of citizen, producer and consumer had actually been realised under Stalin.

The report's most controversial sections were those dealing with the litmus-test issues of the political prisoners and Georgia. Both had in recent months given rise to renewed public outcry. At the end of August the Bolsheviks had put down a rising in Georgia with what even the TUC report accepted was 'disproportionately heavy' bloodshed.[213] Continuing protests regarding the plight of political prisoners were followed in October by news of a hunger-strike at the notorious Solovetsky Island prison-camp. Unable to visit the camp, which was only seasonally accessible, the delegates pharasaically urged the disadvantages of locations lending credence to hostile reports. They did however visit the defendants in the SR show trial, who since the lifting of their death sentence had been held in Moscow's Butirky prison. According to Emma Goldman the delegates were accompanied by two notorious Chekists.[214] One prisoner, Abram Gotz, wrote scornfully that Purcell would doubtless see in this 'old and filthy jail of Tsarist times' a veritable crystal palace.[215] The delegates did duly provide a positive gloss on the conditions, and either Gotz or one of his comrades was cited as priding himself on the 'superiority of the Socialist Boutirka' over that of the Tsars. Though they wanly proposed the alternatives of 'clemency' or exile, the delegates declined to condemn the principle of imprisoning such 'irreconcilables'.[216] Whether through diffidence on the one hand or fear of arrest on the other, the delegates had almost no direct contact with oppositionists except in these most unpropitious circumstances.[217]

In Georgia the delegates adopted a similar position, combining basic support for the regime with some studiedly uncensorious caveats. Purcell himself had no use even for these, and in front of a huge demonstration in Tbilisi made no attempt to nuance his case against what he called the slanders of capitalists and 'quasi-socialists'.[218] Urged on by the Russian and Georgian Mensheviks, the LSI just two months earlier had agreed resolutions of protest on both Georgia and the issue of the prisoners. The shooting of hostages in Georgia in particular had been described as plumbing the 'lowest depths of barbarity'; as one Bolshevik sarcastically observed, every true social-democrat seemed to have two native countries, 'his own and Georgia'.[219] Purcell had his own and Russia, and inevitably these issues predominated in the chorus of protests that followed the delegates' return.[220]

A second, unanticipated legacy of the delegation was the undertaking to establish the relationship between the two movements on a more permanent footing. Already at the Hull TUC Purcell had proposed that the TUC take the initiative in promoting a unity conference between IFTU and the Russians.[221] It was nevertheless on somewhat doubtful authority that he assured the ARTUC that the British were ready to 'force on' the issue if Amsterdam failed to.[222] The Russians naturally took this up with alacrity. By the time the delegates dispersed, a provisional agreement was announced to work together in the cause of unity and Purcell, who was far from sylph-like, must have been amazed to find himself tossed into the air in celebration.[223] As confirmed by the general council, it was this agreement that led to the establishment of the Anglo-Russian Advisory Council at a conference in London in April 1925. Reaffirmed at the subsequent Scarborough TUC, these unavailing efforts to secure IFTU's co-operation persisted until definitively rebuffed in December 1925. Purcell likened the TUC's taking of this initiative to the establishment of the First International on British soil.[224] If he was singled out in the protests that now registered through IFTU, it was not only as the most outspoken of the TUC's Russian delegates, but because of the disregard he was held to have shown for his responsibilities as IFTU president.[225]

On the surface at least, the argument was not primarily about the legitimacy of the Russian unions themselves. In the early postwar period, IFTU had devoted enormous energy to this issue and one might have imagined that its most important function was the exposure of Bolshevik propaganda claims.[226] By the time of the Anglo-Russian campaign, on the other hand, even Oudegeest lent credence to the view that Tomsky, in pursuing international links, was seeking to extricate his movement from the 'tyranny' of the communist party.[227] Oudegeest knew quite well, of course, that this was as much grist to Losovsky's mill as Losovsky's sectarianism was to his. Nevertheless, it was only in December 1925, once the TUC's overtures had suffered a decisive defeat, that Oudegeest returned to the categorical exposure of the Russian unions and refusal to differentiate between Tomsky and Losovsky.[228]

A more persistent concern was with the extension of unity to disruptive elements closer to home. In a sense the two could not be separated, for the TUC's ingenuously pro-Soviet positions provided a form of eagerly grasped partisan ammunition in the more bitterly divided movements on the continent. Purcell, unlike most of his colleagues, was in any case committed to a bigger conception of unity than that with Russia alone. In Dutt's *Labour Monthly* symposium he had used the metaphor of a working-class 'mosaic' to describe the pluralistic conception of unity that he upheld within Britain.[229] At the ARTUC in December he again used this metaphor, but with the suggestion of repairing the 'international mosaic' by the inclusion of the Russians.[230] A similar conception could be applied to the more fragmented labour movements of other European countries. At Hull it was the receipt of messages from communist-led union federations that prompted Purcell to move the bringing together of the different elements of the European labour movement.[231] When he invoked the First International, it was with the sense that Britain might again provide a centre 'about which the various sections – Red, White, Yellow and Green – may be gathered for the purpose of ... Unity'.[232]

Had it been this straightforward, the First International might have lasted longer. Not only was unity inevitably constructed as a partisan demand, but through its own example and practical support the TUC seemed to succour the dissident movements with whom its continental counterparts claimed to be in mortal strife. There were numerous possible causes of tension. A spate of unofficial Russian delegations followed in the wake of the British one. One from Czechoslovakia secured a foreword from Purcell himself, and featured his portrait along with Lenin's.[233] An American one was initially projected during a Purcell speaking tour. One from Germany, where the issue was especially divisive and controversial, had a telegram of greetings read out by Bramley at the Scarborough TUC.[234] The Russian report itself provided an invaluable aid to propaganda. Translation rights were vested in the Russians, at least one communist paper serialised it in its entirety, and Germany alone saw fifty thousand copies 'struck off as a first issue'.[235]

Purcell's launching of the monthly *Trade Union Unity* in April 1925 was thus a particular cause of ill-feeling, as well as a symptom of the sense of marginalisation within IFTU of its British affiliate. Oudegeest maintained a close personal control over the printed *Press Reports* issued by IFTU, excluding even his British co-secretary, J.W. Brown, and provoking repeated complaints which Bramley detailed at great length in February 1925.[236] Constrained in the use of first-person polemic, Oudegeest's preferred device was the reproduction of past or present communist pronouncements that apparently exposed the duplicity and undiminished sense of antagonism that underlay their professions of unity. Losovsky was an especially fruitful source of these, as if the secretaries of the 'red' and 'yellow' internationals had some common institutional interest in the issues that divided them.[237] Even when Oudegeest provided relatively neutral coverage of the Russian issue, he remained adamant that IFTU had to be defended against internal communist manoeuvres from which even the British were not entirely exempt. 'The impertinence of this double-faced Dutchman paralyses our pen', wrote Lansbury, apparently not quite paralysed, and in Britain the sense of resentment went beyond those habitually associated with left-wing causes.[238]

Attracting contributions from across the general council, *Trade Union Unity* has even been mistaken for a TUC organ.[239] Conceived amidst the hostile coverage of the Russian delegation, and the presumed assistance of the Russians in supporting an alternative view, its initial rationale was to provide for a 'British' voice in trade-union affairs and counteract its misrepresentation in organs giving a 'purely German, French, Dutch or Belgian' point of view.[240] Indeed, its two British editors, Purcell and Hicks, were quite prepared to assume a position of international leadership on behalf of the TUC.[241] But there was also the object of a two-way communication: numerous articles were included on other European countries, and Fimmen as their co-editor encapsulated the sense of an alternative trade-union platform that could not be confined within national boundaries.[242] Most of the overseas contributions were from communist or 'minority' sources, and the magazine's working editor Allen Hutt made full use of contacts like Joanny Berlioz, secretary of the Profintern's Latin bureau. There also followed similar publishing ventures in Belgium, the Netherlands and Germany, while the French equivalent *L'Unité* was announced in the communist paper *L'Humanité* with a message of support from Purcell, Swales and Tillett.[243] Oudegeest assailed the ignorance and prejudice of the clearly unwelcome publishing initiative, and complained that Purcell had received no 'instructions' to publish it.[244] Purcell in turn held forth on the 'small bunch of Amsterdam leaders' who saw IFTU as an appendix of the 'Second International' and its dominant German section.[245] Through rival publications the adversarial logic of unity was thus played out in full public view.

One other obvious difference between *Trade Union Unity* and the IFTU *Press Reports* was the wider geographical coverage of the former. Essentially at this time IFTU was a movement of European labour aligned with social democracy. 'Unity' as propounded by Purcell thus combined the challenge both of militants and oppositionists within Europe and of movements at or beyond Europe's peripheries, to which the communists through the Profintern were so much more committed. This wider conception of unity was henceforth to be one of the hallmarks of Purcell's activity. In his Russian speech in December he evoked the image of a single 'great world working class family which recognised no foreigners.[246] At the TUC a few months later he moved a resolution of 'complete opposition' to imperialism, which upheld the principle both of trade-union organisation and the rights of all peoples to self-determination.[247] Delegates approved the resolution by a forty-to-one majority. There was nevertheless an obvious tension between the formal repudiation of empire, sincere as far as it went, and the view of Britain as a centre around which even colonial trade unionists should unite. This ambiguity was at the heart of Purcell's conception of labour internationalism, and may be traced through reactions to the Russian report.

3.5 SOCIAL ANTI-IMPERIALISM

Appearing in 1930, the first Tintin adventure was set in the land of the Soviets. In one scene a British party in plus-fours draw affably on their pipes while natives of ferocious appearance surreptitiously set factory stacks smoking with bails of hay. Needless to say, the object of satisfying the visitors' credulity ('Very nice...') is achieved.[248]

Though the image was captioned 'English communists', its source was an incident supposedly occurring during the TUC visit and described in Joseph Douillet's best-selling *Moscou sans voiles*, which devoted most of its first chapter to the delegation.[249] Seldom indeed can a group of English working men have prompted such widespread comment. Immediate rejoinders to the delegates' report had been issued by the Russian and Georgian Mensheviks.[250] Social democrats everywhere assailed their naivety and irresponsibility.[251] Oudegeest, constrained by his position, referred in general terms to 'pompous journeys' and 'meretricious reports', and the German unions published a direct rejoinder.[252] Anti-socialist opinion was united in hostility. The rebuttal of a Paris-based team of Russian emigrés ran to nearly six hundred pages, and included an introduction in which the former legal marxist Peter Struve underlined the absence in Russia of the economic preconditions of a socialism he no longer believed in.[253]

The most influential statement of the socialist case against the report was that of the LSI secretary Friedrich Adler.[254] A figure unequivocally of the left, indeed the assassin of Austria's wartime premier Count Stürgkh, Adler had been touted as a possible leader of the Austrian communist party before assuming the secretaryship of the Vienna or 'two-and-a-half' international. While Adler thus upheld a critical marxist perspective, his ideal, like that of his party, the Austrian SDAP, remained that of the workers' party as collective instrument and embodiment of political authority. Moving to London when the LSI was formed, Adler had thus been struck at first hand by the porousness and *désorganisation* of the British labour movement.[255]

In both its theoretical and its organisational aspects, it was to this that Adler turned in explanation of the peculiar deficiencies of the TUC report. On the one hand, he cited Engels as to the disabling empiricism and incapacity for theoretical insight of the British.[256] On the other hand, he regarded Young as the delegation's real leader and ascribed the 'Foreign Office' spirit that imbued its findings to the alien social and political background of its advisers. Enthusiasm for

Bolshevism was thus combined with 'the conceit of the bureaucrat in the foreign service, who has two quite distinct standards, one for Britons, who "never shall be slaves", another for the "natives", for the inhabitants of foreign countries, for whom other social institutions, from servitude to slavery, are naturally ordained'. Purcell was therefore an 'incomparably less important' figure than Young and merely lent the report the prestige of his organisation.[257] Condemning the report in the name of international socialism, Adler maintained that its baseness was unparalleled since the 'socialist imperialism' of the wartime SPD.[258]

The paradox was that Purcell also spoke in the name of internationalism and against the double standards that were seemingly incompatible with it. According to Adler, the British saw only the Russians and ignored the problems of other European labour movements.[259] Purcell, on the other hand, challenged those who saw only Europe, at the expense of the wider world, whose vanguard and cynosure Russia was. As he later observed, when he was not being depicted as a 'Moscow manoeuvrer' he tended to be treated as a political simpleton and as a 'child in international affairs'.[260] Nevertheless, he expounded his conception of labour internationalism with a degree of consistency and even cogency that he did not always attain in other contexts. In a longer perspective, his setting of a 'world sense' against a purely 'European sense' is suggestive of that wider ambivalence of the British left from which the mentality of empire was not always absent.[261] It did not exactly breathe the spirit of the Foreign Office, at least such as anybody employed there would have recognised. It did however reflect a deep-seated tension between unity and self-determination, one within which Purcell's identification with the new Soviet Union may itself be located.

The basis of Purcell's outlook was what is sometimes referred to as the rapid industrialisation thesis. In writings like those of J.A. Hobson and H.N. Brailsford, the dynamic of imperialism had become identified since the turn of the century with the export of capital rather than the development of markets. Through their reworking in Lenin's *Imperialism* (1916) these ideas had a profound influence on communist theorists such as M.N. Roy and the Briton Dutt, for whom developments in India exemplified the quickening tempo of colonial development.[262] Fimmen also picked up on this phenomenon in his book *Labour's Alternative*, to which Purcell contributed a foreword in 1924.[263] Purcell would have noticed here the parallel between Fimmen's treatment of colonial development and NAFTA's earlier concerns with cheap labour districts. There was even an echo of Bramley's 'class cohesion' in the conception of 'international capitalism', for which Fimmen was taken to task by Allen Hutt in the *Labour Monthly*.[264] On the organisational form of labour's alternative, Purcell did not see eye-to-eye with Fimmen. Where Fimmen as ITF secretary looked to develop the trade secretariats, Purcell, very much in the spirit of NAFTA, urged the virtues of an 'all-in' international against an 'International Industrialism' of too 'insular' and sectional a type.[265] Where he and Fimmen were at one was in the challenge that they identified with the internationalisation of capitalism.

Perhaps it can be thought of as the argument of social anti-imperialism. In marxist analyses the export of capital tended to be identified with the generation of super-profits, to the benefit either of a labour aristocracy or of the working population as a whole, through the stimulus to domestic consumption or commitments to public welfare.[266] There was however an older tradition, discernible in Marx's own writings, according to which the colonies were maintained at net cost to 'John Bull' himself.[267] Purcell's was not the stance of a little Englander bemoaning the costs that empire imposed upon the public exchequer. Rather, it was from the perspective of the trade unionist, concerned with control of the labour supply, that he condemned the empire on behalf of the 'patient, loyal, hard-working, long-suffering' working class that bore its burdens.

During the period of his IFTU presidency, he delivered three significant pronouncements on the subject: at the first Commonwealth Labour conference in July 1925, at the American Federation of Labour three months later and at IFTU's triennial congress in August 1927. On each occasion, his central theme was that of the 'stupendous industrial development' taking place beyond Europe's borders, as capital not only sought out the cheapest supplies of labour and raw materials but brought to their exploitation the latest plant and forms of technology. What, he asked at the Commonwealth Labour Conference, did colonial wealth or the acquisition of Togoland mean to the East End slum dweller or the toil-worn navvy? 'What, indeed, does this precious Empire mean to the whole working class of this country, whose arduous work and wages of toilsome earnings hardly enables them to drag on from week to week?' Through empire, the 'wealth wrung from the workers of Britain' was invested in cheaper labour, 'black, brown and yellow', sometimes, as in the South African mines, to the exclusion of available white labour.[268] Opposition to the public cost of imperialism were sometimes expressed in terms of its better investment at home.[269] From a trade-unionist perspective, on the other hand, what it required was the logic of solidarity seen at Richill or High Wycombe, but on an international scale:

> If the cotton mills of Bombay had been in London, there is no question but that the Textile Workers Unions would have sent organisers along to organise the mill workers. Why have not the Textile Unions sent organisers to Bombay, Calcutta, Cawnpore, to Southern China and Egypt? Why has not the MFGB sent organisers to India where miners work for sixpence a day? How is it possible for coal produced in South Wales to compete with coal produced in India under such conditions?[270]

Moving the Scarborough resolution six weeks later, Purcell described imperialism as a boomerang for the working class.[271] Harry Pollitt, who seconded the resolution, was to return to the subject in the leisure accorded him by Wandsworth prison, and identified as IFTU's most basic flaw its conception as a 'White Man's International'.[272]

As Howe observes, this was a 'relatively coherent and sophisticated' stance that seemed to reconcile altruism and self-interest.[273] Its ambiguity has not always been fully appreciated. The CPGB's official historian thus described the Scarborough resolution as a 'signal victory for the Marxist approach', and even Howe classifies it as a communist position, clearly distinguishable from rival tendencies like Empire Socialism.[274] There were nevertheless obvious tensions that were arguably inherent in the discourse of trade-union internationalism. One was its relation to labour protectionism. What Purcell referred to a 'sanitary cordon of proper wages and working conditions ... in all countries of the world' was a potentially oxymoronic formulation in which the universalism of the Common Rule ('all the countries of the world') was in a clear state of tension with exclusion and the Restriction of Numbers ('sanitary cordon').[275] As noted in the previous chapter, Purcell had already demonstrated in relation to the McKenna duties that he had no absolute objection to protectionist expedients. In theory, this position had been decisively rejected at the Hull TUC, and the Miners' secretary Cook, whose members had such an interest in outgoing trade, described the protectionist response to cheap imported goods as reactionary and dangerous.[276] Where protectionism took the form of subventions to goods aimed at competitive markets, however, Labour's position was a good deal more ambivalent. Indeed, its greatest industrial victory, rudely interrupting Purcell's participation in the Empire Labour Conference, was the achievement of precisely such a subsidy to British coal exports through the Red Friday solidarity action in 1925. Strongly challenged within the International Miners' Federation, this had contributed directly to the contraction of the German mining industry in 1925-6, and had its constraining effect on international solidarity during the competitive opportunity provided by the subsequent British miners' lockout.[277]

A second tension can be found within the terms of the Scarborough resolution itself. Apparently the commitment was clear, both to an all-in conception of industrial organisation – what Purcell's ally Swales referred to as 'unity among the workers and toilers of the Empire itself' – and to rights of political self-determination extending, as the resolution specified, to complete separation from the empire.[278] Some socialists, on the other hand, might have identified Purcell's sanitary cordon with the empire itself, at least in its hypothetically socialised form. A Commonwealth Labour Group had been formed in 1922 and provided a weekly forum for the airing of such views. One prominent member was the Dundee MP Tom Johnston, whose arguments regarding Indian jute workers were strikingly similar to Purcell's.[279] Another was George Lansbury, whose sponsorship of the group was by the late 1920s combined with that of Willi Münzenberg's communist-sponsored League Against Imperialism.[280]

While Georges Fischer rightly observed in this context how conflicting conclusions could be drawn from the same ideological postulates, it is easy to underestimate how this was possible even for the same individual.[281] Defending the principle of the Commonwealth Labour Conference, initially projected to coincide with the Wembley British Empire Exhibition, Lansbury rejected the idea that the empire could be broken into 'half a hundred little ineffective countries, each run by a nationalist clique'. Instead he proposed its transformation into a United Workers' Republic.[282] Bernard Porter has described this outlook in a felicitous coinage as 'imperio-internationalist'.[283] It is familiar from the South African war and the first invocation of a 'commonwealth of nations' in Shaw's *Fabianism and the Empire* manifesto.[284] Even the CPGB, in the year of the Wembley exhibition, had given some credence to such a viewpoint.[285]

Purcell stopped short of such a position. His view of the emerging nationalist movements nevertheless betrayed a syndicalistic distrust of 'mere politicians' and the threat they posed to existing labour market controls. Regarding India, the focus of such discussions at this time, he not only supported equal union rights and working conditions of a 'British standard', but suggested that self-determination, or 'purely political changes at the top', should be conditional on such undertakings.[286] Fabian imperialists had urged that 'the British flag carry with it wherever it flies a factory code and a standard of life secured by a legal minimum wage'.[287] Purcell's anti-imperialism urged that the removal of the British flag be dependent on the same things. He was certainly not alone in holding to such a view.[288] Nevertheless, he was severely taken to task by Ernest Thurtle, Lansbury's son-in-law and PPS, who held that only an imperialist would claim to see to the Indian workers' interests better than they could themselves.[289]

In responding, Purcell again insisted on the primacy of 'economic freedom' over what he called 'liberal and democratic political ideas'.[290] Unlike the mere bestowal from above of British factory codes, this at least was a call to organised self-activity and a challenge to empire from below. At an Albert Hall rally in support of British communist prisoners, Purcell was described as struggling to project himself in the cavernous auditorium 'until anger at the oppression of his class filled his voice with volume and a sort of harsh fury':

> He told us of fifteen trade unionist murdered in Nicaragua, of wanton class war oppression in South and Central America at the word of British or American imperialism, of a thousand workers in jail in Chile

.... He urged us to remember these others who were fighting as well as our own prisoners.[291]

Impelled by the core value of working-class solidarity, Purcell came through the notions of rapid industrialisation and therefore proletarianisation to articulate the forthright internationalism that we shall find attested in his final address as IFTU president.

Perhaps these were also issues to do with Soviet Russia. Adler expressed his greatest sense of outrage at the section in the TUC delegation's report dealing with Georgia, describing it as a 'burning shame for the Labour Movement'. Noting the similarity in tone with official reports on the British colonies, whose denial of freedom was also justified on grounds of security and material advance, he alleged that every possible argument for imperialism was here advanced with the blessing of British trade unionists.[292] The signs of Young's drafting are certainly apparent in this section of the report. It described intrigue and insurrection as 'inbred in the Trans-Caucasian races' and, with a fastidious sense of irony that only a future baronet could have affected, evoked a region so remote that 'the Russian tax collector, and even the British tourist never penetrated'.[293] Even so, the substantive proposal of a sort of '"Dominion" autonomy', in a multi-national union whose 'practical advantages ... might be considered on material grounds as outweighing the disadvantages', was very much that of the delegation as a whole.[294] In an effusive exchange with Tomsky, the delegation cited the exemplary significance of the 'successful reconciliation of revolutionary principles to the practical requirements of the many races, regions, and religions within the Union'.[295] Indeed, the delegation had stated in Georgia itself that it could function independently only as a 'marionette in the hand of the Great Powers' and that in post-war Europe, with the exception of a few such powers, 'independent States do not exist'.[296]

No wonder the Belgian Vandervelde took exception to this.[297] Even in the *Labour Magazine*, Herbert Tracey felt constrained to note that the same reasoning could be used 'in defence of imperialist aggression ... in the world of capitalist exploitation'.[298] Bertrand Russell too observed that India and Georgia were 'in the same case, though neither Conservatives nor Communists think so'.[299] Lansbury for one had no such concerns. In rejecting the idea of breaking up the British empire into 'half a hundred little ineffective countries, each run by a nationalist clique', it was explicitly on the precedent of the USSR that he proposed instead a United Workers' Republic, exactly as the Tsarist empire now provided its foundation.[300] In offering both a challenge to empire and its successful transformation on a socialist basis, the USSR both appealed to and compounded the ambivalencies already much in evidence on the British left. When Purcell went on his final TUC mission to India, we shall see that they had still not been fully overcome.

NOTES

1. RGASPI 495/100/94, unnamed correspondent to W.N. Ewer, 28 February 1922.
2. G.M. Stekloff, trans. Eden and Cedar Paul, *History of the First International*, Martin Lawrence, 1927, p. 14.
3. Lewis L. Lorwin, *Labor and Internationalism*, New York: Macmillans, 1929, pp. 113-14.
4. Henry Pelling, *Origins of the Labour Party*, Oxford: OUP edn, 1966, p. 118.
5. Stephen Howe, *Anticolonialism in British Politics*, Oxford: OUP, 1993, pp. 77-81; Stephen Howe, 'Labour and international affairs' in Duncan Tanner, Pat Thane and Nick Tiratsoo, eds, *Labour's First Century*, Cambridge: CUP, 2000, p. 127.
6. Douglas J. Newton, *British Labour, European Socialism and the Struggle for Peace 1889-1914*, Oxford: OUP, 1985.
7. Hugh Armstrong Clegg, *A History of British Trade Unions since 1889. Volume 2: 1911-1933*, Oxford: OUP, 1985.
8. Ross M. Martin, *TUC: the growth of a pressure group 1868-1976*, Oxford: OUP, 1980, p. 154 and passim.
9. Hunter, 'British Labour and the International', *New Leader*, 16 January 1925.
10. 202 Hansard fifth series, 18 February 1927, cols 1308-15.
11. Lorwin, *Labor and Internationalism*, p. 17.
12. Stekloff, *History*, p. 19 citing Theodore Rothstein; Lorwin, *Labor and Internationalism*, p. 31.
13. Purcell, '"Our patriotism – loyalty to the working class"', *Plebs*, March 1925, p. 101.
14. Susan Milner, *The Dilemmas of Internationalism. French syndicalism and the international labour movement 1900-1914*, Oxford: Berg, 1990, pp. 17-18.
15. *International Socialist Workers and Trade Union Congress. London, 1896. Report of proceedings, list of British and foreign delegates, and balance sheet*, Twentieth Century Press, n.d. but 1896, pp. 40-1.
16. See *Bolshevism and the British Left*, II, pp. 187-9.
17. See Wayne Thorpe, *'The Workers Themselves'. Revolutionary syndicalism and international labour, 1913-1923*, Dordrecht: Kluwer Academic Publishers, 1989, ch. 2.
18. Christine Collette, *The International Faith. Labour's attitudes to European socialism 1918-1939*, Aldershot: Ashgate, 1998, p. 1; compare with Hunter, 'British Labour and the International', and Purcell, preface to Edo Fimmen, trans. Eden and Cedar Paul, *Labour's Alternative: the United States of Europe or Europe Limited*, Labour Publishing Company, 1924, p. 5. Purcell suggested that there was in Britain 'really no enthusiasm of the type which helps to popularise so vast an instrument as International Working Class Organisation'.
19. Lorwin, *Labor and Internationalism*, p. 1.
20. On this point see Eric Hobsbawm, 'Working-class internationalism' in Fritz van Holthoon and Marcel van der Linden, eds, *Internationalism in the Labour Movement 1830-1940*, Leiden: Brill, 1988, vol. 1., p. 10.

21. Hobsbawm, 'Working-class internationalism', pp. 10-11.
22. Catherine Ann Cline, *E.D. Morel 1873-1924. The strategies of protest*, Belfast: Blackstaff Press, 1980, p. 122; also Sheldon Spear, 'Pacifist radicalism in the post-war British Labour Party: the case of E.D. Morel, 1919-24', *International Review of Social History*, 23, 2, 1978, pp. 193-223.
23. Morel, 'Why "foreign affairs" are home affairs', *TGWU Record*, December 1923, p. 7.
24. Purcell, 59th TUC *Report*, 1927, p. 380.
25. Stekloff, *History*, p. 8 was citing Meyer's *Der Emancipationskampf des vierten Stande* (1874-5).
26. Milner, *Dilemmas*, p. 8.
27. Douglas J. Newton, *British Labour, European Socialism and the Struggle for Peace 1889-1914*, Oxford: OUP, 1985, pp. 96-7.
28. John Logue, *Toward a Theory of Trade Union Internationalism*, Gothenburg: University of Gothenburg, 1980, pp. 17-18.
29. Fritz van Holthoon and Marcel van der Linden, 'Introduction' in van Holthoon and van der Linden, *Internationalism in the Labour Movement*, p. vii.
30. Logue, *Toward a Theory*, pp. 27-9.
31. Jeffrey Harrod *Trade Union Foreign Policy. A study of British and American union activities in Jamaica*, New York: Doubleday & Co, 1972, p. 53.
32. Brockway, *Inside the Left. Thirty years of platform, press, prison and parliament*, Allen & Unwin, 1942, p. 184; NAFTA *Monthly Report*, October 1926, pp. 21-3.
33. NTWF archives 159/3/C/188, Fimmen to Williams, 10 June 1922.
34. See the discussion in 'Introduction: around a life' above.
35. Milner, *Dilemmas*, pp. 15-16 and passim.
36. Purcell, preface to Fimmen, *Labour's Alternative*, p. 5.
37. Logue, *Toward a Theory*, p. 46.
38. Sidney and Beatrice Webb, *Industrial Democracy*, Longmans, 1920 edn, pp. 560-1.
39. See Hobsbawm, 'Working-class internationalism', pp. 9, 14.
40. R.C. Rheiners, 'Racialism on the left: E.D. Morel and the "Black Horror" on the Rhine', *International Review of Social History*, 13, 1968, pp. 1-28.
41. *Manchester Guardian*, 18 January 1917.
42. Labour Party conference *Report*, 1917, p. 89.
43. E.g. NAFTA *Monthly Report*, January 1915, pp. 12-14.
44. NAFTA *Monthly Report*, April 1915.
45. NAFTA *Monthly Report*, March 1916, p. 11.
46. See *Bolshevism and the British Left*, II, p. 134, also ch. 8 below.
47. BWD 19 November 1918*, with note added January 1919.
48. Beatrice Webb diaries, 19 February 1918.
49. Geert Van Goethem, *The Amsterdam International. The world of the International Federation of Trade Unions (IFTU) 1913-1945*, Aldershot: Ashgate, 2006, pp. 18, 22, 26.
50. See for example Tomsky, *Getting Together. Speeches delivered in Russia and England 1924-1925*, LRD, 1925, pp. 71, 109.
51. Newton, *British Labour*, p. 83.

52. L.A. Bather, 'A history of the Manchester and Salford Trades Council', Manchester: M Phil, 1956, p. 121.
53. *Clarion*, 26 January 1906.
54. See for example Friedrich Adler, 'The organisation problems of working-class unity', *Labour Magazine*, May 1926, pp. 64-5.
55. Bruno Naarden, *Socialist Europe and Revolutionary Russia: perception and prejudice 1848-1923*, Cambridge: CUP, 1992, pp. 134, 38 and passim.
56. Oudegeest, 'Not the right way to unity', IFTU *Press Reports*, 1 October 1925.
57. Leon Trotsky, *My Life*, Harmondsworth: Penguin edn, 1975, p. 549.
58. Milner, *Dilemmas*, pp. 67-8.
59. Adolphe Smith, *A Critical Essay on the International Trade Union Congress Held in London, November, 1888*, London: the author, 1889.
60. See chapter 2 above; also Augustin Hamon, *Le Socialisme et le congrès de Londres. Étude historique*, Paris: Stock, 1897, pp. 104-25.
61. Milner, *Dilemmas*, pp. 49-50.
62. Van Goethem, *Amsterdam International*, p. 15.
63. Milner, *Dilemmas*, pp. 41-2.
64. Namely Ransome, Russell, Wells, Lansbury, Brailsford and Clare Sheridan; see André Morizet, *Chez Lénine et Trotski; Moscou 1921*, Paris: La Renaissance du Livre, 1922, pp. xiv-xv.
65. TUC archives 292/20/6, TUC parliamentary committee, London members' minutes, 10 May 1920.
66. Stephen White has provided a detailed description of the delegates' itinerary and organisational arrangements, drawing on both Soviet and British sources: White, 'British Labour in Soviet Russia, 1920', *English Historical Review*, 1994, pp. 621-40.
67. TUC archives 292/20/6, TUC parliamentary committee minutes, 10 and 24 March and 21 April 1920.
68. NA HW12/10/2971, Chicherin to Krasin, decrypted telegram, 15 June 1920.
69. TUC archives 292/31.6/1, Labour Party/TUC international joint sub-committee minutes 9 March and 20 April 1920; Ben Turner, *About Myself*, Humphrey Toulmin, 1920, p. 211; Tanner, *Solidarity*, August 1920.
70. See the accounts in Turner, *About Myself*, pp. 211-31; Margaret Bondfield, *A Life's Work*, Hutchinson, n.d., pp. 190ff.
71. Lenin to Chicherin, April 1920, encl. draft resolution for RCP central committee, cited Richard Pipes, ed., *The Unknown Lenin. From the secret archive*, New Haven & London: Yale University Press, 1997, p. 80.
72. Jean-François Fayet, *Karl Radek (1885-1939). Biographie politique*, Bern: Peter Lang, 2004, p. 330.
73. See 'Corrections and Additions Drafted After a Telephone Conversation Between Lenin, Chicherin and Radek', appended to Lenin's draft resolution, Pipes, *Unknown Lenin*, pp. 80-1.
74. Morton H. Cowden, *Russian Bolshevism and British Labor 1917-1921*, New York: Columbia University Press, 1984, ch. 5.
75. White, 'British Labour in Soviet Russia', p. 635.
76. See Walter Citrine's comments in his *Men and Work. An autobiography*, Hutchinson, 1964, p. 89.
77. *Russian Information and Review*, 7 October 1922, p. 8. For biographical

details and a typical presentation of his industrial credentials, see 'Mikhail Tomsky. A biography', *Communist Review*, September 1925, pp. 208-10.
78. Williams, *Impressions of Soviet Russia*, Amsterdam: ITF, 1920, p. 5.
79. Orlando Figes, *A People's Tragedy. The Russian Revolution 1891-1924*, Cape, 1996, p. 605.
80. Snowden, *Through Bolshevik Russia*, ch. 1. The same account also describes, for example, the unofficial markets (pp. 108-11) of which Figes suggests the delegates were ignorant. Richard Pipes provides a fair and accurate characterisation in his *Russia under the Bolshevik Regime 1919-1924*, London: Fontana Press, 1995 edn, pp. 203-5.
81. Bertrand Russell, *The Practice and Theory of Bolshevism*, Allen & Unwin, 1920, p. 24.
82. Leon Trotsky, *My Life*, pp. 598-9.
83. Marguerite Harrison, *Marooned in Moscow*, Thornton & Butterworth, 1921, p. 177.
84. Turner, *About Myself*, pp. 219-21; also White, 'British Labour in Soviet Russia', pp. 629-30, 638-9.
85. Emma Goldman, *My Disillusionment in Russia*, C.W. Daniel, 1925, p. 59. As on most subjects, Goldman was a less astute observer than Berkman.
86. NA HW12/10/2989, Chicherin to Krasin, decrypted telegram, 15 June; *Daily Herald*, 2 August 1920.
87. NAFTA *Monthly Report*, May 1920, p. 13.
88. Angelica Balabanoff, *My Life as a Rebel*, Bloomington & London: Indiana University Press, 1973 edn, pp. 257-8; Williams, *Impressions*, p. 14.
89. E.g. Purcell speech at ARTUC, 11 November 1924, *Inprecorr*, 16 December 1924, p. 977.
90. Mrs Philip Snowden, *Through Bolshevik Russia*, Cassells, 1920, pp. 48-51.
91. Alexander Berkman, *The Bolshevik Myth (Diary 1920-1922)*, New York: Boni & Liveright, 1925, pp. 137-40.
92. Lenin to Chicherin, April 1920.
93. Bondfield, *A Life's Work*, p. 201; TUC archives 292/31.6/1, Labour Party/TUC international joint sub-committee minutes, 10 November 1920.
94. Guest, 'Russia under the Bolsheviks', *Fabian News*, August 1920, pp. 33-4; *Times*, 1 October 1920; Chicherin to Krasin, 15 June 1920.
95. Berkman, *Bolshevik Myth*, p. 140. For conflict with Guest, see NA HW12/10/2971 and 2989, HW12/11/3177 and 3190, Chicherin to Krasin, decrypted telegrams, 15 and 26 June and 2 July 1920.
96. *British Labour Delegation to Russia, 1920: report*, TUC and Labour Party, 1920, pp. 26-7 and (for first interim report) 28-9.
97. NA HW12/11/3254, Klishko to Krasin, decrypted telegram, 1 July 1920.
98. Russell, *Practice and Theory*, pp. 151-2; also Klishko to Krasin, 1 July 1920. Milovan Djilas's book *The New Class* was published in 1957.
99. Russell, *Practice and Theory*, pp. 113-35; Guest, *Times*, 30 September-4 October 1920.
100. See *Bolshevism and the British Left*, I, p. 204.
101. See *Bolshevism and the British Left*, II, ch. 7.
102. Losovsky, *The Trade Unions in Soviet Russia*, Moscow: All-Russian Central Council of Trade Unions, 1920; *Trade Unions in Soviet Russia. A collection of Russian trade union documents compiled by the ILP Information Committee and the International Section of the Labour*

148   *Bolshevism, syndicalism and the general strike*

       Research Department, LRD/ILP Information Committee, 1920; also 'Trade unionism in Russia', LRD *Monthly Circular*, September 1920, pp. 43-5;. The British Library copy of Losovsky's pamphlet has the handwritten note 'British Labour Delegation, Russia, 1920'.
103. Losovsky in *Trade Unions in Soviet Russia*, pp. 27-9.
104. *Daily Herald*, 7 July 1920.
105. Berkman papers XXV, diary entry 18 May 1920; Russell, *The Autobiography of Bertrand Russell 1914-1944*, Allen & Unwin, 1968.
106. Guest, 'Russia under the Bolsheviks'; *Times*, 4 October 1920.
107. Arthur Marwick, *Clifford Allen. The open conspirator*, Oliver & Boyd, 1964, p. 63; Russell, *Practice and Theory*, pp. 88-91.
108. *British Labour Delegation to Russia*, pp. 119-21.
109. NAFTA *Monthly Report*, April 1920, p. 2-3.
110. Bondfield papers, folder D, typescript draft, 'Industrial organisation and mobilisation of labour'.
111. Chicherin to Krasin, 15 June 1920; *British Labour Delegation to Russia*, pp. 122-5.
112. Williams, *Impressions*, pp. 6, 14; see also Williams, *The Soviet System at Work*, CPGB, 1920. Much of the text of the two pamphlets is identical.
113. Unless otherwise stated, quotation which follow are from NAFTA *Monthly Report*, July 1920, pp. 15-20; August 1920, pp. 17-21; and September 1920, pp. 19-20.
114. *Daily Herald*, 12 July 1920.
115. NAFTA *Monthly Report*, September 1920, pp. 16-17.
116. Williams, *Impressions*, p. 4.
117. NAFTA *Monthly Report*, August 1920; also Snowden, *Through Bolshevik Russia*, pp. 33-5.
118. See e.g. Jane Burbank, *Intelligentsia and Revolution*, New York: OUP, 1986, pp. 78-9; Goldman, *My Disillusionment*, pp. 86-9; Naarden, *Socialist Europe*, p. 394.
119. Bondfield, *A Life's Work*, pp. 202-5.
120. *Communist*, 26 February 1921.
121. ILP archives ILP/4/1923/41, telegram from British Labour delegation to ILP, 11 June 1920, detailing the composition of the proposed delegation.
122. TUC archives 292/947/1, 'An open letter to the workers of England from the Russian Trade Union Delegation in Western Europe', n.d.; also 292/20/6, TUC parliamentary committee minutes, 17 July and 2 September 1920.
123. *Russian Information and Review*, 7 October 1922, p. 8.
124. Tomsky at TUC welcoming dinner, 14 May 1924, in idem, *Getting Together*, p. 58.
125. See TUC archives 292/497/1 for IFTU press articles for circulation by national affiliates, around two-fifths of which deal with Russia.
126. Van Goethem, *Amsterdam International*, pp. 80-1.
127. Labour Party conference *Report*, June 1922, pp. 193-6.
128. *Labour Magazine*, August 1922, pp. 179-82.
129. See for example *Socialist Review*, July-September 1921 (article addressed to MacDonald by the ousted Georgian president Noe Jordania), February 1922 (sixteen-page Georgian supplement), November 1922 (article by Julius Braunthal).

130. MacDonald papers NA 30/69/1166, letter to MacDonald from suppressed London legation of Georgian Workers' Social Democratic Party, 21 March 1922; David Marquand, *Ramsay MacDonald*, Jonathan Cape, 1977, pp. 264-6.
131. TUC archives 292/31.6/1-4, TUC general council/Labour Party NEC joint international committee minutes, 2 May 1922.
132. Stephen White, *Britain and the Bolshevik Revolution. A study in the politics of diplomacy 1920-1924*, Macmillan, 1979, p. 215.
133. IISH SAI 201, LSI Vienna meeting 5-7 June 1924, comments of Adler and Jean Longuet; SAI 206, LSI circular on LSI executive meeting, 30 September; SAI 215, LSI executive meeting, Brussels, 4 January 1925, 'Replies of affiliated parties, *re seat of Secretariat*'.
134. BWD 4 September 1920.
135. BWD 30 June 1918.
136. Baikalov papers, box 2, Snowden to Baikalov, 24 June 1923.
137. The clearest account is in White, *Britain and the Bolshevik Revolution*, ch. 6.
138. See Trevelyan papers CPT 105, Krasin to Trevelyan, 14 June 1923.
139. The British abstained and two 'minor' parties opposed; see André Liebich, *From the Other Shore. Russian Social Democracy after 1921*, Cambridge, Mass.: Harvard University Press, 1997, pp. 161-3.
140. M. Philips Price, 'The Hamburg congress and the new Labour international', *Labour Monthly*, August 1923, p. 85. For Price see *Bolshevism and the British Left*, I, pp. 74-6, 95-6, 158-9.
141. IISH SAI 1712, Adler (?) to Francis Johnson, 31 January 1924.
142. BWD 30 May 1923; Price, 'Hamburg congress', p. 84.
143. Liebich, *From the Other Shore*, pp. 162 and 388 n. 36; Naarden, *Socialist Europe*, pp. 509-14. Liebich states that Abramovich's account was 'entirely consistent with Webb's expressed opinions regarding Russian emigr socialists', but no evidence is provided and it cannot be found in Beatrice's diary entry.
144. NTWF archives 159/3/C/188, Williams to Fimmen, 31 May 1923, Fimmen to Williams 4 June 1923.
145. Van Goethem, *Amsterdam International*, pp. 85-8,
146. TUC archives 292/20/8, TUC general council minutes, 31 October 1923; also Van Goethem, *Amsterdam International*, p. 86.
147. TUC archives 292/901/1, TUC international committee minutes, 10 December 1923, 292/20/8, TUC general council minutes, 12 December 1923.
148. Van Goethem, *Amsterdam International*, p. 89.
149. Catherine Ann Cline, *Recruits to Labour. The British Labour Party 1914-1931*, Syracuse: Syracuse University Press, 1963, pp. 138-9.
150. MacDonald papers (JRULM), RMD 1/14/79, Trevelyan to MacDonald, 6 January 1924
151. *Workers' Weekly*, 11 April 1924.
152. Pierre Broué, *Rakovsky ou la Révolution dans tous les pays*, Paris: Fayard, 1996, pp. 216-16.
153. See e.g. Ponsonby papers Ms Eng hist c. 669/65, Rakovsky to Ponsonby, 12 November 1925, also 19 March 1926; also Raymond A. Jones, *Arthur Ponsonby. The politics of life*, Christopher Helm, 1989, p. 146; Gus Fagan,

150 Bolshevism, syndicalism and the general strike

introduction, in Christian Rakovsky, ed. Gus Fagan, *Selected Writings on Opposition in the USSR*, Allison & Busby, 1980, pp. 34-5.
154. MacDonald papers (NA) 30/69/220 RRO 1 May 1924 citing Zinoviev and Kolarov for the CI to CPGB, 7 April 1924.
155. The document itself indicates that the letter was only 'reported to have been sent' the CPGB.
156. MacDonald papers (NA) 30/69/1171, Newbold to MacDonald 2 June 1926; Tillett, Bramley and Tomsky at TUC welcoming dinner, 14 May 1924, in Tomsky, *Getting Together*, pp. 36-41.
157. Morel papers F8/123, Ponsonby to Morel, 31 July 1924
158. Morel papers F2 3/1, 'How the Anglo-Russian Conference was saved by the Labour back benches. Secret history of the events of August 5, 6, 7, 1924'; Marquand, *Ramsay MacDonald*, pp. 362-3.
159. Ponsonby papers MS Eng. hist. c 683/75, Rakovsky to Ponsonby, n.d.
160. Purcell at TUC welcoming dinner, 14 May 1924, in Tomsky, *Getting Together*, p. 34
161. E.H. Carr, *Socialism in One Country, 1924-1926. Volume 3*, Harmondsworth: Penguin edn, 1972, p. 26 n. 2.
162. Purcell, speeches at Coventry and Manchester reported *Coventry Herald*, 3-4 October 1924 and *Manchester Guardian*, 29 September 1924.
163. 56th TUC *Report*, 1924, pp. 246-7.
164. Tillett, 'The International. Notes on the Vienna conference (June 2nd-6th 1924)', TGWU *Record*, July 1924, p. 6.
165. 56th TUC *Report*, 1924, pp. 383-403; 57th TUC *Report*, 1925, p. 482; MacDonald papers (NA) 30/69 1172, Newbold to MacDonald, n.d. but 1927.
166. TUC *Report*, 1924, p. 395; NA FO 371/10478 N6351/108/38, Hodgson to MacDonald, 24 July 1924.
167. TUC archives 292/20/9, TUC general council special meeting minutes, 16 October 1924.
168. TUC archives 292/947/4, Dogadoff (?) to Purcell for TUC (telegram), 20 July 1924. At its meeting of 28-30 August the ILP NAC agreed to await the TUC's decision before deciding whether an ILP delegation should be included but no further discussion is recorded (ILP archives 3/16).
169. *Daily Herald*, 6 November 1924. Bramley also added a characteristic reference to the co-operative movement, to which he was strongly committed.
170. Printed in *Inpecorr*, 16 December 1924, pp. 977-8.
171. *Workers' Weekly*, 28 November 1924; *Manchester Guardian*, 25 November 1924; TUC archives 292/947/59 for press cuttings.
172. NA FO 37/10487 N8865/530/38, William Peters to Austen Chamberlain, 21 November 1924.
173. NA FO 371/11014, report by Ledward, N 1757/73/38.
174. MRC TUC archives 292/947/13, IFTU general council, 6-7 February 1925, 'Relations with Russia'; Bramley papers, box 1, 'The FSI and the question of unity', trans. of report by Jouhaux to CGT, n.d.
175. Bramley papers, box 1, signed agreement of delegates, n.d.
176. TUC archives 292/20/9, TUC general council minutes, 17 December 1924 and 28 January 1925, special meeting minutes, 29 December 1924 and 12 February 1925.

177. *Russia. The official report of the British trades union delegation to Russia and Caucasia Nov. and Dec. 1924*, TUC, 1925, p. 1.
178. Peters, report on the delegation.
179. TUC archives 292/21.12/1, Bramley to Citrine, 13 November 1924; also Bramley papers, Purcell to Bramley, 22 December 1924.
180. NA FO 371/11014 N 153/73/38, Jerram to Peters; *Krasnaya Gazeta* cutting, 24 December 1924; TUC archives 292/21.12/1, Bramley to Citrine, 28 November 1924.
181. TUC archives 292/947/13, IFTU general council, 6-7 February 1925, 'Relations with Russia'. Bramley's address was published as *Relations with Russia*, Trade Union Unity, 1925.
182. *Inpecorr*, 16 December 1924, p. 978.
183. Peters to Chamberlain, 21 November 1924; TUC archives 292/21.12/1, Bramley to Citrine, 16 November 1924.
184. Purcell, 'The truth regarding the Union of Soviet Republics' in *Inprecorr*, 23 December 1924, pp. 1017-18.
185. RGASPI 495/100/176, unidentified Amsterdam correspondent to A. Valenius, 6 November 1924.
186. See Swales comments on his fellow metalworker Lepse, *Sunday Worker*, 12 April 1925.
187. IFTU general council, 6-7 February 1925, 'Relations with Russia'.
188. GARF 5451/13a/40, ARCCTU to TUC Russian delegation, n.d., January 1925?
189. GARF 5451/13a/41, Bramley to Melnichansky, 9 March 1925; also Bramley to Citrine.
190. *Russia*, p. xxiii.
191. TUC *Report*, 1925, p. 70.
192. See NA KV2/506 for Grenfell's MI5 file.
193. Swales, 'Fred Bramley: remembrance and an appreciation', *Labour Magazine*, December 1925, p. 317.
194. For the mugwumps, see *Bolshevism and the British Left*, I, ch. 5.
195. *Lansbury's Labour Weekly*, 2 July 1927.
196. Trevelyan papers CPT 100, Price to Trevelyan, 12 May 1919.
197. Bondfield papers, folder D, ILP programme sub-committee agenda and papers with Young's memorandum on 'The soviets', 2 July 1920. According to Bondfield, *A Life's Work*, p. 230, Young accompanied the delegation as a journalist.
198. Labour Party archives, ACIQ memoranda Young, 'The reform of the foreign services', July 1918 and 'Reform of diplomacy, May 1921.
199. Trevelyan papers CPT 108, Ponsonby to Young (copy), 12 February 1924. For MacDonald's initially radical intentions, see his *A Policy for the Labour Party*, Leonard Parsons, London: 1920, pp 123-36.
200. Trevelyan papers CPT 96, Young to Trevelyan, 31 October 1924; *New Leader*, 14 November 1924.
201. Sidney Webb to Beatrice Webb, 20 February 1925 in Norman Mackenzie, ed., *The Letters of Sidney and Beatrice Webb*, vol 3, Cambridge: CUP, 1978, pp. 226-7; BWD 20 February 1925 also mentions Trevelyan as a possible author.
202. TUC archives 292/31.6/3, TUC/Labour Party joint international department, advisory committee on international questions, minutes 18

February, 4 March, 20 May and 15 July 1925. The proposals were diluted at MacDonald's behest.
203. Bramley papers, box 1, statement drafted by Young and sent *Daily Herald*, 9 December 1924; also *The 'Zinoviev' Letter. Report of Investigation by British delegation to Russia*, TUC general council, 1925, p. 4.
204. *Lansbury's Labour Weekly*, 3 October 1925.
205. Trevelyan papers CPT 96, Young to Trevelyan, 31 October 1924.
206. *Russia*, pp. 41-59.
207. *Russia*, pp. 3-4, 137-42, 148-9.
208. *Russia*, p. 17.
209. *Russia*, pp. 14-15.
210. *Russia*, p. 10.
211. *Inprecorr*, 16 December 1924, p. 978.
212. *Russia*, pp. 139, 170.
213. *Russia*, p. 211.
214. *Russia and the British Labour Delegation's Report: a reply*, BCDPPR, 1925, p. 20.
215. 'An open letter from Gotz to Eddo Fimmen' (dated 1 February 1925) in *Letters From Russian Prisons*, C.W. Daniel for the International Committee for Political Prisoners, 1925, pp. 217-21.
216. *Russia*, pp. 16-17.
217. According to Turner, oppositionists in Tbilisi were arrested for making contact with Purcell, though Purcell obtained at least their temporary release. See GLDS Goldman to Laski, 23 December 1924; also NA FO 371/11014 N146/73/38, letter to TUC delegation from RSDLP Petrograd Committee, 10 December 1924; IISH SAI 1631, Georgian former union officials incl. Ch. Aldsucheli to TUC general council, 26 April 1925.
218. Different re-translations from the Russian can be found in *Inprecorr*, 23 December 1924, pp. 1017-18; *Workers' Weekly*, 26 December 1924; NA FO 371/10487 N9467/530/38.
219. IISG SAI 206, LSI executive meeting, 28-30 September 1924; Brailsford, *New Leader*, 3 October 1924; G. Valetzki, 'The twenty-one points of the Second International', *Labour Monthly*, October 1925, p. 596.
220. TUC archives 292/913.2/3, TUC/Labour Party joint international department, minutes of LSI bureau and EC and joint meeting with IFTU, 1-6 January 1925; also Bramley papers, box 1 for various protests and responses.
221. 56th *TUC Report*, 1924, pp. 311-19, 404.
222. Purcell speech at ARTUC, 11 November 1924.
223. *Daily Herald*, 27 November 1924.
224. Purcell, '"Our patriotism – loyalty to our class"', p. 102.
225. Oudegeest, 'Purcell in Russia', IFTU *Press Reports*, 18 December 1924; also IFTU general council, 6-7 February 1925, 'Relations with Russia', contribution in Oudegeest.
226. See for example IFTU *Press Reports*, first series, nos 12, 15-16, second series nos 63, 81, 120.
227. Oudegeest, 'Amsterdam-London-Moscow', IFTU *Press Reports*, 14 April 1925.
228. The abandonment of this view can be traced across the three commentar-

ies published in the IFTU *Press Reports* of 10 December 1925 and 21 and 28 January 1926.
229. Purcell, 'Towards a new policy: V', *Labour Monthly*, May 1924, p. 269
230. Purcell, speech at ARTUC, 11 November 1924.
231. 56th TUC *Report*, 1924, p. 404.
232. Purcell, '"Our patriotism – loyalty to our class"', p. 102.
233. *Der Wahrheit eine Gasse. Was sah die tschechoslowakische Arbeiterdelegation in der Sowjetunion?*, Reichenberg: Runge & Co, 1926.
234. 57th TUC *Report*, 1925, p. 534.
235. GARF 5451/13a/41, Citrine to Tomski and Bogadov, ARCCTU, 24 April 1925; Swales, TUC *Report*, 1925, p. 70. The New York *Daily Worker* published the report in daily parts from 25 July to 10 September 1925.
236. 'Meeting of the General Council of the IFTU held 5th February, 1925, at Amsterdam' (IFTU *Press Reports*), contributions of Bramley and Brown. See also TUC archives 292/20/8, TUC general council minutes, 29 December 1924 and 25 March 1925; GARF 5451/13a/41, Citrine and Swales to Oudegeest (copy), 15 June 1925; TUC archives 292/90/1, TUC general council, Paris IFTU congress sub-committee minutes, 11 July 1927.
237. Examples of such usages may be found in the IFTU *Press Reports* of 20 November 1924 and 8 and 29 January 1925.
238. *Lansbury's Labour Weekly*, 30 May 1925.
239. Keith Laybourn, *The General Strike 1926*, Manchester: MUP, 1993, p. 24. Concerns were initially expressed regarding the journal's unauthorised publication of confidential matter; see TUC archives 292/20/9, TUC general council minutes, 25 March 1925.
240. LRD archives, 'Unity an appeal', printed circular, March 1925; see also TUC archives 292/901/1, TUC international committee minutes, 20 January 1925 for concerns about securing an 'accurate and reliable report' of the British contribution to IFTU affairs.
241. See RGASPI 539/3/286, Hicks to Citrine (copy) re possible commission to investigate Bulgarian atrocities, n.d. but 1925. 'I believe that it would do great good, emphasise and strengthen our international relationships with the workers of other countries ... and add to the prestige of the British Trade Union movement for the General Council to instigate this Enquiry and give full publicity to its findings'.
242. Purcell, editorial, *Trade Union Unity*, May 1925, pp. 1-2.
243. Reiner Tosstorff, 'Unity between "Amsterdam" and "Moscow"? Edo Fimmen's relationship to the communist trade union movement' in Bob Reinalda, ed., *The International Transportworkers' Federation: the Edo Fimmen era*, Amsterdam: IISG, 1997, pp. 101-2 and 257 n. 260; NA KV 4/282, 'Aspects of the General Strike, May, 1926'.
244. Oudegeest, 'The fight for the united front', IFTU *Press Reports*, 24 September 1925.
245. Purcell, 'The burning question of international unity', *Labour Monthly*, September 1925, p. 527.
246. *Inprecorr*, 16 December 1924.
247. 57th TUC *Report*, 1925, pp. 553-5.
248. Hergé, *The Adventures of Tintin, Reporter for 'Le petit vingtième', In the Land of the Soviets*, Methuen, 1999 edn, pp. 29-30.

249. Joseph Douillet, *Moscow sans voiles. Neuf ans du travail au pays des Soviets*, Paris: Spes, 1928, pp. 19-20.
250. Liebich, *From the Other Shore*, pp. 170-1 and pp. 390-1, n.33; *The British Trade Union Delegation and Georgia*, Paris: Foreign Bureau of the Social-Democratic Labour Party of Georgia, 1925.
251. See 'Reception of the Russian report', *Trade Union Unity*, April 1925, pp. 11-12; Hunter, 'British Labour and the International'.
252. IFTU *Press Reports*, 11 March 1926; Heinrich Löffler, *Russland in Licht englischer Gewerkschafter*, ADGB, 1925.
253. Struve, 'Introduction' in Michel Fedoroff, ed., *La Russie sous le régime communiste. Réponse au rapport de la délégation des trades-unions britanniques, basée sur la documentation officielle soviétique*, Paris: Nouvelle Librairie Nationale, 1926, pp. 5-15.
254. Friedrich Adler, *The Anglo-Russian Report. A criticism of the report of the British trade union delegation to Russia from the point of view of international socialism*, P.S. King, 1925. Originally published in the Austrian monthly *Der Kampf*, the pamphlet also appeared in French and German editions and its key contentions were taken up by socialists like Léon Jouhaux. A Russian edition published in Berlin carried a forward by the Menshevik Dan.
255. See *Bolshevism and the British Left*, I, p. 112
256. Adler, *Anglo-Russian Report*, pp. 12-13, 39.
257. Adler, *Anglo-Russian Report*, pp. 10-11, 17, 26-7.
258. Adler, *Anglo-Russian Report*, p. 9.
259. Adler, *Anglo-Russian Report*, pp. 7-8.
260. 59th *TUC Report*, pp. 376-7.
261. 59th *TUC Report*, p. 377. For a polemical commentary see Tom Nairn, *The Left Against Europe?*, Harmondsworth: Penguin, 1973, ch. 5.
262. John Callaghan, *Rajani Palme Dutt. A study in British stalinism*, Lawrence & Wishart, 1993, pp. 86-94.
263. Fimmen, *Labour's Alternative*, pp. 52-4.
264. G.A.H., 'Does international capitalism exist?', *Labour Monthly*, November 1924, pp. 693-5.
265. Purcell in Fimmen, *Labour's Alternative*, p. 6.
266. See for example Kautsky, 'The American worker' (1906) in Richard B. Day and Daniel Gaido, eds, *Witnesses to Permanent Revolution. The documentary record*, Chicago: Haymarket edn, 2011, pp. 629-33 on 'English capitalism'.
267. For examples of such arguments from Marx's journalism and correspondence, see Shlomo Avineri, ed., *Karl Marx on Colonialism and Modernization. His despatches and other writings on China, India, Mexico, the Middle East and North Africa*, New York: Doubleday & Co, 1968, pp. 222-5, 345-55, 440-1.
268. *Report of First British Commonwealth Labour Conference*, pp. 76-8.
269. See *HC Deb 5s.*, vol. 191, 18 February 1926, cols 2196-200 for Purcell's opposition to the Anglo-Iraq treaty – a country 'located a long distance from home, in a district which is, so to speak, packed with malaria'.
270. *Report of First British Commonwealth Labour Conference*, pp. 76-8.
271. 57th *TUC Report*, 1925, pp. 553-5.
272. Pollitt papers, prison note book issued 10 April 1926.

273. Howe, *Anticolonialism*, p. 59.
274. James Klugmann, *History of the Communist Party of Great Britain. Volume two: the General Strike 1925-1926*, Lawrence & Wishart, 1969, pp. 297-8; Howe, *Anticolonialism*, p. 65.
275. *Report of First British Commonwealth Labour Conference*, p. 78.
276. 56th TUC *Report*, 1924, pp. 482-4.
277. IFTU *Press Reports*, 4 March 1926; Larry Peterson, 'Internationalism and the British coal miners strike of 1926: the solidarity campaign of the KPD among the Ruhr miners' in van Holthoon and van der Linden, *Internationalism in the Labour Movement 1830-1940*, vol. 2, pp. 465-6, 479-84.
278. 57th TUC *Report*, 1925, p. 553; *Report of First British Commonwealth Labour Conference*, p. 37.
279. Graham Walker, *Thomas Johnston*, Manchester: MUP, 1988, ch. 3.
280. For Lansbury's rationale see his *My Life*, Constable, 1928, pp. 269-74.
281. Georges Fischer, *Le parti travailliste et la décolonisation de l'Inde*, Paris: François Maspero, 1966, p. 14.
282. *Lansbury's Labour Weekly*, 25 July 1925.
283. Bernard Porter, 'Fabians, imperialists and the international order' in Ben Pimlott, ed., *Fabian Essays in Socialist Thought*, Heinemann, 1984, pp. 54-64.
284. Gareth Griffith, *Socialism and Superior Brains. The political thought of Bernard Shaw*, Routledge, 1993, pp. 63-70.
285. Callaghan, *Rajani Palme Dutt*, p. 96.
286. NAFTA *Monthly Report*, August 1924, pp. 22-3.
287. Cited Griffith, *Socialism and Superior Brains*, p. 66.
288. See Fischer, *Parti travailliste*, p. 201.
289. *Daily Herald*, 5 September 1924.
290. *Daily Herald*, 8 September 1924
291. Raymond Postgate, *Lansbury's Labour Weekly*, 13 March 1926.
292. Adler, *Anglo-Russian Report*, pp. 24-9.
293. *Russia. The official report*, pp. 202, 210-11.
294. *Russia. The official report*, p. 217.
295. Bramley papers, box 1, TUC Russian delegation to Tomsky, 25 January 1925.
296. Peters, report on the delegation
297. TUC/Labour Party joint international department, minutes of LSI bureau and EC and joint meeting with IFTU, 1-6 January 1925.
298. 'H.T.' (Herbert Tracey), *Labour Magazine*, March 1925, pp. 501-3.
299. Russell, report of TUC delegation report, *Foreign Affairs*, June 1925, pp. 282-3.
300. He returned to the theme repeatedly following the publication of the report, e.g. *Lansbury's Labour Weekly*, 23 May, 27 June and 25 July 1925.

Chapter four

'Swimming against a flood': Emma Goldman in London

4.1 A HABIT OF TRUTH-TELLING

Adler knew from the start that there was no chance of a Labour Party edition of his brochure.[1] The ILP even declined to guarantee assistance with distribution as requested by its likeliest commercial publisher, Allen & Unwin.[2] Labour's international secretary William Gillies was privately sympathetic to Adler's point of view. The party's press officer Herbert Tracey interpolated his note of 'surprise and criticism' into a two-part review of the TUC report he wrote for the official *Labour Magazine*.[3] Reaction in Britain was nevertheless constrained by the report's official status. Meeting confidentially with Labour Party officers, Adler's assistant Oscar Pollak noted that they dared not precipitate a conflict with the TUC. Clynes, according to Gillies, was the only Labour leader willing to confront the issue.[4] Even MacDonald, despite his private disdain, appears to have made no public criticism. Hostile comment in conservative papers like the *Times* and *Morning Post* merely confirmed the issue's status as a litmus test. Purcell's sole recorded rebuttal of Adler, as if it were sufficiently damning in itself, was to point out that he was favourably quoted in such organs.[5]

There was one exception which confirmed the general rule. This was a body established in London in January 1925 and calling itself the British Committee for the Defence of Political Prisoners in Russia (BCDPPR). Similar committees existed in other countries, and there was some suggestion of the rump SDF taking a similar initiative in Britain.[6] The committee actually established, however, was a personal initiative of the Russian-born American anarchist Emma Goldman. Goldman was certainly qualified for such an endeavour. With her comrade Alexander Berkman she had been among the foreign-born leftists deported to Russia from the USA at the height of the post-war red scare. Though they travelled to Russia as supporters of the revolution, the suppression of the Kronstadt naval mutiny of March 1921 proved a defining moment in their disillusionment in the regime.

Leaving Russia at the end of the year, both Goldman and Berkman produced substantial testimonies alleging the betrayal of the revolution by the Bolsheviks, and it was this that Goldman sought to convey to a British Labour public after arriving in London in September 1924.[7]

It was, she said, like swimming against a flood.[8] There was no prominent British socialist for whom Kronstadt and its aftermath had provided a comparable moment of reckoning, and Goldman found the British Labour press almost entirely closed to her. Overlooked except by her biographers, her encounter with the British left does not bear out the view that the labour movement lacked any basic affinity with the Soviet regime.[9] It provides an outsider's perspective on the relation of Bolshevism and the British left that is worth recovering in its own right, and as a unique sidelight on the political culture epitomised by Purcell.

It was Purcell indeed who personified Goldman's frustrations, and her immediate object was to provide a counter-documentation of repression in response to the TUC report. Born three years and a thousand miles apart, these were lifelong activists living parallel lives on the left whose sole recorded point of intersection was Russia. When they first met in Petrograd in 1920, they apparently parted without antagonism, and four years later Goldman recorded almost affably their reacquaintance.[10] But as Russia was their one point of contact, so with Purcell's second visit it now engendered the strong sense of enmity that is documented in Goldman's papers. Goldman held firmly to the 'Russian gold' view of communist influence, and how it served to 'buy, corrupt and blind' figures like Purcell and his co-delegates.[11] She in turn was accused of moral and material dependence upon the goodwill of Bolshevism's enemies in the west. Neither allegation was entirely without foundation. What they nevertheless fail to explain is why Goldman could not have acted as Purcell did, nor Purcell as Goldman, no matter what the compensations. Conflicting responses to Bolshevism, and the political or financial connections which allowed them voice, must be located instead within the longer political trajectories that brought these ill-matched protagonists face-to-face on Russian soil in the summer of 1920.

There was, first of all, a palpable difference in the character of their internationalism. Born in Kovno, Lithuania, of German-Jewish parentage in 1869, Goldman was partly brought up in St Petersburg and could identify, or be identified, with Russia as a native Russian.[12] This Russian strand, however, was merely one component of her lived internationalism. Growing up speaking Yiddish, German and Russian, Goldman had subsequently learnt French as well as English in the USA, where she migrated with her family as a teenager. Three times she returned to Europe, twice attending international anarchist congresses, and on each occasion addressing political meetings in Britain. Goldman was thus an internationalist by circumstance as well as conviction, and through experiences of exile and deportation rather than the exchange of institutional credentials. There would have been a good deal in common between one of NAFTA's bank-holiday meets and the polyglot anarchist movement that Goldman first encountered in the USA. Nevertheless, if Purcell can be thought of as an insular internationalist, Goldman's by the same token was a form of cosmopolitan internationalism.

At the same time, their contrasting conceptions of social agency may be linked with the heavy sense of American symbolism so often remarked upon as present in Goldman's anarchism.[13] Biography as a rendition of celebrity is one indicator. When exceptionally Bob Smillie set aside the British trade unionist's reticence in this respect, his very title *My Life for Labour* conveyed the primacy of the collective even for the individual. How different in character the enterprise of collation and reconstruction that began with Goldman's own thousand-page autobiography, with its similarly expressive title *Living My Life*. The least panegyrical of Goldman's numerous biographers, Alice Wexler, notes how she had recourse to the labour memoirist's stock scenario of a first confrontation with an employer. The less familiar sequel, however, was not an attempt to rouse her fellows, but Goldman's decision to remove herself from the situation that she found so intolerable.[14] The individualism both of the action and of the form in which it was reconstructed were fully consistent with Goldman's particular articulation of anarchism. Accounts of anarchist thought commonly distinguish between its 'communist' and individualist strands.[15] In theory, Goldman saw her own anarchism as embracing both these strands and reconciling the 'sovereignty of the individual' with the 'theory of social harmony'.[16] She gave energetic support to labour and other social struggles and briefly even promoted a syndicalist league. This, however, was a wash-out, and Goldman was personally ambivalent about the very idea of meaningful collective action. In her own understanding of anarchism neither masses nor mass organisations, but the 'strong, beautiful, uncompromising personality', was accorded a sort of absolute precedence.[17]

Already in St Petersburg Goldman had been captivated by the heroism of the nihilists executed for Alexander II's assassination in 1881.[18] Her later adhesion to anarchism had followed the trial and execution in 1887 of the scapegoated 'Haymarket martyrs', whose dignity and courage in the face of judicial terror she was to invoke throughout her career.[19] With Berkman in 1892 she conceived the attempted assassination of the steel boss Henry Clay Frick, for which Berkman as its executant spent fourteen years in gaol. As registered by Goldman, the act not only demonstrated the sublimity of revolutionary idealism but also exposed the pitiful counterfoil of the 'people' who remained indifferent to such sacrifice.[20] Still more sensational was the execution of the Polish-American Leon Czolgosz for the assassination of

US President McKinley in 1901. Goldman had unwittingly inspired Czolgosz, and he henceforth represented for her the lone, dissenting individual whose actions were beyond all taint of interest or calculation.[21] Once again it served as contrast with the 'mob soul, so appalling in its massiveness', and the image of the revolutionary martyr became a staple of Goldman's oratory and journalism.[22]

In the years following Czolgosz's execution, Goldman came to see that her very notoriety was a resource with which she could take advantage of what she called the American 'craze for celebrities'.[23] From 1903 she organised a regular cross-country lecture tour lasting up to five months. Where once she had embraced the fin-de-siècle cult of the *attentat*, now she used the platform itself as a form of dynamite, and propaganda, not by the deed but as the deed itself. The same bearing of individual witness and affirmation of the absolute integrity of the executant was a quality she now increasingly identified with the iconoclasm of the creative writer. In 1906 she established *Mother Earth*, a 'monthly magazine devoted to social science and literature', and she henceforth regarded it as the *raison d'être* of her work.

The financial basis of such activities provided a further crucial difference with Purcell's trade-union career path. Professionally organised, and charging rather more than nominal sums for admission, Goldman's turn to a form of political performance marked a self-conscious break with proletarian anarchism. Speaking mainly in English, she moved beyond the 'foreign' milieux she now thought cut off from 'native' Americans, and in particular from the native intelligentsia. One staunch supporter observed that she was an 'excellent business woman' as well as orator.[24] Through the construction of a personal platform Goldman avoided the servitude of the salaried propagandist, while generating the funds that made possible her own continuing activism as well as the loss-making *Mother Earth*. It was thus that she explained her antipathy to party organisation:

> I stand outside. I take no pay ... There is no party to back me, but there is no party to say, 'You must do this and you must not do that. You are paid. You owe it to us. You must bow to the majority.' I bow to nothing except my idea of right.[25]

In the goodwill of 'individual friends' of means there were certainly parallels with a British contemporary like Lansbury.[26] In place of the European practice of a subscribing membership, or of the organised producer and consumer, Goldman's activities were nevertheless supported primarily by the paying audience. Like her populist contemporary William Jennings Bryan, hers was an entrepreneurial model of activism, controlled, 'not by a commercial syndicate or a political trust', but by the drawing power of personality.[27]

Not all anarchists were impressed.[28] Drawing on experiences in both America and Britain, Harry Kelly, an intimate of Goldman's, urged the European example of mass agitation against the 'introspective' concern with self-expression to be found in *Mother Earth*. 'Instead of participating in the trade unions, organizing the unemployed, or indulging in soap-box oratory', he complained, 'we rent comfortable halls and charge ten cents' admission. Added to that are, in many cases, ten cents' car fare, and Anarchism has become a luxury.'[29] Goldman justified such work as reaching out to the middle classes and made clear her revulsion from the 'dirty halls in squalid sections' which provided proletarian anarchism's characteristic milieu.[30] It was thus no longer on the most exploited classes that her hopes of emancipation rested, but on the intellectual proletarian who prefigured already a higher form of human consciousness.[31] When Berkman emerged from prison in 1906, he noted the chasm that had opened up between anarchism's 'plain, untutored underworld' and Goldman's development of a form of salon politics.[32]

Within this environment the elitist cast of Goldman's anarchism was further accentuated.[33] Her strong case for 'Minorities versus majorities' (1910) was as much a product of its intellectual moment as Michels's *Political Parties* (1911) or Ford and Foster's *Syndicalism* (1912). On the one hand, it told of the 'individual giants' on whom all human advance depended. On the other, it depicted the 'brainless, incompetent automatons' through whose cravenness and submission these few were 'misunderstood, hounded, imprisoned, tortured, and killed'.[34] Some at first managed to project such attitudes onto Bolshevism itself as a form of directive authority. Even the TUC's report from Russia prompted the *Herald* journalist W.N. Ewer to renewed analogies with H.G. Wells's Samurai order.[35] There was nevertheless little in the report to justify this view, and with Lenin's death in January 1924 brilliance of leadership seemed to give way to the flattening effect of bureaucracy.[36] Stalin, like Tomsky, was its embodiment, and the endorsement of British trade-union officials its certificate of validation. Trotsky was the obvious exception, as even Goldman grudgingly acknowledged.[37] At the same time, Trotsky's progressive exclusion from power only underlined the plight of the dissenting intellectual with whom Goldman so fervently identified.

Though Nietzsche stood the highest of Goldman's literary heroes, it was the playwright Henrik Ibsen who came most readily to mind while she was in Britain in 1924-6. A conservative himself, Ibsen had always had an appeal in anarchist circles. In particular, his play *An Enemy of the People* (1882), sometimes euphemistically rendered *An Enemy of Society*, had prompted public demonstrations of support on its performance in Paris and Barcelona.[38] Epitomised and articulated by its hero, Dr Stockmann, the play depicted the sovereign individual withstanding ostracism and persecution to expose deception in local public life. It not only conveyed the message that there was no higher value than the truth. It also depicted the free-thinking individual who alone recognised this value, and for this was hounded and derided by a bovine 'compact majority'. Goldman saw Stockmann as a 'giant figure' whose heroism lay in 'maintaining a truth against all odds'.[39] Its counterfoil once more was 'the multitude, the vulgar herd, the masses', who to Stockmann's outrage presumed themselves his equals.[40]

Ibsen was definitely hostile to the labour movement. According to Goldman's fellow Nietzschean James Huneker, his vision of the coming century lay in seeing how 'the aristocratic of spirit must enter into combat with the herd instinct of a depressing socialism'.[41] This again was hardly representative of all elements within anarchism. At the international anarchist congress held in Amsterdam in 1907, its most venerable agitator Enrico Malatesta claimed that Stockmann would soon have got off his pedestal had he had to work in a factory. Goldman in response maintained that individualism could be combined with a Kropotkinian social philosophy.[42] Nevertheless, in 'Minorities versus majorities' she upheld the Stockmann view that the minority was always right, and even alluded to the 'compact, immobile, drowsy mass' of Russian peasants that repudiated its own intelligentsia.[43]

Her revulsion against Bolshevism after Kronstadt may perhaps be compared with Ibsen's similar reaction to the Paris Commune. 'I owe this to the revolution, nailed to the Bolshevik cross, to the martyred Russian people, and to the deluded of the world', Goldman wrote in 1921, as she pledged herself to the regime's exposure.[44] More than that, she owed it to herself 'to bear future witness that I had not remained a silent party to the blackest betrayal of the Revolution'.[45] One of her British admirers described it as a 'habit of truth-telling'.[46] That commitment to bearing personal witness was to mean a bruising encounter with the compactness that Goldman found in the British left.

4.2 THAT DAMN FAKE PURCELLE

Goldman arrived in London as the crisis over the Russian treaties was reaching its height. By the time a welcoming dinner could be organised, the Labour government had fallen amidst a virulent campaign to tar it with its Bolshevik associations. Josiah Wedgwood, who presided at the dinner, was an old-fashioned radical now sporting Labour colours. Bertrand Russell, who had already impressed Goldman in Russia, delivered what even the anarchist *Freedom* described as 'the most complete avowal of Anarchist convictions of the evening'.[47] Goldman, in her own words, then exploded a bomb by announcing her intention of devoting her time in Britain to the exposure of Soviet rule.[48] While Russell stated the case against government in general, the *Manchester Guardian* wryly noted, Goldman's stand was against this one form of government alone.[49] 'Of course, the Conservatives rejoice', she confided after the dinner; 'nothing better could have come to them than my declaration of treating the Russian situation'.[50]

She was soon to discover how politically damaging this could prove. In pursuit of her objects Goldman envisaged a committee that would be 'non political, if possible, but of a predominant labour element'.[51] To this end, the 'very brilliant' Harold Laski hosted a meeting to introduce her to figures from the intellectual left, in most cases identified with the ILP.[52] Goldman herself effected further likely connections, but the response in almost every case was negative. Some were straightforwardly antagonistic: like those around the *Herald* who had assisted Goldman in getting into Britain.[53] Others, like Henry Nevinson and the Pethick Lawrences, excused themselves by other commitments or by a primary concern with evils for which their own government was responsible.[54] Even Wedgwood, while at this stage pledging his support, explained that his immediate priority was drafting Labour Party pamphlets on the land question.[55]

The commonest response was a relativising emphasis on the context of Bolshevism, whether that meant Russian history, the hostile international environment or the possible alternatives to the regime which alone seemed presently conceivable. Purcell's old SDF supporter Lady Warwick warned of anything that might play into the hands of Tsarist restorationists.[56] The radical sexologist Havelock Ellis felt that every social condition was affected by the 'social condition that preceded it'.[57] Even Russell, on whom Goldman set such store, declined to sign any statement construable as opposition to Bolshevism itself, on grounds that no better form of government was as yet imaginable in Russia.[58] Enumerating such objections, Laski suggested that the choice before Goldman lay between a 'general attack on Bolshevism', which Laski could not himself support, or a campaign specifically over the prisoners. But even the latter, if it were to be effective, would have to be under some other than Goldman's avowedly 'anti-Bolshevik' auspices.[59]

Such a response was in some ways predictable. Since the Hamburg conference of the LSI, responsible figures in the British labour movement had shown a definite preference for private representations to the Soviets over any such matter of controversy. There was some encouragement for this approach when the formation of the Labour government was followed by an amnesty for defendants in the SR show trial, which Rakovsky ascribed primarily to 'willingness to meet the wishes expressed by Labour Party circles'.[60] As successively Mensheviks, SRs and revolutionary syndicalists sought publicity for similar issues, the stock response in Britain was to pursue the matter in the same discreet and non-confrontational way.[61] This was not necessarily ineffectual: when a commission of enquiry was established over the Solovetsky prisoners, even Abramovich highlighted the contribution of 'our English comrades' as well as the general rousing of European socialist opinion.[62] It was nevertheless clear, as Brailsford put it, that the British stood alone in such matters. Brailsford himself exercised considerable influence as editor of the ILP's *New Leader*. He did not deny what he called the barbaric and alien aspects of Bolshevism, and Goldman was to describe him as the one socialist editor who did not altogether refuse material hostile to the regime.[63] Even so, with Russia currently providing the dominant line of cleavage in British politics, Brailsford thought it politically inconceivable that Labour should join with its fiercest opponents in attacking the Bolsheviks.[64]

Heedless of such signals, Goldman convinced herself that it was the TUC delegates' return from Russia that put paid to her plans. 'The damnable report of Purcelle has already born its rotten fruit', she wrote after the fruitless meeting at Laski's. 'God damn that fake Purcelle.'[65] Lady Warwick had said she was unwilling to act pending the delegates' return.[66] Laski suggested that any campaign would need to develop out of their report.[67] At a predominantly Fabian gathering attended by Goldman, Young arrived in person to eulogise the Soviets.[68] Even Wedgwood now had second thoughts: 'After all Miss G, you are out of Russia too long and Mr Young has been there now, I could not doubt his word.'[69] It was thus that Goldman's campaign came to centre on the rebuttal of the delegation, both in pamphlet form and through a series of public meetings. Like Adler, Goldman criticised the delegates' lack of appropriate skills and independent sources of information. She also stressed the treacherous role of advisers trained in the covering up of state crimes, and thought Young a venal and repulsive 'rat'.[70] What others saw as context, she, again like Adler, saw as the typical double standards of the British by which methods unthinkable at home were seen as tolerable if applied to foreigners.[71]

There was little that was distinctively anarchist about these arguments. It was nevertheless on her anarchist contacts that Goldman, with obvious reluctance, came to depend. Wedgwood had protested at the use of the committee as a personal vehicle and declined to decorate it as a 'dummy shop window figure'.[72] S.E. Morison, an 'American professor who teaches history at Oxford', also disappeared from the committee list, and perhaps had returned to America.[73] The committee's only remaining public figures were the writer Rebecca West and the anarchist union leader John Turner.[74] West was a steadfast supporter and a journalist enjoying prominent connections. She was not, however, experienced in political campaigning, and she muddied the issue by suggesting that Russia, like everywhere else, got the government it subconsciously desired – in this instance, an oriental merging of the individual into the All.[75] Following a launch at London's South Place Institute, Goldman alone addressed a series of meetings in various provincial centres. The best of them was that in Norwich, with its ILP and Socialist League traditions. There was no real organisation, however, and a proposed conference of union officers never took place.[76] The mainstream Labour press offered no support or publicity.

In a double sense, Goldman felt defeated by the pull of party. She quickly discovered that Britons did not share what Russell called the 'unintelligible' American fondness for the paid public lecture. Ostrogorski in his book on the modern party had described its displacement by the partisan public meeting.[77] A propagandist body like the National Guilds League noted how its decline was exacerbated by mass unemployment.[78] In London, the anarchists had reportedly not held an indoor public meeting in years.[79] There were of course alternatives. Turner described his recreation as 'Lecturing for Socs, etc, of workers too poor to pay fees', and Goldman knew from her earlier visits that the outdoor speaking pitch was as British as 'bacon for breakfast'.[80] Indeed, her autobiography refers rather dramatically to the weekly rounds she now undertook, 'from one end of London to the other, in rain, sleet, fog and chill'.[81] There is little evidence of this in her correspondence, where she clearly states her refusal to undertake such forms of propaganda.[82] Nor was there much attempt to link up even with such obvious potential allies as Sylvia Pankhurst.[83] Goldman's political capital was celebrity. She resented the contrivance of a committee and forgot how even in the USA celebrity did not simply attach itself to the individual who desired it.[84] Instead, she complained that the British moved in flocks and shunned any event not sponsored by their own 'society, party or group'.[85] 'Individual endeavour' had no chance, and Goldman concluded that she could never hope to establish herself in Britain.[86]

Party was still more an impediment in the sense of collective loyalty and constraint. The years after 1918 were ones of exceptional volatility in British politics, both of voters and of politicians. Underlying this surface movement there was nevertheless emerging what was almost a two-camps conception of political allegiance, one whose very rawness put a premium on the symbols of cohesion. If only as a shared repulsion of the Conservatives, Russia at this crucial moment thus helped provide the labour movement with a form of rudimentary collective identity. Declining to recycle the Comintern's stock anti-reformist slogans, even the communists noted sarcastically that a Labour Party defending the Russian treaties was 'highly unlikely to inaugurate at this juncture a campaign against Russia'.[87] Conversely, when the twelve communist leaders were imprisoned in 1925, Goldman herself expressed admiration at how the wider labour movement came to their defence in a way inconceivable in the States.[88]

Sometimes she saw this as the hypertrophy of organisation, sometimes as a solidaristic herd instinct. Either way, party as Goldman saw it loosened purse strings, provided a press, mustered an audience and endowed its leading figures with authority. Again and again she complained that in Britain more than anywhere else political lines were 'very rigidly drawn' with everybody 'comfortably tucked away' in a party organisation.[89] Tellingly, she was most readily accepted into the middle-class feminist networks which to some extent cut across these party divisions.[90] These were exemplified by West and by Lady Rhondda, proprietor of the weekly *Time and Tide*, virtually the only left-leaning publication in which Goldman managed to publish.[91] Even at Lady Rhondda's, however, Goldman observed how Labour women were conspicuous by their absence.[92]

Goldman was not oblivious to the pull of party in this wider sense. Pragmatically, she avoided the use of Menshevik sources, and she favoured a clear separation between the cause of revolutionists (to be supported) and that of 'counter-revolutionaries' (best avoided).[93] She cannot have failed to notice that figures like Russell, Laski and Brailsford co-operated with the New York-based International Committee for Political Prisoners and contributed to its publication *Letters from Russian Prisons*. H.G. Wells, who also contributed to the same publication, thought Goldman 'the deviationingist old organiser of futility that ever dressed up in embellishing vanity as benevolence'.[94] What mattered more to ILP-type contributors was that the exposure of Bolshevik prison conditions, however trenchant, should not imply a generalised hostility to the regime itself. Indeed, the editor of the American volume, Roger Baldwin, went somewhat further in characterising Bolshevism as a worthy experiment in social reconstruction whose blemishes alone required correction.[95] At the earlier Hamburg congress, Brailsford and the British delegates did not object to condemning the Bolsheviks' 'continued use of terrorism' within the context of a general resolution which also opposed outside intervention. What they did object to was a separate anti-Bolshevik resolution signalling a 'declaration of war' against the regime itself.[96] Goldman, however, was oblivious to such distinctions, and what most discredited her campaign was not her deviationingism but her perceived convergence with political reaction.

Repeatedly she suggested that she found this convergence a mental agony. 'The Tories have taken a stand against the Communists, in France they are being hounded, the Pope comes out against them', she recorded in a moment of candour. 'And here am I doing the same.' It was a desperate situation and little wonder that 'everybody refuses to join me'.[97] Goldman did not, however, take the one obvious step that might have dispelled any misunderstanding. She had earlier declined to remain in Sweden on condition that she refrain from anti-Soviet propaganda.[98] She was, however, prepared to desist from other forms of propaganda, and in Britain she understood from the start that a Conservative government was 'not likely to bother me as long as I lecture or write on Russia'.[99] Though she claimed to have been unaware of undertakings made on her behalf to refrain from domestic political interventions, she was punctilious in observing just such conditions as a Conservative home secretary might have imposed.[100]

At the inaugural meeting of her committee, Wedgwood, like Russell before him, stressed the need to oppose dictatorship in whatever form it took. Goldman, on the other hand, concentrated on the Bolsheviks alone, and according to the *Times* she underlined the threat that it posed internationally:

> That it was their desire and intention to establish their dictatorship, as conceived and directed by Moscow, in every country was best proved by the fact that ... the Russian Government spent hundreds of millions of roubles for its propaganda in every country.[101]

Labour had just been subjected to a lurid and exaggerated red-scare propaganda unprecedented in British history.[102] Goldman's private apprehensions of a Labour government were not apparently that dissimilar.[103] From New York, Baldwin argued that 'attacked by all the capitalist governments of the world and an issue in their internal as well as external affairs, it is natural that labour and radicals should on the whole be cautious about that which is also attacked by their bitterest enemies'.[104] For reformist socialists in many countries, the bitterest enemy was communism itself and attitudes to Russia were shaped accordingly. To Goldman's clear dismay, it was in Britain that the constraint described by Baldwin was most powerfully felt.

She likened her position to that of Dr Stockmann, reviled and vilified by the very people to whom she had devoted a lifetime of 'complete consecration to the cause of humanity'.[105] She was not, however, so alone as Stockmann. Arriving in Britain, she had promptly written to Berkman of Bolshevism's popularity with the cowardly Anglo-Saxons.[106] The very same morning, however, half of Britain spluttered over its breakfast at the news of the fabricated Zinoviev letter. Two weeks later Goldman herself observed that Bolshevism had 'caught the fancy of the mob'.[107] 'Invitations from Lady So and So' came 'at least several times a week', and for a time she was the favoured guest of 'people who have magnificent homes, with butlers, chauffeurs, and what not, they claim to be intensely interested in light on Russia...'[108] The *Daily Express* had at first pretended horror and amazement on discovering the 'Red Virgin of the Commune' living quietly in a London side street.[109] West, however, badgered its proprietor Beaverbrook into keeping his 'rabbit-witted subordinates' in order, and insisted that Goldman was an 'Anti-Bolsh' eye-witness second to none.[110] In the case of the *Express*, Goldman declined the 'steep sum' offered her on grounds of the paper's sensationalism.[111] The invidiousness of her position remained.

Stockmann had described a party as a sausage-machine, grinding brains together in a single mash.[112] In small-town Norway, or even Bolshevik Russia, perhaps it was. But party in Britain in 1925 was more fundamentally a line of cleavage and dissociation, whose gelling agent on either side was repulsion of the compact mass that confronted it. Biographers of Laski suggest that Goldman's potential supporters were deterred by her associations with extremism.[113] Goldman gave the same impression in her autobiography.[114] If anything the reverse was true. Goldman did not experience universal ostracism, but a society deeply divided over Russia. The force of party in this sense was nowhere better demonstrated than by her anarchist comrades who in theory had no party.

4.3 ANARCHISM AND THE ENGLISH PSYCHOLOGY

Goldman regarded her anarchist comrades with something like contempt. The vigorous movement she had known when previously in Britain had been decimated by forced and voluntary returns to Russia. The monthly *Freedom* was said to have eighty-three subscribers.[115] Thomas Keell, its editor, was a 'living corpse' who left you paralysed when he did not give you fits.[116] Her strongest supporter, William C. Owen, conceived of anarchism in antipathy to socialism and affinity with nineteenth-century liberalism.[117] Otherwise her committee comprised only cadavers: lifeless, uninteresting, uninterested and 'utterly hopeless' when it came to efficiency, vision or enterprise.[118] In Bristol there were glimpses of a livelier tradition, and Goldman spent a fortnight in South Wales addressing meetings in the Rhondda and the anthracite district. Even here, however, support was less conspicuous than communist opposition. Goldman concluded that there was 'no anarchist movement in this country if ever there was one, and … not enough comrades who could, even if they would create a movement'.[119]

The one person whom Goldman would have exempted from these criticisms was the Shop Assistants' official John Turner. Remarkably, Turner was not only the one trade-union leader to support Goldman's committee but a member of the Russian delegation against which its ire was principally directed.[120] It is hard to imagine a more delicate predicament. Five years Goldman's senior, Turner's involvement with anarchism went back, as hers did, to the Haymarket affair. In the days of William Morris, he was already prominent in the anarchist faction of the Socialist League, and twice he went on American speaking tours where he established close relations with Goldman herself.[121] On the first occasion, in 1897, he undertook the first extensive English-language speaking tour there since the Haymarket killings and provided the immediate stimulus for Goldman to do likewise.[122] Six years later, threatened with deportation under laws introduced after McKinley's assassination, Turner was the focus of a free-speech campaign that drew Goldman back into public activity after a short period undercover.[123] Little remembered today, he was a considerable figure for whom Goldman had a genuine respect.

He may also be regarded as a second point of intersection between Goldman and Purcell. In Goldman's recollection, Turner thought his place 'among the rank and file' and refused the lure of 'so-called "public affairs"'.[124] Like Purcell's, on the other hand, his radicalism was that of the full-time union officer, not the grassroots labour activist. An initiator of the United Shop Assistants' Union, in 1898 Turner had become national organiser of the Amalgamated Shop Assistants' Union (ASAU), where he worked closely for a time with Margaret Bondfield, and where his eloquence won the young Mary Macarthur over to union activism.[125] For a few months in 1907 he published the anarcho-syndicalist *Voice of Labour*, including Harry Kelly's 'notes and reflections from America'. He also had some involvement with the ISEL, and like Purcell was later drawn by the idea of industrial guilds and a possible guild of distributive workers.[126] His main preoccupations, however, were indistinguishable from those of any other union official. It was the Webbs' trade-union *History* that he lent Macarthur as a labour movement primer, and in its daily practice Turner's anarchism translated into a decidedly low-key commitment to direct action.

In 1913 he attended the international syndicalist congress in London. According to Wayne Thorpe, Turner was among those who 'virtually vied in rebelliousness' at a closing rally.[127] His congress address nevertheless provided a union officer's gloss on the syndicalist truism that it was 'minorities that always made for progress':

> In the Trade Union movement they had taken up the Syndicalist position almost before the word itself was known; and ... he had worked in a quiet way in that movement, because it gave him an opportunity to express his ideas and opinions. ... He was sorry to say that the rank and file of the Trade Unions were not with the Syndicalists. He was an official of a Trade Union ... and he knew that the members of the Trade Unions were not so advanced as many of the leaders of those bodies ... Syndicalists should not imagine that the masses were with them; it was their work to bring them along; not only by talking, they must ... be willing to do the detail work of the Trade Unions, and they must show that theoretically they understood the position better than their fellows. If they did that, another thirty years might see the triumph of the principles enunciated that week. (Applause.)[128]

Just months before the war that exploded all such vistas, only a compatriot of Sidney Webb's could have spoken from an anarchist platform in quite this way. Goldman observed that Turner was not one of those 'sensational and bombastic reformers' who choked their ideas down your throat.[129] Usually he is described as a moderate; and an anarchist comrade described him as 'one of the most blatant reactionaries with which the Trade Union movement was ever cursed'.[130]

If nothing else, Turner's selection for the TUC's Russian delegation confirmed its representative character. A member of the general council only since 1922, Turner had worked energetically to secure Goldman's entry into Britain and his was the original idea of a reception to present her to a wider audience.[131] Pollitt in a note to Moscow described him as the group's 'only unsatisfactory delegate' and 'by no means sympathetic to the Dictatorship of the Proletariat'.[132] Another note described him as 'the only one who might cause trouble on his return because … there might not be enough "liberty" in Russia'.[133] Through Goldman and other contacts, Turner obtained details of prisoners whose cases could be taken up in Russia. In Russia itself, he was assisted by Sophie Kropotkin, whom as an ardent Kropotkinite he would have known in Britain. He also met the disillusioned former Wobbly Big Bill Haywood, and sought through the delegation to have representations made on behalf of the 'politicals' in the Butyrka prison.[134]

Though constrained by the embargo on individual statements of opinion, Turner moved the BCDPPR's inaugural resolution demanding rights of free expression and association, and he circulated the audience with a report he had compiled on the imprisoned revolutionaries.[135] Subsequently he was also to publish an article on this theme in the UDC monthly *Foreign Affairs*.[136] Given its misrepresentation in some press articles, he also took the opportunity to clarify his view of the regime in an interview with the New York *Daily Forward*. While this registered workers' economic and social gains under the revolution, it also described communism as a reign of terror and alleged that its use of police and espionage was worse even than under the Tsars.[137] The interview was given a wide circulation by the American Federation of Labour, and *Pravda* launched editorially into Turner in what Goldman conceded was 'a most terrible fashion'.[138]

To Goldman's consternation, Turner nevertheless put his name to the TUC report without any dissenting statement. Though he claimed to have had the document 'very considerably' modified, it is difficult to detect his positive input and it specifically repudiated the idea of a reign of terror.[139] On certain points Turner may have exercised an unspoken editorial veto: while the delegates were in Georgia his name had been missing from a declaration endorsing its Bolshevik rulers, and the omission of its more flagrant formulations in the published report may have been one of the 'very important particulars' Turner claimed to have had altered.[140] Even so, his signature helped validate claims with which he must have felt profoundly uncomfortable. Countering IFTU critics, Bramley pointedly observed that the party included members 'in the closest possible association for over thirty years' with Russia's current oppositionists.[141] Understandably, Goldman thought the 'English psychology' strange indeed if Turner could endorse such a document while simultaneously voicing criticisms no less outspoken than her own.[142]

More specifically this was an English labour movement psychology that reflected Turner's union environment in both positive and negative ways. Positively, it meant the recognition of those ties of collective allegiance which Goldman held in such disdain. Turner bristled at her dismissal of his colleagues as a 'crooked gang'. Purcell in particular he thought 'as honest as mistaken – one of the straightest amongst our labour men'.[143] Like many a later communist party organiser, Goldman despaired of this inability of the British union activist to 'stand out against his Trade Union gang'. Out of a misconceived sense of loyalty Turner had consciously and deliberately misrepresented the beliefs to which he otherwise gave such cogent expression. 'He has been a Trade Unionist all his life at the expense of his Anarchism. Now he must pay the price.'[144]

His lifelong trade unionism in any case meant that he was more responsive than Goldman to the vaunted achievements as well as shortcomings of the new Russia. At the South Place Institute, while he condemned the Bolsheviks' appropriation of the revolution, Turner also suggested that Russia's 'great political experiment' promised more than any parliamentary government if only it were disencumbered of the party dictatorship.[145] Goldman found it risible that Turner should have come away impressed by the accessibility of Bolshevik officials and that he 'thought it marvellous that a man whom he used to know in the East End of London … is now a Judge in Moscow'.[146] The disinclination to condemn outright was nevertheless shared by other working-class anarchists. Some months later Goldman met Fred Charles, another veteran Socialist Leaguer, who had spent seven years in prison following the Walsall bomb plot of 1892. For two hours she and Charles had it out over Russia, but he persisted in regarding it as the 'greatest socialist experiment' – always at this early stage it was an experiment – and one that could not have been attempted without the Bolsheviks.[147] Turner meanwhile claimed that he was guided in his stance by 'practically all sections' of the Russian anarchists, and that even these took exception to the manner, though not the substance, of Goldman's criticisms. Goldman in reply denied their competence to make such a judgement given that they were not properly informed as to her activities.[148]

In a negative sense, Turner was anxious throughout to distance his own position on Russia from that of political reactionaries. Bolshevism was not to be attacked to the exclusion of other evils, still less as a way of implicitly condoning them. On behalf of the BCDPPR Turner stressed that its sponsors had the right to condemn the Bolshevik terror precisely because of their opposition equally to tyranny under the Tsars or within the British empire.[149] Like most within the British labour movement, he had no objection in principle to writing for the commercial press. Even so, when he was approached for his views on Russia he demanded equal scope to describe social conditions in Britain and the treatment of political prisoners in Ireland. The condition was naturally refused: his views were sought, said Turner, to 'distract from the infamies of the Government here', and hence provide not a spotlight but a screen. What Turner called a 'sense of proportion' was less an issue of light and shade in Russia, more a recognition that other truths required affirmation and other lies exposure. Pointedly he reminded Goldman of Burke's lamentable role at the time of the French revolution.[150]

Excluded from the left-wing press, Goldman felt she had no alternative but to use the mainstream commercial media. She had already provoked controversy by publishing in the *New York World*.[151] In Britain, similarly, she found in the *Times* and *Sunday Times* both an audience and a necessary source of remuneration.[152] Her committee was in penurious condition and Goldman insisted that she would not have it maintained from reactionary sources.[153] She did not, however, feel that this constraint extended to the reactionary press. '*I will speak out and I will be heard*', she insisted. 'I had stood out on more than one occasion against popular prejudice, and now too I must stand out. There is no other way for me.'[154]

To Goldman it was daring to be a Daniel. To her detractors it was consorting with the lions. 'Vilest of them all', her fellow anarchist Guy Aldred denounced her as a revolutionary scab and traitor.[155] Ethel Carnie Holdsworth expressed her heartfelt concern for the Russian prisoners in the form of verse which she offered *Freedom*. Nevertheless, her husband and political collaborator Alfred Holdsworth expressed his outrage at Goldman's lining up with the 'dirtiest hacks of the dirtiest Press that has ever polluted the minds of the masses'.[156] When Goldman publicised her refusal to address a Women's Guild of Empire branch, Aldred scathingly wondered what sort of revolutionary it was that got invited there.[157] Thankfully Goldman did not also publicise the invitation she received from 'A member of British fascisti'.[158] At her Manchester meeting, an audience member describing herself as an old comrade asked her in broken English if she was 'out for a better living'.[159] Turner's selfdefence also contained the implicit reproach: 'I decline to lend my name *to their game!*'[160] Even Berkman declined to be associated with Goldman's campaign, and thought her position untenable both on principled grounds and on pragmatic ones of not alienating one's primary audience.[161] There can have been few more reactionary home secretaries than the notorious 'Jix', or William Joynson-Hicks, who had occupied that position since the 1924 general election. That Jix left Goldman unmolested underlines just how compromised her position had become.

Her marriage of convenience to the South Wales miner Jim Colton was intended to answer both public and private misgivings.[162] Goldman did not need Aldred to point out how she continued to lecture freely while communists were being deported. 'I knew it was because of my stand on Russia', she confided when at last her marriage secured a British passport, 'and I felt rotten ...'.[163] Even at this stage, there is little evidence of her taking up the 'real work' now open to her on British issues.[164] She had discovered a personally and politically congenial publisher in the anarchist-leaning C.W. Daniel, and at last she had the satisfaction of seeing through an integral edition of her book on Russia.[165] As luck would have it, its publication coincided with the gaoling of the twelve communist leaders, and to some favourable reviewers it seemed to justify it.[166] Goldman described herself as sick with disgust not to be able to take a stand on the prisoners' behalf. In what sense she was 'forced to keep silent' is nevertheless unclear, and it is difficult to reconcile with her compulsion for speaking out.[167] When at last Goldman did so, it was to indicate her exasperation with those who made so much of British prisoners and so little of Russian ones.[168]

Whatever had Turner so entangled, it was not the grip of party or the 'terrific centralisation' of which Goldman complained.[169] Pollak, who like Adler was a member of the Austrian SDAP, was no less critical than Goldman of Purcell, the TUC delegation and what it represented. Nevertheless, his explanation of the phenomenon was the very reverse of hers:

> For the British movement, with its wide and loose organisation, with its broadness of mind and weakness of theory, with its freedom of individual thought and action, a number of men speak who cannot in themselves represent all its shades or currents of thought, nor pledge it beyond a certain limit of general agreement. The Continental party is otherwise. It is a rigid body, marching in closed ranks and guided by a unanimously accepted doctrine which dominates and determines all its actions.

For the continental worker, the appearance of a communist party, however small, seemed an affront to this 'indivisible unit', and its mere existence a shock 'quite unintelligible to his British colleague, accustomed as he is to the variety of organisation and opinion which has made his movement broad and all-inclusive'.[170] In another article, Pollak offered the further astute observation that the delegation represented a reaction against the Labour government of trade-union 'bosses', who in Austria would also have felt more closely bound by their political leadership.[171] Again, it was the perception of communism as existential threat that in other European countries reinforced this closing of ranks. Only in Britain, 'within the safe limits of an old and assured democracy', was communism regarded as 'but a different shade of opinion, adding one other to those already existing'.[172] Some years later Beatrice Webb put the same point in more ideological terms. It was the absence in Britain of the positive creed of 'Continental Marxists', she argued, that spared it the fratricidal destructiveness of doctrinal rivalry – 'the most bitter of all divisions of opinion'.[173] Even here, following the onset of Class Against Class at the end of the 1920s, Beatrice felt by 1932 that the 'silly and hostile little CP' was performing a similar role, and that if only the Comintern were dissolved British Labour would be free to become 'definitely Communist in its faith, and a firm ally of the USSR'.[174] There was never any chance that British labour would be communist in its faith. But at the time of Goldman's visit, as even communists seemed accepted as just another shade of opinion, it did for the time being appear to be the best ally the Bolsheviks had in the western world.

4.4 A NATION OF SHOPKEEPERS?

Goldman's attitude to the English could be characterised as cosmopolitan anglophobia. As an American among Europeans, she noted how Londoners lacked efficiency or speed, and with a wistful remembrance of American typists complained of finding only the same 'slowness and incompetency' as in Germany'.[175] More distinctively English was a dankness of climate and personality, as if in mutually reinforcing conspiracy to afflict her with tedium and lumbago. The weather was enough 'to drive one to utter despair', she wrote, not from Siberia, but from St John's Wood. 'And if added to the rain, gloom and penetrating chill to one's physical being is the English temperament in the face of deep human suffering, then one is altogether paralyzed.'[176] One hardly knows if she meant the Russian prisoners or her sciatica. 'I have met hundreds of people', she confided, 'but not ... one single English person who has shown enough warm ordinary humanity to evince interest in either myself or my work'.[177] Clutching at her throat after meeting them, or seeking solace from the London vapours in a Turkish bath, Goldman endured what she freely described as hell.[178]

There was a further national quality which Goldman characterised as the 'shopkeepers' mind and psychology'.[179] In this she displayed what was more a European than an American sensibility, reflecting her immersion in writers like Nietzsche and their deep-seated depreciation of the commercialism and utilitarianism of the British. Ironically, this critique of the Anglo-Saxon world-view was by this time more commonly directed at America itself. Even within Britain it could be traced back to Dickens and beyond, and Stendhal and Tocqueville had noted how Americans appeared to the English just as the English appeared to the French.[180] While this was to be confirmed in Purcell's impressions of America, Goldman in staring back inverted the image. Occasionally she linked the Anglo-Saxon nations in their incapacity for the heroic.[181] But far more often the English appeared to her, at least in this respect, precisely as Americans did to the English themselves.

More specifically, she made the connection with Labour's Russophilia. Goldman largely heeded Turner's disapproval of depicting the TUC delegates simply as a 'crooked gang' corrupted by Moscow.[182] She did however allege a motivation of material self-interest which they further identified with that of British commerce as a whole.[183] Privately Goldman described Russia as the 'fleshpot for International Capitalism' and the means of putting it back on its feet.[184] Her comrade Max Nettlau thought advisers like Young 'emerited secret service agents' testing the ground for British investments.[185] Goldman herself described the ILP and TUC as middlemen between British investors and Russian monopolists, contriving at once to 'perpetuate the superstition of the masses' and to 'strengthen the desire of British investors to avail themselves of the unlimited opportunities for loot Russia offers'.[186] According to Goldman's autobiography, the ILPer Clifford Allen explicitly preferred such concerns to any commitment to the truth as a value in itself.[187] Once more the argument recalls *An Enemy of the People*, where this higher ideal of truth is set against the petty financial self-interest epitomised by the printer Aslaksen.[188]

From Losovsky in Moscow to Samuel Gompers and the *American Federationist*, this view of Labour's Russian policy was widely advanced at the time.[189] It is also supported in a substantial academic literature. Notably in Stephen White's *Britain and the Bolshevik Revolution*, these primary considerations of trade and employment are amply documented, and the labour movement appears as the virtual instrument of a hegemonic business interest.[190] Purcell himself made frequent allusion to trading arguments in the House of Commons.[191] To coincide with the TUC Russian report, he also put his name to a somewhat technical case for the extension to Russia of the provisions of the Overseas Trades and Trades Facilities acts.[192] Bramley, in his preface, sought to extricate the issue from 'party politics' as one in which capital and labour had a common interest.[193] According to White, even radical elements within the labour movement saw little connection between Russia's professed socialism and their own more utilitarian considerations. As a market for goods produced by British workers, Purcell duly observed in Cinderford, 'it was immaterial whether Russia called itself red, blue, green or any other colour'.[194]

Trade unionists like Purcell do not much figure in these accounts.[195] More importantly, focus on the Russian issue alone, within a tightly confined chronological period, may obscure the distinctly political and even symbolical significance that was attached to Russian trade. It is certainly true that much was made of employment arguments. In connection with its attitudes to empire, P.S. Gupta observed that the most important line of differentiation within the British labour movement was that separating industries which were export-orientated from those which were not.[196] There are parallels here with the claims which some advanced regarding the complementarity of the British and Russian economies, as exporters respectively of manufactured goods and of food and raw materials.[197] Purcell in Coventry stressed the possible boost to employment, particularly in the engineering industry. White also notes how engineering employers were most active in promoting a Russian trade agenda, while a flurry of interest in the ailing guilds movement also saw the projected establishment of a National Engineering Guild as one geared to 'the specific development of Russian trade'.[198] Mining MPs visiting Russia in 1925 were similarly concerned to investigate trading opportunities in both general and sectoral terms.[199] Purcell and Bramley also made a good deal of the comparative disadvantage British industry suffered through its anti-Soviet policies.[200]

That Russia had this intrinsic economic significance was nevertheless far from clear. Between the wars its share of international trade was never more than two per cent, and even Britain, a considerable trading partner, had a massively greater interest in its empire.[201] In 1925, as the level of trade with Russia was beginning to pick up, Baldwin as prime minister dismissed the prospect of large-scale manufacturing exports.[202] From within the UDC tradition, the more sophisticated argument was thus advanced of Russian trade as a stimulus to wider reconstruction. In the pamphlet issued under Morel and Purcell's joint names the ending of Russia's exclusion was thus urged in the interests of a general restoration of European trade, not least the Russo-German trade on which the more substantial Anglo-German trade was seen as depending.[203] Ironically, this could be seen as conducing to Germany's payment of reparations under the Dawes plan, to which left-wing supporters of Russian trade were generally opposed.[204] It certainly sat uneasily with Purcell's distinction elsewhere between Russia as potential customer and a Dawes-compliant Germany as 'full-blooded competitor'.[205]

The trading arguments were therefore highly complex ones. For committed supporters, these were nevertheless somewhat secondary considerations. The origins of Labour solidarity with the Soviets predated any significant prospect of trading activity. Pollitt took issue with Losovsky on this point, evoking a spontaneous movement of solidarity from which the subsequent delegations and trade interventions had all arisen.[206] Certainly, at the time of the first Labour delegation in 1920 the trading issue was peripheral and not associated with the relief of unemployment.[207] Through UDCers like Brailsford and Dorothy Buxton, the conception of Russia as breadbasket and market for manufactured goods was certainly advanced through the Labour Party's Advisory Committee on International Questions.[208] But even in 1924, only one of the nineteen chapters in the TUC report on Russia dealt with foreign commerce.[209]

For proponents like Purcell, Russian trade was therefore less a motive than an argument. As such, its deployment and phrasing varied according to context and audience, and it was especially serviceable in addressing those who had no interest in Russia's claims as socialist exemplar. 'There are other arguments for higher aspects of the question of relations with Russia', ran one characteristic TUC presentation, 'but this economic argument ought to be convincing enough to impress even a Tory diehard'.[210] In a deputation to just such diehards in the Baldwin government, Purcell warned of Russia being pushed 'the other way' if deprived of the 'civilising influences of the West'.[211] This was the 'civilisation through trade' argument which had had much currency in government circles, particularly under Lloyd George, and which was carried into the labour movement by a figure like Frank Wise.[212] Whether or not such lines of argument implicitly recognised the Conservatives' ideological hegemony, they did certainly register that these and not Labour remained Britain's dominant party of government. It did not, however, prevent Purcell, in a rather different context, from simultaneously declaring his hope that British workers, having 'long been fairly conscious of our own strength, may learn from the Russians how to use it'.[213]

Once again, apparent inconsistencies are more readily understandable if viewed as a form of rhetorical strategy varying according to audience or interlocutor. When subsequently western communist parties embraced the cause of east-west trade, nobody believed that trade rather than communism provided the motive-force. Though Purcell, unlike the communists, was answerable to a wider constituency, the same ambivalence is easily discernible. On the eve of the 1924 election, he and Swales issued a statement for the TUC urging full diplomatic and economic relations with Russia. This was not, they insisted, because they approve of the 'policy, methods, or principles of Soviet rule', any more than they supported trade with Turkey on similar grounds.[214] Citing a similar analogy, White suggests that this perfectly encapsulates British Labour's position on Russia.[215] How convincing it was, however, will depend on whether the TUC at any time promoted Turkish trade in any discernible way whatsoever.

To appreciate the specificity of the Russian case it is therefore important to broaden the perspective both geographically and chronologically. Urging the similarity between the TUC's pro-Bolshevism and conventional attitudes to empire, Adler argued that the only difference between Purcell and Jimmy Thomas was that Purcell took his stand with Soviet imperialism and Thomas, notoriously, with his own country's.[216] This, however, was hardly just a matter of personal whim. At the same year's TUC the distinctness of the two positions was underlined when Purcell moved the radical NAFTA resolution for the dissolution of empire, while Thomas was almost alone in opposing it. Arguments regarding the complementarity of the British and Russian economies were certainly predicated on the latter's current underdevelopment. What Adler saw as a colonial mindset could thus be directed at Russia itself as potential market – and indeed the left communist Preobazhensky envisaged the Russian peasants as an internal surrogate for 'colonial robbery' in the interests of the wider Soviet economy.[217] What, on the other hand, had this to do with Purcell?

Where Thomas and Preobazhensky each identified with his own metropolis, it is impossible to make sense of Purcell's Russian commitments except on the basis that he shared with Preobazhensky the ideological conviction that Russia was a workers' state, and as such in many respects sui generis. Where British imperialism was constructed as a threat to workers' conditions – whether to be dealt with by the Common Rule or the Restriction of Numbers, as discussed in chapter three – Purcell could thus simultaneously promote the country's opening up to Russian trade. He did not, moreover, associate this with underdevelopment, but with 'a new economy and a new life, keenly and rapidly adopting ... all the latest developments in science and industry'.[218] The answer to the Restriction of Numbers lay in the promotion of Russian trade within the context of an underconsumptionist diagnosis of current economic ills which implicitly was opposed to protectionism.[219] With appropriate safeguards, as we shall see, such arguments could even be extended to India. The safeguards, on the other hand, were critical: the answer of the Common Rule was that Russia, uniquely, was held to guarantee rising labour standards and the extension of the domain of organised labour. There was force to Adler's argument that the British applied quite different standards to diverse foreigners from those they felt appropriate to themselves.[220] Nevertheless, the logic of Purcell's trade-union internationalism was of a Common Rule or single standard, so that all such differences should be neutralised and as far as possible overcome. There were of course exceptions, but these were mostly confined to those primary sectors, like agriculture, in which British labour was less directly concerned from a producers' perspective.

It was a measure of commitment to the USSR, or to the claims made on its behalf, that the issue of double standards was overlooked in the matter of Russian trade. When later under the Five Year Plan the Soviets sought to make up for lack of credits through cheap exports, Conservatives warned of a 'plot against British Labour' and the throwing of thousands out of work:

Dumped wheat and dumped timber will be followed by the dumping of cotton, wool, steel, and electrical goods. This will mean the ruin of British industry, and reduce the British worker to the same level of degradation as the unfortunate Russian.[221]

Any trade unionist would have recognised these arguments, and Coates in response berated the hypocrisy of those who cared so little for conditions in the British colonies.[222] On the other hand, Coates himself now resurrected the argument, which he certainly would not have urged on British workers, that alleged forced labour signified the planned organisation of socialised labour power and the realisation of the precept, 'He who does not work neither shall he eat'.[223] Whether seen as promise or as threat, the socialism supposedly being realised in Russia could turn partisan lines of argument on their head. The scope for an ideologically neutered discussion of Soviet trade was correspondingly reduced.

To Purcell and Morel, it was a 'self-evident fact' that those opposed to closer relations with the Russians were also opposed to working-class rights and aspirations within Britain itself.[224] Not only did it matter that Russia was red, not blue; for active supporters like Purcell, this was almost the only thing that did matter, even when it came into conflict with his most basic precepts of trade-union action. Purcell was not representative of all labour movement opinion, and the ascendancy of his forthright identification with Soviet Russia proved short-lived. Without this basic instinct of shared interests or ideals, it is nevertheless difficult to see how Russian trade could have acquired its politically defining character in the time that Goldman spent in Britain.

4.5 THE RUSSIAN SUPERSTITION

Goldman's misfortune was that these eighteen months were the heyday of Anglo-Russian trade-union co-operation. The eighth anniversary of the revolution in November 1925 saw a flurry of features in the British labour press. *Lansbury's Labour Weekly* carried a 'What I Saw in Russia' feature and a full-page portrait of Lenin. Brailsford, who contributed, seemed to have cast off earlier inhibitions: both here and in the *New Leader* he saluted the achievement of an elevating social freedom with feelings of veneration 'and even of envy'.[225] The Webbs' friend Susan Lawrence, whose Russian impressions appeared in the *Labour Magazine*, noted that Labour readers knew more about Russia than about any other country.[226] The reopening of the old Tsarist embassy allowed for the further lubrication of such agreeable sentiments and the extension of a select if apparently profligate hospitality. 'Can you beat anything more for corruption?', Goldman observed with understandable disgust, as even Russell figured among the guests of honour.[227]

The suggestion of a 'freeze' in activities may therefore be discounted.[228] Nor can it be said that the labour movement lacked any feeling of political community with its Soviet counterpart.[229] While the Anglo-Russian committee itself was a somewhat desultory affair, the number of group as well as individual visits to Russia is hardly suggestive of a lack of interest. Deputising for Bramley, Citrine played down the significance of such parties by describing them as 'holiday excursions'.[230] That responsibility for trade groupings was vested in the unions concerned was nevertheless a recognition of established trade-union prerogatives, not a sign, as Calhoun suggests, that the British were 'loth to promote informal Anglo-Russian contacts'.[231]

Among the groupings specified by the Russians, the miners were to have been the largest, followed by engineering, textiles, the railways and a number of smaller contingents.[232] Some unions, like the General and Municipal Workers, were opposed on principle to any such arrangement.[233] Nevertheless, delegations in 1925-6 did include one of miners and miners' wives and one of railwaymen. There was also a women's delegation which, though unofficial, was led by Mary Quaile of the TUC general council. Acting as its clerical secretary was Purcell's daughter May, then said to be active in the socialist youth movement and 'helping her father a great deal' in his activities.[234] Also attending as 'advisory delegate' was Zelda Kahan Coates, and the party's published impressions of both Russia and Georgia were entirely congruent with its all-male predecessor.[235] Following Tomsky's appearance at the Scarborough TUC, Hicks and Citrine returned with him to Russia, and Citrine reported back enthusiastically in the left-wing press.[236] Purcell himself did not return to Russia until 1933. According to police reports, he nevertheless made several visits to Paris, where Tomsky was again representing the Soviets in negotiations, and where Purcell is said to have stayed at the Soviet embassy.[237]

Melnichansky had stated a preference for delegations drawn from the 'rank and file', including local union officials.[238] A more targeted approach took advantage of the new Soviet welfare facilities and the appropriation by the unions of previously exclusive resorts. The TUC itself made no formal use of these. Whether for reasons of diplomacy, lack of opportunity or personal preference, even Bramley, who was dying of cancer, was sent instead on a voyage to South America. The Miners' Federation, on the other hand, had been promised five places in a Soviet health resort.[239] Lansbury, making his second Russian trip in 1926, made full use of such facilities and expressed his appreciation in encomiums to the regime.[240]

Also revisiting Russia at this time was the quondam revolutionary Williams, now business manager at the *Herald* and current Labour Party chairman. Ostensibly reporting on the Soviet press, Williams described with relish his journey to Yalta in a 'powerful Benz car' and the 'indescribable' opulence of his surroundings in the summer palace of the Tsars:

> How am I to write about the Press – which is why I am here? ... I felt on leaving London I should want to write and tell the world about my impressions, but the sun is warm, and the water and sun baths are enervating and invigorating at the same time. It is good just to lie with less than nothing on and be baked five minutes on one side and five on the other. The food is all one could desire. We have peaches, plums, strawberries and apricots from the late Nicholas' gardens. I hate to speak of the caviare, but it's just a mid-summer day's dream![241]

What were conferences in Bridlington or even Southport to compare with this? While almost nothing now remained of Williams's left-wing proclivities, his report on the Soviet press enthused about its quality, its varied character, and its 'far-sighted', if not positively ominous, 'understanding of the enormous potentialities of the printed word'.[242]

It is hard to dispute Goldman's view that such relations were corrupting. They certainly did not encourage a concern with the Russian prisoners. When Abramovich prepared a pamphlet on Russian conditions for the LSI's affiliates, James Maxton for the ILP pronounced its allegations 'not sufficiently substantiated' and forwarded them in the usual way to the Soviet embassy. An ILP resolution referred darkly to the 'apparently concerted effort to create an atmosphere of suspicion and hatred' between the two peoples and make Russia 'our next world enemy'.[243] Even Wedgwood, who was active on behalf of the British communist prisoners, now endorsed the communist-sponsored ICWPA, attached to an international executive in Moscow which naturally would have nothing to do with Russian prisoners. 'Was it a crime to work for a government similar to that which existed in Russia?', he declaimed at the ICWPA's inaugural conference, and in echo of Turner added: 'If so we were going back to the "good old days" when it was considered a crime to sympathise with the French Revolution.'[244] When campaigns were launched against the death sentences passed on the Italian-American anarchists Sacco and Vanzetti, Goldman was quick to see the inconsistency with attitudes to Russia. Only too late she saw that her own failure to speak out for these and other non-Russian prisoners was open to no less obvious objections.[245]

Goldman's comrade Max Nettlau held that Russia supplied timorous labour leaders with a vicarious revolutionary identity, allowing them to 'bask in the sunshine of bolshevik revolutionaries ... without doing anything nor incurring risks'.[246] Goldman discerned a similar compensatory political function in the blighted South Wales coalfield, and admitted feeling torn 'to take away the last ray of hope from the unfortunate Welsh slaves in regard to the "Heaven" in Russia'.[247]

Uncompromising recognition of the truth, however, was a value that she put above all others. 'We are so afraid and worried how the Truth about Russia will affect the masses', she wrote to anarchist correspondents, 'that we are willing to wait until it will become rotten with lies'.[248]

It is easy to see how depictions of Soviet Russia became rotten with lies. It is not so clear that the alternative was as simple as Goldman implied. Russell in his book on Russia observed that 'the truth in social questions is not quite like the truth in physiology or physics, since it depends upon men's beliefs. Optimism tends to verify itself by making people impatient of avoidable evils; while despair, on the other hand, makes the world as bad as it believes it to be.'[249] Russell's point was to underline the importance of constructive alternatives to Bolshevism, alternatives which he identified with self-government in industry. On the other hand, he also seemed to anticipate how even shocking untruths about Russia might legitimise optimism and the struggle against avoidable evils in the west. Amidst the enveloping despair of the inter-war years much of the appeal of Soviet communism can be understood in this way. For South Wales miners, and others like them, the idea of a workers' paradise was not just a compensatory fantasy. It was also an antidote to despair and acquiescence, and the reason why, as Goldman gloomily conceded, only the communists carried out any actual revolutionary propaganda.[250]

For centuries normative or exemplary states had been imagined in this way, as repositories of competing social values in the process of present realisation. In the case of the Venetian republic, W.H. Greenleaf proposed that what mattered for outsiders was 'not what Venice was then really like but what ... contemporaries thought it was like'.[251] The same can hardly be said of Bolshevism. Not only was the support of external movements and public figures a crucial source of state legitimation and diplomatic leverage, explicitly expressed in terms of common transnational interests. Presumed actuality also meant the possibility of undermining or disproof, as delegations and commissions of enquiry absorbed enormous energies in a continuous battle of verification and refutation. What contemporaries thought these powers were like was in countless cases subject to moments of dramatic unsettlement, like Goldman's Kronstadt, and thus potentially to disillusionment and political realignment. At the same time, a conscious or unconscious state of denial regarding Bolshevism's darker side was to remain a considerable political phenomenon for decades to come. Optimism both verified and falsified itself, and credulousness and complicity helped consolidate the dictatorship in Russia itself, which consequently invested significant resources to achieve precisely this end.

Goldman's experience in Britain shows how the will to believe which so frustrated her can only fully be understood in the context of a deeply partisan construction of the truth. Discussions of the social rationality of accepted untruth can overlook this partisan dimension, as if society provided some 'generally accepted standard of epistemic rationality' demanding either compliance or descent into the irrational.[252] Shaw had written in this way during the war: one had to accept madness as sanity, since sanity was only the madness on which all agreed.[253] For those who contested the madness of war, on the other hand, the refusal of its legitimising propaganda became both an article of faith and an act of defiance. In the case of German atrocity stories, it has been suggested that there was more truth in Allied propaganda than these critical voices were ever prepared to recognise.[254] But the deep conviction in a 'lying press', as expressed in NAFTA's anti-war manifesto, was not based on detailed knowledge or a capacity for refutation, but on the tendentious character of the partial truths to which alone this press gave voice.[255]

Denial or apologia was also tendentious in character. When Turner and Wedgwood proposed the analogy with the French revolution, they not only relativised the idea of revolutionary dictatorship but implied its transitional character on the basis of the only historical precedent available to them. Bolshevism was thus extenuated, not only by reference to the past, but in anticipation of the democratic future it was believed to be creating. Some predicated this on rising levels of culture and literacy. Susan Lawrence held that there was an inherent contradiction between the simultaneous preaching of insurgency and obedience and that this would inevitably result in the ending of the communists' political monopoly.[256] It is easy to see now that the contradiction might equally be resolved through terror, and western supporters of Bolshevism might certainly have been more sceptical regarding the systematic concentration of power. Nevertheless, just as we now see through the lens of the twentieth-century dictatorships, and what would then have seemed an almost unimaginable scale of atrocities, it is not surprising that contemporaries of Lenin were reassured rather than deterred by the analogy with the short-lived Jacobin terror.

It is easier to be sure of a lie than the truth. Goldman's truth, while corresponding better to Bolshevik realities both presently and tendentially, was politically compromised in two basic ways. Though Havelock Ellis was convinced that she would be bound to protest under any social order, Goldman breathed hardly a word against British capitalism or British imperialism, and her failure to bear witness to truths concerning entire social systems located her within a partisan construction of the truth exactly as it had Allied war propagandists.[257] Goldman herself did not now recognise this dilemma. In her view it was simply an 'irony of fate' that she should carry out the 'kind of work that happens to fit in with the existing Government'.[258] In earlier days she had not seen it this way. In campaigns against Tsarist oppression, even the American police had left her unmolested as long as she confined her speeches to freedom in Russia. Goldman herself had had words of biting satire for those who respected such constraints.[259] Though critics put the most cynical construction on her subsequent compliance with just such restrictions, Goldman's correspondence shows that she really was preoccupied with Bolshevism at the expense of almost every other issue that had previously moved her. Arguably this was politically incapacitating; for holding that conditions in Britain were 'a hundred times better' than in Russia suggested a sort of acquiescence in established power relations, just as the delusion of a Russian heaven could nurture expectations of their transformation.

Russia, of course, was not the only possible heaven. Anarchism itself was not 'true', but a projection of the imagination which provided exactly this hope and spur to resistance. It is easy to see how some anarchists, like Fred Charles, proved susceptible to the particular claims of Bolshevism. Those who resisted these claims, on the other hand, might also feel themselves undeceived in the revolution which had given rise to so deflating an outcome. Harry Kelly had gone into the property business, and was 'simply worn out with the struggle and disillusioned as a result of the fiasco in Russia'; according to Goldman, who understood this perfectly, it took a burning zeal to 'go on believing in the masses after the mess made in Russia'.[260] On leaving the country after Kronstadt, it was to the revolution and the martyred people that she had pledged her exposure of Bolshevism. Now she confided that she had 'no faith left in the people, or the revolution, or our own ideas'.[261] To Ellis she described how she had 'foolishly believed that the principal thing is to get the people to rise against the oppressive institutions and that everything else will take care of itself'. Bolshevism had exposed this as a Bakuninite fallacy, and Goldman placed what hopes remained to her in a longer process of revolution from within.[262] To Berkman she described it simply as the 'collapse of our faith through Russia'.[263]

By the time of her marriage to Colton, even the work on Russia seemed irrecoverable. To support herself, Goldman thought of setting up a gallery or a shampoo parlour to cater for the 'American tourist trade'.[264] Through the British Drama League she did at least discover a paying audience for lectures on the theatre such as had eluded her on more overtly political topics. In a last political effort, she organised a meeting with Pankhurst on the Bolshevik and fascist dictatorships, but the response was as depressing as ever. 'The fact is', Goldman, commented, 'that the Russian superstition holds everybody in its snare'.[265]

Her last hope was provided by her compatriot Lady Astor. A convinced if independent-minded Conservative, Astor encapsulated for the labour movement a certain temptation to social climbing. But she was also well-connected with women's and voluntary organisations; and she was ready to commission from Goldman a book on Soviet destitute children when the coal crisis in Britain itself intervened. Goldman herself expected nothing of the crisis, for the English seemed 'so docile and so overorganized'.[266] Confuted by the General Strike, she did nothing to assist in any lesser capacity once her offer to look after the relief effort was politely declined.[267] Given the plight of the British coalfields, even Astor now thought it impossible to 'go off on Russia' and the arrangement came to nothing.[268]

Goldman in any case had left the country. 'British now', she had done 'as most natives do who can scrape up enough to escape their country's climate', and with the assistance of American friends departed for the French Riviera on 11 May 1926.[269] The General Strike was still in progress; rather than blackleg Goldman took a plane. The Russian superstition had defeated her.

NOTES

1. IISH SAI 974C/5, Pollak to Adler 24 January 1925.
2. IISH SAI 1697 Adler to Clifford Allen, 29 April 1925 and Allen's reply, 4 May 1925.
3. 'H.T.' (Herbert Tracey), *Labour Magazine*, March 1925, pp. 501-3, and April 1925, pp. 540-3.
4. Pollak to Adler 24 January 1925. For Clynes's stance, see e.g. *New Leader*, 21 November 1924; *Labour Magazine*, December 1924, pp. 346-8, *Daily Herald*, 5 February 1925.
5. Purcell, 'The burning question of international unity', *Labour Monthly*, September 1925, p. 527.
6. Baikalov papers, Baikalov to H.W. Lee, 20 January and 3 June 1924, Lee to Baikalov, 17 June 1924.
7. Goldman, preface, in *Russia and the British Labour Delegation's Report: a reply*, BCDPPR, 1925, p. 4.
8. Goldman to Berkman, 16 June 1925 in Candace Falk, *Emma Goldman. A guide to her life and documentary sources*, Chadwyck Healey, 1991. The account here derives in particular from this meticulous microfilm edition (hereafter GLDS). In some cases correspondence in the Berkman and Goldman papers was consulted before becoming aware of this edition, and while it is cited accordingly there is no suggestion that it will not be found in the comprehensive Falk edition. Goldman was not originally an English speaker and her occasional idiosyncrasies of spelling have been silently corrected.
9. Stephen White, *Britain and the Bolshevik Revolution. A study in the politics of diplomacy 1920-1924*, Macmillan, 1979, p. 215 and ch. 8 passim.
10. Goldman, *My Disillusionment in Russia*, C.W. Daniel, 1925, pp. 58-9; GLDS Goldman to Berkman, 2 October 1924.
11. Nettlau papers 158, Goldman to 'Dear Comrades', 15 December 1924 (copy); see also *Bolshevism and the British Left*, I, p. 23.
12. See e.g. *Russia and the British Labour Delegation's Report*; Rebecca West, introduction to Goldman, *My Disillusionment*, p. v. Her Russian identity

had been strongly expressed in her early years in the States, but less so latterly for reasons that will become clear; for her own observations see Goldman's interview with the *New York Sun*, 6 January 1901 in Candace Falk et al, eds, *Emma Goldman: a documentary history of the American years. 1. Made for America, 1890-1901*, Berkeley Cal., University of California Press, 2003, p. 424.

13. See David DeLeon, *The American as Anarchist. Reflections on indigenous radicalism*, Baltimore: Johns Hopkins University Press, 1978, pp. 94-6, 98; George Woodcock, *Anarchism. A history of libertarian ideas and movements*, Harmondsworth: Penguin, 1975 edn, p. 440. Goldman described herself as an American in the truest sense: Goldman, *Living My Life* (1931), New York: Dover edn, 2 vols, 1970, p. 594.
14. Alice Wexler, *Emma Goldman in Exile. From the Russian Revolution to the Spanish Civil War*, Boston, Mass.: Beacon Press, 1989, pp. 142-3.
15. See e.g. Danel Guérin, trans. Mary Klopper, *Anarchism: from theory to practice*, New York & London: Monthly Review Press, 1971, edn, pp. 3-7; David Miller, *Anarchism*, London & Melbourne: Dent, 1984, part 1.
16. Goldman, 'Anarchism: what it really stands for' in her *Anarchism and Other Essays* (1911), New York: Dover Publications, 1969 edn, pp. 57-73.
17. Goldman, 'The child and its enemies', *Mother Earth*, April 1906, p. 7.
18. Goldman, *Living My Life*, p. 28.
19. For a characteristic example see Goldman, 'The crime of the 11th of November', *Mother Earth*, November 1911, pp. 263-6.
20. Goldman, *Living My Life*, pp. 190, 304, 507.
21. See for example Goldman, 'The tragedy at Buffalo', *Free Society*, 6 October 1901 in Falk, *Documentary History*, I, pp. 471-8.
22. Goldman, 'The source of violence', *Mother Earth*, December 1911, pp. 206-8.
23. Material in this paragraph derives from Kevin Morgan, 'Heralds of the future? Emma Goldman, Friedrich Nietzsche and the anarchist as superman', *Anarchist Studies*, 17, 2, 2009, pp. 55-80.
24. William C. Owen, preface to Emma Goldman, *The Crushing of the Russian Revolution*, Freedom Press, 1922, pp. 1-2.
25. Goldman interview, *New York Sun*, 6 January 1901 in Falk, *Documentary History*, I, p. 426; also Goldman, 'Some more observations', *Free Society*, 29 April 1900, ibid, p. 401.
26. Goldman, interview in *New York Sun*, p. 426.
27. Willa Cather cited Michael Kazin, *A Godly Hero: the life of William Jennings Bryan*, New York: Alfred Knopf, 2006, p. 101.
28. See Goldman's comments, *Living My Life*, p. 539; also Hippolyte Havel, 'Biographical sketch' in Goldman, Anarchism and Other Essays, p. 2.
29. Harry Kelly, 'Anarchism. A plea for the impersonal', *Mother Earth*, February 1908, p. 562. For insights into his labour movement experiences in Britain see his contributions in *Mother Earth*, December 1907, pp. 456-7 and August 1913, pp. 180-5.
30. Goldman, 'On the road', *Mother Earth*, May 1907, p. 132.
31. Miriam Michelson, 'A character study of Emma Goldman', *Philadelphia North American*, 11 April 1901, *Documentary History*, 1, p. 443; also Ben L. Reitman, 'The end of the tour and a peep at the next one', *Mother Earth*, September 1913, p. 212.

32. Alexander Berkman, *Prison Memoirs of an Anarchist* (1912), London: C.W. Daniel edn, 1926, p. 493.
33. For a fuller discussion, see Morgan, 'Herald of the future?'.
34. Goldman, 'Minorities versus majorities' in *Anarchism and Other Essays*, pp. 75-84.
35. W.N. Ewer, *Lansbury's Labour Weekly*, 7 March 1925; on this point see *Bolshevism and the British Left*, II, ch. 7.
36. On this see for example Michael Farbman, *After Lenin. The new phase in Russia*, Leonard Parsons 1924.
37. GLDS Goldman to Angelica Balabanov, 15 August 1925.
38. William Archer, 'Introduction to "An Enemy of the People"' in William Archer, ed., *The Collected Works of Henrik Ibsen*, vol. 8, Heinemann, 1907, p. xii; Halfdan Gregersen, *Ibsen and Spain. A study in comparative drama*, Cambridge, Mass.: Harvard University Press, 1936, pp. 53-6.
39. Goldman, 'Light and shadow in the life of an avant-guard', *Mother Earth*, March 1910, pp. 16-27.
40. Ibsen, *Enemy of the People*, pp. 13-6.
41. James G. Huneker, *Egoists. A book of supermen*, New York: Scribners, 1910, p. 348.
42. Goldman, 'The international anarchist congress', *Mother Earth*, October 1907 in Falk, *Documentary History*, 2, pp. 234, 237-9.
43. Goldman, 'Minorities versus majorities', pp. 76, 81-2; Ibsen cited Archer. 'Introduction', p. ix.
44. 'Emma Goldman on the Bolsheviks', *Freedom*, May 1922, p. 31.
45. Goldman, *Living My Life*, p. 881.
46. Owen, preface, pp. 1-2; see also West, introduction to Goldman, *My Disillusionment*, p. v.
47. Wexler, *Emma Goldman in Exile*, p. 94; 'Dinner to Emma Goldman', *Freedom*, November-December 1924, p. 60.
48. GLDS Goldman to Senya Flechine, 28 November 1924; Bertrand Russell, *Autobiography*, Unwin Paperbacks, 1978 edn, p. 356.
49. *Manchester Guardian*, 13 November 1924.
50. Goldman to Senya Flechine, 28 November 1924.
51. Nettlau papers 158, Goldman to Wedgwood, 9 December 1924 (copy).
52. Nettlau papers 158, Goldman to Mrs Hawkes, 13 December 1924, copied to Nettlau, 15 December 1924; GLDS Goldman to Roger Baldwin, 5 January 1925.
53. See Nettlau papers 158, Goldman to Nettlau 15 June 1924, where Lansbury and the *Herald* editor Hamilton Fyfe are mentioned as making representations on Goldman's behalf. Goldman in *Living My Life*, pp. 965-6 claimed that their involvement had been unknown to her.
54. GLDS Nevinson to Goldman, 29 December 1924, Emmeline Pethick Lawrence to Goldman, 11 February 1925, F.W. Pethick Lawrence to Goldman, 18 February 1925.
55. GLDS Wedgwood to Goldman, 9 February 1925.
56. GLDS Frances, Lady Warwick to Goldman, 6 December 1924.
57. GLDS, Ellis to Goldman, 28 March 1925.
58. GLDS Russell to Goldman, 14 February 1925.
59. GLDS Laski to Goldman, 29 December 1924.

60. MacDonald papers (NA) 30/69/1204, unnamed correspondent, evidently Rakovsky, to MacDonald, 22 January 1924.
61. See ILP archives 3/16, NAC minutes, 23-24 February 1924; LSI archives (IISG) SAI 201, Abramovitch at LSI executive, Vienna, 5-7 June 1924; SAI 1715 Adler or Pollak to Brailsford, 1 September 1924; also TUC archives MSS 292/31.6/1.4, TUC/Labour Joint International Committee minutes, 21 May and 18 June 1924.
62. TUC archives MSS 292/947/39, Abramovitch to LSI secretary, 27 October 1924; see also IISG SAI 2595, Adler (?) to Brailsford, 1 September 1924; Brailsford to Adler, 5 September 1924; Brockway to Adler (?), 8 October 1924; TUC archives MSS 292/947/39, William Gillies to Bramley, 1 October 1924; Brockway to Bramley, 8 October 1924; Berzin to Brockway, 11 October 1924; Brockway to Berzin, 24 October 1924.
63. GLDS Goldman to Nettlau 5 April 1926.
64. *New Leader*, 3 October and 14 November 1924.
65. GLDS Goldman to Berkman, 22 December 1924.
66. Goldman, *Living My Life*, pp. 968-9.
67. GLDS Laski to Goldman, 29 December 1924 and Goldman to Roger Baldwin, 5 January 1925; Nettlau papers 159, Goldman to A. Chapiro, 8 January 1925 and Goldman to Rudolf and Milly Rocker, 30 March 1925.
68. Berkman papers IIIa, Goldman to Berkman, 5 January 1925.
69. Nettlau papers 159, Goldman to Nettlau, 2 April 1925; GLDS Goldman to Berkman, 11 March 1925.
70. GLDS Goldman to Berkman, 11 March 1925.
71. *Russia and the British Delegation's Report*, pp. 30-1.
72. GLDS, Wedgwood to Goldman 14 April 1925.
73. Nettlau papers 159, Goldman to A. Chapiro, 8 January 1925.
74. The other committee members were the anarchists Keell, Dryden and Sugg. Only the first of these is mentioned even in John Quail's detailed account *The Slow Burning Fuse. The lost history of the British anarchists*, Paladin Books, 1978.
75. Turner similarly offered relativist judgement: 'Russia is Russia.' West, introduction to Goldman, *My Disillusionment in Russia*, pp. vi-vii; Turner, 'What British Labour saw in Soviet Russia', *American Federationist*, March 1925, pp. 186.
76. GLDS Goldman to Berkman, 5 February 1925; Goldman to John H. Cook, 25 February 1925.
77. M. Ostrogorski, *Democracy and the Organization of Political Parties*, trans. Frederick Clarke, Macmillan, 1902, vol. 1, pp. 412-13.
78. Bedford papers M4, NGL annual report 1920-1, p. 6.
79. GLDS Thomas Keell to Goldman, 6 February 1925.
80. *The Labour Who's Who 1924*, Labour Publishing Co, 1924, p. 174; Goldman, *Living My Life*, p. 163.
81. Goldman, *Living My Life*, p. 972.
82. GLDS Goldman to Minnie Lowensohn, 12 May 1925.
83. Florence Wedgwood suggested addressing local meetings of Labour women but there is no evidence that Goldman was interested (see her letter to Goldman, 5 March 1925).
84. Goldman, *Living My Life*, p. 966 for her resentment.
85. GLDS Goldman to Bayard Boyesen, 5 June 1925.

86. Goldman to Boyesen, 5 June 1925; also Goldman to Saxe Commins, 26 December 1924.
87. RGASPI 495/100/171, Inkpin to ECCI secretariat, 18 September 1924.
88. GLDS, Goldman to Ben Capes, 15 December 1925; also Goldman to Joseph Ishill, 24 November 1925.
89. GLDS, Goldman to Ellis, 27 February 1924 and to Odette Keun, 26 December 1924.
90. Cheryl Law, *Suffrage and Power. The women's movement 1918-1928*, I.B. Tauris, 1997, chs 6-7 and passim.
91. E.g. Goldman, 'The tragedy of the Russian intelligentsia', *Time and Tide*, 31 July 1925, pp. 748-9.
92. GLDS Goldman to Stella Ballantyne, 27 March 1925.
93. GLDS Goldman to Berkman 5 February and 8 June 1925.
94. GLDS Goldman to Nettlau 5 April 1926; Wells to Russell, 7 March 1925 in David C. Smith, ed., *The Correspondence of H.G. Wells. Volume 3: 1919-1924*, Pickering & Chatto, 1998, pp. 189-90.
95. *Letters from Russian Prisons*, C.W. Daniel for the International Committee for Political Prisoners, 1925. Both Isaac Don Levine and Alexander Berkman, who helped compile the material, were confirmed anti-Bolsheviks. Berkman's contribution to the volume, however, was not acknowledged (see Wexler, *Emma Goldman in Exile*, p. 107).
96. *Resolution of the Labour and Socialist Congress held at Hamburg May 21st to 25th 1923*, London: LSI secretariat, 1923, p. 12, resolution on 'International action against international reaction'; Labour Party archives LSI 12/10/1, notes for news services on the congress by William Gillies.
97. GLDS Goldman to Berkman, 20 December 1924 (wrongly dated to 1925 by the editors); also Goldman to Odette Keun, 6 February and 21 May 1925.
98. Theresa Moritz and Albert Moritz, *The World's Most Dangerous Woman. A new biography of Emma Goldman*, Toronto: Subway Books, 2001, p. 24.
99. Goldman to Mrs Hawkes, 13 December 1924.
100. See GLDS Hamilton Fyfe to Goldman, 18 November 1925 and Goldman's reply, 24 November 1925.
101. *Times*, 31 January 1925.
102. See Beatrice Webb's observations to her husband's electors, Passfield papers 4/15, printed letter to Seaham women constituents, 20 November 1924.
103. See her letter to Roger Baldwin, 20 April 1925, cited Wexler, *Emma Goldman in Exile*, p. 106.
104. Baldwin to Goldman, 27 March 1925.
105. GLDS Goldman to Levine, 27 December 1924, Goldman to Wedgwood, 5 May 1925.
106. GLDS Goldman to Berkman, 25 October 1924.
107. GLDS Goldman to Roger Baldwin, 6 November 1924.
108. Goldman to Mrs Hawkes, 13 December 1924.
109. 'Red virgin comes to London', *Daily Express*, 16 November 1924.
110. Beaverbrook papers, BBK/C/322, West to Beaverbook, n.d., November (?) 1924.
111. Goldman to Mrs Hawkes, 13 December 1924.
112. Ibsen, *Enemy of the People*, pp. 160, 184.
113. Isaac Kramnick and Barry Sheerman, *Harold Laski. A life on the left*, Hamish Hamilton, 1993, pp. 224-6.

114. Goldman, *Living My Life*, pp. 970-1.
115. Goldman to Saxe Commins, 26 December 1924.
116. GLDS Goldman to Berkman, 13 and 26 August 1925.
117. See for example his 'Anarchism versus socialism', *Freedom*, September 1921, p. 52 (originally written in 1903 at Goldman's behest).
118. GLDS Goldman to Minnie Lowenshohn, 22 January 1925; Nettlau papers 159, Goldman to Michael A. Cohn, 27 February 1925; GLDS Goldman to Stella Ballantine, 10 February 1925.
119. See Kevin Morgan, 'A splendid field? Emma Goldman in South Wales', *Llafur*, 10, 1, 2008, pp. 47-61.
120. The only union to indicate support was the National Tailors' Union of Subdividisional Workers based in the East End; GLDS C. Horwitch to Goldman, 22 December 1924.
121. Biographical details from Goldman, 'A glimpse of an active career', *Lucifer, the Lightbearer*, 22 October 1901, in Candace Falk et al, eds, *Emma Goldman: a documentary history of the American years. 2. Making Speech Free, 1902-1909*, Berkeley Cal., University of California Press, 2005, pp. 112-14; also Quail, *Slow Burning Fuse*, pp. 244-9.
122. See Goldman, 'The situation in America' (report for international anarchist congress, Amsterdam), *Mother Earth*, November 1907, pp. 378-88.
123. Havel, 'Biographic sketch', pp. 34-5.
124. Goldman, *Living My Life*, p. 346.
125. Margaret Bondfield, *A Life's Work*, Hutchinsons, 1949, p. 47; Mary Agnes Hamilton, *Mary Macarthur: a biographical sketch*, Leonard Parsons, 1925, pp. 7-12.
126. Bedford papers M/15, Turner for NAUSAWC to Margaret Cole, National Guild Council, 16 September 1922.
127. Wayne Thorpe, *'The Workers Themselves'. Revolutionary syndicalism and international labour, 1913-1923*, Dordrecht: Kluwer Academic Publishers, 1989, p. 80.
128. 'John Turner on the declaration of principles', *Syndicalist*, December 1913.
129. Goldman, 'The new inquisition', *Free Society*, 1 November 1903 in Falk, *Documentary History*, 2, pp. 115-16.
130. Christine Collette, The *International Faith. Labour's attitudes to European socialism 1918-1939*, Aldershot: Ashgate, 1998, p. 19; Daniel F. Calhoun, *The United Front. The TUC and the Russians 1923-1928*, Cambridge: CUP, 1976, p. 94; Quail, *Slow Burning Fuse*, p. 247.
131. Nettlau papers 158, Goldman to Nettlau, 15 June 1924; GLDS Goldman to Sophia Kropotkin, 1 October 1924 and Goldman to Berkman, 2 October 1924.
132. RGASPI 534/7/74, Pollitt to Losovsky, 25 September 1924; 495/100/128, Pollitt to MacManus, 25 September 1924.
133. RGASPI 495/100/176, unnamed Amsterdam correspondent to A. Valenius, Moscow, 6 November 1924, encl. letter from presumed British contact, 3 November 1924.
134. GLDS Goldman to Berkman, 25 October 1924; Goldman papers X/2, Turner to Goldman 21 November 1924; GLDS Goldman to Roger Baldwin, 5 January 1925.
135. Nettlau papers 159, typescript report of BCDPPR, South Place Institute, 29 January 1925.

136. Turner, 'Russian prisons', *Foreign Affairs*, May 1925, pp. 255-6.
137. 'What British Labour saw', pp. 184-9.
138. GLDS Goldman to Minna Lowison, 12 May 1925.
139. Goldman papers X/2, Turner to Goldman 13 March 1925; *Russia. The official report of the British Trade Union Delegation to Russia and Caucasia Nov. and Dec. 1924*, TUC, 1925, pp. 16-17.
140. Compare the original declaration in NA FO 37/10487 N9463/530/38 (report on the delegation, 19 December 1924) with *Russia. The official report*, pp. 208-17.
141. TUC archives MSS 292/947/13, report of IFTU general council, Amsterdam, 6-7 February 1925, 'Relations with Russia'.
142. GLDS Goldman to Berkman, 16 March 1925; Nettlau papers 159, Goldman to Nettlau, 2 April 1925.
143. Nettlau papers 159, Turner to Goldman, 29 December 1924 (copy); Goldman to Berkman, 5 February 1925. Turner had less regard for Tillett and thought Bramley stodgy.
144. Nettlau papers 159, Goldman to Odette Keun, 21 May 1925; Goldman to Nettlau, 2 April 1925.
145. Goldman papers X/1/2, Turner, draft of speech moving resolution at South Place Institute, 29 January 1925.
146. Nettlau papers 159, Goldman to A. Chapiro, 8 January 1925.
147. GLDS Goldman to Nettlau, 15 November 1925. For Charles, see Quail, *Slow Burning Fuse*, ch. 6, also Bondfield, *A Life's Work*, p. 47.
148. Goldman papers X/2, Turner to Goldman, 3 March 1925; Turner to Goldman, 13 March 1925; Goldman to Turner, May 1925.
149. Goldman papers X/1/2, Turner, draft of speech moving resolution at South Place Institute.
150. Goldman papers X/1/2, Turner to Goldman, 13 March 1925.
151. Wexler, *Emma Goldman in Exile*, pp. 62-7.
152. GLDS Marie Belloc Lowndes to Goldman, 6 February 1925; Goldman to Berkman, 11 March 1925.
153. See for example Nettlau papers 159, Goldman to Nettlau, 2 April 1925. According to a financial statement dated 6 May 1925 the committee's main sources of income were lecture tickets (c. £67) and pamphlet contributions (c. £40).
154. Goldman to 'Dear Comrades', 15 December 1924.
155. GLDS Goldman to Stella Ballantyne, 14 April 1925 and to Rudolf Grossman, 18 May 1925; Aldred cited Mark Shipway, *Anti-Parliamentary Communism. The movement for workers' councils in Britain, 1917-45*, Basingstoke: Macmillans, 1988, p. 52.
156. *Freedom*, January 1925, p. 3; also October 1924, p. 54
157. GLDS Mrs J.B. Campbell to Goldman, 20 January 1925; 'Declined with thanks', *Freedom*, March-April 1925, p. 18; Aldred, 'The decline of Emma', *The Commune*, May 1925.
158. GLDS 15 November 1924.
159. *Manchester Guardian*, 30 April 1925.
160. Turner to Goldman, 13 March 1925.
161. Goldman to Berkman, 12 and 16 March 1925; also Goldman, *Living My Life*, pp. 936-7.
162. Morgan, 'A splendid field?', pp. 59-61.

163. GLDS Goldman to Stella Ballantyne, 30 June 1925.
164. GLDS Goldman to Berkman, 8 July 1925.
165. GLDS Goldman to Berkman, 28 May, 7 July, 13 and 20 August 1925.
166. GLDS Goldman to Harry Weinberger, 23 October 1925.
167. GLDS Goldman to Berkman, 11 and 16 October 1925.
168. *New Leader*, 27 January 1926. The letter had initially been sent the *Daily Herald*, which did not publish it.
169. GLDS Goldman to Saxe Commins, 26 December 1924.
170. Pollak, 'British Labour and the International: a continental replies', *New Leader*, 23 January 1925.
171. Pollak, 'Amsterdam, Moscow and England', trans. from *Arbeit und Wirtschaft* in Bramley papers, box 1. As Tillett put it (*Some Russian Impressions*), LRD, 1925, p. 17: 'It is good to think that the rank-and-file lions still live to growl at the brayings of those in part responsible for the present debacle.'
172. Pollak, 'British Labour and the International'.
173. BWD, 6 October 1932.
174. BWD, 27 October 1932.
175. Goldman to Mrs Hawkes, 13 December 1924.
176. GLDS Goldman to Odette Keun, 26 February 1925.
177. GLDS Goldman to Frank Harris, May 1925.
178. GLDS Goldman to Berkman 28 May and 30 September 1925. The reference in this case was to Havelock Ellis.
179. GLDS Goldman to Powers Hapgood, 19 November 1925.
180. Antonello Gerbi, trans. Jeremy Moyle, *The Dispute of the New World. The history of a polemic 1750-1900*, Pittsburgh: University of Pittsburgh Press, 1955, pp. 479-80.
181. GLDS Goldman to William C. Owen, 22 June 1926.
182. See Turner to Goldman, 29 December 1924, and compare for example Goldman to 'Dear Comrades', 15 December.
183. Goldman to Levine, 27 December 1924.
184. GLDS Goldwin to Roger Baldwin, 20 April 1925.
185. Berkman papers XIII/1, Nettlau to Berkman, 2 March 1925.
186. Nettlau papers 159, Goldman to Odette Keun, 21 May 1925.
187. Goldman, *Living My Life*, p. 968.
188. Goldman papers 158, Goldman to Nettlau, 21 August 1924.
189. A. Losovsky, *British and Russian Workers*, NMM, 1926, pp. 12-13; 'What, then, of British trade unionism', *American Federationist*, February 1924, pp. 151-3.
190. White, *Britain and the Bolshevik Revolution*, p. 244 and ch. 8 passim; see also e.g. A.J. Williams, *Labour and Russia. The attitude of the Labour Party to the USSR, 1924-34*, Manchester: MUP, 1989, e.g. pp. 19, 35; Wexler, *Emma Goldman in Exile*, pp. 92-3.
191. E.g. 175 Hansard fifth series, 7 July 1924, cols 1895-9.
192. A.A. Purcell, *Anglo-Russian Trade. How it could be immediately increased by the Overseas Trade Acts and Trade Facilities Acts*, Anglo-Russian Parliamentary Committee, (February) 1925.
193. Bramley, preface to Purcell, *Anglo-Russian Trade*, p. 4.
194. *Dean Forest Mercury*, 3 June 1927.
195. See for example White, *Britain and the Bolshevik Revolution*, ch. 8 on 'Soviet Russia and Labourism'.

196. Partha Sarathi Gupta, *Imperialism and the British Labour Movement 1914-1964*, New Delhi: Sage Publications, 2002 edn, p. 3.
197. L. Krassin, 'The problem of Anglo-Russian trade', *Labour Magazine*, July 1923, pp. 106-7.
198. White, *Britain and the Bolshevik Revolution*, ch. 7; Bedford papers M/9, 'Conference between the National Guilds Council and M. Rakovsky of the Russian delegation', 18 January 1924; 'Draft memorandum of the agricultural, building, engineering, furnshing and tailoring guilds (1924)'. Already three years earlier a 'Coventry Engineering Guild' had approached the Russian Trade Delegation regarding work for the Soviet government (see reports and correspondence in Bedford papers M/15). Such considerations were possibly decisive for the smaller number of Conservatives interested in Russian trade, like the maverick Bob Boothby, who visited in April 1926, and in whose Aberdeenshire constituency the Russian fish market was badly missed (see Robert Rhodes James, *Bob Boothby. A portrait*, Hodder & Stoughton, 1991, pp. 79-81).
199. Hansard, fifth series, vol. 175, written question to MacDonald, 23 June 1924; NAFTA *Monthly Report*, September 1924, p. 25; *Sunday Worker*, 6 September 1925; GARF 5451/13a/51, 52; T.I. Mardy Jones, 'Soviet Russia', *Colliery Workers' Magazine*, December 1925, p. 272.
200. Hansard, fifth series, vol. 192, cols 2536-9, 10 March 1926; *Fabian News*, May 1925, p. 20.
201. See Andrew J. Williams, *Trading with the Bolsheviks. The politics of East-West trade 1920-39*, Manchester: MUP, 1992, ch. 2 for an assessment. Williams suggests (p. 5) that Soviet trade was limited in scale but of considerable symbolic importance.
202. TUC 57th Congress *Report*, 1925, p. 166.
203. Purcell and Morel, *The Workers and the Anglo-Russian Treaty. Why the treaty must be ratified*, Anglo-Russian Parliamentary Committee, September 1924, pp. 4-5.
204. See the *Spectator* cited W.P. and Zelda Coates, *A History of Anglo-Soviet Relations*, Lawrence & Wishart/Pilot Press, 1943, p. 170; also for example Keith Middlemas and John Barnes, *Baldwin. A biography*, Weidenfeld & Nicolson, 1969, p. 189.
205. NAFTA *Monthly Report*, September 1924, p. 25.
206. Pollitt, preface to Losovsky, *British and Russian Workers*, p. 9. For a similar chronology, see Brailsford, *New Leader*, 3 October 1924.
207. NAFTA *Monthly Journal*, September 1920, pp. 19-20.
208. See e.g. Labour Party archives, ACIQ memoranda no. 188, Brailsford, 'Unemployment, the peace and the indemnity', 1921; also Dorothy F. Buxton, 'Credits for Russia', *Labour Monthly*, January 1922, pp. 39-52.
209. *Russia*, pp. 71-82.
210. 'Notes and news', *Industrial Review*, April 1927, p. 2.
211. TUC 57th Congress *Report*, 1925, pp. 161-71, delegation of 23 June 1925.
212. See *Bolshevism and the British Left*, II, pp. 190-3, also Wise, 'Russia and British trade', *Labour Magazine*, August 1925, pp. 172-5, for a typical presentation of Wise's trading arguments as an employee of the Soviet co-operatives. More generally, see Williams, *Trading*, pp. 59-71, 88.
213. *Sunday Worker*, 3 May 1925.

214. TUC 57th Congress *Report*, 1925, pp. 337-8; *Manchester Guardian*, 17 October 1924.
215. White, *Britain and the Bolshevik Revolution*, p. 233, citing MacDonald's analogy with the recognition of Mohammedans by Christian governments.
216. Adler, *Anglo-Russian Report*, pp. 24-5.
217. E.H. Carr, *Socialism in One Country 1924-1926*. Volume 1, Macmillan, 1958, pp. 202-6.
218. 45th AFL Convention *Report*, 1925, p. 148.
219. See for example Robert Williams, 'Russia and ourselves', *Labour Magazine*, November 1926, pp. 294-6 which makes a good deal of the rising purchasing powe of the Russian people.
220. Friedrich Adler, *The Anglo-Russian Report. A criticism of the report of the British trade union delegation to Russia from the point of view of international socialism*, P.S. King, 1925, pp. 12-13.
221. Conservative Party archives 22775 d. 50, Conservative leaflets, c. 1930.
222. Tillett, preface to Coates, *Is Soviet Trade a Menace?*, ARPC, 1931, p. 5.
223. Coates, *Is Soviet Trade a Menace?*, pp. 57-9.
224. Purcell and Morel, *Workers and the Anglo-Russian Treaty*, p. 8.
225. Brailsford, 'A tribute', *Lansbury's Labour Weekly*, 7 November 1925; Brailsford, 'After eight years', *New Leader*, 6 November 1925. Just a year earlier Brailsford had stressed Bolshevism's barbarous as well as its heroic qualities (*New Leader*, 14 and 21 November 1924).
226. Susan Lawrence, 'Russia: some impressions and some guesses', *Labour Magazine*, November 1925, p. 293.
227. Goldman to Berkman, 15 November 1925. See ch. 2 above for Herbert Morrison's observations on the same event.
228. Calhoun, *United Front*, p. 164.
229. White, *Britain and the Bolshevik Revolution*, pp. 216, 243-4. Of course the feeling was not universally shared. But Frank Hodges, whose comments on Bolshevism are so often cited in this context, was rapidly losing his own sense of community with the labour movement itself, and certainly did not speak for 'uncompromisingly militant' activists.
230. GARF 5451/13a/41, Citrine to Melnichansky, 29 July 1925 and Bogadov to TUC general council, 3 August 1925.
231. Calhoun, *United Front*, p. 164.
232. Calhoun, *United Front*, p. 164 GARF 5451/13a/40, Melnichansky to Citrine, 6 May 1925; GARF 5451/13a/41, Citrine to Melnichansky, 29 July 1925. There was therefore no question of dealing with 'over two hundred' unions as suggested by Calhoun.
233. GARF 5451/13a/40, P.G. Gevenan, assistant general secretary, NUGMW to A. Kantyshev, president, Russian Municipal Employees' Union, 12 October 1925.
234. GARF 5451/13a/55/37, biography of May Purcell, 1925.
235. GARF 5451/13a/55, declaration of British women's delegation in Georgia, 27 June 1925; *Soviet Russia. An investigation by British women trade unionists April to July 1925*, W.P. Coates for the signatories, 1925, p. 87 and passim. For a hostile account citing Goldman against the delegates, see *Daily Mail*, 8 July 1925.
236. See e.g. Citrine, 'The electric republic', *Sunday Worker*, 29 November and

194   Bolshevism, syndicalism and the general strike

        6 December 1925; 'The New Russia', *Trade Union Unity*, December 1925, pp. 138-40.
237. NA KV 4/282, 'Aspects of the General Strike, May, 1926'.
238. Melnichansky to Citrine, 6 May 1925.
239. Melnichansky to Citrine, 6 May 1925
240. See *Bolshevism and the British Left*, I, pp. 118-9.
241. TUC archives, MSS 292/497/3, Williams to 'Dear everybody', 6 July 1926.
242. Robert Williams, 'Press and propaganda in Russia', *Labour Magazine*, September 1926, pp. 204-6.
243. ILP archives 3/16, 3/17, NAC minutes, 7-8 March and 10 April 1925; LSI archives (IISG) SAI 1700, correspondence between Pollak, Adler and Brockway, February-May 1925.
244. RGASPI 539/3/284, report of ICWPA conference, 12 December 1925; also Bob Lovell, report of meeting of ICWPA London contacts, 10 November 1925.
245. See Moritz and Moritz, *World's Most Dangerous Woman*, pp. 91-2.
246. GLDS Nettlau to Goldman, 22 December 1924.
247. Goldman to Isaac Don Levine 8 April 1925.
248. Nettlau papers 158, Goldman to 'Dear Comrades', 15 December 1924 (copy).
249. Russell, *The Practice and Theory of Bolshevism*, Allen & Unwin, 1920, p. 158.
250. Nettlau papers 159, Goldman to Nettlau, 17 April 1925.
251. W.H. Greenleaf, *Order, Empiricism and Politics. Two traditions of English political thought 1500-1700*, Oxford: OUP, 1964, pp. 236-7.
252. Quentin Skinner, 'Interpretation, rationality and truth' in *Visions of Politics. Volume one: regarding method*, Cambridge: CUP, 2002, p. 37.
253. Shaw to Gorki, 28 December 1915 in Dan H. Laurence, ed., *Bernard Shaw. Collected letters 1911-1925*, Max Reinhardt, 1985, p. 341.
254. John Horne and Alan Kramer, *German Atrocities, 1914. A history of denial*, New Haven & London: Yale University Press, 2001.
255. For the manifesto see ch 1.4 above.
256. Lawrence, 'Russia', pp. 293-5.
257. Ellis to Goldman, 28 March 1925.
258. Goldman to Mrs Hawkes, 13 December 1924.
259. Goldman, *Living My Life*, pp. 330-1; 'Observations and comments', *Mother Earth*, April 1907, pp. 60-1.
260. GLDS Goldman to Joseph Ishill, 10 September 1926.
261. GLDS Goldman to Berkman, 16 June 1925.
262. GLDS Goldman to Ellis, 8 November 1925.
263. GLDS Goldman to Berkman, 10 September 1925.
264. GLDS Goldman to Berkman, 30 August 1925. Eleven years later she recovered something of her vision on visiting Catalonia in the early days of the Spanish revolution. Though neither would have accepted the analogy, she travelled with something of the desperate will to believe that had turned Beatrice Webb in the direction of Soviet Russia. Both, in the crushing of their hopes for the future, had immersed themselves in major projects of autobiographical reconstruction. Both were also ignorant of the language, dependent on official guides and predisposed in favour of what they saw – though ultimately Goldman saw that in Spain too Bolshevism cast its shadow.

265. Nettlau papers 159, Goldman to Nettlau 17 April 1926; also Goldman to Ben Reitman, 15 April 1926.
266. GLDS Goldman to Nettlau, 4 April 1926.
267. GLDS Goldman to Nettlau, 31 May 1926. Goldman later suggested that Turner supported her suggestion and that it was turned down by the TUC (*Living My Life*, pp. 983-4). It is most unlikely that Turner ever took the idea seriously. As a correspondent wrote to Goldman: 'I don't see why you bear a grudge against old Turner, and think he was perfectly justified, under the circumstances, to keep you out of the picture' (GLDS Michael Cohn to Goldman, 26 May 1926).
268. GLDS, Astor to Goldman, 26 May 1926 and related correspondence between them April-May 1926.
269. Goldman, *Living My Life*, pp. 981-4; Wexler, *Emma Goldman in Exile*, p. 127.

Chapter five

The other future?

5.1 THE FUTURE IN AMERICA

In 1906 H.G. Wells concluded his book of travel impressions, *The Future in America*, by reflecting on the wider circulation of this type of literature. Uplifted by America's 'morning-time hopefulness', Wells viewed the recording of such encounters as the means of the world attaining to greater self-awareness, perhaps, in due course, to the World State of which he dreamt. It was not, he wrote, simply America 'that we swarm over and build up into a conceivable process, into something understandable and negotiable by the mind'. Now in India, now in Africa, now perhaps in Germany, this was a work of collective illumination, a literature of 'facts and theories and impressions' aimed at 'getting the world presented'.[1]

No country or regime was alone in giving rise to these facts and impressions; in getting any one part of the world presented, what also had to be negotiated was its changing inter-relationship with the other parts, not least the presenter's own. In its diverse aspects of ideology, culture and inter-state relations, this was pre-eminently the case with the other future represented by Russia. Announcing itself from the outset as both anti-system and nemesis to the west, Bolshevism was impossible to place except through the construction of rivalries, anathemas and alternatives. Notwithstanding the avowed self-sufficiency of Stalin's socialism in one country, comparison remained inherent in the Bolshevik claim to universal validity or exemplarity, and in the multiple forms of emulation and contestation to which this gave rise. Communism in turn drew legitimacy and rationale from the negative image of its competitors. The interconnections between pro-Sovietism and anti-fascism are familiar. Technocratic enthusiasm for Russian hyper-productivism appears as the mirror image of economic breakdown in the west. In an age of rekindled national hatreds and oppressions, the vaunted resolution of the nationalities question offered argument and inspiration. Often discussed in isolation, or as if the only relevant comparator was the religious pilgrimage, the road to Russia in reality was one of a number of possible itineraries which were never merely 'seen' or 'believed', but offered different ways of getting the world presented.[2]

Over the longer twentieth century, the most significant contest was that between communism and America itself. As the defining cleavage of a bipolar world, the later cold war has naturally generated a huge literature, but its origins between the wars rather less of one. Projected in the 'soft' forms of ideological and cultural influence, the earlier rivalry weighed less heavily on Europe than would the construction of rival blocs. It was also, as a result, less relentless and prescriptive, with room for considerable ambiguity cutting across both national and party boundaries. As Wells had recognised, America's claim, like Bolshevism's, was that of an alternative possible future. Though each could also appear as present threat, their fascination for the ailing Europe of the 1920s was, said Beatrice Webb, as two great laboratories of social organisation. The lure or repulsion of Americanism was a crucial factor in the relationship of Bolshevism and the European left, and it is as a competing image of the future, just as Purcell saw it on visiting the USA in 1925, that it is primarily considered here.

A century earlier, in another age of social, political and military convulsions, it had become common to link the emerging powers to east and west as Europe's possible inheritors.[3] Following the Napoleonic wars, Henri Beyle – the novelist Stendhal – envisaged Britain, despite its temporary ascendancy, being reduced to a third-rate power by those beyond the reach of any military threat.[4] In 1835 Tocqueville concluded the first volume of his *Democracy in America* with the image of Russia and America as the coming nations that would 'sway the destinies of half the globe'. Tocqueville's work enjoyed a wide success, and the motif for a time was widely adopted.[5] Beyle had noted America's and Russia's strategic invulnerability; the young Louis Napoleon added the crucial counterpoint of the 'old European centre' as 'a volcano consuming itself in its crater'.[6] The Russian radical Alexander Herzen, after the crises and disappointments of the 1840s, depicted Europe as a passing civilisation, deficient in energy and will-power, and the Americans and Slavs as its likely heirs.[7]

Such imaginings were readily entertained for as long as a sense of crisis in the established European powers combined with anticipation or apprehension of their younger rivals. For decades after 1848, that moment had clearly passed. Europe in the 'age of capital' was in its ascendancy, not its death-throes, and Britain was not yet the fallen colossus that Beyle had imagined. If anything, it was Russia under the last three tsars (1855-1917) which seemed more at risk of consuming itself, or of surviving only at the expense of financial and cultural dependency on the west.[8] Though a substantial public opinion interested itself in Russia's affairs, it was on account of its scandalous, 'medieval' backwardness.[9] Wells in 1906 might hope to find the future in America. Following Japan's military triumph over Russia, he could even be drawn by the idea of a Samurai order. He would not, however, have thought to find Europe's destiny prefigured in Russia itself. Visiting in 1914, he dismissed the Russian Bogey got up by '"advanced" people' in the west. It was nevertheless to Russia's share in a western future that he looked, not Russia as possible image of the future in itself.[10]

Revolution changed all that. By the time that Wells revisited the country in 1920, Europe was once more struggling with the legacy of war and its own failed or aborted revolutions. Mussolini's fascism might also present itself as a sort of rebirth, but in Britain its appeal was to a 'Diehard Tory' element.[11] If jazz-age America seemed to have discovered the key to the affluent society, Bolshevism alone seemed possessed of a comparable dynamism, and on the eve, as Wells put it, of its own 'noble future'.[12] Exceptionally, the German social democrat Kautsky had already discerned this possibility in the revolutionary movement that was to come to the fore in the Russian revolution of 1905. Responding to Werner Sombart's famous exposition of American exceptionalism, Kautsky took issue with the notion that America offered Europeans the image of their own future. Instead he stressed the uneven development of capitalism in its different aspects, agreeing that America represented its highest development economically, but arguing that Russia led the way in the revolutionary movement of the proletariat that stood for the alternative to capitalism. While conceived as an intervention in debates within German social democracy, the argument also had a wider international resonance. Not America alone, Kautsky wrote, but both countries showed Europeans their future: 'it will have a half-American, half-Russian character'.[13]

It was a remarkable anticipation. As Russia achieved its political revolution, it was in Americanism that it saw the other half of the future that it had yet to realise. Both societies envisaged a future of mass production and mass communications, and in a Europe fixated on the idea of the modern it was as harbingers of this new mass society that their images were compared, contrasted and juxtaposed. Many regarded them with a common hostility, or with Spenglerian foreboding for the older Europe.[14] But they could also be presented, as Beatrice Webb perceived them, as 'vital world forces' or 'stupendous social experiments' that left the old world trailing in their wake.[15] Gramsci, in one of his best known writings, described Americanism as the latest phase of industrialism and 'the biggest collective effort to date to create, with unprecedented speed and with a consciousness of purpose unmatched in history, a new type of worker and of man'.[16] Precisely this 'new type of worker and of man' lay at the heart of the issue between Americanism and Bolshevism, just as the cult of speed and sense of purpose can be found in both. 'Both creeds, though they differ in all else', wrote the British communist W.T. Colyer, 'look to the future'.[17]

But if the Bolsheviks themselves felt the pull of Americanism, it was because Bolshevism as yet offered little more than an ethos and aesthetics of mass production. The legacy of economic backwardness was for many years compounded by the effects of war and civil war; not until the late 1920s did Russia even regain its production levels of 1914. Though Krasin in 1920 briefly mesmerised a Fabian audience with the promise of the scientific organisation of industry, not for another decade could the Soviets compete with any credibility on such terms. Bolshevism might aspire to a sort of socialised Americanism. What it represented to the wider world, however, was not half-American, half-Russian, but Russia as alternative to an Americanised future and what Gramsci initially described as the revolution against *Capital*. Kautsky in 1905 had discerned in the Russians a quality missing in America which he described as revolutionary romanticism.[18] British trade unionists may not have put it that way. What nevertheless attracted them to Bolshevism was the recognition it seemingly accorded established labour values and priorities, against the inexorable logic of the capitalist economy. The irony was that Kautsky after 1917 rejected what he now called the 'Tartar' revolution, on the basis that the economic conditions for its fulfilment did not exist.[19] For some in Kautsky's party, Americanism itself provided the alternative. The future was not only contested, but contested according to different measures of value and achievement.

Purcell's pro-Bolshevism and anti-Americanism are consequently impossible to disentangle. His engagement with America comprised just the one visit as fraternal delegate to the American Federation of Labour (AFL) in 1925. With his penchant for controversy he nevertheless exposed the tensions in this relationship as few other visitors could have. The episode is approached here through a broader discussion that confirms the significance of movements across national boundaries, and at the same time of variations in these movements inviting comparative reflection. Bearing the promise of a sort of modernity, but through the maintenance or intensification of existing relations of property and power, Americanism divided both radicals and conservatives in ways that made for shifting alignments across time and space. As such it both complements and illuminates Purcell's view of Soviet Russia.

5.2 FORDISM AND THE LEFT

'There are two ways of acquiring a party reputation as a foreign affairs specialist in the present day political world', observed a contributor to the ILP's *Socialist Review* in 1928. 'If one is conservative one goes to America, spends three hectic weeks being pump-handled by enthusiastic Americans and then comes back and writes a book proving that capitalism is the only possible system, etc, etc. In the other political camp one goes either to Russia or to Geneva.'[20] Geneva, headquarters of the League of Nations and the International Labour Organisation, may be set aside here as of primary interest in matters of international regulation. In both its American and its Russian aspect, on the other hand, this was a distinctly British way of viewing things. Across Europe as a whole, not even Russia gave rise to the simple left-to-right alignment here suggested, and this was still more the case with America.

So far as the left was concerned, the key to such variation ideologically was the differing character and influence of marxism from one country to another. In Germany, where the marxism of the Second International had its deepest roots, it also took its most scientistic, productivist and determinist form. Kautsky in 'The American worker' had proposed a complex relationship between the economic and political preconditions of socialism. In respect of the first of these alone, however, there is no doubt of what Peter Beilharz has called the unrepentant modernism of Kautsky's thinking.[21] Conviction as to the intensification of exploitation under capitalism was matched by insistence on the progressive character and irreversibility of enhanced productive technique and capacity. Such advances gave rise to those immediate forms of class struggle that were inherent in capitalist property relations. But in a longer historical perspective, they were not only the indispensable economic basis for socialism, but the key to the revolution itself, as the development of productive forces came into conflict with the private ownership of the means of production. It was this strand in marxism, as a counsel of economic necessitarianism, that engendered Kautsky's powerful critique of Bolshevism in power as a relapse into utopianism, sustainable only on the basis of coercion.[22] Within conditions of capitalism, on the other hand, the same modernising discourses could descend into technomania and the triumph of capacity over values.[23] Kautsky may once have recognised the force of a sort of political romanticism. But in his validation of the 'irresistible forward march' of machinery and the division of labour, there was little notion of the work process itself as a site of contestation and resistance.[24]

In the very different contexts of the German and the Russian revolutions, these common ideological roots made for a fascination with Americanism across the now bifurcated marxist tradition. Over the centuries America had had many meanings, the sole common factor being its relative disencumberment from history. In an age of ascendant liberalism, it had seemed a world beyond the reach of feudal relations and the forms of deference and subordination to which these gave rise. Little of that allure survived the coming of the trusts. Some indeed attributed the peculiarly naked and brutalised character of American capitalism to the absence of those constraints of feudal or civic obligation that lingered on vestigially in Europe.[25] Instead it was the age-old legacy of craft production, whose roots might also be traced to the middle ages, which in America seemed far more tenuous than in the old world. Still in 1924, when the Railwaymen's leader Cramp set foot in America it was as the 'fulfilment of a dream' in which Emerson, Lowell and the Declaration of Independence came directly to mind.[26] For rather more of Cramp's labour movement contemporaries, Americanism had nevertheless by this time acquired the very different connotations of Taylorism, Fordism and rationalisation.

Taylorism was the theory of 'scientific management' expounded from around the turn of the century by the American engineer Frederick W. Taylor. Fordism, building upon it, was both a model of industrial organisation and the social philosophy extrapolated from it by the Detroit motor manufacturer Henry Ford. The German cognomen of 'rationalisation' was also of transatlantic inspiration; according to a contemporary commentator it was 'without exception linked to the expression "Americanisation" in the European literature', while also carrying connotations of vertical integration and cartelisation.[27] That the idea of rationalisation went into general currency, and was the most widely employed of these terms in Britain from the mid-1920s, serves as reminder that Americanism represented social processes that were neither unique to the USA nor as ubiquitous there as was sometimes suggested. Moreover, though the precise relationship between them was unclear, these concepts were never simply interchangeable. For the historian Charles S. Maier, Fordism and Taylorism were aspects of Americanism, and rationalisation an elaboration of Fordism.[28] For Gramsci at the time, the Taylorist organisation of work processes was the most brutal expression of Fordism as Americanism.[29] The communist Dutt, on the other hand, referred indifferently to 'rationalisation or Americanisation', but nevertheless distinguished this from the more ideological construct – or 'golden mythical pictures' – he identified with Fordism.[30]

Through publications like Ford's *My Life and Work* (1922) these images circulated throughout the Europe of the 1920s, but with receptions that varied both within and across national boundaries. The very 'apostle of Americanism', in the words of the Russian writer Ehrenburg, was Berlin.[31] Mary Nolan's admirable study refers to Weimar Germany's Ford 'psychosis' or infatuation, noting that it sent more investigators to America than any other country, and saw through thirteen printings and 200,000 copies of *My Life and Work*.[32] What mainly distinguished this from the milder British strain of Americanism was not so much its intensity as its assimilation into a broadly social-democratic vision of modernity. The 'purely formal imitation of American labour methods' was rejected by German labour leaders. The dehumanising aspects of US-style Taylorisation were acknowledged, and given the proficiency and ready availability of European labour it was not thought necessary to carry the division of labour to American extremes.[33] Nevertheless, the productivist rationale which Fordism carried on from Taylorism was thought to possess an intrinsic 'progressive' validity, irrespective of its temporary mechanisms of control and distribution.

In Germany communists challenged capitalist rationalisation, and their orientation to its victims has been seen as providing a structural basis for the KPD's sharpening antagonism towards social democracy.[34] The variants of state power, as embodied in the Bolshevik and Weimar regimes, were thus a defining issue for the divided marxist tradition. Productivism, on the other hand, was not, and nor did NEP Russia lag behind with its own Ford psychosis. With *My Life and Work* running through eight editions, Ford's name borne with Lenin's on processions and *fordizatsiya* proclaimed the escape-route from backwardness, this has been described as the moment of Russia's 'rediscovery of America'.[35] Though written in isolation and published only posthumously, Gramsci's 'Fordism and Americanism' was thus indicative of a wider fascination with Americanism as the perfection of technique. Also predicating social advance on the development of productive forces, Gramsci hailed the displacement of customary working practices by a new and superior 'psycho-physical equilibrium', by which a part of the old working class would be 'pitilessly exterminated' from the world of labour – but which, on the other hand, could be fully internalised only on the basis of the workers' own power.[36]

In its Soviet and Gramscian renditions, Fordism, like Taylorism, was essentially a philosophy of rationalised production. This alone, however, could not explain its spell over a Europe whose plight, the reverse of Russia's, was the inability to work even its existing productive resources.[37] Nolan, in her German study, identified consumptionist and ideological as well as productivist readings of Fordism. With its stress on entrepreneurial leadership, the ideological reading clearly buttressed business values.[38] What made Fordism so attractive to sections of the left, on the other hand, was the claim to marry productive technique and organisation to the consumptionist mantra of High Wages.[39] To the extent that social democrats offered a critical perspective on rationalisation in Germany, it was in the insistence on this link with the raising of workers' purchasing power.[40]

Where it failed to offer a critical perspective was in respect of the work process itself. Concerns with 'quality work', which in Britain were a central issue for many guilds enthusiasts, were derided by Gramsci and identified in Germany with the political right.[41] Like Gramsci, who envisaged a work-process so undemanding as to free the mind to explore its own higher reaches, SPD socialists looked beyond the performance of work functions for the flowering of personality. This again was rooted in a Kautskyan ideal, not of the 'freedom of labour', but of freedom *from* labour through machine production, and thus of the opening to all of a 'happy, harmonious culture' such as the Athenians had attained by the achievement of leisure through slavery.[42] Weimar's eight-hour day could be seen as a step in this direction, and a 'German model' briefly presented for possible emulation by British labour.[43] The price, according to Nolan, was that the left abandoned to its opponents any possible discourse about alternative technologies and job satisfaction. 'Work as reality belonged to the proletariat; work as ideology became the distinct preserve of the right.'[44]

In countries like Germany and Britain the same sorts of industry mattered, and they faced many similar problems. In responding to these problems, moreover, European labour movements drew on ideas and experiences circulating internationally, precisely as did Kautsky's pamphlets and later Lenin's. Differing attitudes to Americanism and Bolshevism were not innate but constructed politically in ways that altered over time, and in response to variations in the patterns of party and ideological conflict. For the SPD, whose most basic rivalry was with communism, Americanism offered the answer to the politics of catastrophism and the inevitability of a revolutionary breakdown. Even in France, where the CGT union confederation also experienced a communist breakaway, the left-wing metalworkers' secretary Alphonse Merrheim abandoned his earlier forthright criticisms of Taylorism, and became as forceful a proponent of its precepts as he did an opponent of communism.[45] Probably the most influential advertisement of American methods from the worker's point of view was the work of Merrheim's protégé and sometime fellow CGT official, Hyacinthe Dubreuil, whose book was published in an English edition with the endorsement of the Taylor Institute.[46]

In Britain itself there was no home-grown equivalent. As American success, like the scourge of Bolshevism, was deployed against the labour movement by its traditional enemies, a prevalent left-wing discourse remained of Americanism as threat or cautionary tale. Concerns at the extension of US power, prefiguring Cold War anti-Americanism, were expressed by some in response to the Dawes plan of 1924.[47] This, however, was an entirely secondary theme. In the most uncompromising of the period's critical accounts, Colyer's *Americanism: a world menace*, it was explicitly discounted in favour of the more pervasive 'indirect, unrecognised influence' which Americanism, rather like Prussianism, expressed in its most sharply crystallised form.[48] In part it was an issue of 'work as ideology', in part one of cultural aspiration and its perceived debasement. Each will be taken in turn before we proceed to Purcell's encounter with America in the autumn of 1925.

5.3 WORKERS VS ROBOTS

In 1902, the South African mine-owner Alfred Mosely organised a so-called industrial commission of British trade unionists to the USA.

Published amidst the mounting obsession with national efficiency of Britain's political class, the resulting report was a landmark construction of Americanism as industrial threat and exemplar. Though each member of the (all-male) party contributed notes on his own trade, Mosely, as instigator and sole subscriber, retained the prerogative of setting out its broader conclusions. Notably these focused on the abandonment of 'old' methods and machinery, including the machinery of industrial confrontation, and the harnessing of employees' initiative in the fullest exploitation of labour-saving machinery. The prospect of higher wages and living standards was thus dangled before the British worker as the just reward of co-operation. The 'true-born American', Mosely summed up, 'is a better educated, better housed, better fed, better clothed, and more energetic man than his British brother, and infinitely more sober'. His British brother, one must infer, was ill fed, read and clothed and infinitely more drunk.[49]

Twenty-four years later, the *Daily Mail* organised another 'Trade Union Mission' to the USA. It took its inspiration from the current prime minister Baldwin, who had urged that nothing could better serve trade unionists than establishing how the American worker had come to enjoy the world's highest living standards and levels of productivity.[50] No workmen were as skilled, competent and trustworthy as those in Britain, the US Secretary of Labour informed the visitors encouragingly. 'But you must speed up. Big production is the only hope for you.'[51] Mosely too had traced the secret of American prosperity to the speed and scale of its machinery of production.[52] Continuity between the two initiatives was symbolised by the fulsome backing of the *Mail* party of the sometime Labour MP and ASE general secretary George Barnes, who had been a member of the Mosely commission.

Juxtaposition of these ventures nevertheless reveals significant differences in the framing of the issue. A 'fundamental realignment' in British attitudes to America has been traced to the final decades of the previous century.[53] Conservative denigration gave way to approval, radical sympathies were dissipated, and a shared imperial vision served to mitigate older foreign-policy antagonisms.[54] What the two industrial missions also demonstrate is Americanism emerging more specifically as an employers' refrain, but one intended for workers' consumption and delivered in a spirit of warning and exhortation. By 1926 one may clearly observe the narrowing of this perspective, its more aggressively anti-union character and its diminishing credibility with trade unionists themselves.

Whatever his motives, Mosely had a genuine reformer's interest in America, to which he shortly afterwards organised a similar educational mission. The origin and timing of the *Mail* initiative, in the aftermath of Red Friday, betrayed a more blatant concern to counteract what Barnes called 'outworn theories of class conflict'.[55] Mosely would not have dissented from that aim. He did however succeed in recruiting twenty-three bona fide union officers, including the chairman of the TUC parliamentary committee. Though these may not necessarily have supported his conclusions, only one, the SDFer and London trades council secretary James McDonald, failed to contribute to the resulting publication. The *Daily Mail* had also intended selecting delegates with the 'knowledge and assistance' of their unions.[56] But no such co-operation was forthcoming.[57] Even Barnes by this time had relinquished any standing in the labour movement, and at the time of the *Mail* party Baldwin was writing to cabinet colleagues of his parlous financial position and need for employment.[58] The only other recognisable trade unionist to join the party was the former Patternmakers' secretary William Mosses. Mosses, however, had long since broken his ties with the labour movement, and his union wrote expressly to dissociate itself from the venture.[59] No accredited trade unionist would have travelled for the *Mail* had it offered them a trip to paradise itself. It is as revealing politically that the *Mail* should have sponsored American industrial methods as was its later promotion of the Blackshirts.

What American methods represented was subject to varying interpretations. Mosely's emphasis had been on themes of partnership, profit-sharing and strong but responsible organisation on both sides of industry. Nevertheless, as the idea of scientific management became familiar in Britain, it was in a period, not of partnership, but of mounting industrial unrest. Despite the efforts of some of its advocates, it thus became synonymous with the attack on the 'restrictive' practices and collective organisation that appeared to stand in its way. Already in 1911, the Singer strike at Clydebank provided an early British set-piece battle over 'American' methods.[60] Clydeside employers, indeed, were seen as distinctly autocratic and anti-union almost as their American counterparts were.[61] The most overtly Americanising of them was the combative William Weir, who not only indicted custom, skill and workers' organisation with homilies of transatlantic derivation, but borrowed a factory design from Ford's for his Cathcart foundry.[62]

Promoted by such as Weir, even the welfare aspects of US-style paternalism provoked a healthy cynicism. 'Surrounded by a retinue of "scientific managers" ... workmen are regarded by him as so much raw material for manufacturing pumps!', ran an Ironmoulders' leaflet of 1919:

> The refractory human element that separates the moulder from the pig-iron, or the mechanic from the machine, he would fain repress ... with apparently cheap overalls, and Weir's special dope in the shape of a monthly bulletin, added to the 'Clubs' and such-like 'Welfare' work, honest men are expected to be robbed of their character and reduced to the category of worms![63]

Worms, robots, bags of mails: we shall see that metaphors varied, but the dehumanisation of labour was a constantly recurring theme in the labour movement literature of the 1920s. This commitment to 'work as ideology' – work, that is, as a source of identity and site of contestation that went beyond its mere exchange value – was at least as evident in the new 'producer' ideologies of syndicalism and guild socialism as in the older craft traditions which in other respects they repudiated.

It may, on the other hand, be identified more particularly with trades in which these traditions had the greatest resonance. In tracing the historical roots of the different cultural constructions of labour in Britain and Germany, Richard Biernacki drew particularly on the woollen industry, which was not especially conspicuous in later discussions.[64] In contending that issues of workplace control were more tenaciously defended in Britain than in any other country, Richard Price cited a wide range of examples from the 1850s to the inter-war period.[65] As Mike Savage sums up, through the link between ideas of work and cultures of independence and masculinity, manual labour in twentieth-century Britain was invested with 'distinctive moral values'.[66] While such general observations are certainly valid, more limited articulations, like responses to Americanism, might reflect the real or symbolic influence of particular industrial sectors, varying over time. From this perspective, the overt anti-Americanism of the 1920s may once again be linked with the high visibility of the building and associated trades, whose sectional expediencies and deeper sense of identity it voiced so clearly.[67] More or less coinciding with Purcell's TUC career, the general critique of Americanism had already become more restricted in scope and influence by the end of the decade.

A generation of British socialists had been exposed to ideas of the builder as archetypal craftsman through authors like Ruskin, Morris and Robert Tressell. Even in the German context, Beilharz notes the connection between Kautsky's rejection of a regressive syndicalism and its links with craft production in the building trades.[68] Forms of industrial organisation nevertheless influenced the dominant articulation of such views. Within the International Union of Woodworkers there was a clear contrast between the craft-influenced militancy of NAFTA, initially its sole British affiliate, and the all-embracing German Woodworkers' Union, with its imposing central offices and a membership in Berlin alone more than twice that of NAFTA's nationally.[69] What they did have in common was a breadth of industrial outlook, and the wider influence that derived from this. When the wood worker Leipart in 1920 succeeded Legien as secretary of the German union confederation the ADGB, one consideration was that 'in contrast to most other leaders, his concern with union matters ranged beyond the confines of his own union'.[70]

If that suggests a striking parallel with Bramley, there was by this time no common ground in their attitudes to Bolshevism. In the same way, it was another Woodworkers' official, Fritz Tarnow, who proved the most outspoken exponent in Germany of social-democratic Americanism. Purcell, on the other hand, was an utter stranger to what might be called technological romanticism. In his first parliamentary campaign, in 1910, he had argued that 'Chemical and Mechanical Science' had so far developed as to bring humanity, not blessings but a curse. In his second parliamentary campaign, in 1923, he re-used the passage almost word for word.[71] Within a building trades' environment such sentiments were anything but controversial. As one of Mosely's party had put it, American methods threatened the craftsman's natural pride in 'strength, durability, and finish' and sacrificed years of effort to achieve such workmanship 'in the interests of present-day utility'.[72]

Nothing so infuriated industrial modernisers as this disregard for present utility. The British building worker of the 1920s was seen as the epitome of restrictive practices, and the industry as a whole as one luxuriating in its sheltered status and the imperative social demand for its products. Even Cole recorded the impression that the building industry hardly knew the meaning of a 'reasonable day's work'.[73] With housing now a defining issue of domestic politics, there was no other case in which the issue between craft and technology was so widely represented.[74] Challenged on the unions' alleged exploitation of pressing housing shortages, Labour sought to reconcile social needs and building livelihoods through the 1924 Wheatley Housing Act, which Purcell, as we have seen, regarded as a model. But beyond such necessary counter-claims, there was a qualitatively different perception of the building process as one that could not be reduced to its end product in a spirit of mere convenience.

It was thus that a guild-socialist ethos, not so much obliterating craft values as generalising and democratising them, had its greatest contemporary resonance in this sector.[75] Hicks as bricklayers' secretary could be dismissive of Bramley's more romanticised evocations of the craft spirit. Even Hicks, however, described this same craft spirit as a form of basic 'self respect' in advancing an ideal-type definition of the Webbs' Doctrine of the Vested Interest. 'Would doctors, lawyers, architects, or even dancing masters, look upon "dilution" favourably?' Were they prepared to be handled 'like so many bags of mails'? Was the making of a qualified bricklayer or joiner not also the work of several years?[76] Into the 1930s and beyond, building trades' officials could raise the spectre of a 'twentieth century John Ludd', moved not just by fear of displacement but by a sense of degradation. The Building Trades' president Thomas Barron tapped into this wider discourse in 1930: 'The ordinary Capitalist idea of rationalisation is to reduce costs, to speed up production, to displace men by machines, to remove all semblance of craftsmanship and those things which give men joy in their labour, and to make the few remaining human beings who are left employed into mere mechanical Robots, who, provided they are kept stoked, oiled and trimmed, will give no more trouble than their counterparts which are made of metal ...'[77]

Appropriately, it was Weir who took on what he thought a protected monopoly, through the mass production of prefabricated houses built on Fordist rather than Gropian principles of total product standardisation.[78] Undertaken with the Baldwin government's backing and with Fordist promotional flair, the so-called Weir steel house even generated its own trickle of overseas admirers, particularly from Germany. The economist Julius Hirsch merits special mention as the author of works like *Das amerikanische Wirtschaftwunder* (The American Economic Miracle), and a figure ideologically close to the SPD. In the *Berliner Tageblatt* Hirsch made the familiar equation between mass production and mass enrichment, whatever the implications for the work process. 'The German workpeople will scarcely oppose such an experiment', he concluded. 'If it succeeds, it means, like every economic improvement, both the increase in purchasing power of the masses and the increase in employment ... Moreover, the German trade union – and that is exactly what is noted again and again in England – has never yet resisted economic progress.'[79]

The 'English' unions, by implication, took a different attitude, and with general but not universal labour movement support successfully defeated Weir's innovations. A world of cultural and institutional difference may be traced through these experiments in industrialised building. In Weimar Germany, it was the progressive architect, employed by socialist administrations and drawing on the *Bauhütten* (building guilds), which pioneered the use of new, cheaper and faster methods of construction. The *Bauhütten* themselves achieved their considerable success as social building corporations, accountable to their consumers and (social) investors, but not so concerned with the issues of self-government that moved their British counterparts. Where Weir had Baldwin's backing, the managing director of the *Bauhütten* was Berlin's social-democratic head of city planning, Martin Wagner, who energetically espoused industrialised building methods and left the craft values of the *Berufsethos* to social and political conservatives.[80]

With his usual insight, the *Vorwärts* London correspondent Egon Wertheimer ascribed these differences to the German trade unionist's early induction into marxist concepts. Even if this were often 'mere lip-service', it still meant the ability to see beyond the 'immediately practical' in issues of production and working relations.

> His British brother ... unburdened by theoretical conviction, has a far greater appreciation of immediate realities. Marxist training has given the German leader ability to counteract in his union those medieval craft tendencies that have hampered the British trade union movement even

to this day, and to approve rationalisation as an inevitable process in capitalist development at a time when to the Englishmen ... not only the concept but the process itself seemed more than suspicious.[81]

Gramsci similarly claimed that in Italy it was 'precisely the workers who brought into being newer and more modern industrial requirements and in their own way upheld these strenuously'.[82] Gramsci also held that in the USA it was the AFL, with its craft basis of organisation, that embodied resistance to these necessary innovations.[83] Nevertheless, if the AFL and its German counterpart the ADGB now found the basis for a common understanding, it was in the common belief that organised labour had an interest in these developments. If any national body displayed the craft-based spirit of stubbornness that Gramsci so despised, it was the TUC.

When Ross McKibbin posed the question of why there was no 'marxism' in Great Britain, he used the word interchangeably with 'rejectionism'.[84] McKibbin's starting point was the absence in Britain of the sort of mass rejectionist party apparently exemplified by the pre-1914 SPD. It is nevertheless arguable that it was precisely where marxism took this form that its rejectionism was most obviously attenuated after 1918. Conversely, disencumberment from the disciplines of party could leave intact, not so much a rejectionist articulation of the class struggle, but an abstentionist position on the responsibilities for 'capitalist development' that might have impeded it. In the summer of 1925, both Purcell and Hicks simply declined to suggest possible remedies at a TUC conference on unemployment. 'We are not responsible for the organisation or the absence of organisation of private enterprise in industry', said Hicks. It was the capitalists' system; they should find remedies if they could; the unions should get rid of them if there were no remedies, and defend their members in the meantime.[85]

Except for this last consideration, there were obvious affinities here with the 'utopianism' which, in Robert Skidelsky's judgement, left the second MacDonald government helpless in the face of the same problem of mass unemployment.[86] Of nowhere was it truer than in Britain that the marxist, as Wells put it, adopted Marx as his prophet 'simply because he believes that Marx wrote of the class war, an implacable war of the employed against the employer, and that he prophesied a triumph for the employed person'.[87] For those within this syndicalistic tradition, what Gramsci called the 'inherent necessity' of productive development was simply not the workers' concern for as long as capitalism lasted.

Hostility to American methods was not confined to trade unionists. Views differ as to how far labour's intellectuals shaped, voiced or appropriated the movement's values. They had certainly been exposed to the Ruskin, Morris and latterly Cole tradition, and humane concerns for the work process were expressed in what might be thought unexpected quarters. Though the Fabian ordering of work and leisure apparently resembled the SPD's, Beatrice Webb, even without the influence of Cole, had described scientific management as justifying sabotage.[88] Later Fabian lecturers were confirmed in such misgivings by Ford's example and had a new word for expressing them in the shape of the Čapek brothers' invention of the robot in their play *R.U.R.* (English edition 1923). Three years before Barron, the Webbs' youthful epigone W.A. Robson indicted Ford precisely for having 'robotised' his workers in disregard for the strain, monotony and subjection that this imposed upon them.[89] Herman Finer, having spent a year at an American university, spoke of industrial 'tyranny' as a matter of course.[90] A dissenting presence was S.K. Ratcliffe, a prolific commentator on US affairs, who in the Fabians' 1927-8 lecture series saw in America's 'more enlightened order of capitalists and managers' the makings of a 'new type of civilisation', giving the lie to the Webbian jeremiad of capitalist decay. The prevailing Fabian view may nevertheless be gleaned from the title originally allotted Ratcliffe, 'Industrial feudalism – the capitalist autocracy'.[91]

Americanism had its most obvious resonance with the underconsumptionist economics of the ILP. Already in 1921, Snowden's protégé William Graham cited the example of scientific management and a high-wage economy in his book *The Wages of Labour*.[92] With the ILP's adoption of the Living Wage policy in the mid-1920s, the influence of such an example was more emphatically attested. In 1926, Oswald and Cynthia Mosley went on their own transatlantic fact-finding mission, whose impact Skidelsky compares to that upon the Webbs of their own later search for a new civilisation. As with so many visitors, the Ford works in Detroit was the high point of the Mosleys' itinerary. They returned with the lesson that high wages not only sustained domestic purchasing power but commanded efficiency through the need to circumvent high labour costs.[93] Expositions of the Living Wage struck a similar note, while also noting the role that restriction of immigration played in maintaining American wage levels.[94] Only afterwards were the huge variations in American living standards properly registered as a threat to the high-wage economy from within.[95] In notably pungent chapters published in 1927, Palme Dutt accused the ILP of a wholesale capitulation to the American 'myth', sedulously promoted as a diversion from the class struggle.[96]

What Dutt regarded as incidental objections – to 'the autocracy, opposition to trade unions, etc' – were nevertheless central to the ILP presentation of Americanism.[97] While Mosley, like his German counterparts, did see in a fuller life outside of work the compensation for its increasing monotony, others held that socialism meant the refusal of any such trade-off. Wilfred Wellock was another Midlands Labour candidate who converted to socialism via Morris and Tolstoy.[98] He was also among the ILP Americanisers specifically cited by Dutt.[99]

Writing for the *New Leader* on the basis of a four-month lecture tour, Wellock's dominant impression was nevertheless of the tyranny of production methods that cast men aside like bricks and sacrificed human well-being on the altars of 'quantity, cheapness and speed'.[100] Brailsford, the *Leader*'s editor and a vigorous proponent of the Living Wage, conceded the possibility and even likelihood of US capitalism overcoming poverty through abundant resources and 'intelligent technique'. Even so, he rejected the price of a degrading materialism, and held even well-paid American workers to be 'more helpless under the dictatorship of capital than any impoverished proletariat in Europe which struggles and keeps its own soul'. Labour's object was 'to change the motive of work'. Should it abandon that object for 'an easy material life' it merely hastened its own defeat.[101]

Dutt thought these inconsequential 'ethical' caveats. Two implications may nevertheless be noted. One was that the possibility of capitalism perpetuating itself on such a basis made it only the more imperative to proceed to socialism before it did so. Not socialism or barbarism, as Dutt might have had it, but socialism or Americanism were therefore presented as alternatives, according to a timescale scarcely less peremptory than that of Dutt's catastrophism. The second point is that it was precisely on these ethical grounds that ILP socialists were simultaneously drawn towards the USSR as the counterfoil to Americanism. A year after visiting America, Wellock went to Russia and marvelled in the pervading sense of joy, purposeful anticipation and 'human nature at its best!'[102] Brailsford also visited in 1927 and held somewhat euphemistically that the political system was still in a state of transition. Nevertheless, like Wellock he saluted the removal of inequalities of status and opportunity as having solved the 'greatest of all human problems ... the problem of social freedom', and thus as having removed the heaviest obstacle to the development of the human potential of its people.[103]

Concerns with the status of labour extended beyond the work process to society as a whole. Perhaps, like Perry Anderson, we should think of this as 'proletarian positivity', reflecting a 'distinct hermetic culture' that thwarted socialist direction through very excess of its 'corporatist class consciousness'.[104] Aspirations for a better society were identified with the progress of organised labour, and in the three-volume labour movement *Encyclopaedia* of 1927 entries on all industrial powers except for Russia concentrated exclusively on the character, strength and legal standing of their respective labour movements. Finer's section on the USA thus failed even to mention Fordism in either its productivist or consumptionist reading, but attributed the success of US capitalism to the weakness of legal regulation and collective bargaining procedures.[105] Politically speaking, the same limited outlook was held to be exemplified by the lack of an American labour party and the accommodating spirit of the American unions. A naked class dictatorship, wrote Colyer, had been established 'for purely offensive purposes against ... one of the feeblest and most docile Labour organisations in the world'.[106] The influence of such a literature was to be clearly manifested when Purcell in 1925 addressed that same organisation as fraternal delegate.

5.4 BARBARIANS, PHILISTINES, POPULACE

It is a truism that Americanism and anti-Americanism existed in multiple variants, political, industrial and cultural. Not all things American were assimilated into these constructions, and within America itself there were continuously generated alternatives and counter-narratives by which America was also represented in unAmerican ways. Anti-Americanism of a certain register, for example the political one, might thus prove compatible with enthusiasms for diverse literary and cultural productions: for example, jazz in the Zhdanov era, or the earlier vogue for writers like Jack London and Upton Sinclair. Anti-Americanism therefore did not usually represent an innate or indiscriminate hostility to all things American. Though partly connoting American power, Americanism also stood for wider social or cultural trends which, while held to have originated or reached their highest level in the US, were neither specific to it nor uncontested within its own cultural and geographical borders. It is thus, for example, that the Dutch historian Rob Kroes differentiates between a political anti-Americanism, primarily of the post-war left, and a cultural anti-Americanism that Kroes associates with inter-war conservatives.[107] Tony Crosland ascribed this post-war political anti-Americanism to the need, in what he now believed was a post-capitalist society, to 'find some new and powerful scapegoat to replace the capitalists at home'.[108] Bill Schwarz, conversely, has suggested that the CPGB's cultural anti-Americanism of the same period reproduced the prejudices of the 'traditional European intellectual' and was largely misjudged.[109]

Too clinical a separation of America's different meanings may nevertheless obscure the extent to which these also provided scope for dialogue, adjustment and the massaging of dissensions. More specifically, they may obscure the significance for the British labour activist of a tradition of cultural criticism that cannot straightforwardly be positioned on either left or right. Deriving from Ruskin and Morris, there had become established a clear association between ideas of freedom in work and issues of culture and even aesthetics. How little prepared he was for 'American methods', Dubreuil wryly noted, by his choice of these authors to hone his English-language skills.[110] How well-prepared, conversely, were those deriving from these sources, if not the anathematisation of machine-production, at least a willingness to challenge the 'irresistible' determinism of conventional political economy. Attempts were certainly made to extricate Morris's social philosophy from his 'intellectual Ludditism'.[111] Equally, however, where Morris had asserted the unity of politics, culture and morality, this was upheld in a discourse of anti-Americanism in which industrial standardisation and the pursuit of efficiency seemed inseparable from social homogenisation and the tyranny of the cash nexus.

To the extent that mass production served a mass market, the defence of craft ideals involved similar contradictions to those encountered by Morris in his own attempt at balancing socialist ideals with what inevitably proved to be exclusive forms of production. It was thus the bricklayer on the Mosely commission who deplored the prevalence in America of '"cheap work, and nasty"', and called for more 'artistic' forms of production allowing the workman pride in his craft and 'excellence of character and finish'.[112] Twenty years later, this was very much Purcell's language in launching the Furnishing Guild. Indeed, it was the NAFTA representative on the Mosely commission, Harry Ham, who condemned the sacrifice to mere quantity of any distinctiveness of taste or design. If a hotel required two hundred identical bedroom suites, he conceded that the Briton would be beaten 'by the Yankees'. If, conversely, a mansion required a different style and design of furnishing for each apartment, the work would be produced to a higher standard and more cheaply in Britain.[113] One is reminded of the reluctance of the building trades to countenance the restriction of 'luxury' building as the condition of meeting the post-war housing shortage.[114]

There was also a strain of cultural pessimism that was by no means the monopoly of political conservatives. An illustrious precursor was the poet and critic Matthew Arnold, who touring the States in 1884 had warned of the hardness, materialism and boastfulness of its 'life of business' and its disregard of all that was 'elevated'.[115] Arnold was among the cultural influences on the Fabians that Ian Britain argues have consistently been underrated.[116] It was from Arnold, for example, that the Webbs borrowed the classical dictum to 'choose equality and flee greed', and it provided the basis for their own evaluation of America when they visited a decade or so after him.[117]

Despite a viewing of the technological wonders of the Carnegie steel works, it is notable that, as late as 1898, the Webbs' copious notes on American political arrangements contained so little reference to industrial affairs. There was, however, a characteristic readiness to come to social judgements.[118] Americans, Beatrice reflected, very largely had 'chosen equality', and in this demonstrated the 'most essential part of good breeding'. They had not, however, fled greed; on the contrary, they had elevated 'pecuniary self-interest' into a veritable stampede for money, to the exclusion of any public service ethic and the disregard of intelligence and expertise. By reputation the Webbs should have been as enraptured with efficiency as trade unionists were with high wages. Beatrice, however, thought American bustle a 'dissipation of energy' as compared with the 'leisure loving Englishman' or the methodical German. She also described as 'positively wearisome to the European' the social and intellectual uniformity that she found so difficult to reconcile with America's diversity of population.

Her reflections were published only in the 1960s. As America, rather more than Russia, provided a stock theme for Fabian lecturers in the 1920s, several of them nevertheless struck a similar note. The Belfast-born playwright St John Ervine stressed the 'standardisation' of minds as well as production, and the American propensity to think, move and act in crowds.[119] The nationalisation specialist Emil Davies both acknowledged and viewed with competitive apprehension America's prosperity, but drew consolation from its continuing cultural deference to the Europeans.[120] Finer provided the most sweeping account of cultural abasement and uniformity. Among his several complaints were the prevalence of stealing (from 'trustification to small scale getting by'), the absence of any fixed standard of conduct and the fixation on earning capacity to the detriment of freedom of conduct or opinion.[121] One can only envy a world in which these should appear as peculiarly American traits.

Perhaps this was the unacceptable face of modernity; or perhaps of the philistines and Gradgrinds against whom Arnold had railed, with scarcely greater indulgence towards the mass of his own compatriots. Corresponding with Brailsford, the novelist Richard Church employed authentically Arnoldian cadences in bewailing the 'tidal wave of American barbarism' as the 'back-wash of the laissez-faire 19th Century', imperilling culture with arrogance, megalomania, vulgarity and 'giant-scale philistinism'.[122] As powerful a symbol as Ford was George F. Babbitt, eponymous hero of Sinclair Lewis's withering satire on American business values. It was in Britain that *Babbitt* had its most remarkable success: published within weeks of *My Life and Work* in October 1922, by the end of the decade it had gone through twelve editions compared to the latter's thirteen. One may note in passing that a comparable German response had to await Lewis's more sympathetic portrayal of a US research scientist, *Arrowsmith* (1925), while in America itself his earlier *Main Street* (1920) had caused the greater sensation.[123] Among *Babbitt*'s keenest readers was another Fabian socialist, the popular philosopher C.E.M. Joad, whose book *The Babbitt Warren* restated old antipathies in their most caustic and indiscriminate form.[124] But as the *Labour Magazine*'s reviewer rightly noted, what really exercised Joad was not so much America at all as the 'modern civilisation' emerging unevenly in all industrialised countries, and generating critical responses, like Lewis's, from the heart of America itself.[125]

The discourses of cultural impoverishment and of alienation in work were hardly the emanations of a single hermetic culture. Nor, on the other hand, were they the properties of distinct social constituencies attaching to the labour movement; in many cases they served to corroborate and reinforce each other. The best demonstration of this, published almost simultaneously with *Babbitt* and *My Life and Work*, was Colyer's *Americanism: a world menace*. Colyer by this time was a confirmed communist. Resigning from the Local Government Board over the compilation of the war register, he had moved to New England during the war and was active in the Socialist Party before being arrested in the Palmer Raids and deported back to Britain in 1922.[126] Along with the trade-unionist's refusal of 'industrial serfdom', he railed at philistinism, 'dollar-worship', arrogance, the 'standardisation of human beings' and a general state of 'besotted ignorance and spiritual degradation' unique among civilised nations. He provided Ervine at least with one of his sources, while Finer too could have read there of intellectual conformism, the 'total absence ... of what the Old World knows as "honour"', and a disregard for truthfulness bred of sales ethics. Repelled by American religion, Colyer even provided a curious remembrance of the Anglo-Catholic forms whose exquisiteness of architecture, music and ceremonial had at least associated Christianity with the satisfaction of the human longing for beauty'.[127]

Formerly in the ILP, and now on the CPGB's central training committee, Colyer saw in communism what was ultimately the only alternative to the Industrial Feudalism encapsulated in, but not confined to, America. Prefaced by Tom Mann, boosted in the *Labour Magazine* and *Socialist Review*, revisited in Plebs League lectures and even – who knows? – communist party training schools, his *Americanism* was a compendium of the antipathies at this time circulating on the British left.[128]

5.5 PURCELL IN AMERICA

Wells's building up of such impressions into a 'conceivable process' was never just a question of shedding Wellsian enlightenment; it depended on whose light was shed, and from where. As Rousseau had put it over a century earlier, 'I have been reading books of travels all my life, but I never found two that gave me the same idea of the same nation'.[129] Like other forms of political communication, books of travel required resources. Millions of migrant workers took one-way tickets, usually from east to west. Trade and war demanded diverse forms of free and unfree labour, including soldiering. Rousseau himself might symbolise travel by force in the form of political exile. What Joan Sangster describes as an early form of political tourism nevertheless demanded a budget, some independence and a passport.[130] If involvement in national and even local political networks drew on unequally distributed resources of time, money and skill, how much truer was this of the international traveller. As Doreen Massey writes, 'mobility, and control over mobility, both reflects and reinforces power'.[131] Both long-term migration and short-term swarming were also circumscribed by the entry restrictions that were increasingly imposed by possible countries of destination. First-hand accounts conveyed a quality of authenticity and immediacy which helped to validate competing political myths. Doubtless for this very reason, governments to varying degrees did not regard the right to observe and report across national boundaries as absolute or inalienable.

Passages to America must be viewed accordingly. Waves of nineteenth-century economic migrants included many thousands of Britons, among them figures on both sides of industry such as Samuel Gompers and Andrew Carnegie. Elite connections were epitomised by a flourishing transatlantic marriage market, while possession of a common language encouraged the professionalisation of getting presented on the part of journalists and above all lecturers. Arnold again had been among the pacesetters, inaudibly condescending to thousands at as much as a dollar a head.[132] As self-designated 'transcontinental tour agent for lectures by Men of Fame', the impresario W.B. Feakins had by 1914 put together a whole roster of speakers.[133] A decade later the humorist Steven Leacock complained of a tide of incoming Britons upsetting the transatlantic 'balance of trade in impressions'. The readiness of visitors to reach an instant verdict on Russia was a phenomenon frequently remarked upon. But Leacock exaggerated only slightly when he wrote of arrivals in New York heading away from customs to 'forward to England *from the closed taxi* itself ten dollars' worth of impressions of the American national character'.[134]

Working-class activists were not entirely excluded from such exchanges. Pre-1914 Mann and Hardie were among those taking advantage of Labour's international connections to tour the USA. Speakers on Feakins's books included socialists like Sylvia Pankhurst and Margaret Bondfield, both early visitors to Soviet Russia; and if their fellow lecturer Molly Hamilton thought an American tour the 'lowest of missions', it remained in the 1920s the 'great resource of the intellectual unemployed'.[135] Nevertheless, even the respectable were not assured entry – Pankhurst after her communist phase would certainly not have been – and militant labour activism was repulsed no matter what its place of origin. The Englishman Turner, as we have seen, was the first foreign radical to fall victim to the exclusion laws introduced following McKinley's assassination. Context for Colyer's denunciation of US capitalist 'terror' is suggested by his own arrest and deportation.[136] Lecturers' fees did not guarantee complaisance; if Ratcliffe, their 'prince and doyen', reciprocated in fulsome encomiums to America, Russell, like Brailsford and Wellock, was among those in the Arnold tradition of disdaining easy flattery.[137] Even so, the working-class critic hardly had the chance to make the trip. The *Daily Mail* naturally covered the costs of its own party, Weir was among the employers who assisted, and Dubreuil had the support of the Council of Industrial Relations, financed by the Rockefeller Foundation.[138] The Wellsian passive – getting America presented – obscured who did the getting as much as metaphors of active fabrication exaggerate it in the Soviet case.

There was, however, one regular example of a genuine working-class delegation. Beginning in 1894 on an American initiative, the TUC had for thirty years exchanged fraternal delegates with the AFL, generating contributions to the labour press and the later chapters on America that became as much a standby of the Labour memoirist as the Russian ones.[139] By the 1920s there were similar relations with the Canadian Trades and Labour Congress and more sporadically with the Russian and Indian unions. In each case, the exchanges provided a connection with movements currently absent from IFTU, connections which the TUC might be seen as exercising in a wider interest. Ironically, in 1924 the American link was even cited as an argument for the continuing British incumbency of the IFTU presidency in the person of Purcell.[140]

Already at this point relations between the two movements were cooling. Under the dominant influence of Samuel Gompers the AFL had always rejected political ties. With the formation of a Labour government in Britain, even MacDonald was now portrayed as a political doctrinaire and the ILP as having 'a thorough-going Marxian socialist programme'.[141] British recognition of the soviets, which in America had to wait until Roosevelt's presidency in the 1930s, prompted stirring affirmations of American values, if necessary against 'all the Old World's governments' in their weakness for autocracy.[142] While Tomsky cast his spell over the 1924 TUC, the AFL's fraternal delegate frankly described the unions as a bulwark against Bolshevism.[143] The delegates gave their verdict between them when Purcell was comfortably returned at the head of the poll for the TUC's reciprocating delegation to the AFL convention in Atlantic City the following year.[144]

The AFL's coolness towards the British was matched by a new sense of warmth towards the ADGB. When the German unions in 1923 were faced with organisational crisis due to the collapse of the mark, the AFL under Gompers relaxed its post-war disengagement from European affairs to provide moral and material support. There were many American trade unionists of German origin or descent. This had not, however, prevented anti-German feeling during the war, and there was clear political momentum behind the new understanding. IFTU's German co-secretary Johannes Sassenbach had taken over its correspondence with the AFL, and had adopted a 'friendly and conciliatory tone' to which a shared antipathy to communism contributed considerably.[145] Indeed, the AFL's appeal on behalf of the ADGB in 1923 stressed its vulnerability to the onslaughts of Bolshevism even more than the threat to its traditional economic functions.[146] There was no chance whatever of a half-American, half-Russian strategy of IFTU enlargement. Instead, they appeared as distinct and opposed alternatives that were identified with the Germans and the British respectively.[147]

Intimating that it would welcome closer relations with the ADGB, in 1924 the AFL was for the first time addressed by a German fraternal delegate, the printworkers' official Peter Grassmann, who travelled with the assistance of further American financial contributions.[148] Attending the same convention for the TUC, Swales commented perplexedly on the warmth with which Grassmann was received so soon after the war, while the Russians were just as vigorously rebuffed. The explanation, however, was obvious. As subsequently during the Cold War, national antagonisms were rapidly superseded by a shared rejection of communism, whose characterisation by Grassmann as conspiracy and mental disease drew from Gompers a 'long and eulogistic' response.[149]

By the time that Purcell attended the following year, Gompers had died and been succeeded by the Ohio miners' leader William Green. There was nevertheless complete continuity in regard to these questions. The main burden of Purcell's address to the AFL was the untenability of its 'policy of isolation'. In vivid terms he described the internationalisation of labour markets, and urged that neither US immigration laws nor a White Australia policy could prevent the competition internationally of the products of the labour that was thus excluded. By this time, and in this context, Purcell's was an unequivocal case for labour internationalism over labour protectionism. Moreover, he not only suggested that the AFL take its place in the 'gigantic confraternity of Labor'. He linked this with a concluding peroration exhorting it to send its own delegation to Russia.

But for his lack of German, one might have suspected Purcell of having reading Kautsky's 'American worker'. He did not speak of revolutionary romanticism or of uneven development. He did however commend the 'genius for organization and ... essential grip of things that my class has displayed in Russia'. Purcell conceded that the Americans had been the most advanced in matters of industrial technique and organisation. He also described how the vogue for American films and business methods could be observed in any British town or factory. He did not, however, believe that this alone represented the future:

> I say that you, workers of America, have much to learn from Russia. We must not be afraid of new ideas. It has often struck me that while the Americans have been the most advanced – the most receptive – in ideas concerning mechanical invention and business organization, they have been most slow in accepting new social and political ideas.[150]

The previous year Swales had thought Green cool and deliberate.[151] Now, as Purcell concluded, he swung his fist and shouted defiance of communist machinations while delegates 'rose as one, stomped their feet and yelled their approval'.[152]

Tarnow, there as German fraternal delegate, must have been delighted. Attending as part of a fourteen-strong ADGB party charged with the providing a workers' view of American industry, he steered clear of any possible controversy and offered delegates the agreeable assurance that it was from America itself that their German counterparts were anxious to learn. Indeed, his appearance in the USA coincided with the publication by the ADGB of a direct rebuttal of the TUC's Russian delegation.[153] Tarnow was a convinced opponent of any dealings with the Russians, and a key figure in the IUW majority which three months earlier had had Gossip removed from the Woodworkers' international executive.[154] He was rewarded in Atlantic City with a minute-long ovation; and the portrait photograph by which the *American Federationist* would normally have marked Purcell's appearance was on this occasion displaced by the image of the German visitors.[155]

The contrast was not confined to the convention itself. As the delegates departed, Purcell embarked upon a four-week speaking tour to promulgate his message of international unity. According to Benjamin Gitlow, then a communist organiser, the arrangements were made on George Hardy's proposition for the British Minority Movement and drew on a special fund provided by the Profintern.[156] There was certainly generous coverage in the New York *Daily Worker*, which described Purcell both as a Fighting Englishman and as the head of twenty-two million European trade unionists.[157] When two years later a first American workers' delegation visited Russia, it traced its origins to the 'Purcell fund' first mooted at the end of his tour.[158]

The outnumbering of trade unionists by advisers on the delegation suggests that Purcell had failed to reach the main body of trade-union officials.[159] Nevertheless, the communists even in America were able to mobilise impressive demonstrations of grassroots support. British visitors to the States remarked on the as yet unfamiliar practice of 'organised applause'.[160] Speaking alongside Eugene Debs at the Carnegie Hall, Purcell's ovation lasted some ten minutes, sustained no doubt by the communist element that also booed the meeting's socialist chairman, Morris Hillquit.[161] Coinciding with Purcell's visit, the communist MP Saklatvala had been denied entry to the States to attend the convention of the Inter-Parliamentary Union. The *Washington Post*, while urging Saklatvala's ejection from the British parliament as a national traitor, also demanded Purcell's deportation as an advocate of the world revolution who had somehow evaded applicable exclusion laws.[162] Even Green would not have gone that far. He must nevertheless have been caused further disquiet by the extension of Purcell's trip to Mexico; for Gompers had denied assent to an IFTU delegation proposed by Purcell's ally Brown, which he saw as contravening the notion of a Labour Monroe Doctrine.[163]

There were no such tensions with Tarnow and his colleagues. According to the communists, it was the AFL which took the 'German labor fakers' under its wing and secured their easy entry into American industry.[164] Unlike Purcell, the German visitors observed discretion in their public pronouncements.[165] Guilelessly, they afterwards reported of American employers that 'just a word about our work was enough to let us see whatever we needed to see'.[166] They were also entertained in the White House, and the Secretary of Labour J.J. Davis assured them of every possible assistance. This may also be compared to the following year's *Daily Mail* mission, which had a similar reception. There was also an unacknowledged resemblance to the TUC delegation in Russia, to which in effect this was a sort of response. With what was doubtless a sense of tu quoque, one communist reviewer noted how Tarnow and his colleagues had spent only seven weeks in America and failed to visit the states where its social conditions were worst.[167]

Like the British in Russia, the ADGB report warned against the easy transference of lessons from one society to another. Even Mosses in the *Mail* report, and IFTU in a sceptical assessment of Ford's 'miracle', stressed this point.[168] Nevertheless, the report's conclusions, according to Nolan, threw caution to the wind, and held up America as a textbook embodying the revised laws of capitalist development. The 'theoretical feud' about rising living standards under capitalism had thus been solved thanks to what it did indeed describe as an economic miracle.[169] As 'a counterweight and propaganda object' against the influence of the Soviet economic model, it was thus in a very direct sense a counterblast to the TUC report.[170] Tarnow, who wrote the report's trade-union section, propounded these ideas more fully in a book whose very title, 'Why Be Poor?', was lifted from a chapter in Ford's *My Life and Work*.[171] Tarnow was an orthodox Kautskyan at least to this extent, that he was convinced of the technical necessity of ever more repetitive work, to which workers would the more willingly resign themselves through the achievement of *Lebensfreude*, or happiness beyond the workplace.[172]

Purcell's impressions of America were recorded in his union journal, at public meetings and in the *Labour Monthly*, from whence they found their way into the communist press internationally.[173] The AFL itself was depicted as narrow, exclusive, reactionary and decades behind its British counterpart. But Purcell also took issue with Americanism as supposed industrial model and noted that its keenest exponents were 'employers, servile writers and the like – not workmen'.[174] In Cinderford, where he had great fun with the American cult of bigness, he assured his audience that nothing much could happen in America, nor anything much be learnt there.[175]

Principally, however, Purcell focused on the status and condition of the worker. Rather than offer direct observation, which employers would probably not have granted him, he reaffirmed what effectively were the stock positions of a large section of the British left. It was not therefore the perfection of industrial technique that most impressed him, but the 'spirit of vigorous regimentation' and extreme division of labour. In spite of its 'boasted high wages', Purcell described America's industrial system as a 'monotonous tyranny' in which the worker was so regulated, ordered, disciplined and controlled that it was nothing less than a slave system. Objections had been made to his pro-Soviet sentiments on grounds of democracy.

> 'Democracy' – in the land of the frame-up, the gunman and the spy? 'Democracy' – in the land where negro lynchings and the bludgeoning and murder of workmen striking for their rights have been a part of every-day life these many years? 'Democracy' – in the land where all the forces of the law, the State and the police … are openly and shamelessly at the beck and call of triumphant plutocracy …?

In suggesting that 'mere forms of government' mattered less than what lay behind them, Purcell not only indicted the dictatorship of American capital but implicitly justified that of Russian workers.[176] With the position of organised labour as his measure of value, he underlined the contrast with Calles's Mexico, and specifically with its labour code and its powerful trade-union organisation under Luis Morones.[177]

Purcell's verdict was to be confirmed the following year by Hicks, who as fraternal delegate did visit Detroit and described its workers as dehumanised, robotic and intellectually degraded. Hicks also described the food as adulterated, the press as a bath of slime and the labour movement as a quarter of a century behind the British.[178] While privately conceding American endeavour, he added the proverbial bricklayer's scepticism as to 'whether the return is proportionate to the energy expended'.[179] Hicks did not, however, follow Purcell's lead in communicating such sentiments to the AFL. On the contrary, he soft-soaped the delegates by paying effusive tribute to the municipal, industrial and constructional achievements he had witnessed in the States.[180] As will be seen, Hicks's more emollient attitude appears to have registered if nowhere else with the leadership of IFTU.

For the time being there was nevertheless a clear alignment between the AFL and ADGB to the exclusion of the TUC. Extensive coverage of US affairs in the IFTU *Press Reports* was matched not only by Sassenbach's contributions in the *American Federationist* but by a whole series of articles by ADGB officials.[181] The Wisconsin labour economist Selig Perlman even offered a Gompersite account of German trade-union development as one of progressive extrication from political direction and thus of convergence with the AFL itself.[182] Within the IUW, an observer from the American Carpenters' and Joiners' union was so 'agreeably surprised' by the hostility to communism, which Gossip above all personified, that the union took the relatively unusual step of affiliating to the IUW in January 1926.[183] Two years later Tarnow himself acknowledged what Dutt called the German-American trade-union model in noting the paradox by which movements based respectively on socialism and on the rejection of class conflict nevertheless reached 'identical conclusions in all important and fundamental questions'.[184]

There was also virtual derecognition of the TUC. Writing to Citrine in July 1926, Green implicitly dissociated the AFL from reports by 'unofficial groups and commissions' whom US industrialists had worked hard to direct towards the desired conclusions.[185] Nevertheless, when the *Daily Mail* followed in the steps of the ADGB delegation, it was with the assistance of AFL officers who urged on the visitors the same familiar lessons of efficiency, co-operation and harmony between employers and employed.[186] British contributors to the *American Federationist* were now restricted to those, on whichever side of industry, who were prepared to uphold the same position. Among these were Barnes, the GFTU secretary Appleton and a Rowntree's works manager who looked favourably on scientific management.[187] Not until May 1927 did a contribution (by Margaret Bondfield) again appear from a TUC source.

Almost immediately following the General Strike, a modification of these attitudes to Americanism began to be discernible in the British labour movement. It was as if, as previously in Germany, it was precisely the deflating of alternatives that encouraged such a reappraisal. At the TUC in October Beatrice Webb gloomily characterised it as a 'sort of defeatism and desire to come quickly to terms with the Mammon of Unrighteousness'.[188] Fund-raising for the miners in the States, Tillett now recorded his positive impressions of the efficiency and professionalism of the US labour organiser and of the 'striking new business view of the labour movement' which Green epitomised.[189] When Baldwin invited Bevin onto the government own US industrial commission, Bevin after some deliberation assented, wary of the 'boosting' of American methods but persuaded that it was with these that trade unionists henceforth had to deal.[190] As late as 1929 Wertheimer excluded only Bevin and Citrine from his general strictures regarding the craft-based stubbornness of the British.[191] But it was Bevin and Citrine who were the dominant figures in the phase of trade-union history that was now opening. Purcell, and much of what he stood for, was one of its casualties.

Meanwhile, his America illuminates his Russia in unexpected ways. In 1927 Walton Newbold described the US, as so many did, as 'literally a New World' of the machine, in whose ultra-modern steel mills and hydro-electric plants one 'felt a thrill at having entered into the future in a sense it was impossible to do under the hammer and sickle surmounted regimental banners of the Red Army or amid the thronging peasant hordes of Soviet Russia'.[192] By the 1930s, Russia too began to impress upon its visitors the thrill of a new mass culture of machine production. In Russia itself, the aspiration existed even in the 1920s: among Bramley's papers is a pamphlet in English describing the Central Institute of Work, through which the Russian unions organised the laboratories of time and motion depicted in the pamphlet through text and image.[193] There were no such images in Bramley's TUC report, however. Indeed, there were none of industry at all, nor any real discussion of the organisation of work. A single photograph of 'The Red Army at work' depicted haymaking, doubtless to stoke the factory chimneys in the Tintin strip; but the chimneys themselves were absent. When Lincolns Steffens visited Russia, he famously commented that he had seen the future and it worked. But Steffens was also to write in strikingly similar terms of Mussolini.[194] Seeing the future meant nothing unless you knew which future it was.

The American socialist and fellow-traveller Scott Nearing sized up the fraternal delegates at the Scarborough TUC in 1925. His fellow-Americans were 'comfortable-looking, businessman-like'; they talked of high wages, labour banking, collaboration with employers. The Russian Tomsky, by contrast, was an 'under-sized, stooping product of European proletarian life', speaking of class struggle and the revolution.[195] Personified by Tomsky himself, it was for the under-sized but defiant, not self-assured bigness, that the delegates at Scarborough roared their approval. The flags which so impressed Bramley, and which Newbold so dismissed, signified a future to be realised on their own terms and through the successful prosecution of present conflicts. Marc Lazar has commented that belief in Soviet Russia was not just a matter of 'faith' but a 'symbolic banner' and crucial source of political identity.[196] Bolshevism in the 1920s was a labour activist's or a social reformer's utopia, and a banner of unAmericanism. The lure of its technocratic rationality was to come later.

NOTES

1. H.G. Wells, *The Future in America*, Bell, 1906, pp. 353-9.
2. Compare for example with Rachel Mazuy, *Croire plutôt que voire? Voyages en Russie sovietique (1919-1939)*, Paris: Odile Jacob, 2002, ch. 9; Paul Hollander, *Political pilgrims: travels of western intellectuals to the Soviet Union, China and Cuba 1928-1978*, New York: Oxford University Press, 1981.
3. See for example Antonello Gerbi, trans. Jeremy Moyle, *The Dispute of the New World. The history of a polemic 1750-1900*, Pittsburgh: University of Pittsburgh Press, 1973, pp. 358-72 for the development of Goethe's ideas of America after 1789.

4. Doris Gunnell, *Stendhal et l'Angleterre*, Paris: Charles Bosse, 1909, p. 88.
5. Alexis de Tocqueville, trans. Philip Bradley, *Democracy in America*, Everyman's edn, 1994, vol. 1, p. 434.
6. Napoleon Louis Bonaparte, *Des idées napoléoniennes. On the opinions and policy of Napoleon*, Henry Colburn, 1840, pp. 11-12. For other contemporaneous examples, see Richard L. Rapson, *Britons View America. Travel commentary 1860-1935*, Seattle & London: University of Washington Press, 1971, p. 162; also *Bolshevism and the British Left*, II, p. 144.
7. Franco Venturi, *Roots of Revolution. A history of the populist and socialist movements in nineteenth century Russia*, Weidenfeld & Nicolson, 1960, p. 33.
8. Eric Hobsbawm, *The Age of Capital 1848-1875*, Abacus, 1997 edn, pp. 194-200 and passim.
9. The characterisation is that of S. Stepniak, *At the Dawn of a New Reign. A study of modern Russia*, Chatto & Windus, 1905, pp. vii-xii.
10. See diverse letters to the press September-December 1914 in David C. Smith, ed., *The Correspondence of H.G. Wells. Volume 2: 1904-1918*, Pickering & Chatto, 1998, pp. 379-81, 384-6 and 406-13; also Wells, introduction to Denis Garstin, *Friendly Russia*, Fisher Unwin, 1915.
11. See the contemporary assessments of Gaetano Salvemini and H.B. Usher in H.B. Lees-Smith, ed, *The Encyclopaedia of the Labour Movement*, Caxton Publishing Co, 3 vols, 1926, vol. 1, pp. 283-90; and for an overview of the relevant academic literature Thomas Linehan, *British Fascism 1918-39. Parties, ideology and culture*, Manchester: MUP, 2000, ch. 3, esp. pp. 68-71.
12. David C. Smith, ed., *The Correspondence of H.G. Wells. Volume 3: 1919-1924*, Pickering & Chatto, 1998, pp. 48-9.
13. Kautsky, 'The American worker' (1906) in Richard B. Day and Daniel Gaido, eds, *Witnesses to Permanent Revolution. The documentary record*, Chicago: Haymarket edn, 2011, pp.609-61.
14. Spengler's own writings drew the parallel between them; see for example Spengler trans. Charles Francis Atkinson, *The Hour of Decision. Part one: Germany and world-historical evolution*, Allen & Unwin, 1934, pp. 58-72.
15. BWD, 18 August* and 19 November 1930; also e.g. 10 September 1926 and 28 December 1930; see also *Bolshevism and the British Left*, II, pp. 144-6.
16. Antonio Gramsci (eds Quintin Hoare and Geoffrey Nowell Smith), 'Americanism and Fordism' in *Selections from the Prison Notebooks*, Lawrence & Wishart, 1971, pp. 302-3.
17. W.T. Colyer, *Americanism. A world menace*, Labour Publishing Co, 1922, p. 2.
18. Kautsky, 'American worker', pp. 640-1.
19. See for example Bruno Naarden, *Socialist Europe and Revolutionary Russia: perception and prejudice 1848-1923*, Cambridge: CUP, 1992, pp. 356-62.
20. C.R. de Gruchy in *Socialist Review*, April 1928, cited A.J. Williams, *Labour and Russia. The attitude of the Labour Party to the USSR 1924-33*, Manchester: MUP, 1989, pp. 65-6.
21. Peter Beilharz, *Labour's Utopias. Bolshevism, Fabianism, Social Democracy*, Routledge, 1992, p. 98.

The other future? 225

22. First argued, to Lenin's great ire, in *The Dictatorship of the Proletariat*, Manchester: National Labour Press, 1918.
23. See Charles S. Maier, 'Between Taylorism and technocracy. European ideologies and the vision of industrial productivity in the 1920s', *Journal of Contemporary History*, 5, 27, 1970, pp. 45-54 for the dilemmas of the Weimar SPD.
24. Kautsky, trans. Florence Baldwin, *The Socialist Commonwealth*, Twentieth Century Press, 1909.
25. C. Desmond Greaves, *The Life and Times of James Connolly*, Lawrence & Wishart, 1972 edn, p. 153.
26. 44th AFL Convention *Report*, 1924, p. 158.
27. M. Rubenstein cited Mary Nolan, *Visions of Modernity. American business and the modernisation of Germany*, New York: OUP, 1994, p. 6.
28. Maier, 'Between Taylorisn and technocracy', pp. 27, 54-5.
29. Gramsci, 'Americanism and Fordism', pp. 302-3.
30. Dutt, *Socialism and the Living Wage*, CPGB, 1927, p. 201.
31. Cited John Willett, *The New Sobriety*, Thames & Hudson, 1978, pp. 98-9.
32. Nolan, *Visions*, chs 2-3. 'Ford psychosis' was the phrase of Irene Witte, a contemporary German authority on Taylorism.
33. For an exposition of these arguments for a British readership, see Paul Hertz, 'Labour and rationalisation in Germany', *Labour Magazine*, February 1928, pp. 463-6.
34. As expounded in communist writings at the time; see Nicholas N. Kozlov and Eric D. Weitz, 'Reflections on the origins of the "Third Period": Bukharin, the Comintern and the political economy of Weimar Germany', *Journal of Contemporary History*, 24, 1989, pp. 395-6; Norman LaPorte, *The German Communist Party in Saxony, 1924-1933: factionalism, fratricide and political failure*, Bern: Peter Lang, 2003, pp. 287-94.
35. Richard Stites, *Revolutionary Dreams. Utopian vision and experimental life in the Russian revolution*, New York: OUP, 1989, pp. 146-9; Jeffrey Brooks, 'The press and its message: images of America in the 1920s and 1930s' in Sheila Fitzpatrick, Alexander Rabinowrich and Richard Stites, eds, *Russia in the Era of NEP. Explorations in Soviet society and culture*, Indiana University Press, 1991, pp. 239-44. The theme is emphasised in contemporary accounts like Maurice Hindus, *Humanity Uprooted*, Cape, 1929, ch. 2.
36. Gramsci, 'Americanism', pp. 279, 285-6, 301-3.
37. As argued from their different perspectives by commentators as far apart in their conclusions as the Comintern economist Varga and the German social democrat Fritz Tarnow, for whom see respectively Kozlov and Weitz, 'Reflections on the origins of the Third Period', pp. 392-3 and Tarnow, *Warum Arm Sein*, Berlin: ADGB, 1928, p. 68.
38. Nolan, *Visions*, p. 32.
39. Gramsci's essay does include a section on high wages, but this was incidental to his main argument.
40. Hertz, 'Labour and rationalisation', p. 463; Tarnow, *Warum Arm Sein*, p. 4.
41. See e.g. Joan Campbell, *The German Werkbund. The politics of reform in the applied arts*, Princeton University Press, 1978, pp. 127-9, 158-61.
42. Kautsky, *Socialist Commonwealth*, pp. 27-31; also e.g. Nolan, *Visions*, p. 102.

43. See Aldred Streimer's articles on the German works councils, *Labour Magazine*, October 1922, pp. 275-7 and November 1922, pp. 324-5; also Arthur Henderson on the Federal Economic Council, *Labour Magazine*, July 1922, pp. 116-19.
44. Nolan, *Visions*, p. 100.
45. See Nicholas Papayanis, *Alphonse Merrheim. The emergence of reformism in revolutionary syndicalism 1871-1925*, Dordrecht: Martinus Nighoff, 1985, pp. 65 ff.
46. Hyacinthe Dubreuil, *Standards. Le travail américain vu par un ouvrier français*, Paris: Bernard Grasset, 1929. For biographical details see the entry by P. Fridenson in Jean Maitron and Claude Pennetier, eds, *Dictionnaire biographique du mouvement ouvrier français*, vol. 24, Paris: Les Editions ouvrières, 1986, pp. 63-6.
47. Tillett interpolated a characteristically intemperate note of anti-Americanism into his reflections on the TUC's Russian delegation: *Some Russian Impressions*, LRD, 1925, pp. 17-18. It can be found in the initial communist reactions to the Dawes plan, but seems then to have given way to a more generalised attack on Allied financiers; compare e.g. TUC archives 292/778.2, Pollitt to Bramley, 3 and 26 September 1924 with Pollitt in 57th TUC *Report*, 1925, pp. 544-5; also E.H. Carr, *Socialism in One Country, 1924-1926. Volume 3*, Harmondsworth: Penguin edn, 1972, pp. 479-91.
48. Colyer, *America*, p. 4.
49. *Mosely Industrial Commission to the United States of America, Oct.-Dec., 1902. Reports of the delegates*, Manchester: Co-operative Printing Society, 1903, 'Preface', pp. 5-12.
50. *The Daily Mail Trade Union Mission to the United States. Full story of the tour and members' report*, Daily Mail, 1926, p. 3 and passim.
51. *Daily Mail Trade Union Mission*, pp. 22-3.
52. *Mosely Industrial Commission*, 'Preface', pp. 8-11.
53. H.A. Tulloch, 'Changing British attitudes to the United States in the 1880s', *Historical Journal*, 20, 4, 1977, pp. 825-40.
54. Bradford Perkins, *The Great Rapprochement. England and the United States 1895-1914*, Gollancz, 1969.
55. *Daily Mail Trade Union Mission*, p. 5.
56. *Daily Mail*, 12 February 1926.
57. The one initial indication of such support was from the Blacksmiths', Forge and Smithy Workers' Society, *Daily Mail*, 16 February 1926.
58. Baldwin papers 161/24-9, Baldwin to William Joynson-Hicks, 15 March 1926, also Neville Chamberlain, Arthur Steel-Maitland and others.
59. A. Findlay, letter to *Daily Mail*, 18 March 1926. Findlay, of course, had been a member of the TUC Russian delegation.
60. See Glasgow History Workshop, 'A clash of work regimes: "Americanisation" and the strike at the Singer Sewing Machine Company, 1911' in William Kenefick and Arthur McIvor, *Roots of Red Clydeside 1900-1914? Labour unrest and industrial relations in West Scotland*, Edinburgh: John Donald, 1996, pp. 193-213.
61. See Arthur McIvor, 'Were Clydeside employers more autocratic? Labour management and the "labour unrest", c1910-1914' in Kenefick and McIvor, *Roots of Red Clydeside*, pp. 41-65.

62. W.J. Reader, *Architect of Air Power. The life of the first Viscount Weir of Eastwood 1877-1959*, Collins, 1968, pp. 29-30 and 110-14; Elizabeth Williamson et al, *The Buildings of Scotland: Glasgow*, Penguin, 1990, p. 541.
63. Tom Bell, *Pioneering Days*, Lawrence & Wishart, 1941, pp. 140-6.
64. Richard Biernacki, *The Fabrication of Labor. Germany and Britain 1640-1914*, University of California Press, 1995.
65. Richard Price, 'The labour process and social history', *Social History*, 8, 1, 1983, pp. 57-75.
66. Mike Savage, *Class Analysis and Social Transformation*, Buckingham: Open University Press, 2000, pp. 127-8.
67. Kevin Whitston has challenged Price's presentation with evidence exclusively from the engineering industry ('Worker resistance and Taylorism in Britain', *International Review of Social History*, 42, 1997, pp. 1-24). Conversely, Price's presentation may owe something to his more extensive familiarity with the building trades.
68. Beilharz, *Labour's Utopias*, p. 103.
69. See W. Stephen Sanders, *Trade Unionism in Germany*, FRD, 1916 edn, pp. 43-4.
70. Gerard Braunthal, *Socialist Labor and Politics in Germany. The General Federation of German Trade Unions*, Hamden, Conn.: Archon Books, 1978, pp. 95-6.
71. Purcell, West Salford election address, January 1910, WCML; NAFTA *Monthly Report*, December 1923, pp. 20-1.
72. H. R. Taylor, Operative Bricklayers' Society, *Mosely Industrial Commission*, p. 181.
73. G.D.H. Cole, *Building and Planning*, Cassells, 1945, p. 93.
74. Kevin Morgan 'The problem of the epoch? Labour and housing, 1918-1951', *Twentieth Century British History*, 16, 3, 2005, pp. 227-55.
75. For the guilds and craft, see G.D.H. Cole, *Self-Government in Industry* (1917), Hutchinson, 1972 edn, pp. 206-8.
76. George Hicks, *The ABC of Housing*, AUBTW, 1924, pp. 9-10; *Daily Herald*, 20 September 1923; also Hicks, 'Craft or class. The future of trade union organisation', *Labour Magazine*, November 1922, p. 303. For the Doctrine of the Vested Interest, see Sidney and Beatrice Webb, *Industrial Democracy*, Longmans, 1920 edn, pp. 562-72.
77. NFBTO, 13th annual conference *Report*, 1930, pp. 12 ff.
78. See Kevin Morgan, 'Cutting the feet from under organised labour? Lord Weir, mass production and the building trades in the 1920s', *Scottish Labour History*, 43, 2008, pp. 47-69.
79. Weir papers, DC 96/2/23, translation of article from *Berliner Tageblatt*, 5 June 1926. For Hirsch see Nolan, *Visions*, pp. 19, 68-9, 91, and for other German visitors see D. Dex Harrison in John Madge, ed., *Tomorrow's Houses*, Pilot Press, 1946, p. 119.
80. Nike Bätzner, 'Housing projects of the 1920s. A laboratory of social ideas and formal experiment' in Thorsten Scheer, Josef Paul Kleihues and Paul Kahlfeldt, eds, *City of Architecture, Architecture of the City: Berlin, 1900-2000*, Berlin: Nicolai, 2000, p. 151.
81. Wertheimer, *Portrait of the Labour Party*, Putnams, 1929, pp. 7-8.
82. Gramsci, 'Americanism', p. 292.

83. Gramsci, 'Americanism', p. 286.
84. Reprinted in Ross McKibbin, *The Ideologies of Class. Social relations in Britain 1880-1950*, Oxford: OUP, 1991.
85. *Report of the Trade Union Conference on Unemployment*, TUC general council 1925, pp. 10-11, also pp. 8-9 for the same point made by Purcell.
86. Robert Skidelsky, *Politicians and the Slump. The Labour government of 1929-1931*, Macmillan, 1967.
87. Wells, *Russia in the Shadows*, Hodder & Stoughton, 1920, p. 70.
88. On these themes see *Bolshevism and the British Left*, II, ch. 5.
89. Robson, 'Henry Ford and socialism', *Fabian News*, May 1927, pp. 26-7.
90. Finer, 'Impressions of America', *Fabian News*, February 1926, pp. 9-10.
91. *Fabian News*, December 1927, pp. 62-3. Though the summary does not mention the Webbs by name, Ratcliffe's 'prophecy of four years ago' clearly referred to the Webbs' *Decay of Capitalist Civilisation* (1923).
92. William Graham, *The Wages of Labour*, Cassells, 1924 edn, pp. 43-4, 105-37.
93. Mosley, 'Is America a capitalist triumph?', *New Leader*, 2 April 1926; Robert Skidelsky, *Oswald Mosley*, Macmillan, 1981 edn, pp. 146-50; see also Kautsky, *Socialist Commonwealth*, p. 3; Mosley, *My Life*, Nelson, 1970 edn, pp. 185-209.
94. See the summary in the *Daily Herald*, 1 October 1926.
95. See for example 'Cheap labour peril in the USA', *Industrial Review*, February 1930, p. 13; 'How are things in the United States?', *Industrial Review*, March 1930, p. 3.
96. R. Palme Dutt, *Socialism and the Living Wage*, CPGB, 1927, pp. 154-86.
97. Dutt, *Socialism*, p. 173.
98. See his autobiography *Off the Beaten Track*, Tanjore: Sarvodaya Prachuralaya, 1961.
99. Dutt, *Socialism*, pp. 156-7.
100. Wellock, 'America as a school for socialists', *New Leader*, 26 March 1926. Wellock even included an anticipation of the American slump which Dutt should have found congenial.
101. Brailsford, 'Can capitalism save itself?', *New Leader*, 26 March 1926.
102. Wellock, *Off the Beaten Track*, pp. 60, 94-5, 102 ff.
103. Brailsford, *How the Soviets Work*, New York: Vanguard Press, 1927, pp. 156-7; also F.M. Leventhal, *The Last Dissenter. H.N. Brailsford and his world*, Oxford: OUP, 1985, pp. 205-7.
104. Perry Anderson, 'Origins of the Present Crisis' (1964) in his *English Questions*, Verso, 1992, pp. 33-6.
105. Lees-Smith, *Encyclopaedia of the Labour Movement*, vol. 3, c. 1927, pp. 266-73.
106. Colyer, 'American capital and British Labour', *Labour Monthly*, October 1922, pp. 230-1.
107. Rob Kroes, 'The Great Satan versus the Evil Empire. Anti-Americanism in the Netherlands' in Rob Kroes and Maarten van Rossem, eds, *Anti-Americanism in Europe*, Amsterdam: Free University Press, 1986, pp. 37-42.
108. C.A.R. Crosland, *The Future of Socialism*, Cape, 1956, p. 195.
109. Bill Schwarz, '"The people in history". The Communist Party Historians' Group, 1946-1956' in Richard Johnson et al, eds, *Making Histories. Studies in history-writing and politics*, Hutchinson, 1982, p. 81.

110. Dubreuil, *Standards*, pp. 105-6.
111. The phrase of the arts-and-crafts architect C.R. Ashbee, cited Nikolaus Pevsner, *Pioneers of Modern Design. From William Morris to Walter Gropius*, Harmondsworth; Penguin, 1960 edn, p. 26.
112. *Mosely Industrial Commission*, p. 178.
113. *Mosely Industrial Commission*, p. 210.
114. See for example Hicks, *ABC of Housing*, p. 8.
115. Matthew Arnold, *Discourses in America*, Macmillan, 1885, pp. 64-7.
116. Ian Britain, *Fabianism and Culture: A Study in British Socialism and the Arts c. 1884-1918*, Cambridge: CUP, 1982.
117. See *Bolshevism and the British Left*, II, p. 75. The Webbs might also have found in Arnold (*Discourses*, pp. 50-1) their stock character of the 'average sensual man'.
118. All citations from David A. Shannon, ed., *Beatrice Webb's American Diary*, University of Wisconsin Press, 1963, pp. 142-52.
119. Ervine, 'Some impressions of America', Fabian News, April 1923, pp. 14-15. For Ervine's Fabianism, see Laura Arrington, 'St John Ervine and the Fabian Society: capital, empire and Irish home rule', *History Workshop Journal*, 72, 1, 2011, pp. 52-73.
120. Davies, 'America revisited', *Fabian News*, March 1925, pp. 10-11.
121. Finer, 'Impressions of America', *Fabian News*, February 1926, pp. 9-10.
122. Brailsford papers, Church to Brailsford, 19 October 1926.
123. Mark Schorer, *Sinclair Lewis. An American life*, New York: McGraw Hill, 1961, pp. 357, 422.
124. Though Joad had been expelled from the Fabian Society in 1925, this was on account of his sexual conduct, not his political beliefs, and he rejoined the society in 1943.
125. *Labour Magazine*, November 1926, p. 324.
126. Biographical details from *Workers' Weekly*, 12 September 1924.
127. Colyer, *Americanism*, esp. chs 1 and 6-9. 'Americanism and world dominion' is dealt with in the book's penultimate and shortest chapter and is very much a subsidiary theme.
128. A similar presentation, drawing on articles in the *Yorkshire Factory Times* and carrying a preface by Colyer, was Joe Walker, *Bloody American Capitalism. Its murder of labour*, Bradford: Socialist and Labour Press, 1924.
129. J.-J. Rousseau, trans. Barbara Foxley, *Émile* (1780), Dent: 1911 edn, pp. 414-15.
130. Doreen Massey, *Space, Place and Gender*, Cambridge: Polity, 1994; see also Joan Sangster, 'Political tourism, writing and communication; transnational connections of women on the left, 1920s-1940s' in Pernilla Jonsson, Silke Neunsinger and Joan Sangster, eds, *Crossing Boundaries. Women's organizing in Europe and the Americas 1880s-1940s*, Uppsala: Uppsala University, 2007, pp. 95-115.
131. Sangster, 'Crossing boundaries: women's organizing in Europe and the Americas 1880s-1940s' in Jonsson, *Crossing Boundaries*, p. 17; also Pernilla Jonsson, 'On women's account: the finances of "bourgeois" women's organizations in Sweden, England, Germany, and Canada, 1885-1924' in Jonsson et al, *Crossing Boundaries*, pp. 157-86.
132. Matthew Arnold to Fan Arnold, 28 October and 27 November 1883 in

George W.E. Russell, ed., *Letters of Matthew Arnold 1848-88*, Macmillan, 1895, vol. 2, pp. 225 and 231.
133. See his headed notepaper, 1911-12 at www.elizabethfreeman.orgIPDF/suffrage/feakins-big.pfd, accessed 12 August 2009.
134. Stephen Leacock, *My Discovery of England*, Bodley Head, 1922, pp. 13-14; also William Henry Chamberlin, *Russia's Iron Age*, Duckworth, 1935, p. 338 for a Soviet equivalent of the same stereotype.
135. M.A. Hamilton, *Remembering My Good Friends*, Cape, 1944, p. 225.
136. Colyer, 'American capital and British Labour', *Labour Monthly*, October 1922, pp. 230-1.
137. Hamilton's characterisation of Ratcliffe, *Remembering*, p. 225; also A. Emil Davies, *Fabian News*, February 1933, pp. 7-8 for the cordial approval of Ratcliffe's lectures 'in strong contrast' to some other British visitors.
138. See the Maitron entry by Fridenson, p. 64.
139. Examples by TUC fraternal delegates include John Hodge, *Workman's Cottage to Windsor Castle*, Sampson, Low & Marston; Robert Smillie, *My Life For Labour*, Mills & Boon, 1926; Margaret Bondfield, *A Life's Work*, Hutchinson, n.d.
140. *Labour Magazine*, March 1924, p. 525.
141. See Gompers's editorials in the *American Federationist*, April 1924, pp. 324-7 and June 1924, pp. 487-9.
142. 'Though others fail', *American Federationist*, December 1924, pp. 990-2.
143. Peter J. Brady, TUC 1924 *Report*, p. 385.
144. The election was keenly contested and in 1924 there were twelve candidates. Unusually, Purcell received more than two millions votes, considerably more than four other members of the general council combined.
145. Lewis L. Lorwin, *Labor and Internationalism*, New York: Macmillan, 1929, p. 270.
146. *American Federationist*, January 1924, pp. 92-3. The appeal followed a letter to the AFL from the IFTU officers Jouhaux, Mertens, Leipart, Oudegeest and Sassenbach.
147. See Oudegeest's comments TUC archives 292/947/15, TUC general council and IFTU EC joint meeting, 1 December 1925.
148. For the background see *ADGB Jahrbuch 1924*, Berlin: ADGB, 1925, pp. 203-4.
149. Swales, 'Lessons from trans-Atlantic trade unionism', *Labour Magazine*, February 1925, pp. 454-5; Grassmann in 44th AFL convention *Report*, 1924.
150. 45th AFL Convention *Report*, October 1925, pp. 139-43; *Washington Post*, 8 October 1925.
151. Swales, 'Lessons', p. 454.
152. *Washington Post* and *New York Times*, 8 October 1925.
153. See *Daily Mail*, 26 October 1925. The pamphlet was Löffler's *Russland in Licht englischer Gewerkschafter*, which the *Mail* warmly commended, along with Goldman's *My Disillusionment in Russia*. It seems likely that the example of the ADGB helped inspire the *Mail*'s own American delegation the following year.
154. NAFTA *Monthly Report*, August 1925, pp. 23-4; *Sunday Worker*, 5 July 1925.

155. 45th AFL Convention *Report*, 1925, p. 108; *Amerikareise deutscher Gewerkschaftsführer*, p. 9.
156. Gitlow, *I Confess*, New York: E.P. Dutton, 1940, pp. 292-4.
157. New York *Daily Worker*, 7 November 1925.
158. Though Gitlow suggested that the Purcell fund was chimerical, contemporary reports do refer to collections at meetings of up to $1000 (*New York Times*, 18 November 1925) and these were said to provide the original basis for the fund (New York *Daily Worker*, 24 November 1925).
159. See *Russia After Ten Years. Report of the American trade union delegation to the Soviet Union*, New York: International Publishers, 1927, p. 7. Various members of the delegation had to find 'part or all of their own expenses'.
160. See Bondfield, *A Life's Work*, p. 109 for an earlier description.
161. *New York Times*, 12 October 1925; also New York *Daily Worker*, 17 November 1925 for a similar ovation.
162. *Washington Post* editorials, 7 and 9 October 1925.
163. Lorwin, *Labor and Internationalism*, pp. 298-300.
164. New York *Daily Worker*, 6 October 1925; William F. Dunne, *Sunday Worker*, 4 April 1926.
165. The New York *Daily Worker* (6 October 1925) alleged 'an ironclad pact … not to talk for publication'.
166. *Amerikareise deutscher Gewerkschaftsführer*, p. 9.
167. A. Friedrick, 'Amerika-Literature', *Die Revolution*, July 1926, p. 607. In fact, half of the delegates spent eight weeks in the States, and one of them nearly eleven.
168. *Daily Mail Trade Union Mission*, p. 85; IFTU *Press Reports*, 21 October 1926, Economic Supplement: 'Ford's miracle'.
169. *Amerikareise deutscher Gewerkschaftsführer*, p. 253.
170. Friedrick, 'Amerika-Literature', p. 605.
171. Tarnow, *Warum Arm Sein*, ch. 3.
172. Tarnow, 'Das Berufsethos des Arbeitnehmers', *Die Arbeit*, June 1929, pp. 374-84.
173. E.g. *Die Rote Fahne*, 26 February 1926.
174. Purcell, 'Capital and Labour in the USA', *Labour Monthly*, February 1926, pp. 93-6.
175. *Dean Forest Mercury*, 4 December 1925; also NAFTA *Monthly Report*, December 1925, pp. 22-3.
176. Purcell, 'Capital and Labour'.
177. Purcell even suggested comparison with the Russian workers after their own revolution, before drawing back from such claims, perhaps on the advice of communist editors; compare for example NAFTA *Monthly Report*, December 1925, p. 23 with Purcell, 'Mexico and the workers', *Trade Union Unity*, March 1926, pp. 39-40. For the communist repudiation of such views as expressed by Swales, see *Communist Review*, October 1925, pp. 246-8.
178. Hicks, 'America Today', *Labour Magazine*, December 1926, pp. 349-51.
179. TUC archives 292/973/20, Hicks to Citrine, 14 October 1926.
180. TUC archives 292/973/20, cutting from 46th AFL convention *Report*, 6 October 1926.
181. Sassenbach's contributions appeared in the February, July and November

1926 issues. ADGB officials contributing in 1925-6 included W. Muschte, Gertrud Hanna (three times) and Franz Wendel (twice).
182. Selig Perlman, 'German trade unionism', *American Federationist*, October 1925, pp. 898-903. For Perlman's conception of 'organic labour' see Leon Fink, *Progressive Intellectuals and the Dilemmas of Democratic Commitment*, Cambridge, Mass.: Harvard University Press, 1997, pp. 67-77.
183. W.L. Hutcheson, 'Woodworkers' International Congress', *American Federationist*, January 1926, pp. 47-8; Lewis L. Lorwin and Jean A. Flexner, 'The International Union of Woodworkers', *American Federationist*, July 1926, p. 846.
184. Tarnow cited IFTU *Economic Supplement*, 22 September 1927 in Dutt, 'The "New Course"', *Labour Monthly*, December 1927, p. 726.
185. TUC archives 292/973/36, W. Green, AFL, to W. Citrine, TUC, 30 July 1926.
186. *Daily Mail Trade Union Mission*, pp. 9, 17, 22-3, 44; *Daily Mail*, 18 February and 11 March 1926.
187. See *American Federationist*, July 1926, pp. 793-7; February 1927, pp. 165-70; and May 1927, pp. 562-6.
188. BWD, 12 October 1926.
189. TUC archives 292/252.61/49, Tillett report for TGWU officers, 21 August 1926.
190. Alan Bullock, *The Life and Times of Ernest Bevin. Volume one. Trade union leader 1881-1940*, Heinemann, 1960, pp. 357-62.
191. Wertheimer, *Portrait*, pp. 7-8.
192. Newbold, 'Working conditions in America', TGWU *Record*, April 1927, p. 266.
193. *The Central Institute of Work. An outline of work and methods*, ARCCTU, 1925.
194. See e.g. *The Autobiography of Lincoln Steffens*, New York: Harcourt, Brace & Co, 1931, chs 20-1.
195. Scott Nearing, *British Labor Bids for Power. The historic Scarborough conference of the Trades Union Congress*, New York: Social Science Publishers, 1925, p. 27.
196. Marc Lazar, *Le Communisme: une passion française*, Paris: Perrin, 2005 edn, pp. 51-2.

Chapter six

The General Strike

6.1 THE STRIKE AS SOCIAL MYTH

More than any other event it was the nine-day General Strike of May 1926 that destroyed Purcell as a partisan figurehead. Even as the strike was getting underway, Beatrice Webb described it as the death gasp of direct action and moment of reckoning for 'windbag revolutionary Trade Unionism'.[1] As it ended in defeat and recrimination, this became established as a truism in both Labour folklore and academic historiography. Margaret Cole in the 1940s described it as 'the last throw of "insurrectionism", of "direct industrial action"'.[2] Hugh Gaitskell in the 1950s saw it as demolishing 'the absurd "myth" of syndicalism'.[3] C.L. Mowat in *Britain Between the Wars* described it as a 'catastrophe' brought about by 'extremists' and retrieved by the 'forces of moderation'.[4] Chief among these moderate forces was Ernest Bevin, who usually emerges as the episode's tough-minded and windbag-deflating thaumaturge. In Bullock's authorised biography of Bevin, appearing in 1960, Purcell and his ilk provide the necessary counterfoil. 'Unlike those who had talked of Direct Action for years, but were unequal to events when the time for action came, there was at least one man on the General Council who grasped what had to be done and did it.'[5]

Whether or not biography necessarily tends to a 'great man' view of history, it can seem that way when only great men have biographies written, and when biographers are consumed by their greatness.[6] The biography of Bevin and autobiography of Citrine have had precisely such an influence on the historiography of the inter-war trade-union movement. Rightly, the General Strike is seen as the decisive moment in the emergence of this pairing as the dominant figures in the next phase of the TUC's development. What is less well understood is that the strike itself was not so much the last throw of insurrectionism as the instrument by which this leadership was imposed. Accounts deriving from Bevin and Citrine have been one source of this misunderstanding. But the issue has also been confused by the claims to paternity of the action immediately advanced from the militant left, and more specifically from within the CPGB.

This double mythology has first of all to be registered as mythology if the politics of the strike is to be properly understood. The solidarity displayed in May 1926 would not have been possible without the syndicalistic agitations of the preceding period; nor indeed should the influence of this environment on Bevin and Citrine themselves be understated. Nevertheless, the instrument wielded by the TUC was not that envisaged by those who had 'talked of Direct Action for years'. It was Bevin's conception alone, on the basis of no serious study of such a literature. It was also geared more to the adjustment of formal and informal union hierarchies, and to the centralisation of union power, than to the effectiveness of the strike instrument itself. As a means of pressure on the government it was abysmally ill-conceived and ineffective, and as a consequence even Bevin's customary self-assurance was temporarily dented. It was Bevin, nevertheless, who immediately took the initiative in shaping a narrative of the strike in which his own conceptions of discipline and collective authority were central. The strike must be seen as a calculating exercise in the rationalisation of the TUC and as the prelude to its engagement with a wider process of rationalisation in industry.

Purcell's role in the strike was thus at once more substantial and less influential than is usually recognised. His contribution as chairman of the crucial Strike Organisation Committee (SOC) has invariably been downplayed in favour of Bevin's and in the most recent academic study he is somehow lost sight of completely.[7] On the other hand, the suggestion that Purcell and his allies had promoted the idea of a general strike in any consistent way is impossible to substantiate convincingly. The discussion here once more tries to locate Purcell within a wider picture, but one which looks very different with Purcell now placed at its centre. The alleged fixation of trade unionists on the idea of a general strike is first of all considered, along with the practical considerations which shaped the theory and emerging practice of the wide-scale solidarity action. The TUC's notorious lack of preparation for the strike may then appear more readily explicable in view of the prevalent uncertainty as to the character of any such action and even which body should be responsible for organising it. Alternative strategies, not necessarily more effective, were consequently considered and dismissed at a very late stage. It was Bevin who then prevailed; and bound by a policy of Bevin's making, Purcell was too wholly committed to the TUC, whether out of loyalty or career interest, to give voice to his misgivings at the resulting debacle. Unwilling or unable to account for himself, within two years he had ceased to count for anything in any national capacity.

One must begin with the idea of the general strike itself. Beatrice Webb in her diary referred only to a 'proletarian distemper' originating with Tom Mann and now having run its course. In subsequent accounts, however, the idea of solidarity is rendered more or less synonymous with that of the general strike. Already in 1927 G.D.H. Cole wrote that a 'General Strike "myth"' had haunted British labour since the early days of syndicalism.[8] Ross Martin in his later history of the TUC agrees that this idea had 'gripped the imagination of trade union leaders to an extraordinary degree'.[9] Twice, according to Cole, the threat of such a strike had forced concessions from the government: over Russia in 1920 and over the coal industry at the time of the 'Red Friday' solidarity action of July 1925.[10] With the full enactment of a national solidarity strike the following year, an ex post facto discourse of the general strike was straight away established as rallying cry or cautionary tale, and Purcell himself in the immediate aftermath gave voice to it.[11]

What evidence was there of this beforehand? Georges Sorel in his *Reflections on Violence* had described the general strike as a social myth or 'body of images' evoking the class struggle in its most fully realised form.[12] In Britain, according to the communist Arnot, while this 'did not even get any very wide circulation … (except amongst those whom it frightened), it undoubtedly helped to create a strong propaganda … for strike action on the widest possible scale, regarded simply as a means of winning particular strikes'.[13] This is entirely accurate and indicates a proper sense of proportion. Describing 1926 as the syndicalists' 'last throw', on the other hand, shows little regard for the interplay of the symbolic, the motivational and the realisable in the employment of such rhetorical strategies. Richard Hyman cites J.E.T. Eldridge as to the impossibility of regarding strikes as a single category of social action.[14] The same was just as true of the general strike as sub-category, and Sorel himself insisted on its diverse forms and objects, not all of which met the syndicalist desiderata of the 'proletarian general strike'.[15]

This was evident internationally in the lack of any obvious correlation between syndicalist influence and the general strikes that did occur. Hitherto these had mostly featured in countries with well-organised and centralised social-democratic labour movements such as Belgium and Sweden. In Germany, where the SPD momentarily espoused such a tactic, it was against this 'pedantic schema of a demonstrational mass strike … artificially commandeered by party and trade union' that Rosa Luxemburg projected the idea of the spontaneous mass strike after the example of the Russian strikes of 1905.[16] Even Cole, whose pre-war *World of Labour* provided one of the few serious discussions of the tactic in Britain, noted the vagueness of the concept and the need to distinguish between such variants as the political, economic or anti-militaristic general strike and the social general strike of the syndicalists. According to Beatrice Webb, it was Cole himself who had helped to introduce the proletarian distemper into Britain. Far from being haunted by such apparitions, however, Cole in 1913 described the general strike as a 'grotesquely unpractical' importation which even Mann declined to propagate.[17]

For some of Mann's associates it carried a greater symbolic weight. Goldman's anarchist comrade Sam Mainwaring had in 1907 launched a short-lived paper *The General Strike*. Dissident marxists promoted the idea within the ISEL, and the Manchester syndicalist conference chaired by Purcell in 1912 carried a unanimous resolution for the 'Revolutionary General Strike'.[18] Whether in the ISEL constitution, its May Day proclamations or its exposition of basic syndicalist precepts, it is nevertheless difficult to find much support for such a notion. Mann himself, as Cole rightly indicated, made little of the issue. Mann's syndicalism was conceived as a way of transforming the existing unions, and the general strike was no more than a subsidiary, hypothetical element in its repertoire. Of the fourteen ISEL lectures Mann advertised in 1912, none had this as its theme, and if challenged Mann tended to stress the strength of organisation and workers' solidarity that would obviate the very need for strikes.[19] His view that not even the general strike would be necessary when labour was universally organised recalls the similar objections of socialist politicians on much the same grounds.[20] In what is still the most expansive account of the General Strike in Britain, W.H. Crook in 1931 dug out a passage of Mann's supposedly identifying 'THE GENERAL STRIKE of national proportions' with 'the actual Social and Industrial Revolution'.[21] Tellingly it is a mis-citation, initially by the Webbs, and what Mann actually referred to was a strike of *international* proportions, hence underlining its presently visionary character.[22]

Perhaps Mann also had in mind the one British example of the persistent advocacy of the general strike. This, which had nothing to do with syndicalism, was its promotion by Keir Hardie and the pre-1914 ILP as a form of international action against the threat of war. Careful documentation of the campaign shows that this was neither a mark of Hardie's naivety, nor did it presuppose any facile assumption of the tactic's current practicability. Rather the intention was 'educative' and 'persuasive': a form of leverage or even bluff whose immediate potency, Hardie averred, was that 'the very threat of the possibility of such a strike would make statesmen pause'.[23] Hardie died in 1915, knowing the bitter sense of deflation when it did no such thing. Had he lived a little longer, he might nevertheless have felt that the seeds had taken root when in August 1920 the TUC-Labour Party Council of Action, including Purcell, successfully threatened a national 'down tools' over military intervention in Russia.

Hardie even anticipated a 'universal strike' over economic issues, and two years before the establishment of the 'Triple Alliance' of coal and transport unions he told an audience in Mountain Ash that 'if there were going to be trouble in the mines and on the railways it would be good to have them out at the same time'.[24] Remarkably, when the *Syndicalist* the following year published open letters to the Miners' and Railwaymen's delegates, then meeting separately in conference, it failed to propose any such common forms of action.[25] It is a simple matter of record that Hardie had more to say on the matter than Mann, and even as memorialised by the ILP served posthumously to legitimise such forms of action. When a popular edition of Hardie's authorised biography by William Stewart appeared shortly after Red Friday, a reviewer thus observed once more how Hardie had 'supported the idea of a general strike believing that the more effectively it was organised the less need would there be for putting it into operation.'[26] At the Hull TUC in 1924, there was unanimous support when the Miners revived the idea of a general 'holiday' against war, of which Hardie had been the foremost British proponent.[27]

Among British syndicalists the general strike idea probably had its greatest currency immediately after the First World War. Through publications like the weekly *Solidarity* and Jack Tanner's pamphlet *The Social General Strike* militants were introduced to ideas of such an action circulating among the 'Latin races' and others.[28] Mann by now was secretary of the ASE and repeatedly urged that workers should 'cease to function as workers' to secure their demands, though without actually spelling out what this involved.[29] Only after his retirement from union office in 1921 did he make his one real attempt to launch a campaign around the general strike idea. Focusing on the issue of unemployment, he addressed a series of public meetings in the spring of 1923, including one in Manchester chaired by Purcell, and also took his arguments to conferences of the RILU and the National Unemployed Workers' Committee Movement (NUWCM).[30] Mann by now was a CPGB member as well as president of the RILU British bureau. Nevertheless, he appears to have been acting largely on his own initiative. When he met with approval at the RILU conference, having described its existing resolution as too 'tame', the communist *Workers' Weekly* drily wondered whether delegates 'appreciated all that was involved'.[31] Attending the NUWCM conference for the CPGB, J.T. Murphy similarly warned that 'the class war is a much more serious thing than a three days general strike'.[32] Mann's brochure on the issue was published independently, and initial editorial support in the *Workers' Weekly* was not followed up, except as applied to that year's May Day stoppages.[33]

What nobody had in mind was an indefinite strike. One of the variables Sorel mentioned was that of duration. Reflecting debates in Germany, Werner Sombart's typology of general strike forms also distinguished the demonstration strike of brief duration, the pressure strike and the revolutionary strike.[34] Both socialist and syndicalist advocacy in Britain confirms the importance of these distinctions. When Hardie promoted the anti-war strike, he had in mind a demonstration strike. When he urged the common action of miners and railwaymen, it was on the assumption that two days would be enough to secure a living wage.[35] With their commitment to working within the unions, this was an assumption shared by Mann and his communist comrades, from whom there was little perceptible echo of Luxemburg's more open-ended conception of the revolutionary mass strike. When Mann returned to the theme in 1923, he countered the idea that the workers themselves would be hardest hit by disavowing the notion of a long and costly dispute in favour of 'a series of shorter stoppages'. In no case should these exceed three days, or at very most a week. 'Probably one day will be ample ... and a few weeks after, another day, or half-a-day, according to requirements'.[36] Mann was to revive the idea of intermittent stoppages two years later in support of the twelve communist prisoners.[37] Avoiding the need for strike pay, they would in theory make it easier to sustain a grassroots militancy and counteract the dampening effect of a finance-conscious bureaucracy. Mann even suggested that 'nothing in the nature of resistance to authority is entertained'; the workers were to 'stay at home and play with the kids'.[38]

As briefly taken up by the CPGB, it was the symbolic demonstration strike that was intended, most obviously in the form of the May Day stoppage as 'preparation and earnest of the greater struggle'.[39] In surprisingly Sorelian accents the CPGB pronounced that the General Strike was 'not the end of capitalism or the beginning of a new order' but 'the declaration of the power of the working class':

> It is the visible demonstration of the workers, not only to the capitalists, but to themselves, that society depends upon their own force every day and every minute, and that, if they stop all the life and work of the world stops.[40]

Purcell too, while not overestimating the likely response, upheld the traditional NAFTA position that May Day should be celebrated in this way as far as possible.[41] Well into the popular-front period, downing tools on 1 May was promoted by communists as a form of 'mass political strike' as symbolic action.[42]

The vindication of militant solidarity in the summer of 1925 might have been enough to put the general strike back on the agenda. Not only had the government's climbdown on Red Friday demonstrated the potentialities of such an action, but the strictly temporary nature of the subsidy it granted the coal industry suggested that a further such showdown was inevitably to be expected. Even during the summer's coal crisis, however, there had been surprisingly little discussion of the general strike as such. It had not, *contra* Cole, provided the threat that lay behind Red Friday; the embargo had. In the case of heavily interdependent sectors, this might seem tantamount to a strike, and at the time of Red Friday the TUC had warned of a possible general railway stoppage.[43] For the most part, however, demands for solidarity with the miners failed to specify forms of support, and the TUC had indicated that most unions would be expected to contribute only financially.[44] It was precisely for this reason that Bevin steered towards the shared commitment of a general stoppage, which he expressly saw as an alternative to the targeted embargo tactic and not as a stronger variant of it.

With the embargo tactic having met with temporary success, the general strike if anything slipped even further from view. The Miners' secretary Cook is frequently depicted as the most extravagant of the lefts – Gordon Phillips refers to his 'unbridled public prophecies of a general strike' – and the *Sunday Worker* was one of his regular platforms. Cook did not, however, promote a general stoppage there, and at the Scarborough TUC in 1925 he urged the strengthening of the general council's powers precisely in order to 'avoid a struggle' and 'save a general strike':

> He appealed to the Congress to learn the lesson of the miners' struggle. Surely the time had come when they should realise that the day of the long struggle had gone by. Miners knew what long struggles were. But men could not fight on empty stomachs. It was necessary that they should realise the importance of organising scientifically so that they would not have to fight on the empty stomachs of the women and children.[45]

Few delegates could have known what he meant by long and short. In March 1926 Cook addressed the issue of 'The coal crisis and the way out' for the *Labour Monthly*, but the nearest he got to any concrete proposal was 'united defence of the workers'.[46] A *Plebs* feature introduced by Cook included eight contributions from different coalfields, but this too got no further than a generalised call for solidarity with the miners. At best there was the South Walian S.O. Davies's anticipation of the impending 'supreme clash'.[47] Another Plebs symposium, on prospects for 1926, again failed to anticipate the coming crisis; Hicks alone addressed the general issue of co-ordination; Dutt, with the waywardness that occasionally made him seem like a seer, dealt with the fight against fascism.[48] Subsequent to the reissue of Cole's *World of Labour* in 1919, it is difficult to trace any sign of comparative or theoretical reflection on the general strike, either in labour's research and publishing activities or as occasioned by appropriate conference resolutions. Whatever exceptions remain to be traced, they can hardly have impinged much on contemporaries, who were not after all engaged in researching them.

The communists' position was hardly more explicit. There was subsequently some claim that the launching of a general strike was a 'partial victory' for communist policy imposed upon a reluctant right wing.[49] It is impossible to document this pressure, and even Klugmann's official history cites little more than anticipations of a coming 'fight' or 'battle'.[50] It is likely that there was even a conscious decision to avoid anything more specific. Exceptionally, in the week before Red Friday the *Sunday Worker* had called for a '*General Strike, here and now, organised by the TUC*'.[51] Following the government climb-down, Murphy took up the issue in the *Communist Review*, but made no attempt to vindicate this position. On the contrary, he warned that a threatened general strike must either develop into the fight for power itself, and thus into civil war, or else that it represented the bluffing by the leaders of 'both themselves and the workers'.[52] Not only did Murphy offer no suggestion here of such an imminent fight for power, but in the eight months that followed before the expiration of the government subsidy this was the last such allusion to the general strike in the CPGB's theoretical journal. Less than a week before the actual realisation of the general strike, Murphy warned with perfect clarity against exaggerated expectations of its revolutionary possibilities.[53] As Andrew Thorpe has shown, it was the Comintern, not the CPGB, that tended to talk these matters up.[54]

Tom Mann, according to one biographer, had 'done more over the years than anybody else to propagate the idea of the General Strike'.[55] None was better qualified to stiffen the sinews of such a movement; and with the CPGB's leadership depleted by the arrests in October 1925, and Pollitt's removal to Wandsworth prison, Mann's role as NMM president acquired an added significance.[56] It was therefore rather more than what the same biographer describes as a 'mild irony' that Mann should have missed this climacteric of his life's work through attending to a routine commitment in Moscow.[57] Emma Goldman, while also claiming to have propagated the General Strike 'for 25 years', actually left the country while it was still happening; Mann got back just after it had finished.[58] Two cheers for the despised union bureaucrats who at least managed to turn up at the right time. Passed over in the communists' collective memory, Mann's dereliction of duty underlines the paradox of Moscow subventions, which simultaneously freed revolutionaries from material cares and encumbered them with bureaucratic ones.[59] But it also shows how little every communist effort was focused on *der Tag*.

Had Purcell been a socialist intellectual, the nuances of so ambiguous a commitment might have attracted an essay in hermeneutics. Even as a mere trade unionist, if he talked of Direct Action, it is worth trying to establish what he understood by it. Already within the Furnishing Trades he had made clear his preference for 'short, sharp and sweet fights over a big area', as against long and costly localised struggles meeting at best with partial success.[60] Generalised over different trades, as opposed to the different localities within his own trade, this suggested something on the lines of the demonstration strike, with doubtless somewhat exaggerated ideas of its likely impact. During the food crisis of the later war years, Purcell argued for a national stoppage, first of a day, then two, then three – by which time he believed the objects of the action would have been secured.[61] In February 1919 he played a small part in the Belfast general strike over working hours, attending at least one strike committee meeting. With all but the linen industry at a standstill, no local press except a strike bulletin, and pickets assisting in maintaining order, he would later describe this as the greatest general strike in British history; and he suggested at the time that its re-enactment in twenty other cities would be enough to secure the workers' emancipation.[62] The local outcome, to the manifest discontent of some strikers, was a working week somewhat longer than that demanded, and a return to work as disciplined as the stoppage itself.[63]

As Purcell's activities came to focus on the TUC general council, in which many vested their hopes of a centralised industrial authority, he admitted that his talk of large-scale actions could be seen as tending to the idea of a general strike. On one occasion he suggested that wages would have to chase prices 'until the system itself is wrecked'.[64] The usual caveat nevertheless remained: 'the threat of a general strike would be more powerful than the operation of one'.[65] As TUC chairman during the first MacDonald government, Purcell made little even of the threat. When a Locomen's strike cast a shadow over the government's formation, and on relations between the different rail unions, Purcell chaired the TUC's mediation committee and likened its successful intervention to that of an industrial League of Nations.[66] He and Bramley also settled a dispute in the Southampton shipyards, at a mass meeting that Bramley euphemistically described as 'somewhat difficult'.[67] The object of such interventions, as Purcell observed of the rail dispute, was to minimise the danger to other trades while encouraging managers and workers 'to attempt to hammer out arrangements mutually satisfactory to each'.[68] His TUC profile was not that of a bitter-ender, but of a 'successful arbitrator'.[69]

In Dutt's 1924 *Labour Monthly* symposium, even direct action figured little as a theme. Cook came closest in urging the interdependency of the major industrial groups and the impossibility of the miners acting without effect upon their fellow trade unionists.[70] Nevertheless, in a context so conducive to expressions of militancy, these seven contributions from the trade-union left had contained no single positive reference to the general strike. Hicks and Williams, indeed, specifically distanced themselves from the tactic.[71] Though Purcell also failed to mention the issue, he did inimitably evoke the spirit of the demonstration action that might or might not succeed:

> The chief thing should be to go in and get something; if it comes off well, good – if not, well, come again – and again – and again.
>
> ... how many times (according to our position in the Industrial Line) have some of us, if not all, taken sections of our class up the side of the

mountain, shown them the promised land, and then – now back – down again.

Of course, we all have, and correctly so, we have always been bigger than we thought we were.[72]

Looking bigger than you actually were was a form of brinkmanship requiring agility at times of crisis and resourcefulness in defeat. Purcell in 1926 appeared on the face of it to have neither. In March that year, moving the resolution at an Albert Hall rally in support of the communist prisoners, his speech was drowned in 'furious cheerings' as he promised that the general council would willingly undergo the same tribulations in rising to the challenge of solidarity with the miners.[73] It was to be his last such ovation in a national venue.

The miscalculation was not entirely his. In his diary of the General Strike, Citrine observed that the 'silent of power of labour' had always been envisaged as forcing a speedy reckoning, and that he had never before heard it suggested that a general strike could last 'even a fortnight'.[74] All contemporary evidence confirms this. In the idea of the demonstration strike, as intermittently articulated by the proponents of direct action, there was a significant element of myth-making or simple bluff, very different from the attritional approach of the miners.[75] Labour's misfortune in May 1926 was that the principal architect of the strike was not primarily moved by such considerations. Indeed, he was actively hostile to such a conception and those elements within the labour movement that supported it.

6.2 THE DYNAMICS OF SOLIDARITY

Cole's classification of the general strike by its objects was one possible line of differentiation. Others, of more immediate practical significance, were the issues of who was to come out, under whose authority or co-ordination, with what forms of support, and for how long. Except at a local level, few examples existed of the truly general stoppage involving the principal utilities and productive sectors, such as Purcell had observed in Belfast.[76] Nor did the organisation of similar actions necessarily presuppose their direction by a form of universal trade-union authority. In the years before the British General Strike, there were in fact two rival conceptions of the industrial general staff believed indispensable to such an action. The first, deriving from the 'Triple Alliance' first established in 1913, was that of a co-ordinating body of the unions principally involved in such an action, initially conceived as the rail, coal and transport sectors. Martin's minimal definition of a general strike as involving these groups alone would exclude such famous examples as the Belgian general strike of 1913. It does however convey the centrality in Britain of this notion of the 'Triple' or 'Industrial' Alliance, notwithstanding the devastating exposure of its internal stresses at the time of Black Friday, 1921, when the miners had been left to fight alone.[77] The relationship of this instrument to the wider conception of councils of action, and to the vesting of authority in the TUC general council, was nevertheless ambiguous. Clegg's view was that the TUC was at least spared the competition of rival centres, 'especially now that the Triple Alliance had disappeared'.[78] In reality, the alliance concept remained in abeyance, and at the time of the coal crisis in 1925-6 the issue between these different centres of co-ordination had still to be resolved.

The anomaly in this respect of the TUC was that it not only implied a role for sections having limited capacity for such forms of action, but even accorded them a disproportionate share of the central authority it represented. The CPGB secretary Inkpin described the TUC lefts as being 'released from the necessity of carrying out all their promises ... by the fact that in the main they are the representatives of the smaller unions'.[79] One might have imagined that Inkpin had never issued a slogan without personally attending to its implementation. The point was hardly applicable in any case to Hicks' sixty thousand Building Trades' members, whose record of significant industrial conflict including a recent national strike and lockout.[80] Such activities were nevertheless relatively self-contained; the building trades were clearly peripheral to large-scale solidarity actions and might even be seen as offering leadership from outside the sectors most involved, as craft-based unionists like Mann and Burns had the dockers a generation earlier. Bevin, however, was the very last person to take such pretensions equably. Urged to action by the blue-blooded C.P. Trevelyan, he once remarked that he would bring out the dockers once Trevelyan mobilised the Lord Lieutenants.[81] He could have said the same about French polishers.

Possible tensions can be traced already during the 1922 engineering workers' lockout. Despite the expectations vested in the new TUC general council, it seemed scarcely better equipped to intervene effectively than its predecessor the parliamentary committee. Beyond a common concern with the abuse of overtime, the building and furnishing trades had no direct involvement in the dispute. Nevertheless, it was Hicks and Purcell who moved a significant extension of the general council's powers, to include 'negotiative power', financial assistance, sympathetic strikes and a 'National Down Tools' if required. A 'special and uniform Rule' was also proposed committing the unions in a national emergency to 'follow exactly what lead was given by their accredited representatives on the General Council'.[82] Milder resolutions on these lines were heavily defeated at the 1922 and 1923 TUC conferences, and it was only in 1924 that Hicks, now seconded by Cook, successfully moved such an undertaking.[83] It is odd to infer, as Clegg did, that 'the left had been converted to the policy of the right'; nor can the resolution necessarily be dismissed as what Phillips called 'an inexpensive gesture of solidarity'.[84] Hicks, in defining the 'moral and material support' that was envisaged, specifically mentioned only financial assistance.[85] Nevertheless, the resolution was immediately interpreted within the TGWU as empowering the general council to declare a general strike on its own responsibility.[86]

That this was followed by a sustained effort to resuscitate the Triple Alliance suggests that a Purcell-Hicks general staff may have been regarded with a degree of apprehension. By his own account Bevin was not at first enthusiastic when the MFGB proposed a new 'Industrial Alliance' in the summer of 1924.[87] That in due course he had the main hand in fleshing out the idea suggests that it may be seen as response or counterweight to a strengthened TUC, not just as its complement. The Alliance was conceived as embracing engineering as well as mining and transport workers, and already by February 1925 the TGWU had concluded a 'unity agreement' with the AEU. By the summer a draft constitution for the alliance made clear its assumption of a central co-ordinating role closely resembling the provisions originally proposed by Hicks and Purcell for the general council itself.[88]

While ostensibly not intended as a rival to the TUC, the Alliance expressly provided for its constituents' collective autonomy without further reference to a wider authority and according to a closer (if limited) proportionality from which unions peripheral to its objects were excluded.[89] At the same time, attendance at the TUC's mining and transport sub-committee was far worse than at the other sectional sub-committees, and 'practically no items for consideration' were submitted by the rail or transport unions.[90] As Bevin put it with his customary directness, 'when the fight does come in our Movement, under this Alliance for the period of the dispute, the Executive of the Alliance becomes virtually Controller of that Movement'. One of his own union supporters even thanked him ironically for demonstrating 'that all past Trade Union Congresses had been of no real value to the Trade Union Movement'.[91] Significantly, the principle of the Alliance had never been brought before the TUC. Indeed, at the Hull TUC in the summer in which it was first conceived, Bevin, astonishingly, failed to make a single intervention on any issue whatsoever.

The significance of Red Friday, from this point of view, was as a demonstration of what for the time being remained the sole available authority of the TUC. As a miners' lockout threatened, hostile efforts were made, as Bevin put it, to 'play the Alliance off against the General Council'.[92] In practice, the Alliance had yet to agree its constitution and the Miners had no real option but to refer the dispute to the general council. 'The new Alliance is not ready and cannot function for this dispute', Bevin explained to a TGWU delegate conference fortuitously assembling as the crisis reached its height. Delegates were therefore asked to vest immediate authority in the general council while approving the Alliance as a long-term arrangement.[93] While the implication of a temporary transfer of power was clearly understood, the union resolved even now merely 'to co-operate' with the general council: a language markedly different from that with which it described the Industrial Alliance.[94] The TGWU was indispensable to any solidarity action, and when the general council had organised the transport embargo that secured a temporary coal subsidy and a government court of enquiry, Bevin had been quick to claim the achievement as his own.[95] Nevertheless, he was at best ambivalent about the embargo tactic, and he continued to maintain that the Alliance was 'bigger than the immediate dispute' and part of 'a constructive change in the Trade Union Movement itself'.[96]

This, however, was the general council's moment, and more specifically that of the general council left. The *Herald*'s appellation 'Red Friday' went into immediate currency; and in the run-up to the Scarborough TUC in September 1925 *Lansbury's Labour Weekly* carried a two-page spread, 'Back the General Council', which it boldly emblazoned with the hammer and sickle.[97] One resolution agreed 'the overthrow of capitalism', another the commitment to international trade union unity; a third, as we have seen, 'complete opposition' to British imperialism. MacDonald's triumph at the following month's Labour Party conference only accentuated the contrast; as did his identification of Red Friday with the forces that 'sane, well-considered, thoroughly well examined Socialism feels to be probably its greatest enemy'.[98] Both hopes and forebodings were for the time being focused on the general council, and Mann himself saluted 'Hicks, Purcell and Swales' for the bold stand taken domestically, as already internationally.[99] According to Max Beer, this was 'the highest point yet reached by post-Chartist Labour in Great Britain'.[100] Purcell in his union journal held out the vision of 'a huge offensive disarming the oppressor completely'.[101] As reported in the American communist press, he also claimed that 'all the elements for revolution' were now coming together.[102]

Bevin was naturally more circumspect. When the call was made at Scarborough to extend the general council's powers, he warned that its recent success did not give it licence to 'take on all the troubles' of the movement.[103] As late as November he omitted any reference to the TUC in detailing how the Industrial Alliance would 'bring within its purview all the wider problems of industry'.[104] Even so, Red Friday, in Hicks's words, had 'mark[ed] the point when a large union handed over the conduct of its struggle to a centralised power outside its own executive committee'.[105] The TUC's Special Industrial Committee (SIC) had been set up in June 1925 to deal with the crisis in the coal industry. This was now to remain in existence, with Hicks, though not Purcell, a prominent member, until its re-establishment as the Negotiating Committee on the very eve of the General Strike. Given the powers and status now accruing to the general council, Bevin finally determined to be at the centre of it. At Scarborough, unlike Hull, no other delegate spoke so often from the floor, and Bevin now joined Tillett as one of the two uncontested transport workers' representatives on the general council.[106] With the resumption of their seats by Thomas and Bondfield, there was thus at once a strengthening of the TUC moderates and a closer alignment with the larger unions. Fatefully, however, this did not include the miners, whose president Herbert Smith withdrew from the general council and was not replaced by Cook until 1927. Those who did represent the MFGB in the meantime racked up more unexplained absences than any other members, and during the General Strike itself they excluded themselves from its proceedings entirely.[107]

As Bullock rightly noted, Scarborough beneath the surface thus represented 'the end rather than the beginning of a new mood in the trade unions'.[108] Bramley's death followed just a few weeks later. Swales was succeeded as chairman by the unflappable secretary of the Iron and Steel Trades, Arthur Pugh. Immediately the TUC's interlocutors with the Russians were held more closely to account, and at the December general council they were quietly corrected for having exceeded their authority.[109] It was at this point, as noted in chapter two, that Purcell spoke out vehemently against communist splitting activities, which the communists for their part attributed to the shock he had received at the general council.[110]

It is not therefore surprising that the issue of solidarity was to be posed as much in terms of discipline and control as of how to maximise its effectiveness. In the syndicalist agitations with which the general strike is usually linked, the emphasis was on rank-and-file initiative and an 'organic tendency to Industrial Solidarity' requiring neither strike funds nor a 'complicated labour union organisation'.[111] Rather than a general strike per se, they looked to the replication at national level of the 'spontaneous or demonstration stoppage' intended to 'call attention to the urgency of the workers' feelings of grievance' and hasten the conclusion of satisfactory negotiations.[112] Even when Mann did turn to the idea of the general strike, he implied a wholly independent movement of the militant rank and file, comprising, he estimated, perhaps a fifth of current trade unionists.[113] Similarly, as a way of supporting the communist prisoners he preferred a twenty-four hour 'rest cure' to synchronised shorter strikes requiring 'a highly disciplined power of organisation which may militate against its application'.[114]

One result of Red Friday, as even Mann now saw it, was nevertheless to validate the idea of a central command structure that could mobilise the movement's 'whole strength' behind the miners.[115] The point of the Industrial Alliance was that the principal party to any dispute must equally vest its authority in the higher body. Hicks himself drew this lesson from Red Friday, and within the TGWU the corollary was also noted that the 'test of discipline' would need to be imposed 'not only upon those sections which are called out, but also upon those which the General Council decide shall remain at work'. There must, it went on, 'be no rushing in'.[116] The strength of the General Strike was to be the brilliant improvisation of centralised machinery. Its weakness was to be the subordination to this machinery of all local and sectional initiative.

6.3 STRIKE DISCUSSIONS

For six months after Red Friday it remained unclear which body would be responsible for any future action. The communists warned that the Alliance could not take the place of the general council, and urged the revision of its constitution to bring it under the latter's direction.[117] Even so, as late as 7 February the *Sunday Worker* could feature Mann looking to the general council without referring to the Alliance, while Cook overlooked the TUC in urging 'an Alliance of Unions – the Industrial Alliance'.[118] Even after 1926 Cook continued to refer to the Alliance as if it had been the intended vehicle of solidarity.[119] Bevin, less plausibly, now claimed never to have been keen on the concept, and stressed his authorship of the original draft upon which the general council had been based.[120]

Nevertheless, Bevin's strong advocacy at the time was picked up by the left-wing press, and the TGWU was least of all responsible for the initiative's failure.[121] In November 1925, the NUR withdrew from the discussions. In December, the general council assumed responsibility for any future solidarity action. In February 1926, the MFGB was advised by its solicitors that the Alliance included provisions that were in conflict with its own rule book.[122] Only at this point did the Miners approach the TUC for regular meetings, as the emphasis henceforth shifted decisively to the general council and to the Special Industrial Committee it had established the previous July.[123] As late as April 1926 the TGWU's conception of 'a Central Body' was one requiring the Miners to vest their authority in a wider negotiating committee which in turn should be composed 'primarily of representatives of those who would be involved to the greatest extent in a struggle'.[124] Eschewing any reference to the general council, this assumed – as Bevin put it later – 'the basis of the new Alliance constitutions'.[125] Discussion of the Industrial Alliance helped create the climate of mental preparedness in which a significant demonstration of solidarity could take place. Organisational preparedness, on the other hand, was hardly assisted by this basic confusion as to whose responsibility this ultimately was.[126]

Citrine noted afterwards that the MFGB had not set out clearly its own expectations. He also made much of a memorandum he drew up in January 1926 which supposedly addressed the TUC's own lack of preparedness and which is widely cited in the literature on the strike.[127] The document was nevertheless confined to generalities, and Gordon Phillips was surely right to question the impression Citrine gave of an unavailing attempt to focus minds on practicalities.[128] It was commonly understood that there could be no successful repetition of the Red Friday action. Red Friday had however demonstrated the possibility, perhaps the necessity, of drawing selectively from the repertoire and discourse of the general solidarity movement. Immediately after the government's climb-down, Citrine had warned of further attacks to come, in which the 'large-scale industrial dispute' would increasingly take the place of the detached individual strike or lockout.[129] There were, however, any number of ways of prosecuting the large-scale dispute, and wide variations in the expectations of different sections of the movement, or articulated on their behalf.

The problem of a general strike, as it turned out, was not primarily one of securing initial support, but the fact that both the scope and duration of effective action varied considerably according to different employment situations. This might have been better understood from previous actions had it not been obscured by the language of betrayal. In his essay on the General Strike, Martin Jacques noted that the four main real or prospective solidarity actions of the period all involved the miners as the key section around whom other groups of workers periodically rallied in struggle.[130] Viewed another way, what this also shows us by default is that solidarity actions in the coalfields were of practically no use to other workers. In Tanner's fantastical exposition, the miners were the decisive force which through unreplenished coal stocks would close down all power and communications in as little as a week.[131] But there were no such coal shortages by 1921, as the aftermath of Black Friday demonstrated. Rather, it was rail and transport workers who could exercise immediate pressure on the miners' behalf. 'Let the railwaymen strike. They need no help', said the General Workers' president J.R. Clynes; 'but what measure of help can railway workers give to others, or should [they] give to others if they say they will stop every train and, in support of other workers cease to move an engine?'[132]

What Clynes called the 'inevitable inequalities' of mutual support generated persistent tensions within the Triple or Industrial Alliance. Before the war, even militant railwaymen began to cavil at demands 'to pull other people's chestnuts out of the fire'.[133] When a majority of coalfields voted for 'a general Trade Union strike' to secure coal nationalisation in March 1920, the unions as a whole rejected this by a nearly four-to-one majority.[134] In the national railway strike of 1919, just as Clynes suggested, the rail unions declined to press for sympathetic action under the terms of the Triple Alliance; within days half the pits had in any case been stopped merely by their own action.[135] Duration was thus crucially bound up with issue of who was to be called out, and ideas of solidarity were intricately bound up with the sectionalist perspective of different groups of workers. As the rail strike began in 1919, the Locomen's leader Bromley entertained the idea of a 'long and severe struggle' of up to six weeks.[136] Although the action was settled on favourable terms, it was nevertheless clear after just nine days how vulnerable to counter-measures the rail unions actually were. Hardie had said that the government might get Royal Engineers to run the trains, but that they 'could not blackleg the collieries and it might be arranged that neither colliers nor railwaymen should settle without the others'.[137] Hardie of course was a miner; had he been a railwayman, it might have been clearer that they could not always afford to wait.

Such differences of perspective were invoked with some insistence in the wake of Black Friday. As the rail and transport unions were accused of having abandoned the miners to their fate, Williams, as secretary of the Transport Workers' Federation, offered a wide-ranging defence. The miners, he said, were effectively 'blackleg-proof' in their closed and homogeneous communities. As a result, they were not only able to sustain long strikes, but otherwise incapable of threatening any serious effect on the wider economy. Transport workers, conversely, were vulnerable to strike-breakers and obliged to make an immediate impact, which at the same time was facilitated by the absence of any equivalent to the stockpiling of physical goods. This in turn was reflected in union structures and decision-making procedures. While transport workers prioritised the 'utmost celerity' of movement, the miners maintained cumbersome balloting procedures that could barely deliver meaningful solidarity except at such notice as allowed the unhurried mobilisation of strikebreakers in other sectors.[138]

Similar points were made by Jimmy Thomas to the Railwaymen and it is obvious that this could serve as bureaucratic apologia.[139] It is also clear, however, that variations in the psychology and practicalities of industrial action undoubtedly did make its effective co-ordination a somewhat daunting enterprise. Despite his identification with the TUC lefts, Bromley by 1926 was one of the most decided advocates of a more limited and targeted approach to solidarity action; indeed, his preference was to meet such commitments through the union's cheque-book. Even the right-winger Thomas was bolder than that, though he similarly held that the railways could not be held up indefinitely: 'if they did not win in 10 days they were done'.[140]

At the conference of union executives called to account for the General Strike and its calling off, Citrine referred tantalisingly to there having been 'three courses that we could have pursued', before being diverted from enumerating them.[141] It is possible that he had in mind the meeting of TUC and Labour Party officers which he convened on 18 February 1926, the day before the crucial meeting between the

SIC and representatives of the MFGB. Those attending the meeting included the Labour Party secretary J.S. Middleton; its press officer Herbert Tracey; and the TUC's own research and publicity officers, respectively Walter Milne-Bailey and Will Henderson. Collectively these represented the new breed of bureaucratic officer, without distinct leadership ambitions or associations with militancy. Once filed away, their deliberations were easily forgotten and Citrine in his autobiography was more concerned to demonstrate his own prescience. They nevertheless underline the fact that there was nothing preordained about the form of action undertaken in May 1926.

Just prior to the meeting Citrine had produced a document on essential services which again distinguished between two types of industrial action. In the 'basic and productive industries', where the effects of disputes were 'not so speedily discernible' and had little impact on a wider public, these tended to be protracted in character. In the 'transport trades', conversely, a '"social inconvenience" factor' immediately obtruded on the public and a dispute had therefore to be short, sharp and decisive. 'I have heard it stated', Citrine recorded, 'that unless a railway strike is won in 48 hours, it will inevitably be lost'.[142] It was not Citrine, however, but Herbert Tracey who followed through this logic in setting out the three possible courses of action, with an incisiveness missing in Citrine's document:

1. An appeal to the whole Movement to support the Miners after three or six months of struggle.
2. An appeal to the Transport and Railwaymen as the 'Storm Troups' of the whole Movement to join with the Miners and be supported financially by the other Unions.
3. A policy of sharp, sudden and speedy blow at the vitals of the Nation.

The second option meant a variation on the Red Friday embargo, against which the government had clearly now made adequate precautions. In apparently indicating his preference for the third option, Tracey did not therefore confine himself to the transport trades:

> An even more revolutionary alternative to a National Stoppage was to arrange with the Unions who could inflict the maximum amount of inconvenience and even danger on the community as a whole ... such as electrical power workers and telegraphic and postal workers, which really affect the whole mechanism of business and trade.

A stoppage of power workers, Tracey concluded, could be effective in three days; and the mere signal that they could organise such a stoppage offered the unions' best chance of bringing the government to reason.[143] Citrine himself was a former officer of the Electrical Trades Union (ETU). He might have added that the union's capacity for immediately effective action had been demonstrated a few years earlier in securing the continuing use of the Albert Hall for political rallies.[144] But there is no record that he did so.

Of South Walian origin, a former Methodist preacher and writer on the *Christian Commonwealth*, Tracey was a protégé of Arthur Henderson's and a functionary dependable enough to have been entrusted with the official *Book of the Labour Party*.[145] S.G. Hobson, who thought much of Tracey's qualities of spiritual and political insight, believed that they might have been voiced more freely but for his official responsibilities.[146] Even so, within what was as yet a relatively new apparatus the different strands of socialist opinion were far less constrained in expression than would subsequently be the case. Tracey in 1925 not only contributed to the communist-edited press. In expounding a philosophy of labour he showed considerable empathy for the stoppage of essential industries or services 'as a means of reminding the community at large that its most important members are the ordinary unidealised average men and women who work', and who could bring the community to a standstill.[147]

Citrine wanted nothing of it. He had originally defined the issues for the meeting as 'a policy of avoidance of a stoppage' and 'a policy if the stoppage took place'. Now he moved that discussion be confined to the first of these only, and at the following day's liaison meeting with the MFGB presented his own memorandum, whose boldest and most explicit proposal was 'to examine in the closest degree the situation and to determine upon some form of preparation'.[148] From this point on, according to John Lovell, Citrine made virtually no contribution to the SIC, and it is simple supposition to suggest, as Lovell does, that his reticence was somehow forced upon him.[149] At the TUC's subsequent post-mortem, Citrine maintained that the general council had never set about preparation of a general strike, and 'would have failed most lamentably if they had'.[150]

The coal subsidy had consequently just three days to run when the TUC on 27 April at last set up a Ways and Means Committee (WMC) to consider the planning of any possible action. By now it was clear that the general council alone had the authority to co-ordinate and direct it. It was also generally accepted that its only conceivable forms were those of the limited strike or coal embargo or of the general 'pressure' or 'demonstration' strike. No clear signals from the left suggested any different. The 2 May issue of the *Sunday Worker* included both a stop press announcement of the calling of the General Strike and a CPGB manifesto, now obviously superseded, demanding only a transport embargo and a stoppage of the 'lying capitalist press'.[151] In the official party organ the *Workers' Weekly*, the acting Minority Movement secretary George Hardy did call if necessary for 'a general strike of all unions capable of rendering the miners' assistance'. However, even this message was compromised by another vague party manifesto, and by an article by Tom Wintringham which took for granted the prospect of a coal embargo, and which, in the spirit of the demonstration strike, suggested that this would be relaxed for essential services once the initial impact had been made.[152]

The action actually undertaken by the TUC on 4 May differed materially from anything previously envisaged. It was to be of unspecified duration; it was neither general, nor confined to unions 'capable of rendering the miners' assistance', but rested on what Phillips called a 'somewhat random' choice of participants; and its effective deployment as a weapon was undermined by the unfathomable decision to pull these forces out in two 'waves' or stages fully a week apart.[153] Presented to the conference of executives on 29 April, the strategy had been drawn up by the WMC, whose key members were Purcell as chairman and Bevin as secretary. It is to Bevin alone, however, that one must ascribe a strike plan that defied strategic logic and was least of all of syndicalist or communist provenance.

In its own way, it was a demonstration strike. Luxemburg in *The Mass Strike* had been ambivalent at best about the self-contained demonstration strike, enacted on command and 'directed by the conductor's baton of a party executive'.[154] Against the strike conceived as instrument she had defended a protean conception of unfolding struggle that was beyond the scope of central initiation or direction – the mass strike, almost, as synonym for the great unrest.[155] Bevin's idea, however, was precisely to wield the conductor's baton, and thus bring under central direction the pressures from below in which Luxemburg saw the promise of revolution, but Bevin only the threat to Labour's claim to a wider voice in the ordering of society.

Peter Weiler expresses the common view that '[a]fter the General Strike ... Bevin played a crucial role in turning the labour movement toward a corporatist path and away from direct action'.[156] In reality, the strike itself was the paradoxical instrument of this process, and is almost impossible to make sense of on any other basis. Bevin's clear and explicit priorities were the involvement of wide sectors of the movement in a shared collective responsibility under strong central leadership, displayed as much in the ability to restrain trade-union members as that of mobilising them. If this was a demonstration, it was directed as much as anything at the labour movement itself. So soon after the carnage of the trenches, it is a matter of wonderment how readily labour movement figures adopted the language of armies and general staff, as if these were quite untarnished as a model of effective leadership. Very few, however, can have used this analogy so freely as did Bevin during the period of the General Strike.[157]

Where others favoured an action that would be short and sharp, Bevin stood for breadth and stamina. The case for breadth meant not so much the massing of weight as the sharing of responsibility: like the French general Joffre favouring action at the Somme to make sure the British did not avoid their obligations. On these grounds Bevin had developed a rooted objection to the embargo tactic as falling principally upon the transport unions, and exposing them at once to victimising employers and allegations of betrayal. The idea of a general strike consequently had a certain currency within the TGWU, and Bevin did not afterwards hold the TUC line of referring to it only as a 'national' stoppage.[158] At a meeting of TGWU officers directly after the dispute, he reported how, 'as usual', there was a 'lot of talk on the General Council by people who thought they were not going to be involved. When the Council decided it was necessary to support the Miners I personally made up my mind that it had to be a much wider dispute than anything attempted before....'[159] This sense of resentment against 'non-participating heroes' was strongly expressed in a summary of the TGWU position by the Bevinite loyalist and passenger transport section secretary Harold Clay. In Clay's enumeration of the strike's rationale, this consideration is given clear precedence over that of bringing greater pressure to bear on the government. The tactic's effectiveness as a form of leverage upon the government is indeed hardly mentioned except incidentally in disposing of alternative strategies.[160] On the premise that any future action 'would have to be on wider shoulders', Bevin would not allow of a partial strike or the leaving of 'small groups of men' to bear the weight of any action.[161]

Bevin's conception was therefore of a 'selective strike on a national scale', to be extended by stages if not initially successful.[162] This also assumed the feasibility of a strike of considerable duration. Bevin's rationale, as Citrine recorded it, was that in transport strikes he had learnt not to reach the maximum of strength too quickly and risk a drift back to work.[163] The strategy did succeed in maintaining momentum and on these grounds it had some defenders.[164] Nevertheless, even the first wave of industries was so defined as to reduce and even minimise the strike's immediate effectiveness. On the one hand, the stoppage in 'productive' industries like iron and steel would have little impact. The specific and unanticipated inclusion of building, in which longer stoppages were the norm, was simply incomprehensible except as a test of its leaders' rhetoric.[165] On the other hand, potentially decisive stoppages of transport and the public utilities were so circumscribed as self-evidently to dampen their impact. In respect of Citrine's earlier distinction, power supplies were withheld from 'basic and productive industries', where the immediate impact would be slightest, while at the same time the '"social inconvenience" factor' was as far as possible minimised. The same rationale underlay the proposed exemption of the transport of food, on which issue Citrine recorded 'practically open strife' between the TGWU and NUR.[166]

The Fabians' motto was to wait patiently but strike hard. Bevin's was to strike early, impressively and with flaccidity. He did however understand as well as any syndicalist the mobilising power of rhetoric.

Repeatedly in discussions of the Industrial Alliance, he had invoked the 'altar of industrial unity' as if demanding a form of self-immolation.[167] In the run-up to Red Friday, he depicted solidarity even in defeat as a strengthening of labour's sinews in a longer struggle:

> After all, when the Napoleonic Wars finished, when the Crimean War finished, when the Franco-German war finished, our fathers and forefathers in each instance were driven back in the industrial arena to horrible conditions. For the first time in the history of the world there is a great disciplined army of labour in this country – the greatest army in the world ... It has no parallel anywhere, and if it can be organised and directed, it will go down in history as an epoch. We shall not win material gains out of the struggle immediately ... but the demonstration of power will usher in an era of constructional effort to follow which will lay a sound basis for the generations to come.[168]

Again, when Bevin addressed the assembled union executives immediately before the General Strike he conjured up an action whose validity did not derive from its immediate effectiveness at all: 'We look upon your "Yes" as meaning that you have placed your all upon the altar of this great Movement', he told them, 'and having placed it there, even if every penny goes, if every asset goes, history will ultimately write up that it was a magnificent generation that was prepared to do it rather than see the miners driven down like slaves. (Cheers.)'[169] The parallel with First World War generals is uncanny, and this extraordinary rigmarole is reproduced in almost every history of the strike.[170] Cook, who might have scripted it, would recall it as the evidence of betrayal, and Bevin himself as the mark of his determination.[171] Only Bullock, whose no-nonsense hero was the scourge of windy assertion, overlooked it entirely.[172]

There had of course been other possible ideas regarding the weapons available to the TUC. 'Action must be short and swift, quick, determined and energetic, and there must be complete unity in their ranks', Purcell had told a meeting the week before the WMC convened. 'Their attitude was to lay bare the capitalistic system and to attack the capitalist at every point ...'[173] On the WMC itself, Purcell observed more cautiously that weak demand and under-employment meant that the capacity to hurt employers in industries like furnishing and engineering was limited. He therefore cited Bromley's proposal of a 'couple of days' hold-up, but universally applied: 'If they had the organisation behind them, they could use that as a threat. It assumed they had the power to authorise throughout the length and breadth of the land, everybody to move at a given moment.'[174]

Bevin was dismissive: entirely disregarding the symbolic aspect of any such action, he commented that half the industries closed on bank holidays anyway without causing any dislocation.[175] Bevin's solution was to lengthen the holiday, when it might have been better logic to consider which activities could not be interrupted even for a day. Also on the committee was Jimmy Rowan, Citrine's former boss at the ETU. Rowan was not a 'left' and had no time for syndicalist 'piffle'.[176] At the WMC he nevertheless proposed a temporary shutdown of utilities from which he anticipated an immediate impact through the closing of West End theatres and clubs – not least the gentleman's club of the House of Commons. As a sympathetic instant history of the strike put it, 'the failure even for a short while of the light would have reduced Mayfair and St James's to hysteria'.[177]

Rowan's position was consistent with that of his union at the start of the strike. Given the impracticability of maintaining power for essential services while withholding it from industry, the ETU so interpreted its strike instructions as to try to stop the power stations.[178] Citrine observed that 'they could not discriminate between lighting and power'.[179] Another of the instant strike histories described the aim more positively as 'to "hasten the victory"'.[180] Though the instructions were countermanded, similar tensions were replicated locally, and the ETU afterwards supported a resolution very critical of the way in which the strike had been called off.[181] A similar instinct can be seen in the building trades, whose instructions to come out unless engaged on 'housing and hospital work' caused considerable dissension and what Clay described as putting the telescope to the blind eye.[182] Hicks's union the AUBTW thus employed the slogan 'If in doubt – all out', which it candidly admitted was an interpretation of the instructions 'differ[ing] somewhat from that of other unions'.[183] Indeed, the AUBTW was definitely hostile to the authority which the general council had vested in the allegedly more temporising NFBTO.[184] 'As we felt that the fight had to be short and sharp', it reported afterwards, 'we were concerned more with finding excuses for bringing men out ... than in finding reasons for keeping them in'.[185] Rowan in his annual report to ETU members described the partial character of the action as its greatest weakness.[186]

In one respect alone did Bevin urge the full and immediate application of the unions' collective strength. When the WMC first convened, the very first of his list of priorities was the calling out of the print unions, followed in descending order by the transport workers, paper workers and productive industries, with the power workers coming only fifth. Citrine, following Red Friday, had noted as a point for future decision: '*Press Censorship.* Insistence, through printing Unions, on allowing workers' case to be stated truthfully in the press.'[187] Mann for the left had thought it inconceivable that they would churn out 'hogwash' at the behest of media magnates.[188] Nevertheless, the proposal simply to shut down the press entirely was Bevin's. He justified it by recalling how two years earlier he had refused the *Morning Post* paper unless it carried articles in support of striking dockers. He also reasoned that this 'was a very serious proposition for the Press, because the drop in circulation would take months to get back'.[189] Where the circulation was to go during a general stoppage is unclear, and of course no such fall occurred. Nor is it clear in any case how this salutary effect on the press was to assist the miners if no newspapers were appearing.

No other decision of the general council was so 'very unexpected', in Citrine's words, so obviously half-baked, or so widely criticised afterwards.[190] Some emphasised the loss of any opportunity to appeal to a wider public, now left exposed to the BBC and Churchill's 'hate-breathing' *British Gazette*.[191] As Allen Hutt observed, the lessons were forgotten of the 1919 railway strike, in which a sophisticated media campaign was for the first time conducted for the unions by the LRD, and in which the printing trades undertook to ensure the proper ventilation of the workers' case.[192] Others, like Alex Gossip, regarded the cessation of the Labour press in particular as a 'lamentable error'.[193] There were many applications for exemption of such publications, and the failure to grant them was certainly not an oversight.

It is tempting to see the blanket press closure as Bevin's hit at the London Society of Compositors, which at Scarborough had struck a discordant note in condemning the idea of being dragged into general solidarity actions.[194] But it was also transparently an exercise in discipline and centralisation, and the expedient of a single unrivalled TUC organ was like a metaphor for Bevin's conception of the labour army. Herbert Tracey, who in one account is now depicted as a sort of TUC censor-in-chief, described the objection to bringing in 'all sorts of other issues' and the 'confusion and beclouding of the mind of the movement' that would have been likely had Labour papers had the opportunity of 'presenting the Trade Union case each from its own point of view'.[195] In similar circumstances, the highly centralised Belgian labour movement had maintained its authority through the minutest control of oral and written propaganda. It was at least a step in this direction, not only to subject the TUC's *British Worker* to such intensive oversight, but to require of local organisations that they confine their statements to material issued by the central publications committee without unauthorised 'comment or interpretation'.[196] This again is an issue which Bullock overlooked.[197] For the official *Daily Herald*, which Bevin came to refer to as 'my paper', it was not a hopeful augury.[198]

This was not so much a syndicalist distemper as a bureaucratic emetic to get it out of the system. 'One thing the strike did', Clay argued, 'was to prove how foolish and inaccurate guides were the people who were always preaching "General Strike" as the panacea ... The response was greater than they had ever imagined and yet the forces on the other side did not capitulate in three or four days as they had confidently predicted ...'[199] Bevin made a similar point, and Citrine subsequently ridiculed Mann's conception of the 'short and sharp protest strike'. But there had of course been no attempt to exercise the maximum pressure at the outset of the strike. Bevin did afterwards concede that any future re-enactment would require the complete closing down of transport and a speedier resolution. The inference drawn from this, however, was that it made the general strike an unusable instrument except as a preamble to a struggle for power which nobody at the TUC intended, or arguably had ever intended.[200]

Bevin was to describe the action as 'the finest disciplined movement that the world has ever seen'.[201] Clay repeatedly invoked the qualities of 'discipline and order' by which it had displayed a character possible in no other country.[202] The object, quite explicitly, was to channel and direct the flow of solidarity, not simply to express it: exactly as Bevin within the TGWU asserted a strong central leadership whose anathema was the unofficial action. The decision to call a general strike had given 'point and direction' to a widespread feeling that might otherwise have given rise to spontaneous and ungovernable outbursts of militancy. It was, in a word, Bevin's alternative to 'widespread unofficial fighting in all parts of the country, which would have produced anarchy in the Movement'. As Bevin very aptly reminded his officers, 'you always have to be sure you can control it!'[203]

That Bevin's conception prevailed owed a good deal to his force of personality. It was also true that, whenever he stood up to speak in such circles, it was as if he carried a card vote representing a third of a million transport workers. There was a revealing episode after the strike when NAFTA was accused of having sought exemption to carry out certain non-essential works. More revealing than the charges themselves, which were apparently without foundation, was how the issue had been treated on the general council as a 'bit of a joke' against Purcell, and how Thomas now goaded Gossip with having 'very little knowledge' of strikes on any scale.[204] May 1926 marked the passing of the notion that the moral and political direction of such a movement could be assumed by the militant representative of a union that had no significant role to play in it. In the long term it was a decisive step towards the dominance of the big battalions. In the short term Purcell continued to exercise a significant responsibility in the strike itself. But that has almost disappeared under what sometimes seems a veritable cult of Bevin's personality – one to which, as with most such cults, Bevin himself was not behindhand in contributing.

6.4 THE NINE DAYS

Bullock's account of the strike draws heavily on an anonymous item appearing a fortnight afterwards in the *Yorkshire Evening News*. This depicts Purcell and Hicks as 'budding Lenins' and fire-eaters lacking the most basic political courage. Bevin, on the other hand, was the strike's 'big man':

> It was his quick brain and natural genius for organisation that saved the strike from being a complete fiasco. Within half an hour of the Council's decision to call the strike he had dictated the plans and instructions that were to be laid before the conference of the executive committees of all the unions. Fresh from his agile brain came the scheme for the organisation and administration of strike headquarters. All through the first week, cool and unflurried by anybody or anything, he kept the machine of his making smoothly at work. He could be called 'The Dictator of Eccleston-square', to whom all appealed and sought advice. His word was absolute.[205]

Carefully preserved in Bevin's papers, by an author boasting 'intimate contact with the whole tragic episode', the document occasions no curiosity in Bullock as to the relation of author to subject, or how it found its way into the provincial press.[206] Already in the several instant histories of the strike, Bevin's role in the creation and operation of a central strike machinery is singled out, though in less extravagant terms.[207] The item is also consistent with Bevin's own estimation, acerbically transcribed by Citrine, that with his unrivalled experience and constructive brain 'the Deity had specially ordained him to run the first general strike in Great Britain'.[208] But direct supporting evidence is, in the nature of things, elusive. According to Citrine, any attempt to register individual decisions was swiftly abandoned by the general council. Few surviving records are even initialled, and after the third day no minutes were taken of key committees for fear of possible future legal actions.[209] Bevin appearance as the strike's generalissimo may nevertheless be tested against some other sources than his own cuttings collection.

Of the committees established for the duration of the crisis, two had a particular significance. The Negotiating Committee (NC) was a continuation of the Special Industrial Committee established the previous July and with a similar personnel, notably including Thomas. The Strike Organisation Committee (SOC), established on 5 May, was successor to the WMC, which had itself been reconstituted as the Power and Orders Committee (POC) on 1 May, and whose extended prerogatives included responsibility for the improvised strike machinery.[210] As temporary fulcrum of the TUC's authority, the SOC in theory exercised extensive powers. These included oversight of general council members, receipt of twice-daily committee reports and general responsibility for the 'whole strike organisation and direction'.[211] On 4 May Citrine recorded Bevin's suggestion that 'he, personally, should be put in charge of the Strike Organisation'. He also noted that the proposal occasioned a 'good deal of straight speaking' and open sarcasm.[212] Bevin was not, as a result, brought onto the Negotiating Committee, and neither he nor Purcell had any part in the discussions which in due course provided a pretext for terminating the action in the shape of the Samuel Memorandum.[213] The view that Bevin provided the strike's 'driving force and direction' therefore rests upon his role on the SOC. Gordon Phillips, an authoritative historian of the strike, described the committee as a vehicle for his personal direction with just 'a greater show of protocol'.[214] Bullock recorded that Purcell as its chairman was overshadowed from the start.[215]

Though it seems well established in the literature that Bevin instigated the SOC and persuaded the general council to entrust it with the conduct of the strike, the original source of this information is unclear.[216] Indeed, the committee's surviving records indicate that Purcell actually moved the resolution constituting the SOC on the morning of 5 May, and that he presented the first of its reports the same evening. They also record that Bevin had attended neither of the previous two days' meetings of the POC that might have agreed such a proposal.[217] Having attended its first two meetings on 1 and 2 May, Bevin's nominal role as secretary appears to have been taken up by the acting assistant secretary A.A. Firth. This would hardly be surprising. Unlike Purcell, Bevin led one of the unions principally involved in the action. The secretary of the Railway Clerks' Association, in a similar if less onerous position, described the intense pressure of having to attend to his own union as well as commitments at the general council.[218] Bevin's proud boast was that he had left the TGWU to run itself. With his famously controlling and even proprietorial attitude towards the union, it is nevertheless hard to believe that he could have abandoned these responsibilities for those at the TUC with such instantaneous effect.[219]

Within the TUC's culture of collective responsibility, which Bevin shared but also aspired to personify, some may in any case have been grateful for the counterweight of Purcell's more familiar presence on its committees. 'I have a hazy recollection that it was Purcell', Bromley recalled of one issue that was referred to the SOC. 'But that may be because Purcell reported so often, I do recollect that Bevin reported on some occasions.'[220] Citrine's recollection was similar: 'On several occasions Mr Purcell by himself was making decisions; also at other times Mr Bevin made decisions by himself, but practically on no occasion can I remember the full Committee, or anything like a quorum of the Committee, being present.'[221] One may well believe that Bevin saw his role as SOC secretary as providing him with the leverage over the dispute that he sought.[222] But one must also heed Bevin's own warning, vis-à-vis the Negotiating Committee, that no single personality could dominate a committee of individuals 'who have been at it all their lives'.[223]

Reports like that in the *Yorkshire Evening News* therefore need treating with caution. Control of the dominant strike narrative was a matter of acute political importance, and Bevin least of all underestimated it. Citrine recorded his account of a visiting group of east London MPs, led by Susan Lawrence in 'a state of hysteria' and Lansbury only slightly less so. As they begged for the issuing of essential service permits, Bevin (no doubt firmly and with his chin thrust forward) told Lansbury it was no use urging militant action and then 'squealing at the first shot'. Citrine agreed with him at least about the 'screeching frenzied leader-writers conception of the General Strike', which we have seen is so difficult to document in any detail.[224] One may nevertheless wonder what an accurate minute of the exchange would have recorded. Where Labour authorities like Lansbury's Poplar refused to implement the government's emergency arrangements, it was in any case entirely appropriate that they should have referred to the general council.[225] The deep-seated antipathies were already evident which Bevin would express with similar innuendo during the 1935 Labour conference.[226]

The *Yorkshire Evening News*'s insider offered a similar view of Purcell. 'When the secret news came to the Council that steps were being taken for their arrest ... it was the men who had been known as "Left Wingers" who seemed to show the greatest concern', the article insinuated. 'The speeches of men like George Hicks and A.A. Purcell, both of whom ... pride themselves on their revolutionary leanings, were for once without revolutionary fervour.'[227] As it happens, Purcell, accompanied by Cook, addressed a rally in Gloucester at precisely this stage of the strike. He did indeed stress that its aims were industrial, not political, and that they did not include the overthrow of capitalism. He also warned of martial law and of the militarisation of the government's response. It was not, however, with a view to backing down. 'They had asked the people to form a trade union police corps and that would be done. ... the TUC had made up their minds for a very grim struggle in the next few days. They were behind the miners and must make them win ... in order to be in a position to remove the brutality of the present system'.[228]

It is impossible to reconcile such conflicting accounts. According to Citrine, it was Bevin who at this point proposed the cessation of minute-taking in a 'state of considerable perturbation'.[229] As the strike gathered momentum without prospect of resolution, Citrine also recorded how Bevin appeared to 'recede in forcefulness' as Thomas advanced.[230] The ILPer John Paton, who was helping out in Eccleston Square, described him as almost disappearing from view, 'tearing his hair in a secret fastness' and communicating through notes under the door.[231] Less obviously partisan is the diary entry later published by Ben Turner, who as a fellow member of the SOC described Purcell as 'cool and careful, a devil for work', and Bevin as also a great worker – but 'twitchy'.[232]

No doubt Bevin had reason to be twitchy. As even his press contacts conceded, it was once Bevin took in the financial implications for the TGWU that his thoughts turned from prosecuting the strike to settling it.[233] By the fifth day Citrine depicted him as in one breath demanding 'constructive proposals for a settlement' and in the next declaiming that it 'could not be settled for at least three or four weeks'.[234] Bevin himself admitted that he had originally counted on a possible three-week strike, which he eventually came to see was unsustainable. Bevin also associated Purcell with this estimate, and this was repeated by Phillips, who contrasted this with the Building Trades' position.[235] All the evidence we have seen nevertheless demonstrates that Purcell had consistently upheld the latter position. As a Ministry of Labour review of the strike recorded, it was quickly apparent that time was not on the strikers' side but on the government's.[236] Robert Taylor has recently suggested that it was actually Thomas who demonstrated 'what little strategic sense the TUC appeared to possess'.[237] It certainly was not Bevin. The strike as conceived by the TUC was a miscalculation, and it was Bevin's alone.

There was no damage, however, to his reputation. If he momentarily lost his nerve, Bevin had more than regained it by the end of the strike. He was quick to account for himself to his union, took the lead in speaking for the TUC, and by the time that the conference of executives reconvened after the miners' lockout spoke with undisputed authority on behalf of the SOC. Purcell, on the other hand, lapsed into what detractors described as a 'cowardly silence'.[238] Immediately after the strike he described it as a 'great CLASS demonstration' and a sign of its potential 'if well and powerfully directed'.[239] He was never to make it clear, however, whether it had been well and powerfully directed. In a movement whose philosophy, values and historical mission were deeply teleological, claims and counter-claims to leadership were crucially dependent on the ability to construct convincing narratives of vindication or betrayal. Purcell had never in his career been able to make much sense of defeat. Abstention from the post-strike debate now exposed his lack of any continuing political or industrial base. What must have been a crisis of political identity can only be reconstructed, however imperfectly, from his actions in the months that followed.

6.5 A MELANCHOLY COMPARISON

In November 1926, Purcell spoke as so often before at a packed-out Albert Hall. Writing in *Lansbury's Labour Weekly*, Raymond Postgate noted the 'persistent, melancholy comparison' between his appearance there in March, 'with his voice tearing to the last ends of the hall, to an audience impatient with enthusiasm and admiration', and his faltering delivery now, 'with obvious effort', to an unresponsive audience. Though Purcell at last earned a cheer by saluting Cook, the unspoken question remained: 'When will you tell, when can you tell, why the strike was called off?' As Pollitt took his place on the platform, the audience rose, 'literally they rose', to sing *He's a Jolly Good Fellow*.[240] There was no overt hostility, but Pollitt afterwards described Purcell as 'feeling his position very acutely' and wanting to meet with the CPGB's political bureau to discuss it.[241]

In the six months since the strike's calling off the miners had fought on alone. Even the moral support of the wider labour movement was constrained by the difficulty of upholding the miners' claims without implicitly repudiating the general council's decision to terminate the action. From rallying cry to recrimination, the expectation of solidarity now gave rise to resentment on both sides that could not but further jeopardise the miners' cause. Initial attempts to justify the general council had focused on allegations of a government breach of faith. In *Lansbury's Labour Weekly*, Swales, Hicks and Tillett, all members of the Negotiating Committee, offered an abject defence of the 'courageous gesture of peace' which a duplicitous government now misrepresented as surrender.[242] Cook, however, pulled no punches about the general council in a pamphlet he produced with the communists' assistance; and when the Negotiating Committee produced its own version of events for the reconvened conference of union executives scheduled for the end of June, it now presented the obduracy and lack of loyalty of the Miners' themselves as having been the obstacles to a satisfactory settlement and the reason for the strike being called off.[243] It was Purcell who, with the MFGB's support, moved an embargo on publication of the report for as long as the lockout continued.[244] This was agreed, and the conference of executives postponed, only after the Miners agreed to reciprocate, and Cook to withdraw his pamphlet from circulation. 'Action first, criticism afterward' was a plausible response, and a degree of constraint was reluctantly respected even by the communists.[245] It meant that Purcell could dispose of the strike issue in just a column in his union journal.[246] Hicks cited the pressure on union finances in cancelling the delegate conference at which he might have been held accountable by his own union members.[247] But equally the opportunity of individual TUC leaders to justify or extenuate their position was also lost.

In some sections of the general council there was an unabashed antipathy to the Miners. As if oblivious to its undertakings, Bromley published the key sections of the NC report in his union journal, and in a bilious personal exchange he impressed upon Cook that 'once the cleavage between the miners and the other unions took place ... there was *not the slightest possible hope of success* no matter how long yourself and others persuaded the miners to suffer'.[248] There was even some suggestion of Purcell having taken a similar view. He had after all accompanied Bevin in conveying to the Miners the terms on which the general council had called off the strike.[249] Though he then travelled to Amsterdam to arrange continued international support, either past or unabated animosities meant that the visit resulted in no clear directions whatsoever. Contemporary notices show that the TUC had 'emphatically expressed its wish' that existing solidarity actions be maintained. Nevertheless, IFTU subsequently insisted that it had never received any such application, and that Purcell had expressly advised the raising of loans as providing a quicker source of support than a conventional relief movement.[250] On the information of the Belgian miners' leader Alfred Lombard, Smith, with Cook's support, accused Purcell of having actively discouraged any further assistance to the miners.[251] Despite Purcell's denial, and Smith's grudging retraction, it took further weeks of delay before Purcell at last headed a European fundraising delegation whose other members were drawn from the MFGB.[252] Even now, the IFTU secretary Sassenbach remained implacable in ascribing to Purcell either incompetence or deliberate connivance with the communists.[253]

The idea that Purcell did not support the Miners' continuing struggle can nevertheless be discounted. On Lombard's authority Smith alleged that he taken the position that the Miners' present predicament was the result of their having failed to heed the TUC's advice. There is nothing in Purcell's behaviour within Britain that appears to corroborate such a view. When the Negotiating Committee's report came before the general council, it was he who raised the issue of the MFGB's representation at the meetings with the supposed intermediary Herbert Samuel that led to the strike's conclusion.[254] This of course was precisely the grievance of the Miners themselves. Purcell did not regard the outcome of the strike as a 'victory', as one recent account suggests.[255] In a passing indiscretion he even referred to it as a 'debacle'.[256] Goaded by his opponents, his parliamentary invective took on a clearly compensatory function. Vindication of the strikers' orderly methods segued into the promise of further strikes, of wider scope and illimitable brilliance. Jeering Tory supporters of a 'Tsarist Government' – the most bestial, brutal and murderous known to history – were warned: 'You will get it in good time my friends!'[257] When the issue of Russian financial support came up, Purcell expressed his regret at the TUC's decision to decline such assistance and once again aligned himself with the Miners in supporting their decision to accept it. Whether or not any of the money came from the Soviet state was a matter on which he expressed total indifference, given the scale of Britain's earlier intervention against the Soviets. 'I am bound to confess I have had to bring in money for the trade union movement', he added obliquely, 'and I suppose we can resort to these means again'.[258]

Such a stance was justified by Purcell as that of a 'very old' trade unionist and working-class internationalist. Like so much in the connection in Russia, it might equally be seen as a top-down bureaucratic arrangement and a distraction from the lack of practical support within Britain. Where just a few months earlier Purcell's rhetorical flourishes could be seen as a way of developing and expressing the idea of working-class solidarity, after May 1926 there was a painful dislocation from any commensurate capacity for action or even threat of action. The Miners' central demand was for a coal embargo, and it was by supporting such an embargo that the general council 'lefts' were called upon to demonstrate their good faith. But it hardly now mattered whether they did or not. While Purcell intimated his support for some 'bigger' action than fundraising, such as a possible miners' march to London, he pointed out that only the transport workers could deliver an embargo, which was a measure in effect of the TUC's impotence.[259] Neither the rail unions nor the TGWU referred these matters to the general council, and the Miners themselves approached these unions direct. Bevin, of course, had been clear from the start that the point of a general strike was precisely as an alternative to the embargo. Even in disintegration, the idea of the Industrial Alliance nevertheless persisted, if only in the prerogative to withhold solidarity. Bevin had succeeded to this extent, that non-participating heroes were once more put in their proper place as bystanders.

Purcell's dilemma was that he had nowhere else to go. When, some weeks after the General Strike, he and Hicks at last ventured into print in the *Sunday Worker*, an accompanying leaderette asked what sign they could give that they had not been in a united front in treachery with Thomas.[260] Few of the *Sunday Worker*'s readers would have found the question surprising. The Russians were accusing the TUC of cowardice and a 'deliberate infringement of the elementary duty of class solidarity'.[261] Purcell's own trade union registered the 'nasty feeling of having been betrayed'.[262] Among his parliamentary constituents the sentiment was applauded that leaders could 'come and shout on the platform' but were afraid of the power entrusted them.[263] Nevertheless, the standing of the TUC lefts depended crucially on the moral and material credit extended them by the communists and those around them. Cook still believed it indispensable. With the arrogance of youth, or of their Russian connections, the communists recorded how he 'fairly grovelled with terror' when they hauled him over the coals for having set up a Miners' paper with the ILP's assistance; or how he became 'hysterical' when they took issue with his more accommodating moments as Miners' secretary.[264]

With a similar revulsion against the old constraints, *Trade Union Unity*'s 'factotum', Allen Hutt, now expressed his view of Hicks and Purcell as 'fat, lazy, cowardly drunkards'.[265] Perhaps there were attempted adjustments behind the scenes, for after a three-month hiatus the magazine resurfaced mysteriously for a final August issue, before disappearing completely. In wavering towards Pollitt after the Albert Hall rally, Purcell showed that he knew who could get him a cheer. Nevertheless, while Cook remained on terms with the communists for a further three years, the breach with Purcell was immediate and irrevocable. He not only went round 'vowing vengeance' against the *Sunday Worker* but never again wrote for the communist press.[266] The *Trade Union Unity* subvention was evidently withdrawn, and in September Purcell also announced his withdrawal from the LRD executive. As if anticipating the labour movement's later proscriptions, from this point on he had no association with any broader campaign in which communists had an animating role.[267]

This might have been his basic loyalism, or it might have been an instinct of self-preservation. Its basis was in any case spelt out in a parting encounter with the Russians staged in Paris at the end of July. It was Purcell who moved that the TUC take up the Russian suggestion of a meeting to review current relations between the two movements.[268] No doubt there is a connection here with the brief resuscitation of *Trade Union Unity*. Nevertheless, Purcell was no more willing than his colleagues to allow the legitimacy of the Russian unions' criticisms of the TUC. These had been published at the beginning of June, and even the CPGB had taken exception to them, while Purcell described them as innuendoes of the blackest order.[269] To his constituents in the Forest of Dean he had observed somewhat cryptically that 'another general strike might be of a different type and the methods employed ... somewhat different'.[270] Faced with what he clearly saw as outside criticisms, he nevertheless offered a staunch defence of the calling off of the strike 'at a time when the traditions of the British trade union movement demanded it, namely when [it] reached its zenith'. He again conceded such mistakes as the refusal of Soviet financial support. Nevertheless, he made no attempt to differentiate his own positions, but offered an unreserved defence of his colleagues as a body:

> If you try to dismember and split the General Council you will get nowhere ... Sometimes we discuss a question and the vote is twelve to twelve. At the next meeting the same question is raised again and the same people vote seventeen for and five against. ... There may be a majority and a minority but the question is finally passed unanimously, as it should be. We have neither Rights nor Lefts. The development of the trade union movement in Great Britain follows along lines entirely different from those in other countries. This may be very strange peculiarities of the British movement but such it is and it cannot be helped.[271]

Purcell's only real prospects by this time were either through his membership of the general council, which, as it then appeared, depended on the other unions; or as a backbench Labour MP. It is difficult to imagine that he could have settled for the latter, and the TUC was all that was left.

Of course, this meant a united front with Thomas: that was the conception of unity which the TUC had extended to the Russians, and which had provided Purcell himself with such room for manoeuvre. Those who through their union controlled their trade group nominations had an independent organisational base; Purcell, on the other hand, had little with which to withstand these shifting alignments and voting patterns. The sentiments of the majority were clear. On an apparently diplomatic pretext, Tomsky had missed or been excluded from the Paris encounter at which Purcell spoke so frankly.[272] At the Bournemouth TUC, for which he was denied a visa, Tomsky nevertheless submitted a fraternal communication of unrestrained invective. According to a communist observer, the roar of approval when the general council rebutted him was 'enough to frighten anyone!'[273] Whether frightened by it, or loyally booming from the platform, it was Purcell who the following spring moved that no useful purpose would be served by a meeting of the ARJAC following the government raid on the Arcos official trading organisation.[274]

There was one sphere of activity in which Purcell did successfully restore his public standing. That he alone on the general council also represented a mining constituency must have made the aftermath of the strike more painful still. Ben Turner, whose predicament most nearly resembled his, wrote in June 1926 of his own deep discomfort to be 'surrounded by 7000 Miners' while the TUC remained inactive.[275] In Purcell's case, expectation and corresponding disillusionment was nevertheless of a qualitatively different order. The local Miners' agent Jack Williams had been one of his stalwart supporters. Even in the shock of the strike's ending Williams reserved his judgement on Purcell's personal role. As a Minority Movement supporter he nevertheless described the action as an abject surrender and betrayal, to the manifest approval of local audiences.[276] In contrast with his general reticence, Purcell agreed to give account of himself at two local public meetings, though he made sure that reporters were excluded and he declined to put his case in the local press.[277] There was some suggestion afterwards that he 'blamed the TUC' for letting the miners down. At the second of the meetings he was followed by Nat Watkins, secretary of the Miners' Minority Movement, who certainly did put the 'workers' point of view' against the '"weak-bellied" attitude of members of the General Council'.[278] In fact, Purcell suggested that a case could and would be made for the general council, and argued that the issue of an embargo lay with the unions concerned – at least until they realised the dream of 'one big Union'.[279] Of his several attacks on the government and prophecies of further general strikes, local reporters provided liberal evidence of audience approval. But no such approbation was recorded when he defended the TUC.[280]

Validation of his continuing commitment to the miners' struggle was provided by his involvement in fund-raising and his reported donation of a large part of his parliamentary salary. As a gesture of good faith or reparation this was evidently not without effect. At another FDMA meeting Williams expressed disgust at the 'rabbits' of the general council for failing to impose an embargo; a general staff that 'ran away and left their army' would normally expect to be court-martialled, and the miners had no-one to look to but themselves in their struggle. Though Bromley alone was mentioned by name, it seems remarkable that Purcell not only shared Williams's platform but was described as well-received when he stood up next to speak.[281] He continued to donate substantially from his parliamentary salary and, with his wife Sarah playing a more public role than at any other time in his career, he provided the campaigning support of the traditional labour agitator. By his own reckoning he addressed nearly seventy meetings in the Forest of Dean alone, and by his actions he evidently won over at least the activist section of his constituency.[282]

For a generation to come, the General Strike provided a source of memory and political capital that helped to clarify the lines between official Labour and its challengers, through competing narratives of responsibility, accountability and betrayal. Occurring when the post-war revolutionary crisis had passed, in a country in which its flame had only ever flickered dimly, the strike provided a delayed occasion for the clearer separation of reformism and communism such as was already so pronounced in a country like Germany. The general council had its story, largely entrusted to Bevin. So too had Cook and Smith for the Miners; and there was an assortment of left or right narratives culminating in the communist tale of betrayal which, both nationally and internationally, helped renew and accentuate its rejection of reformism. Purcell, on the other hand, produced neither vindication nor alibi, and the incapacity to do so was to make him seem a broken figure politically.

At the beginning of 1927 he even let slip an interest in the second-order position of TUC assistant secretary; on the advice, one suspects, of candid friends he at least spared himself the humiliation of a rebuff.[283] When the Tory Trades Disputes Bill was published in the spring in a spirit of unabashed retribution, Purcell breathed implausible defiance in the form of a projected campaign that would squeeze the government so effectively 'that there need be nothing left to them but "their eyes to cry with"'.[284] The TUC committee in which he vested these hopes organised a large campaign of meetings entirely without effect, and the 'talk of fighting to the death &c' was dismissed even within his own union as 'so much bunkum'.[285] A happier occasion followed when the FDMA made fulsome presentations to Purcell and his wife for their efforts in the miners' interest. They would not prove forgetful, said Williams, 'of the large number of meetings he held in the Forest of Dean, and ... throughout the country in our support, the amount of money he individually collected, and the personal financial contributions he made ... and the tremendous energy and enthusiasm he displayed in our cause ... We have every confidence in him as ... the outspoken champion of our rights and liberties'.[286] Discredited as a national figure, Purcell was to return to precisely this model of grassroots campaigning when he withdrew from parliament less than two years later.

There was one last moment in the spotlight. On 29 July 1927 the Trades Disputes Act had passed into law without disturbance. Three days later Purcell delivered his presidential address to the triennial congress of the IFTU in Paris. Two observations may be made about his speech. The first is that it now described the strikes and lockouts culminating in the General Strike as an offensive weapon, not of the workers, but of the ruling capitalist class.[287] The second is that it saw the crucial sites of resistance to that class, no longer in Britain itself, but in the so-called subject races.[288] The first of these sentiments marked the closing of a chapter, and Beatrice's proletarian distemper having run its course. The second marked the opening of another, and the finale of Purcell's career.

NOTES

1. BWD, 4 May 1926.
2. Margaret Cole, *Growing Up Into Revolution*, Longmans, Green & Co, 1949, p. 119; also idem cited James E. Cronin, *Industrial Conflict in Modern Britain*, Croom Helm, 1979, pp. 129-30.
3. Philip M. Williams, *Hugh Gaitskell. A political biography*, Cape, 1979, p. 19.
4. Charles Loch Mowat, *Britain Between the Wars 1918-1940*, Methuen, 1968 edn, pp. 284-5.
5. Alan Bullock, *The Life and Times of Ernest Bevin. Volume one: trade union leader, 1881-1940*, Heinemann, 1960, pp. 318-20, 345-6.
6. For a discussion of this theme, see Kevin Morgan, '"Colourless, dry and dull": why British trade unionists lack biographers and what (if anything) should be done about it', *Mitteilungsblatt des Instituts für soziale Bewegungen*, forthcoming, 2013.
7. Keith Laybourn, *The General Strike 1926*, Manchester: MUP, 1993.
8. G.D.H. Cole, *A Short History of the British Working-Class Movement. Volume 3: 1900-1927*, Allen & Unwin, 1927, pp. 211-12.
9. Ross M. Martin, *TUC: the growth of a pressure group 1868-1976*, Oxford: OUP, 1980, p. 175. A similar impression is given in other accounts, e.g. Margaret Morris, *The General Strike*, Harmondsworth: Penguin, 1976, pp. 173-83.
10. G.D.H. Cole, *A History of the Labour Party from 1914*, Routledge & Kegan Paul, 1948, pp. 179-91.
11. E.g. *Dean Forest Mercury*, 11 June 1926, NAFTA *Monthly Report*, June 1926, pp. 20-2.
12. Sorel, trans. T.E. Hulme, *Reflections on Violence*, Allen & Unwin, 1915, pp. 131-9

13. Arnot, *The General Strike May 1926: its origin and history*, LRD, 1926, p. 3.
14. Hyman, *Strikes*, Fontana, 1977 edn, p. 19.
15. Sorel, *Reflections on Violence*, pp. 151, 171, 173-4.
16. As Luxemburg noted: 'In no country in the world ... was the mass strike so little "propagated" or even "discussed" as in Russia'; see Luxemburg, trans. Patrick Lavin, *The Mass Strike* (1906), Merlin Press edn, n.d., p. 17; also Carl E. Schorske, *German Social Democracy 1905-1917. The development of the great schism*, Cambridge, Mass.: Harvard University Press, 1955, p. 57.
17. G.D.H. Cole, *The World of Labour. A discussion of the present and future of trade unionism*, Bell, 1913, pp. 193-204.
18. *Syndicalist*, December 1912, pp. 4-5; see also E.J.B. Allen, 'Politicians and the General Strike', *Syndicalist*, February 1912.
19. *Syndicalist*, July 1912; Mann, 'Syndicalism at work', *Syndicalist*, March-April 1912. See also e.g. 'What is syndicalism?', *Syndicalist*, March-April 1912; 'Workers of the World Unite! May Day, 1912', *Syndicalist*, May 1912; ISEL constitution and objects, *Syndicalist*, July 1912.
20. See e.g. Luxemburg, *Mass Strike*, pp. 11-12; Tanner, *Social General Strike*, p. 2.
21. Webb, *The History of Trade Unionism*, p. 658; Crook, *General Strike*, pp. 216-17.
22. Mann, 'What we syndicalists are after', *Syndicalist*, January 1912.
23. Douglas J. Newton, *British Labour, European Socialism and the Struggle for Peace 1889-1914*, Oxford: OUP, 1985, ch. 10.
24. Accrington *Observer and Times*, 30 September 1911.
25. 'Open letter to the Miners' and Railwaymen's delegates', *Syndicalist*, October 1912.
26. ILP archives 7/8/1,'Vox', 'J. Keir Hardie. A man of the people', *Labour's Northern Voice*, 30 October 1925 (press cutting).
27. 56th TUC *Report*, September 1924, pp. 429-30. The communists would have opposed had the resolution not seemed so congruent with Tomsky's fraternal address (RGASPI 495/1/140, Petrovsky to Manuilsky, n.d. but September 1924; translation from Russian courtesy Francis King).
28. Tanner, *The Social General Strike*, WSF, 1919, p. 2 and passim. Tanner's pamphlet was based on that of the German syndicalist Arnold Roller of the same title.
29. Branko Pribićević, *The Shop Stewards Movement and Workers' Control 1910-1922*, Oxford: Blackwells, 1959, pp. 51-2.
30. *Manchester Guardian*, 23 April 1923.
31. *Workers' Weekly*, 21 April 1923.
32. *Workers' Weekly*, 21 April 1923.
33. Mann, *Power through the General Strike*, Co-operative Printing Society for Tom Mann, May 1923; *Workers' Weekly*, editorial, 14 April 1923 and CPGB EC manifesto, 28 April 1923.
34. Wilfrid Harris Crook, *The General Strike. A study of labor's tragic weapon in theory and practice*, Chapel Hill: University of North Carolina Press, 1931, pp. 221-3.
35. Accrington *Observer and Times*, 30 September 1911.
36. Mann, *Power through the General Strike*, pp. 6-7. 10-11.

37. *Sunday Worker*, 10 January 1926.
38. Mann, *Power Through the General Strike*, p. 7.
39. CPGB EC manifesto, *Workers' Weekly*, 28 April 1923.
40. *Workers' Weekly* editorial, 21 April 1923.
41. Purcell, 'Solidarity of the working class is the meaning of May Day', *Trade Union Unity*, May 1925, pp. 17-18.
42. Kevin Morgan, *Against Fascism and War. Ruptures and continuities in British communist politics 1935-41*, Manchester: MUP, 1989, pp. 148-9.
43. 57th *TUC Report*, September 1925, p. 177; and for a similar point TUC archives 292/252.62/106, Fimmen to Citrine, 5 May 1926.
44. See 57th *TUC Report*, September 1925, pp. 179-80 for the TUC's embargo notice.
45. 57th *TUC Report*, September 1925, pp. 384-5.
46. Cook in the *Labour Monthly*, March 1926, pp. 157-62.
47. 'The coal crisis', *Plebs*, March 1926, pp. 82-9. See also Davies, 'The industrial armistice', *Colliery Workers' Magazine*, September 1925, pp. 199-200.
48. '1926: what will it bring for Labour?', *Plebs*, January 1926, pp. 3-11. The other contributors were Purcell (international trade-union unity), Wilkinson (parliament in 1925), John Jagger (working-class education) and Winfred Horrabin (the 'problem of the unattached supporter'). Hicks did anticipate a further necessary concentration of power in the general council, but on lines which he claimed it was difficult as yet to specify.
49. C.B., *The Reds and the General Strike*, CPGB, 1926, pp. 21-2.
50. James Klugmann, *History of the Communist Party of Great Britain. Volume two: the General Strike 1925-1926*, Lawrence & Wishart, 1969, pp. 34-5, 42-6.
51. 'Our policy', *Sunday Worker*, 26 July 1925.
52. Murphy, 'The nine months truce', *Communist Review*, September 1925, pp. 212-13.
53. For example: 'Those who do not look for a path along which to retreat are good trade union leaders who have sufficient character to stand firm on the demands of the miners, but they are totally incapable of moving forward to face all the implications of a united working-class challenge to the state.' (*Workers' Weekly*, 30 April 1926.)
54. Andrew Thorpe, *The British Communist Party and Moscow, 1920-43*, Manchester: MUP, 2000, pp. 92-3.
55. White, *Tom Mann*, pp. 208-9.
56. Thorpe, *British Communist Party*, p. 90 for the impact of the arrests.
57. White, *Tom Mann*, p. 208.
58. GLDS Goldman to Leon Malmed, 24 May 1926.
59. See e.g. Dona Torr, *Tom Mann*, Lawrence & Wishart, 1944 edn, p. 46 for a typical communist presentation.
60. NAFTA *Monthly Report*, October 1912, pp. 14-15.
61. NAFTA *Monthly Report*, February 1918, p. 14.
62. NAFTA *Monthly Report*, March 1919, pp. 11-13; Purcell, 'Four great demonstrations', *Labour Magazine*, July 1924, pp. 182-3.
63. Conor Kostick, *Revolution in Ireland: popular militancy 1917-1923*, Pluto, 1996, ch. 3; James Hinton, *The First Shop Stewards' Movement*, Allen & Unwin, 1973, p. 308.
64. NAFTA *Monthly Report*, October 1920, p. 20.

The General Strike

65. *Manchester Guardian*, 20 October 1921.
66. *Manchester Guardian*, 30 January 1924; 56th TUC *Report*, 1924, pp. 128-31; for the dispute see David Howell, *Respectable Radicals. Studies in the politics of railway trade unionism*, Aldershot: Ashgate, 1999, pp. 293-309.
67. 56th TUC *Report*, 1924, pp. 134-5.
68. *Manchester Guardian*, 30 January 1924.
69. *Russia. The official report of the British trades union delegation to Russia and Caucasia Nov. and Dec. 1924*, TUC, 1925, p. ix.
70. A.J. Cook, 'Towards a new policy: VI. Trade unionism at the cross roads', *Labour Monthly*, June 1924, pp. 337-41.
71. Hicks, 'An immediate industrial charter', *Labour Monthly*, February 1924, pp. 77-8; Williams, 'Towards a new policy: IV', *Labour Monthly*, April 1924, pp. 213-14.
72. Purcell, 'Towards a new policy: V', *Labour Monthly*, May 1924, p. 268.
73. Raymond Postgate's report, *Lansbury's Labour Weekly*, 13 March 1926.
74. Citrine, *Men and Work*, p. 188 citing diary entry for 9 May 1926.
75. See Citrine's comments, Citrine papers 1/8, 'The General Strike', 11 February 1928.
76. Hardie referred to the universal strike. Luxemburg also cited examples of local general strikes 'in the literal meaning of those words' but did not confine her discussion to these (*Mass Strike*, p. 24). See also Alf Barton, *The Universal Strike*, Sheffield: BSP, 1912.
77. Martin, *TUC*, p. 165 n. 1.
78. Hugh Armstrong Clegg, *A History of British Trade Unions since 1889. Volume 2: 1911-1933*, Oxford: OUP, 1985, p. 310.
79. See for example RGASPI 495/100/240, Inkpin for CPGB CEC, typescript statement on 'The "Left Wing" movement', c. October 1924.
80. Settled on terms which caused some rank-and-file discontent, this was a factor in the in the AUBTW's temporary disaffiliation from the NFBTO in 1925.
81. Peter Weiler, *Ernest Bevin*, Manchester: MUP, 1993, p. 67.
82. TUC archives 292/20/7, TUC general council minutes, 21 March 1922.
83. Martin, *TUC*, pp. 191-2.
84. G.A. Phillips, *The General Strike. The politics of industrial conflict*, Weidenfeld & Nicolson, 1976, p. 19; Clegg, *History*, p. 380.
85. 57th TUC *Report*, September 1925, pp. 347-50.
86. A. C. J., 'Trades Union Congress – I', TGWU *Record*, September 1924, pp. 29-30.
87. Bevin, speech at TGWU No 1 Area, 1 January 1927, TGWU *Record*, January 1927, p. 177.
88. See William McLaine's summary, 'AEU and the Alliance', *Sunday Worker*, 31 January 1926. The provisions were: '1. Negotiation. 2. Financial assistance. 3. Partial sympathetic action. 4. Sympathetic action by stages. 5. Complete sympathetic action.'
89. For the constitution of the alliance, an explanatory memorandum and the debate at the TGWU's 1925 biennial conference, see TGWU *Record*, August 1925, pp. 11-18. For the argument that it was intended as a means of strengthening the general council, see Cook, 'A call for unity', *Sunday Worker*, 30 August 1925.

90. TUC archives 292/28/1, 'Memorandum of the functions of committees showing origins, terms of references, etc', 1924.
91. TGWU delegate conference, July 1925, TGWU *Record*, August 1925, pp. 14, 16, contributions of Bevin and Bro. Warren.
92. Bevin, TGWU delegate conference, July 1925, TGWU *Record*, August 1925, p. 7.
93. Bevin, TGWU delegate conference, July 1925, TGWU *Record*, August 1925, p. 7.
94. TGWU delegate conference, July 1925, TGWU *Record*, August 1925, p. 7.
95. TGWU archives, 126/EB/GS/8/25, 'Coal dispute and General Strike', rough notes of statement of Bevin, TGWU National Docks Group, 22 July 1926.
96. Bevin, TGWU delegate conference, July 1925, TGWU *Record*, August 1925, p. 13.
97. *Lansbury's Labour Weekly*, 5 September 1925.
98. See Marquand, *Ramsay MacDonald*, Cape, 1977, pp. 423-9.
99. 'Tom Mann's lead', *Sunday Worker*, 9 August 1925.
100. Beer, 'Scarborough and Liverpool', *Sunday Worker*, 11 October 1925.
101. NAFTA *Monthly Report*, September 1925, pp. 24-5.
102. *Daily Worker* (New York), 31 October 1925.
103. 57th TUC *Report*, September 1925, pp. 388-9; TGWU *Record*, September 1925, p. 34.
104. Bevin. 'Industrial Alliance, TGWU *Record*, November 1925, p. 84.
105. 'From sectionalism to the united front', *Sunday Worker*, 23 August 1925.
106. Bullock, *Ernest Bevin*, p. 255, mentions that Bevin's provision with an assistant freed him to take on wider responsibilities, but this was hardly the decisive consideration.
107. The calculation excludes other absences explained by illness, involvement in industrial disputes or other TUC business; see 57th TUC *Report*, September 1925, p. 352.
108. Bullock, *Life and Times*, p. 283.
109. Calhoun, *United Front*, p. 203.
110. RGASPI 495/100/74, unnamed correspondent (Rothstein?) to 'Max', 29 December 1925; 495/100/303, 'Humboldt' information report, stamped 12 January 1926 (translation from German courtesy Julie Johnson).
111. 'Workers of the World Unite!', *Syndicalist*, May 1912.
112. Hyman, *Strikes*, pp. 23 ff.
113. Mann, *Power Through the General Strike*, pp. 10-11, also *Manchester Guardian*, 23 April 1923.
114. *Sunday Worker*, 10 January 1926.
115. Mann, 'Prepare for battle', *Sunday Worker*, 7 March 1926.
116. 'The biennial delegate conference', TGWU *Record*, August 1925, Harold Clay's contribution.
117. B. Williams, 'The Miners and the Industrial Alliance', *Communist Review*, December 1925, p. 376; also 'Editorial view', *Communist Review*, February 1926, pp. 437-8.
118. Mann, 'Don't allow them time!' and Cook, 'Keep ranks!', both *Sunday Worker*, 7 February 1926.
119. Cook, 'The issues before the Swansea TUC', *Labour Monthly*, September 1928, p. 529.

120. TGWU archives, 126/EB/TG/6, TGWU general officers' conference, Shornells, Abbey Wood, 19-21 February 1927, Bevin's contribution.
121. See the long exposition of Bevin's reprinted from the TGWU *Record* in the *Sunday Worker*, 22 November 1925.
122. Clegg, *History*, p. 403.
123. See e.g. Cook, *Sunday Worker*, 21 February 1926; also Mann, 'Prepare for battle', *Sunday Worker*, 7 March 1926; 'The miners' next move', *Sunday Worker*, 14 March 1926; editorial on 'The engineers', *Sunday Worker*, 21 March 1926. For the SIC see John Lovell, 'The TUC Special Industrial Committee: January-April 1926' in Asa Briggs and John Saville, eds, *Essays in Labour History 1918-1939*, Croom Helm, 1977, pp. 36-56.
124. Bevin papers 126/EB/GS/4/8, 'The coal mining crisis 1926. Position of the Transport & General Workers' Union', 26 April 1926.
125. 'Coal dispute and General Strike', rough notes of Bevin.
126. Compare for example with the recent claim that the general council 'carried along only by the Triple Alliance, undertook no preparation whatsoever' (Sue Bruley, *The Women and Men of 1926. A gender and social history of the General Strike and miners' lockout in South Wales*, Cardiff: University of Wales Press, 2010, p.2). Cook's own later formulation ('Issues before the Swansea TUC') was that the attempt to rebuild the Alliance was almost completed and 'would have been brought into play … but for the decision of the General Council to stand by the Miners on May 1'.
127. Citrine, *Men and Work*, pp. 145-53; also e.g. Lovell, 'The TUC Special Industrial Committee, January-April 1926', pp. 38-9. Lovell describes this as a well-known memorandum, but this was primarily because of its subsequent advertisement by Citrine himself.
128. Phillips, *General Strike*, pp. 86-7; compare with Clegg, *History*, p. 395; Martin, *TUC*, p. 200; Bullock, *Life and Times*, p. 290.
129. Citrine, 'Lessons from the mining dispute', *Labour Magazine*, September 1925, pp. 198-200.
130. Martin Jacques, 'Consequences of the General Strike' in Jeffrey Skelley, ed., *The General Strike, 1926*, Lawrence & Wishart, 1976, p. 379. Jacques also mentioned the Hands Off Russia movement, discounted here as it did not raise questions of inter-union solidarity.
131. Tanner, *Social General Strike*, p. 11.
132. 57th TUC *Report*, September 1925, p. 387.
133. Clegg, *History*, p. 115.
134. G.D.H. Cole, *Labour in the Coal-mining Industry (1914-1921)*, Oxford: OUP, 1923, pp. 116-21.
135. See Philip S. Bagwell, *The Railwaymen. The history of the National Union of Railwaymen*, Allen & Unwin, 1963, ch. 15.
136. Cited Crook, *General Strike*, p. 256.
137. Accrington *Observer and Times*, 30 September 1911.
138. Williams, *The British Transportworkers' Federation and the Triple Alliance*, Amsterdam: ITF, 1921, pp. 4, 7, 10-11, 26; Williams, 'What Labour wants' in Ethel Snowden et al, *What We Want and Why*, Collins, 1922, pp. 44-7; Ken Coates and Tony Topham, *The Making of the Labour Movement. The formation of the Transport and General Workers' Union 1870-1922*, Nottingham: Spokesman, 1994 edn, p. 779.

274 Bolshevism, syndicalism and the general strike

139. Howell, *Respectable Radicals*, pp. 252-3.
140. Meeting on 'Mining crisis', 18 February 1926, contribution of Will Henderson.
141. *National Strike Special Conference: report of proceedings*, 20-21 January 1927, TUC, 1927, pp. 43-4.
142. Citrine papers 1/7, 'Essential services during trade disputes', copy of memorandum dated 16 February 1926.
143. TUC archives 292/252.61/4, report of meeting on 'Mining crisis', 18 February 1926.
144. See George Lansbury, *The Miracle of Fleet Street. The story of the Daily Herald*, Victoria House Printing Co and Labour Publishing Co, 1925, pp. 58-65.
145. There is a biographical cuttings file at the TUC Library Collections.
146. S.G. Hobson, *Pilgrim to the Left. Memoirs of a modern revolutionist*, Edward Arnold: 1938, pp. 246-7.
147. Tracey, 'Defend free speech', *Sunday Worker*, 18 December 1925 and 'Is work a curse?', *Labour Magazine*, February 1925, p. 464. Subsequently Tracey came to stress the affinities between direct action and fascism; see his 'Introduction' to H.W. Lee and E. Archbold, *Social Democracy in Britain. Fifty years of the socialist movement*, SDF, 1935, pp. 21-4.
148. TUC archives 292/252.61/4, report of meeting on 'Mining crisis', 18 February 1926; Citrine, *Men and Work*, p. 148.
149. Lovell, 'TUC Special Industrial Committee', p. 41.
150. *National Strike Special Conference*, pp. 41-2.
151. *Sunday Worker*, 2 May 1926. In the absence of any such action, the paper also proposed a sort of spontaneous demonstration from below ('The biggest fight of all!', ibid).
152. Hardy, 'Mobilise all force behind the miners!' and T.H. Wintringham, 'Once more – form councils of action', *Workers' Weekly*, 30 April 1926.
153. Phillips, *General Strike*, pp. 134-5. Even among those who accepted the basic principle concern was expressed at the delayed calling out of the second wave (e.g. Gossip, *Sunday Worker*, 23 May 1926).
154. Luxemburg, *Mass Strike*, pp. 58-9, 71. While suggesting that through its conscious direction this represented the 'highest and most mature form of the mass strike' (p. 45), her main emphasis was on the hollowness and artificiality of such an action.
155. Luxemburg, *Mass Strike*, p. 43.
156. Weiler, *Ernest Bevin*, p. viii.
157. Hamilton Fyfe, *Behind the Scenes of the Great Strike*, Labour Publishing Co, 1926, pp. 71-2; Citrine, *Men and Work*, pp. 179-80, diary entry for 5 May 1926.
158. E.g. 'Reflections on the passing year', *TGWU Record*, December 1926, pp. 144-5; Bevin, speech at TGWU No 1 Area, 1.
159. TGWU archives 126/EB/65/7, Bevin, statement to TGWU area secretaries' conference, 27 May 1926.
160. TGWU general officers' conference, Shornells, Clay's paper 'The industrial upheaval. Its effects and lessons'.
161. TGWU general officers' conference, Shornells, Bevin's contribution; 'Coal dispute and General Strike', rough notes of Bevin; Bevin, 'The miners' dispute and the General Strike, 1926', p. 242.

162. Morris, *General Strike*, p. 22.
163. Citrine, *Men and Work*, p. 179.
164. E.g. Raymond Postgate, Ellen Wilkinson and J.F. Horrabin, *A Workers' History of the Great Strike*, Plebs League, 1927, p. 36.
165. Mowat, *Britain*, p. 311 conceded that it was 'rather an irrelevancy ... done to give encouragement and a sense of solidarity to the transport men'.
166. Citrine, *Men and Work*, p. 180.
167. See for example 'Biennial delegate conference', pp. 7, 15.
168. 'Biennial delegate conference', p. 8.
169. *The Mining Situation. Report of a special conference of executive committees of affiliated unions held in the Memorial Hall, Farringdon St., London, on Thursday, April 29th, Friday April 30th, and Saturday, May 1st, 1926*, TUC General Council: 1926, p. 34.
170. E.g. Morris, *General Strike*, p. 24; Weiler, *Ernest Bevin*, p. 43; Allen Hutt, *The Post-War History of the British Working Class*, Gollancz, 1937, p. 131; R. Page Arnot, *The Miners: years of struggle. A history of the Miners' Federation of Great Britain (from 1910 onwards)*, Allen & Unwin, 1953, p. 417; Postgate, *Workers' History*, p. 17.
171. A.J. Cook, *The Nine Days*, London, privately published, 1926, p. 7; Bevin, 'The miners' dispute and the General Strike, 1926', TGWU *Record*, May-July 1926, p. 240.
172. Bullock, *Life and Times*, p. 306.
173. *Dean Forest Mercury*, 23 April 1926.
174. TUC WMC minutes, 28 April 1926.
175. TUC WMC minutes, 28 April 1926.
176. John Lloyd, *Light and Liberty. The history of the Electrical, Electronic, Telecommunication and Plumbing Union*, Weidenfeld & Nicolson: 1990, p. 83.
177. Postgate, *Workers' History*, p. 37.
178. See NA LAB 2/1207/1, 'History of the General Strike', n.d. (late 1926?), pp. 35-6 for the impracticality of the instruction.
179. Citrine papers 1/7, copy diary entry 3 May 1926.
180. Fyfe, *Behind the Scenes*, p. 55.
181. Morris, *General Strike*, pp. 37-8, 417-19; Phillips, *General Strike*, p. 265.
182. Morris, *General Strike*, p. 34; Phillips,*General Strike*, pp. 140-2; Clay, 'The industrial upheaval'.
183. AUBTW archives, 78/AU/1/1/9, AUBTW executive council special meeting, 20 May 1926, report of EC sub-committee on General Strike.
184. AUBTW archives, copy correspondence of Citrine, for TUC strike organisation committee, and AUBTW president George Waddell, 11 May 1926.
185. AUBTW archives, report of EC sub-committee on General Strike; also 78/AU/3/1/1, AUBTW circular 'to divisional organisers, councils, district committees & branch officers', (12) May 1926.
186. Cited Lloyd, *Light and Liberty*, p. 181.
187. Citrine papers 1/7, 'Mining crisis, July, 1925'.
188. National Minority Movement, *Report of Second Annual Conference*, 29-30 August 1925, NMM 1925, p. 11.
189. TUC WMC minutes, 28 April 1926.
190. Citrine papers 1/7, copy diary entry, 29 April 1926.

276   Bolshevism, syndicalism and the general strike

191. Cole, *Short History*, p. 208; also TUC archives 292/252.62/4, 'General Strike 1926. Chief criticisms of the General Council', 5 July 1926; Fenner Brockway, 'A diary of the General Strike', *Socialist Review*, June 1926, p. 10; Kingsley Martin, *The British Public and the General Strike*, Hogarth Press, 1926. Ellen Wilkinson as a supporter of the policy believed the BBC was too obviously biased to be effective (introduction to Scott Nearing, *The British General Strike*, New York: Vanguard Press, 1927, p. xiv).
192. Bagwell, *Railwaymen*, pp. 392-5; Hutt, *British Trade Unionism. An outline history*, Lawrence & Wishart, 1941, p. 111; Williams, *British Transportworkers' Federation and the Triple Alliance*, p. 21.
193. *National Strike Special Conference*, p. 53.
194. 57th TUC *Report*, September 1925, pp. 382-5; see also TUC archives 292/252.62/114, F.H. Curtis to TUC general council, 3 May 1926, for the LCS's concern at handing over its constitution 'lock, stock and barrel' to the general council.
195. Herbert Tracey, 'Freedom of the press. Did the unions stifle independent opinion?', *Labour Magazine*, July 1926, p. 108; Fyfe, *Behind the Scenes*, p. 33.
196. William Mellor, '"The British Worker" May 5-May 17 1926', *Labour Magazine*, July 1926, pp. 109-11; Postgate, *Workers' History*, p. 36.
197. Bullock did provide the otherwise inexplicable information that the Tory *Morning Post* had in 1924 extended Bevin an 'invitation' to use its columns (p. 240). Regarding the closing down the press (p. 320) he provides the telling formulation that 'Bevin [singular] never pretended that they [plural] did not make mistakes'.
198. Bullock, *Life and Times*, p. 589; Weiler, *Ernest Bevin*, p. 79.
199. Clay, 'The industrial upheaval'.
200. TGWU general officers' conference, Shornells, Bevin's contribution; Citrine papers 1/8, 'The General Strike', 11 February 1928; Clay, 'The industrial upheaval'.
201. Bevin, 'The miners' dispute and the General Strike, 1926', *TGWU Record*, May-July 1926, p. 243.
202. Clay, 'The industrial upheaval'.
203. TGWU general officers' conference, Shornells, Bevin's contribution; Bevin, 'The miners' dispute and the General Strike, 1926', p. 243.
204. TUC archives 292/262.62/48, 'Committee of Investigation re statement made by Mr J.H. Thomas, MP', 24 November 1927, contributions of Andrew Conley and Thomas.
205. TGWU archives 126/EB/GS/7, cutting from *Yorkshire Evening News*, 27 May 1926; Bullock, *Life and Times*, p. 319.
206. One wonders whether the 'Mr Curraugh' mentioned as Bevin's main press contact in a contemporary minute (TUC WMC minutes, 28 April 1926) might have been the F.N. Curran who edited the *Yorkshire Evening News*.
207. Cook, *Nine Days*, p. 16; Fyfe, *Behind the Scenes*, pp. 30-1, 71-2.
208. Citrine papers 1/7, copy diary entry, 9 May 1926.
209. Citrine papers 1/7, copy diary entry, 5 May 1926.
210. TUC archives 292/252.62/19, TUC general council minutes, 30 April 1926. Five of the six members of the Ways and Means Committee remained on the Power and Orders Committee.

The General Strike 277

211. TUC archives 292/252.62/19, TUC general council minutes, 10 a.m. 5 May 1926.
212. Citrine, *Men and Work*, p. 178 citing diary entry for 4 May 1926.
213. Though Samuel had chaired the coal commission set up after Red Friday, his role as intermediary in the General Strike had no official standing and there was never any undertaking by the government to honour the terms of any agreement reached.
214. Phillips, *General Strike*, p. 139; also e.g. Laybourn, *General Strike*, p. 51; Patrick Renshaw, *The General Strike*, Eyre Methuen, 1975, pp. 170-1.
215. Bullock, *Life and Times*, p. 318.
216. Clegg, *History*, p. 404; Phillips, *General Strike*, p. 139; Bullock, *Life and Times*, p. 318.
217. TUC archives 292/252.62/19, TUC power and organisation committee minutes, 3 and 4 May 1926.
218. TUC archives 292/262.62/48, 'Committee of Investigation re statement made by Mr J.H. Thomas, MP', contribution of A.G. Walkden, 24 November 1927.
219. TGWU general officers' conference, Shornells. For Bevin's 'sense of ownership', see Weiler, *Ernest Bevin*, pp. 35, 66, 79.
220. 'Committee of Investigation', contribution of Thomas; also 292/225.62/19, 'Procedure of meetings of Central Strike Committee', item dated 10 May 1926.
221. 'Committee of Investigation'.
222. Citrine papers 1/7, copy diary entry, 5 May 1926
223. 'Coal dispute and General Strike', rough notes of Bevin.
224. Citrine papers 1/7, copy diary entry, 7 May 1926.
225. 'History of the General Strike'; John Attfield and John Lee, 'Deptford and Lewisham' in Skelley, *General Strike*, p. 269. There is no mention of the incident in biographies of Lansbury
226. See *Bolshevism and the British Left*, part 1, pp. 120-1.
227. Cutting from *Yorkshire Evening News*, 27 May 1926.
228. *Gloucester Citizen*, 8 May 1926. Cook failed to address the meeting because of leaving for a meeting of the Mineworkers' International in Brussels.
229. Walter Citrine, *Men and Work*, diary entry for 7 May 1926.
230. Citrine, *Men and Work*, p. 184.
231. John Paton, *Left Turn!*, Secker & Warburg, 1936, pp. 257-8.
232. Ben Turner, *About Myself 1863-1930*, Humphrey Toulmin, 1930, p. 314.
233. Cutting from *Yorkshire Evening News*, 27 May 1926. The paper referred to a figure of 'well over £1,000,000' though Bevin's estimate of the final cost to the TGWU was around £600,000 (126/EB/GS/7, Bevin to N. Nathan, International Transportworkers' Federation, 4 June 1926). Other unions were similarly affected: from around £60,000 in the case of the AUBTW to £935,000 in the case of the NUR (Bagwell, *Railwaymen*, p. 495).
234. Citrine, *Men and Work*, pp. 178-91, citing diary entries for 4, 7 and 9 May 1926.
235. 'Coal dispute and General Strike', rough notes of Bevin; Phillips, *General Strike*, p. 135 and n. 3; also Citrine, *Men and Work*, p. 196.
236. 'History of the General Strike'.

237. Robert Taylor, 'Citrine's unexpurgated diaries, 1925-26: the mining crisis and the national strike', *Historical Studies in Industrial Relations*, 20, 2005, p. 70.
238. CPGB PB statement, 12 May 1926, cited James Klugmann, 'Marxism, reformism and the General Strike' in Skelley, *General Strike*, p. 79.
239. NAFTA *Monthly Report*, June 1926, pp. 20-2. Hicks expressed almost identical sentiments in AUBTW *Trade Circular and Monthly Reporter*, June 1926.
240. *Lansbury's Labour Weekly*, 13 November 1926.
241. RGASPI 534/7/32, Pollitt to Losovsky, 10 November 1926.
242. *Lansbury's Labour Weekly*, 22 May 1926.
243. See *Mining Dispute National Strike. Report of the General Council to the Conference of Executives of Affiliated Unions, 25th June, 1926*, TUC, 1927.
244. TUC archives 292/252.62/34, notes on general council discussion of Negotiating Committee report, 17 June 1926.
245. See e.g. RGASPI 495/100/303, Earl Browder to unnamed correspondent, 2 September 1926 enclosing details of an NMM resolution of 27 August accepting the need for 'ruthless criticism' but 'in such places and at such times as are not likely to militate against the possibilities of bringing the miners' strike to a successful conclusion and operate against the future welfare of Anglo-Russian unity'. Kuusinen for the Comintern presidium warned that British communists were 'losing the TEMPO' (494/100/305, letter to CPGB CC, 11 September 1926).
246. NAFTA *Monthly Report*, June 1926, pp. 20-2.
247. See e.g. C. Ewart Street, letters, AUBTW *Trade Circular and Monthly Reporter*, June 1926, p. 32 and August 1926, p. 101; AUBTW Manchester No 1 branch resolution, AUBTW *Trade Circular and Monthly Reporter*, September 1926, p. 31.
248. TUC archives 292/252.61/8, Bromley to Cook, 13 September 1926. For similar observations repudiating the Miners' attritional approach to industrial disputes, see Howell, *Respectable Radicals*, pp. 279-80.
249. 'Coal dispute and General Strike', rough notes of Bevin; Citrine, *Men and Work*, p. 196 citing diary entry for 10 May.
250. TUC archives 292/252.61/48, P.J. Schmidt, Amsterdam to Citrine, 15 September 1926 citing IFTU press reports of 18 and 19 May 1926 (German and Dutch editions); 292/252.61/47, IFTU *Press Reports*, 1 July 1926, cutting, and IFTU circular to national centres and ITSs, 8 July 1926; also Sassenbach for IFTU to TUC, 9 August 1926. IFTU's claims were aired in the socialist press by the Dutch 'unity' supporter Schmidt, who later retracted them; see his 'The effect of the strike on the Continent', *Socialist Review*, July 1926.
251. TUC archives 292/20/10, TUC general council minutes, 22 June and 28 July 1926.
252. TUC archives 292/252.61/8, Smith to Purcell, 30 July 1926.
253. TUC archives 292/252.61/50, Sassenbach to Citrine, 10 September 1926. Purcell visited the Scandinavian countries, Netherland, Germany and Switzerland.
254. Notes on general council discussion of Negotiating Committee report, 17 June 1926.
255. John McIlroy, 'Memory, commemoration and history – 1926 in 2006',

Historical Studies in Industrial Relations, 21, 2006, p. 66. Phillips, on whom the assertion is supposed to rest, recorded Purcell's view that the rank-and-file response to the strike had represented a victory in itself (p. 271), which is of course a different claim.

256. NAFTA *Monthly Report*, June 1926, pp. 20-2.
257. 197 Hansard fifth series, 7 July 1926, cols 2193-4; 199 Hansard fifth series, 26 October 1926, cols 771-3.
258. 197 Hansard fifth series, 5 July 1926, cols 1814 ff; also his opposition to the government's Foreign Contributions Bill, 202 Hansard fifth series, 18 February 1927, cols 1308-15.
259. NAFTA *Monthly Report*, July 1926, pp. 22-3.
260. *Sunday Worker*, 13 June 1926.
261. The text as translated from *Izvestia* can be found in TUC archives 292/943/29.
262. NAFTA *Annual Report and Balance Sheet* for 1926, p. 3. For immediate responses on similar lines see Gossip, *Sunday Worker*, 23 May 1926 and NAFTA *Monthly Report*, June 1926, pp. 3, 8.
263. *Dean Forest Mercury*, 21 May 1926.
264. RGASPI 495/100/303, Rothstein to Max (Petrovsky), n.d., May or June 1926; 595/100/356, Stewart to Murphy, 24 September 1926.
265. LRD archives, LRD executive minutes, 2 September 1926; NA KV4/282, 'Aspects of the General Strike, May 1926', compiled by New Scotland Yard, June 1926, p. 21 citing Allen Hutt to R. Palme Dutt. For Hutt and *Trade Union Unity* see ch. 2 above. Hutt singled out the role of Hicks rather than Purcell on the general council.
266. RGASPI 495/100/356, Bob Stewart to ECCI secretariat, 8 July 1926.
267. See for example RGASPI 495/100/567, CPGB secretariat, report on 'The Cook-Maxton movement' signed MacDonald (J.R. Campbell), c. 5 September 1928.
268. TUC archives 292/20/10, TUC general council minutes, 14 July 1926.
269. For the CPGB see Thorpe, *British Communist Party*, pp. 96-103.
270. *Dean Forest Mercury*, 11 June 1926.
271. TUC archives 292/947/22, verbatim proceedings of ARJAC meeting, Paris, 30-31 July 1926.
272. Calhoun, *United Front*, p. 274.
273. RGASPI 495/100/356, Andrew Rothstein to J.T. Murphy, 14 September 1926.
274. TUC archives 292/901/1, TUC international committee minutes, 23 May 1927.
275. TUC archives 292/252.61/2, Turner to Citrine, 30 June 1926. Turner was candidate and former MP for the Batley and Morley constituency, but had lost the seat in 1924, to regain it in 1929.
276. *Dean Forest Mercury*, 21 May 1926.
277. *Dean Forest Mercury*, 4 and 11 June 1926.
278. Letter from 'A Forester', *Dean Forest Mercury*, 11 June 1926; RGASPI 534/7/33, Nat Watkins, 'The situation in Cinderford relative to the lock-out', n.d. but 28 May 1926.
279. *Dean Forest Mercury*, 9 and 16 July 1926.
280. See for example *Dean Forest Mercury*, 11 June and 9 July 1926.
281. *Dean Forest Mercury*, 21 May, 9 and 16 July 1926.

282. *Dean Forest Mercury*, 11 June and 17 December 1926, 27 December 1935.
283. Was he led astray by Citrine's rhetorical expression of regret that he should have turned away from his primary focus on union affairs? See *Dean Forest Mercury*, 5 November 1926, also 14, 21 and 28 January and 11 February 1927.
284. *Dean Forest Mercury*, 6 May 1927; NAFTA *Monthly Report*, April 1927, p. 23.
285. NAFTA *Monthly Report*, July 1927, pp. 11-12.
286. *Dean Forest Mercury*, 24 June and 8 July 1927.
287. Purcell, *Workers of the World – Unite!*, ILP, 1927, pp. 4-5, 14.
288. Purcell, *Workers of the World*, pp. 4-5.

Chapter seven

Internationalist swansong

7.1 LOOKING TO THE EAST?

By the time that he addressed the IFTU delegates in Paris, Purcell appeared to the communists to have 'completely disappeared'.[1] In the Commons too he hardly spoke, and except in his union journal it is henceforth difficult to find much record of his views. Paris was the exception and an occasion designed to bring out his combative instincts. As the IFTU congress convened only triennially, this was the first such opportunity for the continental delegates to hold his presidency to general account. The British, on the other hand, arrived determined on an organisational overhaul that would have spared only Purcell himself and his sole IFTU ally, the British joint secretary Brown.[2] Probably Purcell felt secure in the TUC's prerogative to nominate the president. In any case, this was his opportunity to work off three years of rebuffs and condescension. His presidential address not only described the organisation as weak in finance, power, influence and even discipline.[3] It also reaffirmed Purcell's by-now familiar conception of trade-union internationalism, and the centrality within it of the Russians – whom only miserable follies and intrigue had served to keep excluded from IFTU.[4] These were the arguments that had so stirred up the AFL convention in 1925. But combined with such criticism of his own organisation, the sense of provocation was even greater.

The CGT secretary Léon Jouhaux was first to his feet. Jouhaux's biographers depict him as a figure anxious to counteract the German influence within IFTU, but constrained by the insularity and indifference of the British.[5] In reality, these were secondary tensions which in this period were subordinated to a shared anti-communism most immediately targeted at Purcell and the TUC. Lorwin thus characterised the Paris congress as a battle of 'Berlin versus London', and in this the French, the Germans and the smaller European affiliates were at one.[6] Repudiating Purcell's address on behalf of his colleagues, Jouhaux thus met with 'prolonged cheers', and was quickly supported by other members of the IFTU executive.[7] Further uproar ensued when Brown, the sole dissentient, produced a letter revealing the factional way in which Jouhaux and Oudegeest had conspired to head off British initiatives over Russia. Oudegeest hit back wildly, describing the Britons as 'agents of Russia'. The German Grassmann, heading the commission set up to investigate the issue, demanded discipline and compliance with the majority. When Oudegeest was then exonerated, an unusually animated Citrine described it as a whitewash, and Oudegeest in turn accused him of acting like an examining magistrate.

From Purcell's first international congress to his last, they took their anthem at its word, 'the last fight let us face'. Purcell himself exited precipitately when the condition of a poorly hand deteriorated over a dinner break. The congress then rejected his renomination as president and even voted Hicks in his place, as if to underline the personal character of the issue.[8] Brown and Oudegeest resigned, Sassenbach remained as sole secretary, and Jouhaux concluded proceedings with a defiant panegyric to Oudegeest alone.[9] Socialist papers like *Le Populaire* further aired the criticisms of Purcell, and there was a personal attack by Adler in the LSI *Bulletin*. When Sassenbach added his voice as fraternal delegate to that year's TUC, he even referred darkly to 'outsiders' at IFTU's head.[10] Purcell, offered a right of reply, described his systematic exclusion from responsible functions and the atmosphere of intrigue, condescension and hostility to which he attributed the soured relations between the two bodies.[11] Supported by his colleagues, as he had always supported them, he was not replaced as IFTU president and the resulting stalemate lasted almost a year.

As usual, Purcell's remarks on Russia had provoked particular controversy. There was even innuendo as to the real authorship of his address, 'and what this person's relations were with Moscow'.[12] Even so, Russia had occupied only a small part of the speech. Substantially, this revisited the themes of Purcell's earlier expositions of internationalism at the Commonwealth Labour Conference and the AFL, as discussed in earlier chapters.[13] Despite the cooling of relations with the communists, it bore the continuing imprint of these past associations as well as that of Fimmen's influence. Even so, in the different possible inflexions between protectionism and internationalism, it tilted more decisively to the latter than any previous speech of Purcell's. The ILP, which issued it as a pamphlet in its own right, described it as the 'biggest and boldest utterance' delivered at a labour conference in several years.[14] Russia certainly featured; but more even than by Russia itself, its radicalism was expressed in the metamorphosing of the idea of the subject races in the course of the Chinese revolution, as this had developed from the time of the Shanghai general strike in May 1925. Indeed, the successive adjustments in this final phase of Purcell's labour internationalism may to some extent be seen as a shift in perspective from India to China, and then back again.

From 1924, as E.H. Carr records, China had eclipsed India in the eastern thinking of the Comintern.[15] Zinoviev in February 1926 went even further in suggesting that the revolutionary centre of gravity that had earlier shifted from Germany to Britain had now moved on to China.[16] The coming together of China's national and social revolutions, respectively embodied in the Kuomintang and Chinese communist party, was nevertheless broadly co-terminous with the period of the Anglo-Russian committee, and provided the other great exemplification of the unity strategy pursued by the Comintern in the mid-1920s. Oudegeest thought China a communist hobby-horse, and it was apparently during his absence or indisposition that Brown in mid-1925 seized the chance to publicise through IFTU the upsurge of labour militancy that signalled the arrival of the revolutionary left as a significant component of the struggle.[17] Purcell and Brown also issued an IFTU solidarity resolution that was closer on the one hand to current RILU policy, and on the other to the resolution on China moved at the Scarborough TUC by the NAFTA communist Alf Tomkins.[18]

'End your speech by a declaration of unity with the Chinese workers and peasants', Willi Münzenberg advised the ILPer Brockway at the founding conference of the League Against Imperialism (LAI) in February 1927.[19] Purcell must have had Münzenberg at his ear every time he spoke. Tensions within the Kuomintang were by this time reaching breaking point, and the spring of 1927 saw the brutal suppression of the workers' movement in Shanghai and Canton. The Chinese revolution nevertheless remained as yet a beacon to the left, which agitated against outside intervention to the exclusion of any clear awareness of the internal threat.[20] In the winter of 1926-7, Tom Mann was part of a three-man 'International Workers' Delegation' whose appeals were couched in precisely these terms.[21] Even into August, as Purcell delivered his Paris speech, the delegation's positive reports continued to filter into the left-wing press, leading to subsequent allegations of a conspiracy of silence regarding the Kuomintang's turn against the communists.[22] From education to the curse of war, Purcell himself had latterly turned almost every constituency speaking topic to the subject of China.[23] It had even occasioned a rare parliamentary intervention, in the lapidary form of the repeated interjection of the words 'Poison gas!' into a speech by the Conservative MP and chemicals manufacturer Sir Alfred Mond.[24] In Paris too, Purcell's allusions to China were considerably more frequent than those to Russia.[25]

The main burden of his Paris speech was once again the internationalisation of the world economy and the new forms of competitive threat to which this subjected the labour movements represented in IFTU. The two great tendencies of modern capitalism were the movements respectively of production and of labour to where the conditions of exploitation generated most profit. The movement of production was the preponderant one, and at the AFL convention in Atlantic City had been cited by Purcell to show the futility of simply blocking labour migration.[26] Nevertheless, it was the example of direct labour competition in the shipping industry that Purcell now used to illustrate his points. That may be suggestive of Fimmen's influence, which was to be demonstrated in pioneering attempts at extending the ITF beyond its European heartlands. To the example of the Indian textile worker which he had cited at the Commonwealth Labour Conference, Purcell now added that of the Chinese seaman, whose face-to-face encounter with his British counterpart posed the issue of international labour competition in its most immediate and inescapable form.

The tension between labour protectionism and labour internationalism, also evident within the ITF itself, now appeared to have been adjusted decisively in favour of the latter. With the Chinese labour agitations of the early 1900s China had become the focus of a racialised variant of labour protectionism.[27] Purcell himself, in 1924, had led a TUC deputation to the Board of Trade demanding the prohibition of 'Chinese and cheap Asiatic labour' on British ships west of Suez and urging the repatriation of such labour as was thereby made unemployed.[28] This was a staple of labour protectionism, pursued in parliament by O'Grady already before the war.[29] Alluding rather obliquely to these earlier pressures, Purcell in Paris glossed over his own past position. Nevertheless, he stated clearly the alternative position that recognised the mobility of employment as well as labour. Should cheaper labour be excluded from British ships, competitive advantage would merely pass to concerns where labour organisation was weaker, and the inexorable logic of the market thus leave the fundamental issue of undercutting unresolved. In the world market that now existed, this was happening in numerous sectors, with the shifting of production to countries employing labour at subsistence or near-subsistence level. The only answer, said Purcell, was to 'think and act internationally'.[30]

This was where 1917 retained its epochal significance, as now refracted through China itself. 'Think of China today, and how we conceived it to be three short years ago', Purcell declared. He meant that China should be thought of, not as a source of cheap labour, but as the country in which the 'genius of revolution' was most visibly stirring.[31] Here again a shift may be detected. In addressing the Scarborough TUC two years earlier, Swales had drawn the parallel between present-day China and the Britain of the Combination Acts a century or more earlier.[32] This was a familiar theme, like a trade unionist's variation upon the Webbian distinction between adult and non-adult races.[33] In a movement propelled by the sense of forward momentum, it suggested a form of unfair competition between the present-day worker and conditions successfully consigned to the past, compounded in some cases by the language of racial threat. Purcell himself had presented the Indian workers in somewhat lurid terms on his return from Russia in 1924. 'Illiterate, ill-paid, badly clothed, frightfully housed and fed', he warned, 'they may, one day, sweep away their Anglo-Indian masters from their midst and in their frenzy excite the teeming millions of the East into an anti-Western attack, the thought of which is sufficient to make the world shudder'.[34]

The sense of temporality in Purcell's Paris speech was nevertheless very different. In Paris if anywhere one should be able to recognise a city on the eve of revolution, and, 'just as the world learnt from Paris during the past century and a half', so now it was Europe's turn to learn from the cities of China. Purcell described how the hopes and expectations of his generation of socialists had until 1914 been vested in the established labour movements of the west. A 'long and painful embryonic process in the womb of Capitalism' had at that time seemed a prerequisite, both organisational and ideological, for the changes that would bring about socialism.[35] That was what had changed in 1917. What Russia and now China demonstrated was the export of *Capital* and not just capital. Ideas as well as production recognised no national boundaries, and the newly proletarianised workers of the east did not just follow in the wake of their western counterparts, but stood upon their shoulders. 'Just as new industrial fabrics are set up in the backward countries, beginning at the apex of capitalist development in the older capitalist countries, so the ideas given currency amongst those workers are the latest, the most modern, in working-class organisation, in the tactics and strategy of the class struggle, and in Socialist theory.' Indeed, because the ideological agencies of capitalism were as yet less well developed, even the ignorant or illiterate – he did not quite say the wretched of the earth – enjoyed greater mental freedom with which to discern their own true interests than did the urban proletariat of the developed world.[36]

The ambiguities of Purcell's labour internationalism had by no means disappeared. Vigorously challenging Eurocentrism, he did so as a matter of indispensable self-interest for IFTU's European affiliates, according to notions of class formation and political development deriving from their own experience. The image of insurgent China was like a reflected image of a European prototype, whose universalisation carried a notion of cultural and organisational transfer which in this case was effected by Moscow. Purcell's approval of Chinese nationalism was symbolised in the figure of Sun Yat-Sen, whom he saluted for the adoption of social goals akin to, and absorbed from, western labour movements and the Bolsheviks.[37] With the rapid development of such a movement in China, Purcell saw in Imperialism and Nationalism two contrarieties standing face to face.[38] Sun, however, had died in 1925. The Kuomintang in reality stood face to face with the labour movement itself.

Continuing uncertainties were confirmed by the turn from China once more to India. Even as Purcell addressed the Paris congress, the Chinese revolution had clearly stalled and post-mortems quickly followed.[39] India, conversely, was becoming the focus of renewed attention. In November 1927 the British government appointed the Simon commission to investigate the constitutional position in India. Controversially, this included Labour members, notably Clement Attlee, but no Indians. There were also at this time redoubled communist efforts focusing on the development in India of a militant industrial movement. Ironically, given the open hostility they now displayed towards him, the communists had also had a hand in Purcell's final mission for the TUC, as senior member of a two-man delegation which travelled to India in November 1927. Nearly two years earlier, the CPGB and Minority Movement had been directed to push for just such a delegation, which should be 'favourable to the left-wing', to the All-Indian Trades Union Congress (AITUC). Purcell was at that time a member of the TUC's Indian Affairs committee, and while objecting that there was insufficient time to make the necessary arrangements that year, he indicated his willingness in principle to go as delegate.[40] As so often, it was a NAFTA resolution that gave him his opportunity, against the recommendation of the general council, at the 1927 TUC.[41] Immediately beforehand Sassenbach had launched his attack on pretended experts on trade unionism 'in the Far East or in Russia'. Some may have seen the mission as a vote of confidence in Purcell. Others must have thought of sending him to India only because they could not think of anywhere further away.

He was accompanied by the Distributive Workers' official Joseph Hallsworth, and over four months in the sub-continent they travelled fourteen thousand miles together. Hallsworth was far less experienced in such issues than Purcell, nor were there any technical advisers. Purcell may therefore be assumed to be the principal author of the report issued on their return. The inclusion of grainy, snapshot-quality photographs added a note of authenticity that contrasted markedly with the Potemkin-village-style images provided three years earlier by official Soviet agencies.[42] Possibly there was also assistance from the ILP secretary Brockway, who travelled separately to attend the AITUC but shared a cabin home enlivened by Purcell's 'jovial comradeship'.[43] Key points of reference were recent British delegations representing jute and textile workers, and Purcell and Hallsworth focused, as these had, on industries comparable with Britain's and potentially competing with them.[44]

The moral drawn was the familiar one of organisation as the answer to undercutting. As the TUC put it in advertising the delegation's findings, '25,000,000 Sweated Indian Workers a Menace to European Wage Standards'.[45] An India Office memorandum dismissed the visitors' findings as of those too readily shocked and ignorant of India's 'immemorial customs and conditions'.[46] This, of course, might have been precisely their value. Purcell is supposed to have said that as a younger man he would have gone back to play his own part in organising the Indian workers.[47] The TUC in any case never carried through a proposed scheme of joint British and Indian trade-union organisers.[48] There is no doubt, however, of the lasting impression made on Purcell. He was active from the start as president of the India Labour Committee, founded in 1930. Subsequently he was described by Khrishna Menon as an 'extremely good friend' of the India League, which under Menon's direction functioned as the main lobby within Britain for India's national cause.[49]

How he built up India into a Wellsian 'conceivable process' had not been transformed in quite the same way as his ideas of China had.[50] On the one hand, there was in both countries the same breakneck industrialisation. On the other hand, trade-union organisation in India remained weak and dependent on outside support. This was symbolised by the role performed there by lawyers and other professionals, to whom Purcell initially reacted with considerable hostility. Exceptionally, there survives a personal letter he sent Tom Mann at the midpoint of his tour. In such a correspondence, reaffirming continuities with their earlier syndicalism, it was the 'pleader' whom Purcell frankly regarded as 'the villain of the piece':

> He has hooked himself on the embryonic organisations everywhere, then with the terrible illiteracy he is easily monarch of all he 'says and does', but being a lawyer, he does other things always of a doubtful kind … His economic basis being such that he can easily see the employers point of view when demanding a reduction in wages, or the 'gate to more'. I have sized him up particularly, he is a viper …[51]

No such sentiments can be found in the delegation's published report. On the contrary, the analogy with industrialising Britain was revived, and the pleader's role compared in more generous terms with that of outsiders like Owen and the Christian socialists in the early days of British trade unionism.[52] Once again, diachronic analogy served as shorthand for organisational immaturity and a lack of self-sufficiency.

In a period in which European labour had already achieved a degree of basic political leverage, there was also a corresponding shift in the view of the role to be played by the state. From a syndicalistic perspective, trade-union struggle was intrinsically to be preferred to the social reformer's 'manna from heaven' because it developed the working-class capacity for self-emancipation. This view, for example, was expressed in reaction to the ILP's Living Wage proposals by Purcell's close political ally Ellen Wilkinson.[53] Statist emphases, as in the Webbs' case, tended conversely to address the interests of groups apparently lacking the present capacity for such forms of collective agency, either replacing these or, more positively, assisting in their development.[54] Seeing the Indian workers in their 'frightful distress', Purcell himself now adopted such a view. Writing to Mann he had denounced the 'frightful morass of political poltroonery' which he identified with the Swarajists, or Indian nationalists.[55] Back in Britain he argued that India was suffering less from 'what is known as Imperialism' than from 'stomach trouble', and that strong unions mattered more than did a constitutional settlement. Thus alone would the Indian workers become 'masters of the situation in their own working class house, rather than servants in the house of the sweating Nationalists who exist ... at the present time'.[56] The state, in this case a colonial state, provided a source of possible redress as well as oppression.

In the emphasis on trade-union organisation Purcell at least avoided what Victor Kiernan described as Labour's 'purely bureaucratic' response to India.[57] The old suspicion of political institutions was nevertheless significantly compromised. In the delegates' published report, stress was placed upon the stimulus to union organisation provided by the ILO, as well as the unions' current dependence on outside financial support.[58] In expanding upon these themes in parliament, Purcell emphasised the role that even the British government could play in assisting the necessary collective organisation of the workers. Translating under-consumptionist arguments to the level of the empire, he not only had in mind Indian wage levels, but also housing and education projects that could stimulate the British economy while addressing scandalous social ills in India itself.[59] 'Is it too much to ask that out of Great Britain – the one land which has made so much profit from its associations with India, no matter what the history books may say – a really practical and lasting form of help may be afforded to over three hundred millions of human beings ... sufficient in number to set going the wheels of world industry at high speed?'[60] In the role assigned to developing markets, viewed in far more benign terms than the export of capital, the parallel may again be noted with earlier controversies concerning Russian trade. More immediately, there were parallels with the position of the moderate Clydesider Tom Johnston, Morel's successor as MP for Dundee, who two years earlier had fulfilled a similar commission for the Jute and Flax Workers' Union. In Johnston's case, it was made quite explicit that underconsumptionist analysis and hostility to nationalist employers did not imply a 'little Englander' approach, but rather the endorsement of imperial ties and heavy involvement in the Commonwealth Labour Group.[61]

It has been suggested that Purcell may have believed the development of industrial organisation necessarily antecedent to political representation, as it had been in Britain.[62] For one of his syndicalist instincts and political formation, another explanation is possible. In

Paris, Purcell had cited British trade unionism and German social democracy as alternative exemplars of labour's development.[63] He would certainly have bristled at the suggestion that British labour's way was in any way preliminary to its German counterpart's. Believing in the distinct pre-eminence and superiority of industrial organisation, he nevertheless allowed for a potentially progressive role for the British state in India according to a sort of law of uneven development. The Fabian overtones of the argument were unmistakeable. Overlooking for once their past antagonism, the Labour poltroon MacDonald was quick to see the serviceability of Purcell's arguments, and the exposure therein of Swaraj-supporting employers just as much as British ones.[64]

Originating in a spirit of unity, the visit precipitated Purcell's final break with the communists. The principal vehicle for communist activities in this field was the League Against Imperialism, which, as so often, had a wider basis of support in Britain than in any other country. In addition to Brockway, Lansbury and Wilkinson were also among those attending the LAI's founding conference in 1927, along with the IFTU secretary Brown.[65] NAFTA meanwhile showed its support by allowing the league temporary use of its own address for correspondence.[66] Purcell, however, was conspicuous by his absence, and at the Cawnpore session of the AITUC that he attended in November he was instrumental in forestalling its possible affiliation to the LAI.[67] As IFTU showed so little interest in India, Purcell's affirmation of the TUC's credentials in this context implied a rivalry primarily with the Profintern. His report with Hallsworth urged, as if even-handedly, that action could not wait upon 'the caprice of various international units'.[68] Dutt, on the other hand, described activities such as theirs as those of 'agents of imperialism' and scathingly cited IFTU's ambition of bringing India into the orbit of 'European trade unionism'.[69] At the AITUC in 1929, a range of communist-sponsored policies were adopted, including affiliation with the LAI. To this extent, the Purcell-Hallsworth mission had failed.

By this time the communists had alienated or repudiated every significant political ally they had had within the British labour movement. This was the infamous 'Class Against Class' approach, and Purcell, through his activities in India, was one of the first to be denounced. Already Indian communists reportedly extended Brockway a warmer welcome as a 'sincere Leftist' than they would 'such Right leaders as Hallsworth and Purcell'.[70] The scandalous Meerut conspiracy trial, following the arrest in March 1929 of thirty-one communist and other labour activists, provided a starker test of loyalties. The trial itself was a charade, and pending its outcome some four years later the prisoners were effectively held in detention. Nevertheless, the TUC offered them no practical support, and, as the AITUC aligned itself more closely with communist policy, gave its backing to the breakaway All-India Trade Union Federation instead. When even Purcell challenged the prisoners' union credentials, he was roundly attacked for his 'dirty innuendoes'.[71] Officially, the TUC cited its private representations to the India Office and offered mealy-mouthed extenuations of the arrests, to which it declined to apply 'Western' notions of justice.[72] One can hardly miss the resemblance to the similar double standards it had allegedly shown towards the Russian prisoners – though the presence of three Britons among the prisoners suggests that such double standards were not entirely based on nationality or ethnicity.[73]

Purcell's predicament was like a metaphor for the 'double closure' or pincer movement of official social democracy and communism.[74] Lacking any secure base in either, he now found himself isolated even within his own union. Amidst the growing trade-union hostility to the communists, NAFTA had at least retained its radical edge. In 1928 it even concluded an agreement with its Russian counterpart, which Gossip presented as a continuation of the Anglo-Russian unity movement at trade level.[75] Purcell, however, had no part in this, indeed he was actively marginalised. Following the 1927 TUC he declined to sign the NAFTA delegates' report which alleged that 'reaction open and unashamed' had dominated the proceedings.[76] The following year Tomkins, as the union's London district organiser, opposed Purcell in the ballot for the one NAFTA official sent as delegate. With strong support from the capital, he narrowly defeated him.[77] Without naming any names, Gossip in the following issue of the *Labour Monthly* aimed a gratuitous sideswipe at the renegade who was 'a thousand times more reactionary than the one who has never made pretences to be more than an ordinary easy-going leader', and at the 'rabidly excitable individual' who always let the workers down when it came to the test.[78] Neglect it as he might, NAFTA had ultimately provided the basis for all of Purcell's activities at national and therefore international level. As he was now ineligible for the TUC general council, it was therefore out of unexplained necessity that he at last withdrew his nomination for the IFTU presidency.[79] As if by positive collusion between NAFTA's communists and IFTU's anti-communists, the crisis in the IFTU leadership was resolved and Purcell's international career brought ignominiously to a close.

The following year he withdrew from his candidacy in the Forest of Dean. Explaining his decision, he cited 'personal and domestic causes', which according to his agent included the expense of working a constituency in which he had latterly spent far less time.[80] With the exception of his speech on India, he had also barely contributed in the House of Commons. The only issue on which he showed something of the old energy was a campaign on behalf of a woman constituent, Alice Pace, who had been wrongly accused of murder, and for whom Purcell helped generate funds, publicity and a Private Member's Bill to make better legal provision for the defence of 'poor persons'.[81] It was as if he were returning to the straightforward campaigning issues on which he had built his career, and through which he had latterly endeavoured to redeem himself during the miners' lockout. Nothing so far suggests that he was forced out of his candidacy either by his union or by his constituency. Nevertheless, in the 1929 election he took his NAFTA sponsorship to the Moss Side division of his adopted Manchester. A vigorous campaign, he said, was thwarted only by the 'Catholic end' of the constituency.[82] Moss Side, however, was a hopeless prospect, recently uncontested by Labour and failing even to send a delegate to party conference.[83] Effectively, the campaign marked Purcell's retirement from national political life. Weeks later he accepted the position of full-time secretary to the Manchester and Salford Trades Council.[84]

NAFTA by this time was a veritable cock pit. Symbolically, the CPGB's break with Cook had severed the last remaining link between the communists and the TUC lefts.[85] Pushed at once by Moscow, and by intransigents within its own ranks, the CPGB's sectarianism was taken to extravagant lengths. Within NAFTA itself, Tomkins left the party in 1929, one of several tested militants to do so. The struggle against these 'pseudo-lefts' had by 1930 seen the extinction of any Minority Movement influence on NAFTA's executive. Warnings against 'comrades in official positions', of whom none now existed, were insistent but superfluous.[86] When NAFTA condemned 'His Majesty's "Labour Government"' over Meerut, the *Daily Worker* dismissed it as 'a typical mean "Left" manoeuvre' and downright treachery.[87] No NAFTA delegates attended the 1930 RILU congress, apparently because of its provision for the representation of non-unionised workers. Gossip complained to Losovsky of 'ill-advised and premature strikes', 'never ending mass meetings' and a disregard for both 'Generalship' and self-sacrificing local officers.[88] The communists would in due course to pull back from the brink and set about rebuilding the party's industrial base. NAFTA in any case retained its militant credentials. But it never again mattered to anybody outside the furnishing industry.

7.2 SEARCHING FOR TRUTH IN RUSSIA

It certainly ceased to matter for the TUC. In 1924, the Menshevik Abramovich had described British Labour as a 'bulwark of bolshevism'.[89] How different things were a decade later when Pollitt described the ageing Swales as the only general council member with any interest in closer relations with the Russians.[90] As trade-union unity returned to the IFTU agenda, the pressure was now most of all from France where even Jouhaux was learning to work with communists. In Germany, where the ADGB had gone down to the last without fighting, the Nazis had destroyed the trade-union movement. London now filled the role once played by Amsterdam and Berlin, and the TUC was viewed by communists as the main obstacle to unity internationally.[91] Goldman's compact majority now seemed as if turned on its head.[92] In the year that Hitler crushed the unions, the TUC affirmed the equivalence of Nazism and Soviet communism with the 'overwhelming' support that it had previously shown for the Soviets themselves.[93] Rather than a gradual evolution, the shift had been signalled with extraordinary rapidity as early as 1927. In June that year the Soviet ambassador Voikov had been assassinated in Warsaw. Immediately the Bolsheviks blamed British machinations and demonstrated their defiance by executing some two dozen white-guardists held in Russian prisons.[94] As relations through the Anglo-Russian committee deteriorated, a more critical stance towards the Soviets had already begun to surface in the British Labour press.[95] Now, it was as if a general sense of constraint had been lifted. The ILP's *New Leader* denounced the executions; Lansbury and Maxton telegraphed their opposition; Herbert Morrison in the *Labour Magazine* wrote of blood-lust; and the TUC itself condemned the degradation of civilised life.[96] For several years the former Bolshevik Anatoly Baikalov, heading a self-styled 'Group of Social Democrats in London', had vainly solicited Labour support for campaigns against the Soviet regime.[97] Now at last he felt that British Labour had definitely determined upon fighting communism.[98] Purcell in his Paris speech had referred only to Voikov's assassination, not the ensuing reprisals.[99] But this was now as little the TUC's position as it was that of IFTU itself.

There are several possible lines of explanation for this belated change of heart. Changing circumstances were one, as the NEP gave way to Stalin's iron age.[100] Rejection and vituperation by the Bolsheviks was clearly another.[101] That Hicks, along with Swales, sought to moderate anti-Sovietism is also suggestive of how the changing generational composition of collective bodies influenced the shaping of such issues.[102] There was also, of course, the marginalisation of the smaller left-wing craft unions. At the 1933 TUC, Tomkins as NAFTA delegate offered opposition to the democracy versus dictatorship line in the best traditions of his union. Two years later he moved the resolution on the united front. No such resolution was ever carried, however; and when Tomkins, like Purcell before him, stood for the general council, he received the merest fraction of the vote of the successful candidates.[103]

Critically bound up with these wider issues was the role of strategically positioned individuals. Relatively small-scale personnel changes had allowed Purcell his pro-Soviet moment in 1924-5. Similar shifts, but of greater scope and durability, now hurried through its conclusion. When Morel died in November 1924, the UDC, according to

A.J.P. Taylor, was left like sheep without a shepherd.[104] One could hardly refer in such a way to Bramley's passing, at the same early age of fifty-one, just eleven months later. It did however represent the abrupt excision from office of the sort of generational experience which Bramley personified. Embedded in the ecumenical culture of the pre-war labour movement, Bramley was among a cohort of leaders whose political socialisation attenuated faction and legitimised pluralism. Even the communists were initially assimilated through an image of the radical life-cycle by which their very excesses recalled the militant youths of the current generation of leaders.[105] In correspondence on Bramley's death or in later reminiscences, communists like Pollitt and Albert Inkpin each drew on this common stock of memories as if offsetting later party differences.[106]

Citrine, as Bramley's successor, was a very different character. From the formative milieu of the early 1920s he retained a strong sense of the unions' independent functions. While still assistant to Bramley he had scathingly compared the limited demands of political activism with the more substantial commitments of the trade unionist.[107] He had also reminded Cole that, if trade-union aims and structures needed reformulating, trade unionists were quite capable of doing this themselves.[108] Fully committed to the unions, Citrine rejected the logic of the pendulum swing, exactly as Bramley might have done. However, where Bramley described as a continental import the 'new and strange' notion of the labour movement's 'wings', Citrine favoured just this delineation of the distinct prerogatives and functions of what he believed were 'two different spheres'.[109] Relinquishing the claim to a sort of labour movement primogeniture, Citrine's pursuit of a corporate trade-union interest was more narrowly focused than in the past, but at the same time less likely to be drawn into such political entanglements as did not assist its further progression within the ambit of the state.

The significance of such differences was accentuated by the centralisation of authority. Displacing what had been a rough-and-ready collegiality, Citrine's ideal was the trade-union boss whose distinctive personal profile did not so much offset the power of the apparatus as rest firmly upon it. At first sight, the TUC's monthly *Industrial Review*, launched in January 1927, epitomises what was henceforth its prevailing bureaucratic ethos. As if on the precedent of the *British Worker*, its contents were mostly contributed by TUC officers and included no provision for debate or controversy. In place of the biographical portraits that Tracey had previously contributed to the *Labour Magazine*, the life-history approach was applied only to individual unions or trades councils conceived of as collective actor. Citrine's name alone stood out, through the front-page feature which for a time bore his facsimile signature, and which in December 1928 was displaced by a personal Christmas message.[110] Nothing captures his style of leadership better than his acceptance of a knighthood from the National Government in 1935. On the one hand, it symbolised an active engagement with governments of whatever political persuasion, disregarding the legitimation this offered Labour's opponents in an election year. On the other hand, while it was clearly bestowed in respect of Citrine's trade-union functions, its acceptance was justified as a purely personal matter in which wider consultation was neither necessary nor appropriate.[111]

The concentration of authority was particularly marked in the international field. When Purcell at last withdrew as nominee for the IFTU presidency, Citrine took his place, in recognition supposedly of 'services ... rendered to the International Movement'.[112] He not only combined the earlier roles of Bramley and Purcell, as TUC secretary and IFTU president, but did so continuously until IFTU's dissolution seventeen years later. Discussions of trade-union internationalism routinely stress the role of such individuals. In a much-cited phrase, Jeffrey Harrod described them as 'virtually unencumbered by membership interest or demands', and it was certainly the case that particular elements within heterogeneous movements secured hold of key institutional levers like those of representation and publicity.[113] As Pollak observed, during the period of Purcell's ascendancy the British labour movement's 'wide and loose organisation' and 'freedom of individual thought and action', meant that individuals spoke for British labour who could not in themselves represent 'all its shades or currents of thought'.[114] Purcell himself acknowledged precisely this limitation.[115] It did not cease to be one just because of Citrine's relative longevity.

Attitudes to Bolshevism were a case in point. Visiting with Hicks in October 1925, Citrine had made no secret of his enthusiasm for what he saw in Russia.[116] Nevertheless, he was already the following year known to be 'specially interested' in the views of Russian oppositionists.[117] Tracey also interpolated a sceptical note into the *Labour Magazine*, which then became a feature of the *Industrial Review*.[118] The role of such figures within the apparatus should not be underestimated. There was nothing in Britain like the spoils system which Purcell alleged to exist in the AFL.[119] Nor, however, was there democratic oversight of staffing arrangements, and the minutiae of appointments procedures assisted the construction of traditions over time. The Bristolian H.W. Lee, a few years Purcell's elder, had been a full-time Hyndmanite loyalist from his teens, as SDF secretary and later editor of the weekly *Justice*. True to Hyndman and his memory, Lee continued to identify with European social democracy against every form of 'impossibilism', from war resistance and direct action to Bolshevism itself.[120]

When the ailing *Justice* folded in 1925, Lee was appointed to the TUC's Far Eastern sub-committee, and his tracking of Comintern policy played its part in the TUC's repudiation of its Indian counterpart in 1930.[121] On good terms with Citrine, Lee also provided a similar service regarding Soviet Russia itself. Even at the height of Labour's Russian superstition he had struggled ineffectually to counteract its influence, offering Adler what assistance he could and noting wryly that the anarchist Turner wished to get in touch.[122] Lee was Baikalov's one steadfast supporter, and they even planned an anti-Bolshevik press bureau, which then fell victim to the 'wave of sympathy' that followed the TUC delegation's return from Russia.[123] Three years later, they revived the proposal in almost identical form, but as a press service primarily to the TUC itself. Through Baikalov, Lee sought to document Comintern activities in Britain and its connections with the Meerut prisoners.[124] From both Bolshevik and Menshevik sources, he also provided Citrine with the documentation he required to contest the pro-Soviet coverage of the *Herald* and Coates's Anglo-Russian Parliamentary Committee.[125]

Was this the recovery of an old tradition or the emergence of a new one? Citrine recognised the constraints of his 'representative capacity', and he wanted no acknowledgement in Baikalov's *In the Land of Communist Dictatorship* (1929).[126] His primary concern was with those aspects of Soviet communism that most impinged on trade unionists, such as the introduction of one-man management in 1929.[127] The effectiveness of this type of argument may be gauged by Pollitt's request by 1934 that the USSR enter the ILO 'as an *employer*'.[128] The unleashing of stalinist repression following the Kirov murder at the end of that year then provided another watershed moment. On Hicks's motion, the National Council of Labour sent a delegation of protest to the Soviet embassy that provoked an intemperate response from the ambassador Maisky.[129] The monthly *Labour*, successor to the *Labour Magazine*, ended a period of diplomatically ignoring Russia by publishing witheringly effective commentaries by another former Bolshevik, Peter Petrov.[130] Baikalov with some hyperbole described it as the ending of a seventeen-year 'conspiracy of silence'.[131]

It was in these circumstances that Citrine set about a return visit to Russia that provides both afterword and comparator to the delegations of the 1920s. The differences in form are striking. Supposedly Citrine was travelling in a 'purely private' capacity.[132] He did so, however, as a salaried official, who was certainly not using his annual leave, and as the invitee of the Russian unions. He also had immediate access to the labour press, and a TUC pamphlet was compiled from the articles he published in *Labour* on his return.[133] Nevertheless, his findings were primarily disseminated through a highly personalised travelogue, *I Search for Truth in Russia*, issued by a commercial publishing house.

The medium and the message were in this instance as one. Adler had criticised the earlier TUC delegation for the empiricist mindset that meant everything being taken at face value and nothing ever glimpsed beneath the surface. On the other hand, it was precisely this native empiricism that made for the quality of first-hand observation that

Citrine had found so lacking when the Webbs' *Soviet Communism* appeared the previous year.[134] A communist critic called him 'you-can't-diddle-me Sir Walter', whose method was to observe 'every place that looks as if it needs a coat of paint' and make a note of it.[135] Richard Crossman claimed that in a workman's flat 'nothing escapes his eye, least of all the electric wiring', and that often Citrine saw more than he was meant to.[136] In just this period, Mass-Observation would seek through similar methods to get behind the idea of the domestic 'public' or public opinion. A fellow documentarist, Citrine's understated use of the diary method subverted the Webbian dependence on official sources through the careful notation of piece rates, working conditions, living spaces and missing plugs. His book has been described as 'displaying the continuing romantic Russophilism of British Labour'.[137] In reality, its clear rejection of this Russophilia was based on the negation of the revolutionary and other forms of romanticism by which for decades now this sentiment had been animated. As far as the TUC was concerned, it meant the chapter opened up by the Russian revolution was now definitely closed.

But Citrine did not, any more than Purcell, speak for the movement as a whole. The TUC by November 1927 would not have accepted an invitation to attend the Bolsheviks' tenth anniversary celebrations. Brockway as ILP secretary declined to take part because of the 'hundreds of Socialists' lingering in Soviet prisons.[138] Even so, the British delegation that did attend was surpassed in size only by those from Germany and France, and it was manifestly representative of a significant body of trade-union opinion.[139] Through writing around the life of Purcell, the chapters in this volume have focused specifically on this current of trade-union sentiment. But as was earlier seen in the case of the Webbs, for many within the British labour movement the road to Russia was only just opening up. After a railway journey in 1929, Harry Pollitt recorded that Labour's ultra-moderate assistant secretary, Jim Middleton, was 'extraordinarily well-informed' about the Five Year Plan, and thought it 'the most gigantic thing that had ever been undertaken'.[140] The crisis of 1931 provided further stimulus to such interest across the whole spectrum of the labour movement.[141] If anything, it was the Labour Party under Lansbury and Attlee that evinced a greater sympathy with the Soviets. Beatrice Webb in 1935 noted the 'exclusively labour' character of Soviet embassy functions and claimed that it was 'the only great house in London at which the left wing meets each other! even some of the right wing of labour party but not Citrine or Transport House officials'.[142] Morrison himself so far overcame his earlier misgivings as to attend, and in a series of *Daily Herald* articles described how his own, often unsuspected 'sense of romance' had been stimulated by visiting the USSR.[143]

Russia itself was hardly standing still, and what it represented to these disparate currents of attraction and repulsion was as much subject to redefinition as attitudes to India or China or Germany. In 1935 the Webbs cited Tomsky's pamphlet *The Trade Unions, the Party and the State* to demonstrate the very real authority of the unions in the Soviets' new civilisation.[144] Nothing could have better demonstrated the inadequacy of a research method perfected in an environment of incremental change. Though the pamphlet was by this time only eight years old – barely a blink in the Webbian time-scale of gradualism – the intervening years had seen a second revolution from above, resulting in the categorical suppression of such trade-union functions as a western trade unionist might recognise. The theme of the unions' enhanced standing was not lost sight of, but it was henceforth identified with such novel and even alien phenomena as socialist competition and Stakhanovism.[145] To both practical and symbolic effect, Tomsky himself, the embodiment of union claims and aspirations, had been stripped of his official responsibilities in 1929.

Whatever the image the Soviets now sought to project, it was not the stooping fellow-worker in struggle that Scott Nearing had perceived in Tomsky at the Scarborough TUC. Better than the frailty of a human frame, or the elusive intimacies of personal colloquy, a more characteristic export of the 1930s was Vera Mukhina's enormous *Worker and Collective Farm Girl* that towered over the Paris exhibition of 1937. Such a figure of the new proletarian man and woman excited not just solidarity but a sense of awe and distance. Already when the illustrated monthly *Russia Today* was launched in 1930, productivist feats were celebrated with an American sense of scale and tempo. 'Putting a hustle into it!', ran a caption for the first State Clock Works. 'In the old Russia time was of little consequence. But Time, Punctuality and Speed are the essence of the tremendous Socialist Construction under the Five Years' Plan.'[146] This was not what the average NAFTA activist had seen in Russia, and it would be worth exploring how far conflicting images persisted in the proliferation of delegations and travel groups from the late 1920s.[147] Nevertheless, it was with the socialism of gigantomania and the hated stopwatch that the Soviet achievement was now identified. Morrison in 1933 described this as its 'sweeping character' that appealed so powerfully to one's liking of 'big things'.[148] It was against just this cult of bigness that Purcell had reacted in America, at the time that he was Labour's best-known visitor to the USSR. But by the time he made his final visit, also in 1933, there were no bands to receive him and nobody was any longer interested in what he had to say.

NOTES

1. RGASPI 495/100/254, Inkpin to Bennett (Petrovsky), 7 June 1927.
2. TUC archives MSS 292/901/1, TUC international committee minutes, 17 March 1927.

3. Purcell, *Workers of the World – Unite!*, ILP, 1927, p. 16.
4. Purcell, *Workers of the World*, pp. 8-9, 17.
5. Bernard Georges and Denise Tintant, *Léon Jouhaux dans le mouvement syndicale français*, vol. 2, Paris: Paris Universitaires de France, 1979, pp. 56-63.
6. Lewis L. Lorwin, *Labor and Internationalism*, New York: Macmillan, 1929, pp. 365-9.
7. *Report of Proceedings of the Fourth Ordinary Congress of the IFTU*, Amsterdam: IFTU, 1927, p. 35.
8. In abstaining from the voting process the British delegation was joined by those from South Africa, Canada and Palestine.
9. *Report of Proceedings of the Fourth Ordinary Congress of the IFTU*, pp. 50-1, 79 ff, 92-7.
10. 59th *TUC Report*, 1927, pp. 345-8.
11. 59th *TUC Report*, 1927, pp. 376-81.
12. Corneel Mertens cited Geert van Goethem, *The Amsterdam International. The world of the International Federation of Trade Unions (IFTU), 1913-1945*, Aldershot: Ashgate, 2006, p. 71, n. 160.
13. See chs 3.5 and 5.5. above.
14. *New Leader*, 5 August 1927, cited Purcell, *Workers of the World*, p. 1.
15. E.H. Carr, *Socialism in One Country, 1924-1926. Volume 3*, Harmondsworth: Penguin edn, 1972, p. 730.
16. Cited Jean-François Fayet, *Karl Radek (1885-1939). Biographie politique*, Bern: Peter Lang, 2004, p. 533.
17. Brown, 'The labour disturbances in Shangai' and 'The real causes of the Chinese disturbances', IFTU *Press Reports*, 18 June and 2 July 1925; and compare with Oudegeest's implied comparison with Japan, 'Communist abuse of Japanese labour leaders', IFTU *Press Reports*, 20 August 1925.
18. Lorwin, *Labor and Internationalism*, pp. 319 and 321; 57th *TUC Report*, 1925, pp. 487-8.
19. Brockway, *Inside the Left. Thirty years of platform, press, prison and parliament*, Allen & Unwin, 1942, pp. 167-8.
20. On this see Tom Buchanan, *East Wind. China and the British left, 1925-1976*, Oxford: OUP, 2012, ch. 1.
21. E.g. 'Appeal of the international workers' delegation in China', *Inprecorr*, 7 April 1927, p. 467.
22. See Chushichi Tsuzuki, *Tom Mann, 1856-1941. The challenges of Labour*, Oxford: OUP, 1991, ch. 13; also Mann, 'My visit to China', *Labour Monthly*, August 1927, pp. 483-9 and the contributions by the American Earl Browder in the journal's July and September issues.
23. *Dean Forest Mercury*, 7 January, 4 February, 8 and 29 April, 6 May 1927.
24. NAFTA *Monthly Report*, January 1927, pp. 23-5 and February 1927, pp. 22-4; 204 Hansard fifth series, 6 April 1927, col. 2123.
25. As a rough-and ready indicator, in the ILP edition of the text there are thirty references to Russia, Russians and Russian place-names and sixty-seven to China and the Chinese.
26. 45th AFL Convention *Report of Proceedings*, October 1925, pp. 141-2.
27. See Buchanan, *East Wind*, pp. 13-21.
28. 56th *TUC Report*, 1924, pp. 97-104.

29. E.g. 27 Hansard fifth series, 28 June 1911, col. 426.
30. Purcell, *Workers of the World*, pp. 10-12.
31. Purcell, *Workers of the World*, pp. 4-5.
32. 57th TUC *Report*, 1925, p. 72.
33. See for example *Bolshevism and the British Left*, II, p. 36. For the currency of formulations like Swales's, see for example Pollitt papers, prison note book issued 10 April 1926.
34. Purcell, '"Our patriotism – loyalty to the working class"', *Plebs*, March 1925, p. 102.
35. Purcell, *Workers of the World*, p. 7.
36. Purcell, *Workers of the World*, pp. 4-8.
37. Purcell, *Workers of the World*, p. 6.
38. NAFTA *Monthly Report*, January 1927, pp. 23-5.
39. E.g. M.N. Roy, 'The lessons of the Chinese revolution', *Labour Monthly*, November 1927, pp. 660-8
40. RGASPI 534/7/32, 'Black' (Hardy) to Alexander (Losovsky), 11 January 1926 and to George Allison, 11 January 1926.
41. 59th TUC *Report*, 1927, pp. 382-4; NAFTA *Monthly Report*, June 1928, p. 29.
42. Purcell and Hallsworth, *Report on Labour Conditions in India*, TUC general council, 1928.
43. Brockway, *Inside the Left*, pp. 182, 184.
44. Purcell and Hallsworth, *Report*, pp. 28-32. The exclusion of the vast field of agriculture was justified on the plausible grounds of lacking either the time or the 'particulars' (p. 42).
45. *Industrial Review*, June 1928, p. 3.
46. India Office Library I/E/7/1522, unsigned memorandum 'Report on labour conditions in India', 1928.
47. W.P. Coates in Anglo-Russian Parliamentary Committee *News Bulletin*, 97, 4 January 1936.
48. Marjorie Nicholson, *The TUC Overseas. The roots of policy*, Allen & Unwin, 1984, pp. 158-60.
49. Krishna Menon papers, box 10, file 6/37, Menon to Waughray, 15 May 1932 (with thanks to Paul Kelemen for this reference); Stephen Howe, *Anticolonialism in British Politics. The left and the end of empire, 1918-1964*, Oxford: OUP, 1993, p. 128; Georges Fischer, *Le parti travailliste et la décolonisation de l'Inde*, Paris: François Maspero, 1966, p. 273.
50. See ch. 5.1 above for Wells and the impact of America.
51. Torr papers CP/Ind/Torr/8/3, Purcell to Mann, 23 January 1928. For the links with their earlier syndicalism see ch. 1 above.
52. Purcell and Hallsworth, *Report*, p. 13.
53. *Lansbury's Labour Weekly*, 6 June 1925.
54. On these themes, see *Bolshevism and the British Left, II*, chs 4-5.
55. Purcell to Mann, 23 January 1928.
56. 220 Hansard fifth series, 2 August 1928, cols 2539-46; also *Dean Forest Guardian*, 20 April 1928, for a constituency speech on very similar lines.
57. V.G. Kiernan, *Marxism and Imperialism*, Edward Arnold, 1974, p. 239.
58. Purcell and Hallsworth, *Report*, p. 12.
59. 220 Hansard fifth series, 2 August 1928, cols 2539-46; *Dean Forest Guardian*, 20 April 1928.

60. Purcell and Hallsworth, *Report*, p. 43.
61. Graham Walker, *Thomas Johnston*, Manchester: MUP, 1988, ch. 3.
62. See Nicholas Owen, *The British Left and India, 1885-1947*, Oxford: OUP, 2007, pp. 156-7.
63. Purcell, *Workers of the World*, p. 7.
64. Partha Sarathi Gupta, *Imperialism and the British Labour Movement 1914-1964*, New Delhi: Sage Publications, 2002 edn, pp. 114-15.
65. Howe, *Anticolonialism*, pp. 71-7.
66. NAFTA *Monthly Report*, November 1927, p. 10.
67. Jean Jones, 'The anti-colonial politics and policies of the Communist Party of Great Britain 1920-1951', Wolverhampton PhD, 1997, p. 97.
68. Purcell and Hallsworth, *Report*, p. 43.
69. Dutt, 'Notes of the month', *Labour Monthly*, June 1928, p. 340.
70. A. Fenner Brockway, *A Week in India (and three months in an Indian hospital)*, New Leader, 1928, p. 17.
71. *Daily Worker*, 22 and 26 May 1930; Bradley papers, CP/Ind/Brad/4/5, Manchester Meerut Defence Committee, 'Reply to Mr A.A. Purcell's charge against the Meerut prisoners', n.d. but May 1930. For the Meerut trial, see the special note by John Saville in Joyce M. Bellamy and John Saville, eds, *Dictionary of Labour Biography*, vol. 7, Macmillan, 1984, pp. 84-91.
72. 'The question of the guilt and innocence of those charged ... is one necessarily in abeyance while the trial ... is proceeding. The long drawn-out proceedings extending over many months, and the fact that the accused have been kept in custody for more than a year and have still to undergo some months of confinement, are matters which, according to Western notions, may not reflect credit upon judicial proceedings in India. But there is no evidence that the accused have in any way been singled out for persecution, or that they have had these serious charges brought against them because of their Trade Union activities.' (62nd TUC *Report*, 1930, p. 189.)
73. The three Britons were Ben Bradley, Philip Spratt and Lester Hutchinson, who had been arrested three months after the other defendants.
74. See *Bolshevism and the British Left*, I, p. 12.
75. NAFTA *Monthly Report*, May 1928, pp. 2-3, 8.
76. NAFTA *Monthly Report*, October 1927, p. 23.
77. NAFTA *Monthly Report*, May 1928, p. 7.
78. Gossip, 'The fourth congress of the RILU', *Labour Monthly*, June 1928, p. 358.
79. TUC archives 292/901/1, TUC international committee minutes, 11 May 1928, incl. Purcell to Citrine, 10 May 1928.
80. NAFTA *Monthly Report*, March 1929, pp. 20-1; *Dean Forest Mercury*, 28 January 1927 and 27 December 1935.
81. For details of the case see John Carter Wood, *The Most Remarkable Woman in England. Poison, celebrity and the trials of Beatrice Pace*, Manchester: MUP, 2012. My thanks to Dr Wood for the sight of relevant chapters.
82. NAFTA *Monthly Report*, June 1929, p. 28.
83. Declan McHugh, *Labour in the City. The development of the Labour Party in Manchester, 1918-31*, Manchester: MUP, 2006, pp. 75 and 201-2.

84. In challenging Howard's more sober assessment of Labour Party organisation in the 1920s (see *Bolshevism and the British Left*, I, ch. 5) McHugh describes Purcell's candidacy as that of a longstanding local activist financed by the local party. Of course, it was neither.
84. NAFTA *Monthly Report*, September 1929, p. 23. Achieving a creditable poll of nearly a third of the vote, Purcell needed a strong Liberal performance, as in 1923, to have had any realistic chance of success. It is just possible that he calculated on this, but he can hardly have been deceived as to the likely outcome.
85. See 'Cook's revolutionary break with the revolutionary working class', *Labour Monthly*, June 1929, pp. 342-8.
86. RGASPI 534/7/48, Mahon to RILU secretariat, January 1930; George Allison to Woodworkers' IPC and RILU Anglo-American section, 21 February 1930.
87. *Daily Worker*, 20 and 21 May 1930.
88. RGASPI 534/7/48, Allison to RILU Anglo-American section, 21 February 1930; Gossip to Losovsky, 4 and 27 June 1930; Allison to RILU Fifth World Congress organising committee, 23 July 1930
89. André Liebich, *From the Other Shore. Russian Social Democracy after 1921*, Cambridge, Mass.: Harvard University Press, 1997, p. 177.
90. RGASPI 495/100/951, Pollitt to 'Dick', c. November (?) 1934.
91. RGASPI 495/2/234, Arnot at Comintern presidium, 25 September 1936. My thanks to Barry McLoughlin for this reference.
92. For the compact majority see ch. 4.2 above.
93. 65th TUC *Report*, 1933, pp. 318-40. The Labour Party manifesto 'Democracy versus dictatorship' had been adopted earlier the same year.
94. See the Soviet government communique 'To the whole working population of the Soviet Union! To the toilers of the whole world!', *Inprecorr*, 16 July 1927, pp. 725-6.
95. See for examples W.W. Henderson, 'Fractions and frictions', *Labour Magazine*, October 1926, pp. 246-8.
96. *New Leader*, 17 June 1927; 'Comrade Rykov's answer to Lansbury, Maxton and Brockway', *Inprecorr*, 7 July 1927, pp. 873-6; Herbert Morrison, 'When "left" is "right" and so righted is wrong: is British Labour having a little too much Russia?', *Labour Magazine*, July 1927, pp. 102-3; TUC archives 292/20/11, TUC general council resolution, 22 June 1927.
97. For biographical details see Liebich, *From the Other Shore*, pp. 178-9; also Baikalov, *I Knew Stalin*, Burns Oates, 1940, autobiographical preface.
98. Baikalov papers box 2, Baikalov to Philip Snowden, 11 October 1928.
99. Purcell, *Workers of the World*, p. 17.
100. For which contrast see William Henry Chamberlin, *Russia's Iron Age*, Duckworth, 1935.
101. For references to the alienating effect of such criticisms see e.g. Baikalov papers, H.W. Lee to Baikalov, 22 December 1927; RGASPI 495/100/951, Pollitt to 'Comrade P[iatnitsky?]', 26 October 1934.
102. As claimed for example in the *Daily Worker*, 2 August 1933.
103. E.g. in 1933 186,000, as against over three million each for Hicks and Frank Wolstencroft of the Woodworkers.
104. Cited Howe, *Anticolonialism*, p. 51, n. 76.

105. Bromley for example expressed such views even after the General Strike, which in other respects has been described as his Rubicon; see AFL 46th Convention *Report*, 1926, pp. 132-3, also David Howell, *Respectable Radicals. Studies in the politics of railway trade unionism*, Aldershot: Ashgate, 1999, pp. 278-9. For Swales's similar observations, also to an uncomprehending American audience, see AFL 44th Convention *Report*, 1924, pp. 156-7.
106. TUC archives 292/21.12/3, Pollitt for National Minority Movement to TUC general council, 13 October 1925 and Inkpin for CPGB political bureau to Arthur Pugh, 12 October 1925; Pollitt, *Serving My Time: an apprenticeship to politics*, Lawrence & Wishart, 1941 edn, p. 51.
107. Citrine papers 1/1, 'Sidney Webb and the Trades Union Congress', diary notes dated 29 December 1924.
108. Citrine, 'Theorists and facts', *Lansbury's Labour Weekly*, 4 July 1925.
109. Bramley, 'Impressions of the Scarborough Trades Union Congress', *Labour Magazine*, October 1925, p. 246; Citrine papers 1/8, 'Speech on the "industrial crisis"', Tottenham Trades Club, 8 March 1926.
110. Pressure was evidently brought to bear and the personal note toned down, with the following year only a much shorter 'New Year's Message' co-signed by the current TUC chairman.
111. See his speech in 67th TUC *Report*, 1935, pp. 429-32; also Citrine, *Men and Work*, Hutchinson, 1964, ch. 19. 'Ruth is almost in tears, says we had better join the Communists!', Hugh Dalton recorded of the impact upon a by no means congenitally leftist Labour household. (Ben Pimlott, ed., *The political diary of Hugh Dalton 1918-40, 1945-60*, Cape 1986, p. 188, entry for 3 June 1935.)
112. Citrine, *Trade Unionism in Modern Industry*.
113. Jeffrey Harrod, *Trade Union Foreign Policy. A study of British and American union activities in Jamaica*, New York: Doubleday & Co, 1972, pp. 59-61.
114. Pollak, 'British Labour and the International: a continental replies', *New Leader*, 23 January 1925.
115. 45th AFL Convention *Report*, 1925, p. 140.
116. Citrine, 'The New Russia', *Trade Union Unity*, December 1925, pp. 138-40, and 'The electric republic', *Sunday Worker*, 29 November 1925.
117. TUC archives MSS 292/947/6, Gillies to Citrine, 30 September 1926.
118. Compare for example 'Trade unionism in Soviet Russia', *Labour Magazine*, March 1926, pp. 522-4 and 'Problem of trade union structure. Industrial organisation in Russia and Sweden', *Industrial Review*, October 1927, pp. 4-5. Commendation of Anton Karlgren's 'intensely critical' account of Bolshevism (May 1927) was by December 1929 extended into unabashed attacks on 'catastrophic communism' drawn from German sources.
119. Purcell, 'Capital and Labour in the USA', *Labour Monthly*, February 1926, p. 97.
120. For a characteristic exposition, see his *The 'Dictatorship of the Proletariat'. An address to the annual conference of the National Socialist Party, August, 1919*, Twentieth Century Press, 1919.
121. See Lee's articles 'Disruption in the All-India TUC', *Industrial Review*, January 1930, p. 3; 'Rift in the Indian trade union movement', *Industrial*

Review, April 1930, p. 4, on which the relevant section in the 62nd TUC *Report*, 1930, pp. 190-1 was based.
122. IISH LAI 1693/13, for correspondence of Lee and Adler, October 1924 and April-May 1925, regarding the *Herald*'s treatment of Georgia and plans to distribute Adler's attack on the Russian delegation.
123. Baikalov papers, Lee to Baikalov, 14 December 1924.
124. E.g. Baikalov papers, Lee to Baikalov, 12 April 1929.
125. TUC archives 292/947/54, Citrine to Pat Coates, Anglo-Russian Parliamentary Committee, 20 October 1928; also Baikalov papers, Citrine to Baikalov, 23 October 1933.
126. TUC archives 292/947/8, Citrine to L'Estrange Malone, 23 March 1936.
127. TUC archives 292/947/54, ARPC *Weekly Bulletin*, 10 October 1929 with accompanying critique;
128. Pollitt to 'Comrade P[iatnitsky?]', 26 October 1934.
129. TUC archives 292/947/12, NCL deputation to Soviet embassy, 31 December 1934. The suggestion that Labour was condoning anti-Soviet 'terroristic activities' was omitted from the published version of Maisky's statement.
130. The change is signalled in the magazine's editorial, January 1935, p. 99. Among Petrov's several contributions to *Labour* between April 1935 and April 1938 were two specifically on trade unionism (November 1937) and the wage system (February 1938).
131. Baikalov papers, Baikalov to Citrine, 30 December 1934.
132. Citrine, *I Search for Truth in Russia*, Routledge, 1936, pp. vii-x and passim.
133. Citrine, *A Trade Unionist Looks at Russia*, TUC general council, 1936.
134. See his review in *Labour*, January 1936, pp. 106-7.
135. T.A. Jackson, 'A worm's-eye view of Russia', *Labour Monthly*, September 1936, p. 576.
136. Crossman, 'The faith of British socialism', *New Statesman and Nation*, 6 April 1940, p. 466.
137. Collette, *International Faith*, p. 29.
138. Brockway, open letter to A.I. Rykov, *New Leader*, 4 November 1927; also IISH SAI 1717, Brockway to Adler, 3 November 1927 for the correspondence that now existed with the LSI on such issues.
139. See the biographical questionnaires in GARF 5451/13a/518.
140. RGASPI 495/100/619, Pollitt to Bell, 18 September 1929; also Baikalov papers, Baikalov to Lee, 15 May 1929, for Middleton's hostile attitude to Baikalov.
141. John Callaghan, 'British Labour's turn to socialism in 1931', *Journal of Political Ideologies*, 14, 2, 2009, pp. 115-32.
142. BWD, 1 March 1935.
143. See Bernard Donoughue and G.W. Jones, *Herbert Morrison. Portrait of a politician*, Weidenfeld & Nicolson, 1973, pp. 226-7 for Morrison's six articles of September-October 1933.
144. Sidney and Beatrice Webb, *Soviet Communism. A new civilisation*, Longmans, 1937 edn, p. 219.
145. See for example the chapter on 'The power of the trade unions' in Pat Sloan, *Soviet Democracy*, Gollancz, 1937, pp. 60-78.
146. *Russia Today*, July 1930, p. 9.

147. For a contrasting presentation of Soviet industry by a former London NAFTA activist, see 'British worker's Moscow broadcast', *Russia Today*, January 1932, p. 5.
148. Donoughue and Jones, *Herbert Morrison*, pp. 226-7.

Epilogue:
a claim-making performer

Purcell died at his home in Crumpsall, Manchester on 24 December 1935. His final years had marked a return to local campaigning themes, as if his moment in the spotlight had never happened. From the 'massacre on the roads' and case against high flats, to the threat to civil liberties and the 'stunt' of family allowances, his trades council position provided him with a vehicle for the most varied concerns.[1] The old breadth of perspective also remained, with an internationalism now justified as the connection between thinking global and acting local.[2] The confidence in thinking and acting as one had nevertheless gone.

In the 1929 election Purcell had offered a straightforward collectivist programme; indeed, he virtually paraphrased the original Fabian *Essays* in describing half of Britain's industries – he included education and the armed forces – as already 'organised in one form or another as socialist undertakings'.[3] His sponsorship of Hobson's *House of Industry*, published two years later, was less a flickering of guild socialism than an ineffectual detour through the territory of the Webbs' 'social parliament'.[4] From Russia itself he returned telling less of workers' self-government than of a new municipalism and civic spirit, again evoked in terms indistinguishable from the Webbs'.[5] Initially Purcell had taken up his trades council responsibilities with the vision of a co-ordinating centre that would encompass labour's diverse industrial, political, co-operative and educational aspects;[6] in 1931 he organised an impressive 'People's Congress', which attracted some two thousand delegates and prompted a revival of the old socialist language of catastrophism.[7] Nevertheless, with the announcement three years later of a county federation of labour parties, confounding the principle of inclusiveness to which Purcell had in some sense been committed all his life, he was powerless to resist – indeed, he suggested that the clearer distinction between political and industrial organisation might free up the unions for their own integral functions.[8] This was the logic of administrative convenience, and Citrine himself could not have expressed it any better.

In one way he died just too soon. As his ashes were being laid to rest, the current issue of the *Labour Monthly* hailed the Webbs' *Soviet*

Communism as a political event.[9] In the issue immediately following, the younger communist functionary John Mahon, a sometime zealot for Class Against Class, paid substantial tribute to Purcell himself.[10] The united front had returned, if only one were still about to enjoy it. According to Mahon, Purcell had attained the highest level that a trade unionist could without entering the 'camp of Communism'. Tomsky, having made it to the pinnacle, committed suicide six months later, following his supposed implication in the first Moscow show trial. It was rumoured that he had kept a diary of his disillusionment which he had thought of sending Citrine, before destroying it in an unavailing instinct of self-preservation.[11] One wonders how Purcell might have figured in such a document, and whether he would also have merited such a trust. Fimmen was to collapse with a stroke, disillusioned by the purges, and henceforth rejected all association with the communists.[12] Mann and Tillett, on the other hand, were in Red Square for the revolution's twentieth anniversary, as for thirteen hours workers, soldiers, tanks and planes passed by in a 'magnificent celebration of efficiency in all departments'.[13] There is nothing to suggest that Purcell would not also have relished this further display of gigantomania.

One might question whether the highest form of political consciousness was to be found in communism. One can concede that, wherever it was to be found, Purcell had not attained it. Mahon observed that his thoughts on the outcome of the General Strike 'must have been bitter'. But he also noted that these thoughts were nowhere to be found in Purcell's speeches or writings.[14] Forty years earlier, Katherine Glasier's composite portrait of Purcell's generation of union organiser had captured perfectly its sense of irresistible upward momentum, and of a movement of the future which had only to maintain its faith and purpose to realise that future. '"Lose here, win there"', is our only motto, he says ... At the moment of surrender he may have been white to the lips, but the next day will find him cheery and undaunted in another part of the country, carrying on his campaign and enrolling hundreds of recruits by the sheer energy of his confident eloquence.'[15] This was the mindset of a movement with all before it and a world to win. But it left not even the vocabulary to describe more basic setbacks and disappointments, of a kind that the socialist of the 1890s could scarcely even have dreamt of. Already by the time of his death, Purcell's limitations were clear.

The lack of this quality of retrospection helps explain why so few of the activists of his generation register in any considerable biographical detail. A few may have felt compelled to document their careers through motives of personal or factional vindication. The very notion of an irresistible forward movement seemed to demand some sort of narrative of progression, whether at the individual or the collective level. Purcell, however, left a life without conscious trace, as if one simply moved on from it as he moved on from one campaign to the next. There is doubtless an intrinsic paradox in trying to reconstruct such forms of activism in the shape of a biography for which no provision was made. One cannot even call it a 'usable' past, like one of Purcell's good-looking pegs to hang one's advocacy upon.[16] Nietzsche once wrote that it was a 'refined and at the same time noble piece of self-control to praise only where one does *not* agree – for in the other case one would be praising oneself, which is contrary to good taste'.[17] Left-wing history writing, biography in particular, is not always free of this surrogate self-regard. With Purcell at least there is no such temptation, and his pastness now appears beyond resuscitation.

There is something in his history, even so, that is worth recovering, in the spirit of E.P. Thompson and his poor stockinger or deluded Southcottian.[18] Some years ago it was fashionable to talk of taking the Labour Party 'back to its ethical roots'.[19] Tony Wright, who had made a close study of Britain's socialist traditions, suggested in 1994 that nothing now remained of socialism's 'doctrinal baggage', or of the belief that it held the key to history, or of the link once assumed with the working class as social agent. All that that was left, said Wright, was what was most essential to socialism, namely its ethic of community and mutual responsibility.[20] Purcell's political baggage may not all be worth retrieving, and his confidence in the future has been confounded by the future itself. Nevertheless, if there is one thing which the experience of New Labour made clear, it is that there can be no ethic of mutual responsibility without the democratic social agency that will make it happen. A socialism rooted in the organisation of male manual workers will not reappear, and its exclusions and limitations are too familiar to need much emphasis here. Nevertheless, what was also integral to their socialism was the affirmation of an ethic of responsibility in an activist stance towards the world around them, and a militant refusal of remediable social ills and of the relations of power and subordination from which they were and are inseparable.

Reflecting on the British 'invention' of the social movement in the early nineteenth century, Charles Tilly described its 'para-electoral' forms of agitation as representing the displacement of more spontaneous, immediate and effective forms of mobilisation by a distinctly more mediated set of 'claim-making performances', co-ordinated by special-purpose associations or political entrepreneurs.[21] Foremost among these claim-making performances were precisely those – demonstrations, meetings, strikes, slogans, symbols and committees – which to socialists of Purcell's generation defined the 'struggle' to which they were so tirelessly committed. Tilly was not enthused by these later movements and was clearly sceptical as to the gains that were thereby achieved. In his celebration of the localised, the face-to-face and the unmediated, the comparison might be made with the rank-and-filist historiography of shopfloor activities that eluded formal structures of representation, or with the reaction against an ossified labour movement on the part of the social movement theorists of the post-1968 period.[22]

Activist-officers like Purcell would have justified their forms of activity as those appropriate to social evils that were systemic, impersonal and national or international in scope. It was precisely on these grounds, however, that their diverse forms of civic and industrial activism were themselves now subordinated to the disciplines of party, as a form of organisation that was parastatist or at least paragovernmental in character. In the Labour Party's case, the disciplines and mentality were precisely those of a prospective party of government. In the case of communists and fellow-travellers, identification with the Soviet system of government had a similar constraining effect. A key theme emerging in *Bolshevism and the British Left* is that in Britain the two processes were more closely interconnected than in most European countries, as the Labour and communist parties took shape more or less simultaneously. It is in this context that one may better understand the diversity and volatility of so many political trajectories in this period, and why Bolshevik Russia should have struck a chord with different elements of the left for such varying reasons, in varying circumstances and at different times.

The Webbs, of course, turned to communism when their world fell apart and there seemed nothing else to cling to. Purcell, by contrast, embraced it from the outset, as another part of the campaign, in another part of the country which, as Paine had put it, was the world itself. One wonders whether he was always so undaunted as he seemed; but if his brain ever whizzed and ached, as Beatrice Webb's did, there was no diary in which to record it, only perhaps a glass with which to indulge the trade unionist's weakness for palliatives.[23] Whatever the tests to which it was subjected, there is little sign in either case that they could have given up the hopes that they had invested in Bolshevism. Purcell, therefore, was no more a simple victim of the double closure than were the Webbs themselves; or if he was, he must also be regarded, as they must, as among its agents. Even so, in the vigour and undauntedness of the plebeian social agencies to which he contributed, a more enduring example also remains. David Marquand has recently evoked the protean, plural nature of British democracy, and criticised the fallacy of a shallow presentism that ignores the richness and diversity of such a history.[24] It is in claim-making performances that both embodied and demanded an ethic of mutual responsibility that the legacy, not of Purcell, but of his generation remains.

NOTES

1. *Manchester Guardian*, 7 October 1930, 1 October 1934 and 18 January 1935; Purcell, *The Massacre on the Roads*, MSTC, 1935.
2. E.g. *Trades Councils and Local Working-Class Movement*, p. 5.

Epilogue 309

3. Moss Side division election literature, Purcell election special, Purcell brochure: 'A souvenir'.
4. Alfred M. Wall and A.A. Purcell, foreword to S.G. Hobson, *The House of Industry. A new estate of the realm*, P.S. King, 1931, pp. vii-xxviii; also David Blaazer, 'Guild socialists after guild socialism: the Workers' Control Group and the House of Industry League', *Twentieth Century British History*, 11, 2, 2000, pp. 147-53.
5. Purcell, *Days in Leningrad. Notes on a visit to Leningrad, August 1933*, MSTC, 1933.
6. Purcell, *The Trades Councils and Local Working-Class Movement*, MSTC, 1930, p. 10 and passim; MSTC 63rd *Annual Report*, 1929-30, pp. 4-5.
7. See MSTC *Annual Report*, 1931-2, pp. 5-8.
8. *Manchester Guardian*, 27 August 1934.
9. Dutt, 'A landmark of the British labour movement', *Labour Monthly*, January 1936, pp. 3-26.
10. J.A. Mahon, 'A.A. Purcell: a champion of working-class unity', *Labour Monthly*, February 1936, pp. 101-9. For the 'Young Turks' characterisation see Nina Fishman, *The British Communist Party and the Trade Unions, 1933-45*, Aldershot: Scolar, 1995.
11. Baikalov papers, Baikalov to Citrine, 19 November 1938.
12. Koch-Baumgarten, 'Edo Fimmen', pp. 59, 65. Fimmen appears to have been most affected by the predicament of Willi Münzenberg.
13. Tom Mann, 'Seeing socialism' and Ben Tillett, 'Mighty democracy', *Labour Monthly*, January 1938, pp. 27-30.
14. Mahon, 'A.A. Purcell', p. 103.
15. Sidney and Beatrice Webb, *The History of Trade Unionism*, Longmans, Green & Co, 1896 edn, pp. 463-4.
16. See ch. 1. above.
17. Friedrich Nietszche, trans. R.J. Hollingdale, *Beyond Good and Evil*, Penguin, 2003 edn, #283.
18. Thompson, *The Making of the English Working Class*, Gollancz, 1963, pp. 12-13.
19. See Tony Blair's preface to Anthony Wright, *Socialisms*, Routledge, 1996 edn.
20. Wright, *Socialisms*, p. 136.
21. Charles Tilly, *Popular Contention in Great Britain 1758-1834*, Cambridge, Mass. & London: Harvard University Press, 1995, ch. 8.
22. For the former, see ch. 2 above; for the latter, Claus Offe, 'New social movements: challenging the boundaries of institutional politics', *Social Research*, 52, 4, 1985, pp. 817-68.
23. For Beatrice's misgivings, see *Bolshevism and the British Left*, II, pp. 242-3.
24. David Marquand, *Britain Since 1918. The strange career of British democracy*, Weidenfeld & Nicolson, 2008.

Bibliography

PUBLIC RECORDS (National Archives, Kew)

Cabinet papers (CAB)
Foreign Office (FO)
Decrypted telegrams (HW12)
Ministry of Labour (LAB)

ORGANISATIONAL RECORDS

Amalgamated Union of Building Trade Workers, MRC
Cabinet papers, National Archives
Comintern archives, RGASPI
Communist Party of Great Britain archives, LHASC
Conservative Party archives, Bodleian Library
Dictionary of Labour Biography files, Hull History Centre
Independent Labour Party, BLPES
International Federation of Trade Unions, IISH
International Transportworkers' Federation, MRC
Labour Party archives, LHASC
Labour Party, York DLP, York City Archives
Labour Research Department archives, LRD, London
Labour and Socialist International, IISH
MOPR archives, RGASPI
NAFTA archives, Working Class Movement Library
Profintern archives, RGASPI
Stockport Trades Council and Labour Party records, Stockport Central Library
Transport and General Workers' Union, MRC
TUC archives, MRC

PERSONAL PAPERS

Anatoly Baikalov papers, Columbia University, Rare Book and Manuscript Library
Stanley Baldwin papers, Cambridge University Library
Lord Beaverbrook papers, Parliamentary Archives
J.P. Bedford papers, Nuffield College, Oxford

Alexander Berkman papers, IISH
Siegfried Bettmann papers, Coventry City Record Office
Margaret Bondfield papers, TUC Library, London Metropolitan University
Ben Bradley papers, LHASC
Fred Bramley papers, TUC Library, London Metropolitan University
Walter Citrine papers, BLPES
Richard Crossman papers, MRC
Emma Goldman papers, IISH
Wal Hannington papers, LHASC
G. Allen Hutt papers, LHASC
David Lloyd George papers, Parliamentary Archives
Ramsay MacDonald papers, John Rylands University Library, Manchester
Ramsay MacDonald papers, National Archives
V.K. Krishna Menon papers, Nehru Memorial Library, Delhi
E.D. Morel papers, BLPES
Max Nettlau papers, IISH
H.W. Nevinson papers, Bodleian Library, Oxford
J.T. Walton Newbold papers, John Rylands University Library, Manchester
Philip Noel Baker papers, Churchill College Archives, Cambridge
Graham Pollard papers, Bodleian Library, Oxford
Harry Pollitt papers, LHASC
Arthur Ponsonby papers, Bodleian Library, Oxford
Jack Tanner papers, Nuffield College, Oxford
Dona Torr papers, LHASC
C.P. Trevelyan papers, University of Newcastle Library
Sidney and Beatrice Webb (Passfield) papers, BLPES
William Weir papers, Glasgow University Archives

SECONDARY SOURCES (BOOKS AND ARTICLES)

Peter Ackers, 'More Marxism than Methodism: Hugh Clegg at Kingswood School, Bath (1932-39)', *Socialist History*, 38, 2011

V.L. Allen, *Trade Union Leadership: based on a study of Arthur Deakin*, Longmans, Green & Co, 1957

Perry Anderson, *English Questions*, Verso, 1992

Ralph Anstis, *Four Personalities from the Forest of Dean*, Coleford: Albion House, 1996

Allan Antliff, *Anarchist Modernism. Art, politics and the first American avant-garde*, Chicago & London: University of Chicago Press, 2001

R. Page Arnot, *The Miners: years of struggle. A history of the Miners' Federation of Great Britain (from 1910 onwards)*, Allen & Unwin, 1953

Laura Arrington, 'St John Ervine and the Fabian Society: capital, empire and Irish home rule', *History Workshop Journal*, 72, 1, 2011

John Attfield and John Lee, 'Deptford and Lewisham' in Skelley, *General Strike*

Philip S. Bagwell, *The Railwaymen. The history of the National Union of Railwaymen*, Allen & Unwin, 1963

Rodney Barker, *Education and Politics 1900-1951. A study of the Labour Party*, Oxford: OUP, 1972

Logie Barrow and Ian Bullock, *Democratic Ideas and the British Labour Movement 1880-1914*, Cambridge: CUP, 1996

L.A. Bather, 'A history of the Manchester and Salford Trades Council', Manchester: M Phil, 1956

Nike Bätzner, 'Housing projects of the 1920s. A laboratory of social ideas and formal experiment', in Scheer et al, eds, *City of Architecture, Architecture of the City*

Zygmunt Bauman, trans. Sheila Patterson, *Between Class and Elite. The evolution of the British Labour movement: a sociological study* (1960), Manchester: MUP edn, 1972

Frank Bealey and Henry Pelling, *Labour and Politics 1900-1906. A history of the Labour Representation Committee*, Basingstoke: Macmillan, 1958

Peter Beilharz, *Labour's Utopias. Bolshevism, Fabianism, Social Democracy*, Routledge, 1992

Stefan Berger, 'Working-class culture and the labour movement in the South Wales and the Ruhr coalfields, 1850-2000: a comparison', *Llafur*, 8, 2, 2001

Russell A. Berman, 'Anti-Americanism and Americanization', in Stephan, ed., *Americanization and Anti-Americanism*

Richard Biernacki, *The Fabrication of Labor. Germany and Britain 1640-1914*, University of California Press, 1995

David Blaazer, 'Guild socialists after guild socialism: the Workers' Control Group and the House of Industry League', *Twentieth Century British History*, 11, 2, 2000

David Blaazer, *The Popular Front and the Progressive Tradition. Socialists, Liberals and the quest for unity, 1884-1939*, Cambridge: CUP, 1992

David Blankenhorn, '"Our class of workmen". The Cabinet-makers revisited', in Royden Harrison and Jonathan Zeitlin, eds, *Divisions of Labour. Skilled workers and technological change in nineteenth century England*, Brighton: Harvester, 1985

Gerard Braunthal, *Socialist Labor and Politics in Germany. The General Federation of German Trade Unions*, Hamden, Conn.: Archon Books, 1978

Asa Briggs and John Saville, eds, *Essays in Labour History 1886-1923*, Basingstoke: Macmillan, 1971

Ian Britain, *Fabianism and Culture: A Study in British Socialism and the Arts c. 1884-1918*, Cambridge: CUP, 1982

Jeffrey Brooks, 'The press and its message: images of America in the 1920s and 1930s' in Fitzpatrick et al, *Russia in the Era of NEP*

Sue Bruley, *The Women and Men of 1926. A gender and social history of the General Strike and miners' lockout in South Wales*, Cardiff: University of Wales Press, 2010

Tom Buchanan, *East Wind. China and the British left, 1925-1976*, Oxford: OUP, 2012

Joseph Buckman, *Immigration in the Class Struggle. The Jewish immigrant in Leeds 1880-1914*, Manchester: MUP, 1983

Alan Bullock, *The Life and Times of Ernest Bevin. Volume one: trade union leader, 1881-1940*, Heinemann, 1960

Jane Burbank, *Intelligentsia and Revolution*, New York: OUP, 1986

Daniel F. Calhoun, *The United Front. The TUC and the Russians 1923-1928*, Cambridge: CUP, 1976

John Callaghan, 'British Labour's turn to socialism in 1931', *Journal of Political Ideologies*, 14, 2, 2009

John Callaghan, *Rajani Palme Dutt. A study in British stalinism*, Lawrence & Wishart, 1993

Joan Campbell, *The German Werkbund. The politics of reform in the applied arts*, Princeton University Press, 1978

E.H. Carr, *Socialism in One Country, 1924-1926. Volume 1*, Basingstoke: Macmillan, 1958

E.H. Carr, *Socialism in One Country, 1924-1926. Volume 3*, Harmondsworth: Penguin edn, 1972

Frank Carr, 'Municipal socialism. Labour's rise to power' in Bill Lancaster and Tony Mason, eds, *Life and Labour in a Twentieth Century City: the experience of Coventry*, Coventry: Cryfield Press, n.d.

William J. Chase, *Workers, Society, and the Soviet State. Labor and life in Moscow 1918-1929*, Urbana & Chicago: University of Illinois Press, 1987

Roy Church and Quentin Outram, *Strikes and Solidarity. Coalfield conflict in Britain 1889-1996*, Cambridge: CUP, 1998

Hugh Armstrong Clegg, *A History of British Trade Unions since 1889. Volume 2: 1911-1933*, Oxford: OUP, 1985

Catherine Ann Cline, *E.D. Morel 1873-1924. The strategies of protest*, Belfast: Blackstaff Press, 1980

Catherine Ann Cline, *Recruits to Labour. The British Labour Party 1914-1931*, Syracuse: Syracuse University Press, 1963

Alan Clinton, *The Trade Union Rank and File. Trades councils in Britain 1900-40*, Manchester: MUP, 1977

Jean-Louis Cohen, *Le Corbusier and the Mystique of the USSR. Themes and projects for Moscow 1928-1936*, Princeton University Press, 1992

Stephen F. Cohen, *Bukharin and the Bolshevik Revolution. A political biography 1888-1938*, Oxford: OUP edn, 1980

Peter Dahle Colbenson, 'British socialism and anti-semitism, 1884-1914', Georgia State University: PhD, 1977

G.D.H. Cole, *A History of the Labour Party from 1914*, Routledge & Kegan Paul, 1948

Christine Collette, *The International Faith. Labour's attitudes to European socialism 1918-1939*, Aldershot: Ashgate, 1998

Morton H. Cowden, *Russian Bolshevism and British Labor 1917-1921*, New York: Columbia University Press, 1984

Krista Cowman, *Women of the Right Spirit. Paid organisers of the Women's Social and Political Union (WSPU) 1904-1918*, Manchester: MUP, 2007

James E. Cronin, 'Coping with Labour, 1918-1926' in James E. Cronin and Jonathan Schneer, eds, *Social Conflict and the Political Order in Modern Britain*, Croom Helm, 1982

James E. Cronin, *Industrial Conflict in Modern Britain*, Croom Helm, 1979

James E. Cronin, 'Strikes and the struggle for union organization: Britain and Europe' in Wolfgang J. Mommsen and Hans-Gerhard Husung, eds, *The Development of Trade Unionism in Great Britain and Europe 1880-1914*, Allen & Unwin, 1985

Wilfrid Harris Crook, *The General Strike. A study of labor's tragic weapon in theory and practice*, Chapel Hill: University of North Carolina Press, 1931

Ralph Darlington, 'British syndicalism and trade union officialdom', *Historical Studies in Industrial Relations*, 25/26, 2008

Richard B. Day and Daniel Gaido, eds, *Witnesses to Permanent Revolution. The documentary record*, Chicago: Haymarket edn, 2011

David DeLeon, *The American as Anarchist. Reflections on indigenous radicalism*, Baltimore: Johns Hopkins University Press, 1978

Bernard Donoughue and G.W. Jones, *Herbert Morrison. Portrait of a politician*, Weidenfeld & Nicolson, 1973

Candace Falk et al, eds, *Emma Goldman: a documentary history of the American years. 1. Made for America, 1890-1901*, Berkeley Cal., University of California Press, 2003

Candace Falk et al, eds, *Emma Goldman: a documentary history of the American years. 2. Making Speech Free, 1902-1909*, Berkeley Cal., University of California Press, 2005

Candace Falk, ed., *Emma Goldman. A guide to her life and documentary sources*, Chadwyck Healey, 1991 (microfilm)

Jean-François Fayet, *Karl Radek (1885-1939). Biographie politique*, Bern: Peter Lang, 2004

Barry Feinberg and Ronald Kasrils, eds, *Bertrand Russell's America. His transatlantic travels and writings. Volume one: 1896-1945*, Allen & Unwin, 1973

David Feldman, *Englishmen and Jews. Social relations and political culture 1840-1914*, New Haven & London: Yale University Press, 1994

Orlando Figes, *A People's Tragedy. The Russian Revolution 1891-1924*, Cape, 1996

Leon Fink, *Progressive Intellectuals and the Dilemmas of Democratic Commitment*, Cambridge, Mass.: Harvard University Press, 1997

Georges Fischer, *Le parti travailliste et la décolonisation de l'Inde*, Paris: François Maspero, 1966

Nina Fishman, *The British Communist Party and the Trade Unions, 1933-45*, Aldershot: Scolar, 1995

Nina Fishman, *Arthur Horner: a political biography*, Lawrence & Wishart, 2 vols, 2010

Sheila Fitzpatrick, Alexander Rabinowrich and Richard Stites, eds, *Russia in the Era of NEP. Explorations in Soviet society and culture*, Indiana University Press, 1991

Hwyel Francis and David Smith, *The Fed. A history of the South Wales miners in the twentieth century*, Lawrence & Wishart, 1980

François Furet, trans. Deborah Furet, *The Passing of an Illusion: the idea of communism in the twentieth century*, Chicago & London: University of Chicago Press, 1999,

John Garrard, *Democratisation in Britain. Elites, civil society and reform since 1800*, Basingstoke: Palgrave, 2002

Antonello Gerbi, trans. Jeremy Moyle, *The Dispute of the New World. The history of a polemic 1750-1900*, Pittsburgh: University of Pittsburgh Press, 1955

Martin Gilbert, *Plough My Own Furrow*, Longmans, 1965

Glasgow History Workshop, 'A clash of work regimes: "Americanisation" and the strike at the Singer Sewing Machine Company, 1911' in Kenefick and McIvor, *Roots of Red Clydeside*

Geert Van Goethem, *The Amsterdam International. The world of the International Federation of Trade Unions (IFTU) 1913-1945*, Aldershot: Ashgate, 2006

Geoffrey Goodman, *The Awkward Warrior: Frank Cousins, his life and times*, Davis-Poynter, 1979

José Gotovitch and Mikhaïl Narinsky, eds, *Komintern: l'histoire et les hommes. Dictionnaire biographique de l'Internationale communiste en France, Belgique, au Luxembourg en Suisse et à Moscou (1919-1943)*, Paris: Les Editions de l'Atelier, 2001

C. Desmond Greaves, *The Life and Times of James Connolly*, Lawrence & Wishart, 1972 edn

Halfdan Gregersen, *Ibsen and Spain. A study in comparative drama*, Cambridge, Mass.: Harvard University Press, 1936

W.H. Greenleaf, *Order, Empiricism and Politics. Two traditions of English political thought 1500-1700*, Oxford: OUP, 1964

Gareth Griffith, *Socialism and Superior Brains. The political thought of Bernard Shaw*, Routledge, 1993

Clare Griffiths, *Labour and the Countryside. The politics of rural Britain 1918-1939*, Oxford: OUP, 2007

Richard Griffiths, *Fellow Travellers of the Right. British enthusiasts for Nazi Germany 1933-39*, Oxford: OUP, 1983 edn

Danel Guérin, trans. Mary Klopper, *Anarchism: from theory to practice* (1965), New York & London: Monthly Review Press, 1971

Doris Gunnell, *Stendhal et l'Angleterre*, Paris: Charles Bosse, 1909

Partha Sarathi Gupta, *Imperialism and the British Labour Movement 1914-1964*, New Delhi: Sage Publications, 2002 edn

Jeffrey Harrod *Trade Union Foreign Policy. A study of British and American union activities in Jamaica*, New York: Doubleday & Co, 1972

James Hinton, *The First Shop Stewards' Movement*, Allen & Unwin, 1973

Eric Hobsbawm, 'Working-class internationalism' in van Holthoon and van der Linden, *Internationalism in the Labour Movement*, vol. 1

Paul Hollander, *Political pilgrims: travels of western intellectuals to the Soviet Union, China and Cuba 1928-1978*, New York: Oxford University Press, 1981

Fritz van Holthoon and Marcel van der Linden, eds, *Internationalism in the Labour Movement 1830-1940*, Leiden: Brill, 2 vols, 1988

Bob Holton, *British Syndicalism 1900-1914. Myths and realities*, Pluto, 1976

John Horne and Alan Kramer, *German Atrocities, 1914. A history of denial*, New Haven & London: Yale University Press, 2001

Stephen Howe, *Anticolonialism in British Politics. The left and the end of empire, 1918-1964*, Oxford: OUP, 1993

Stephen Howe, 'Labour and international affairs' in Duncan Tanner, Pat Thane and Nick Tiratsoo, eds, *Labour's First Century*, Cambridge: CUP, 2000

David Howell, *British Workers and the Independent Labour Party 1888-1906*, Manchester: MUP, 1983

David Howell, *MacDonald's Party. Labour identities and crisis*, Oxford: OUP, 2002

David Howell, *Respectable Radicals. Studies in the politics of railway trade unionism*, Aldershot: Ashgate, 1999

Richard Hyman, *Strikes*, Fontana, 1977 edn

Ben Jackson, *Equality and the British Left. A study in progressive thought 1900-64*, Manchester: MUP, 2007

Martin Jacques, 'Consequences of the General Strike' in Skelley, *General Strike*

Robert Rhodes James, *Bob Boothby. A portrait*, Hodder & Stoughton, 1991

Jeremy Jennings, *Syndicalism in France. A study of ideas*, Basingstoke: Macmillan, 1990

Edward P. Johanningsmeier, *The Forging of American Communism. The life of William Z. Foster*, Princeton, N.J.: Princeton University Press, 1994

Gareth Stedman Jones, *Outcast London. A study in the relationship between classes in Victorian society*, Penguin edn, 1984

Raymond A. Jones, *Arthur Ponsonby. The politics of life*, Christopher Helm, 1989

Pernilla Jonsson, 'On women's account: the finances of "bourgeois" women's organizations in Sweden, England, Germany, and Canada, 1885-1924' in Jonsson, Neunsinger and Sangster, *Crossing Boundaries*

Pernilla Jonsson, Silke Neunsinger and Joan Sangster, eds, *Crossing Boundaries. Women's organizing in Europe and the Americas 1880s-1940s*, Upssala: Upssala University, 2007

Michael Kazin, *A Godly Hero: the life of William Jennings Bryan*, New York: Alfred Knopf, 2006

John Kelly, *Trade Unions and Socialist Politics*, Verso, 1988

John Kelly and Edmund Heery, *Working for the Union: British trade union officers*, Cambridge University Press, 1994

William Kenefick and Arthur McIvor, *Roots of Red Clydeside 1900-1914? Labour unrest and industrial relations in West Scotland*, Edinburgh: John Donald, 1996

V.G. Kiernan, *Marxism and Imperialism*, Edward Arnold, 1974

James Klugmann, *History of the Communist Party of Great Britain. Volume one: formation and early years 1919-1924*, Lawrence & Wishart, 1967

James Klugmann, *History of the Communist Party of Great Britain. Volume two: the General Strike 1925-1926*, Lawrence & Wishart, 1969

James Klugmann, 'Marxism, reformism and the General Strike' in Skelley, *General Strike*

William Knox, ed., *Scottish Labour Leaders 1918-1939. A biographical dictionary*, Edinburgh: Mainstream, 1984

Sigfrid Koch-Baumgarten, 'Edo Fimmen – iron fist in a silken glove: a biographical sketch' in Reinalda, *The International Transportworkers' Federation*

Conor Kostick, *Revolution in Ireland: popular militancy 1917-1923*, Pluto, 1996

Nicholas N. Kozlov and Eric D. Weitz, 'Reflections on the origins of the "Third Period": Bukharin, the Comintern and the political economy of Weimar Germany', *Journal of Contemporary History*, 24, 1989

Isaac Kramnick and Barry Sheerman, *Harold Laski. A life on the left*, Hamish Hamilton, 1993

Rob Kroes, 'The Great Satan versus the Evil Empire. Anti-Americanism in the Netherlands' in Kroes and van Rossem, *Anti-Americanism in Europe*

Rob Kroes and Maarten van Rossem, eds, *Anti-Americanism in Europe*, Amsterdam: Free University Press, 1986

Norman LaPorte, *The German Communist Party in Saxony, 1924-1933: factionalism, fratricide and political failure*, Bern: Peter Lang, 2003

Cheryl Law, *Suffrage and Power. The women's movement 1918-1928*, I.B. Tauris, 1997

Jon Lawrence, *Speaking for the People. Party, language and popular politics in England, 1867-1914*, Cambridge: CUP, 1998

Keith Laybourn, *The General Strike 1926*, Manchester: MUP, 1993

Marc Lazar, *Le Communisme: une passion française*, Paris: Perrin, 2005 edn

H.W. Lee and E. Archbold, *Social Democracy in Britain. Fifty years of the socialist movement*, SDF, 1935

F.M. Leventhal, *The Last Dissenter. H.N. Brailsford and his world*, Oxford: OUP, 1985

Moshe Lewin, 'Pourquoi l'Union soviétique a fasciné le monde' (1997) in *Manière de voir: le Monde diplomatique*, 100, 2008

André Liebich, *From the Other Shore. Russian Social Democracy after 1921*, Cambridge, Mass.: Harvard University Press, 1997

Marcel Liebman, 'La pratique de la grève générale dans le Parti ouvrier belge jusqu'en 1914', *Le Mouvement social*, 58, 1967

Marcel van der Linden, 'Second thoughts on revolutionary syndicalism', *Labour History Review*, 63, 2, 1998

Marcel van der Linden and Wayne Thorpe, eds, *Revolutionary Syndicalism. An international perspective*, Aldershot: Scolar Press, 1990

Marcel van der Linden and Wayne Thorpe, 'The rise and fall of revolutionary syndicalism' in van der Linden and Thorpe, *Revolutionary Syndicalism*

Thomas Linehan, *British Fascism 1918-39. Parties, ideology and culture*, Manchester: MUP, 2000

John Lloyd, *Light and Liberty. The history of the Electrical, Electronic, Telecommunication and Plumbing Union*m Weidenfeld & Nicolson, 1990

John Logue, *Toward a Theory of Trade Union Internationalism*, Gothenburg: University of Gothenburg, 1980

Lewis L. Lorwin, *Labor and Internationalism*, New York: Macmillan, 1929

John Lovell, 'The TUC Special Industrial Committee: January-April 1926' in Asa Briggs and John Saville, eds, *Essays in Labour History 1918-1939*, Croom Helm, 1977

Ian MacDougall, ed., *Militant Miners*, Edinburgh: Polygon, 1981

L.J. Macfarlane, *The British Communist Party. Its origin and development until 1929*, MacGibbon & Kee, 1966

Stuart Macintyre, *A Proletarian Science. Marxism in Britain, 1917-1933*, Cambridge: CUP, 1980

Norman Mackenzie, ed., *The Letters of Sidney and Beatrice Webb*, vol 3, Cambridge: CUP, 1978

Declan McHugh, *Labour in the City. The development of the Labour Party in Manchester, 1918-31*, Manchester: MUP, 2006

Arthur McIvor, 'Were Clydeside employers more autocratic? Labour management and the "labour unrest", c1910-1914' in Kenefick and McIvor, *Roots of Red Clydeside*

Ross McKibbin, 'Arthur Henderson as Labour leader' in McKibbin, *The Ideologies of Class*

Ross McKibbin, *The Evolution of the Labour Party, 1910-1924*, Oxford: OUP, 1983 edn

Ross McKibbin, *The Ideologies of Class. Social relations in Britain 1880-1950*, Oxford: OUP, 1991

Ross McKibbin, 'Why was there no marxism in Britain?' in McKibbin, *The Ideologies of Class*

Sean McMeekin, *The Red Millionaire. A political biography of Willy Münzenberg, Moscow's secret propaganda tsar in the west*, New Haven & London: Yale University Press, 2005

Charles S. Maier, 'Between Taylorism and technocracy. European ideologies and the vision of industrial productivity in the 1920s', *Journal of Contemporary History*, 5, 27, 1970

Sylvia R Margulies, *The Pilgrimage to Russia. The Soviet Union and the treatment of foreigners, 1924-1937*, Madison, Wisconsin: University of Wisconsin Press, 1968

David Marquand, *Britain Since 1918. The strange career of British democracy*, Weidenfeld & Nicolson, 2008

David Marquand, *Ramsay MacDonald*, Jonathan Cape, 1977

Arthur Marsh and Victoria Ryan, *Historical Directory of Trade Unions*, vol. 3, Aldershot: Gower, 1987

Peter Marshall, *Demanding the Impossible. A history of anarchism*, HarperCollins, 1993 edn

Roderick Martin, *Communism and the British Trade Unions 1924-1933. A study of the National Minority Movement*, Oxford: OUP, 1969

Ross M. Martin, *TUC: the growth of a pressure group 1868-1976*, Oxford: OUP, 1980

Arthur Marwick, *Clifford Allen. The open conspirator*, Oliver & Boyd, 1964

Doreen Massey, *Space, Place and Gender*, Cambridge: Polity, 1994

Frank Matthews, 'The building guilds' in Briggs and Saville, *Essays in Labour History 1886-1923*

Rachel Mazuy, *Croire plutôt que voire? Voyages en Russie soviétique (1919-1939)*, Paris: Odile Jacob, 2002

Joël Michel, 'Corporatisme et internationalisme chez les mineurs européens avant 1914' in van Holthoon and van der Linden, eds, *Internationalism in the Labour Movement 1830-1940*

Keith Middlemas and John Barnes, *Baldwin. A biography*, Weidenfeld & Nicolson, 1969

Robert Keith Middlemass, *The Clydesiders. A left wing struggle for parliamentary power*, Hutchinsons, 1965

David Miller, *Anarchism*, London & Melbourne: Dent, 1984

Barbara Miller Lane, *Architecture and Politics in Germany 1918-1945*, Cambridge, Mass.: Harvard UP, 1968

C. Wright Mills, *White Collar. The American middle classes* (1951), New York: Oxford University Press, 1956 edn

Susan Milner, *The Dilemmas of Internationalism. French syndicalism and the international labour movement 1900-1914*, Oxford: Berg, 1990

Lewis Minkin, *The Contentious Alliance. Trade unions and the Labour Party*, Edinburgh: Edinburgh University Press, 1991

Barbara Mitchell, 'French syndicalism: an experiment in practical anarchism' in van der Linden and Thorpe, *Revolutionary Syndicalism*

David Montgomery, *The Fall of the House of Labor. The workplace, the state and American labor activism 1865-1925*, Cambridge: CUP, 1987

James Moran, *Natsopa: seventy-five years. The National Society of Operative Printers and Assistants (1889-1964)*, Heinemann, 1964

Kevin Morgan, *Against Fascism and War. Ruptures and continuities in British communist politics 1935-41*, Manchester: MUP, 1989

Kevin Morgan, 'A splendid field? Emma Goldman in South Wales', *Llafur*, 10, 1, 2008

Kevin Morgan, 'British guild socialists and the exemplar of the Panama Canal', *History of Political Thought*, 28, 1, 2007

Kevin Morgan, '"Colourless, dry and dull": why British trade unionists lack biographers and what (if anything) should be done about it', *Journal for the History of Social Movements/Zeitschrift für die Geschichte sozialer Bewegungen*, 2013

Kevin Morgan, 'Cutting the feet from under organised labour? Lord Weir, mass production and the building trades in the 1920s', *Scottish Labour History*, 43, 2008

Kevin Morgan, 'Heralds of the future? Emma Goldman, Friedrich Nietzsche and the anarchist as superman', *Anarchist Studies*, 17, 2, 2009

Kevin Morgan, *Harry Pollitt*, Manchester: MUP, 1993

Kevin Morgan, 'The problem of the epoch? Labour and housing, 1918-1951', *Twentieth Century British History*, 16, 3, 2005

Kevin Morgan, *Ramsay MacDonald*, Haus, 2006

Theresa Moritz and Albert Moritz, *The World's Most Dangerous Woman. A new biography of Emma Goldman*, Toronto: Subway Books, 2001

Dylan Morris, 'Labour or socialism: opposition and dissent within the

Independent Labour Party 1906-1914 with special reference to the Lancashire division', Manchester, PhD, 1982

Margaret Morris, *The General Strike*, Harmondsworth: Penguin, 1976

Charles Loch Mowat, *Britain Between the Wars 1918-1940*, Methuen, 1968 edn

Bruno Naarden, *Socialist Europe and Revolutionary Russia: perception and prejudice 1848-1923*, Cambridge: CUP, 1992

Tom Nairn, *The Left Against Europe?*, Harmondsworth: Penguin, 1973

Douglas J. Newton, *British Labour, European Socialism and the Struggle for Peace 1889-1914*, Oxford: OUP, 1985

Kenneth Newton, *The Sociology of British Communism*, Allen Lane, 1969

Marjorie Nicholson, *The TUC Overseas. The roots of policy*, Allen & Unwin, 1984

Claus Offe, 'New social movements: challenging the boundaries of institutional politics', *Social Research*, 52, 4, 1985

Emmet O'Connor, '"Sentries of British imperialism?" The question of British-based unions in Ireland', *Socialist History*, 29, 2006

M. Ostrogorski, *Democracy and the Organization of Political Parties*, trans. Frederick Clarke, Macmillan, 1902

Jean-Michel Palmier, trans. David Fernbach, *Weimar in Exile. The antifascist emigration in Europe and America*, Verso, 2006

Nicholas Papayanis, *Alphone Merrheim. The emergence of reformism in revolutionary syndicalism 1871-1925*, Dordrecht: Martinus Nijhoff, 1985

Henry Pelling, *Origins of the Labour Party*, Oxford: OUP edn, 1966

Bradford Perkins, *The Great Rapprochement. England and the United States 1895-1914*, Gollancz, 1969

Larry Peterson, 'Internationalism and the British coal miners strike of 1926: the solidarity campaign of the KPD among the Ruhr miners' in van Holthoon and van der Linden, *Internationalism in the Labour Movement 1830-1940*

Nikolaus Pevsner, *Pioneers of Modern Design. From William Morris to Walter Gropius*, Harmondsworth: Penguin, 1960 edn

G.A. Phillips, *The General Strike. The politics of industrial conflict*, Weidenfeld & Nicolson, 1976

Ben Pimlott, *Labour and the Left in the 1930s*, Allen & Unwin, 1986 edn

Richard Pipes, *Russia under the Bolshevik Regime 1919-1924*, Fontana Press, 1995 edn

Richard Pipes, ed., *The Unknown Lenin. From the secret archive*, New Haven & London: Yale University Press, 1997

Bernard Porter, 'Fabians, imperialists and the international order' in Ben Pimlott, ed., *Fabian Essays in Socialist Thought*, Heinemann, 1984

Greg Power, *Representatives of the People? The constituency role of MPs*, Fabian Society, 1998
Branko Pribićević, *The Shop Stewards Movement and Workers' Control 1910-1922*, Oxford: Blackwells, 1959
Richard Price, 'Contextualising British syndicalism, c.1907-c.1920', *Labour History Review*, 63, 3, 1998
Richard Price, *Masters, Unions and Men: work control in building and the rise of labour 1830-1914*, Cambridge: CUP, 1980
Richard Price, '"What's in a name?" Workplace history and "rank and filism"', *International Review of Social History*, 34, 1989
I.J. Prothero, *Artisans and Politics in early Nineteenth-Century London: John Gast and his times*, Folkestone: Dawson, 1979
John Quail, *The Slow Burning Fuse. The lost history of the British anarchists*, Paladin Books, 1978
Pierre Broué, *Rakovsky ou la Révolution dans tous les pays*, Paris: Fayard, 1996
W.J. Reader, *Architect of Air Power. The life of the first Viscount Weir of Eastwood 1877-1959*, Collins, 1968
Hew Reid, *The Furniture Makers. A history of trade unionism in the furniture trade 1865-1972*, Oxford: Malthouse Press, 1986
Bob Reinalda, 'The early years of the ITF (1896-1914)' in Reinalda, *International Transportworkers' Federation*
Bob Reinalda, ed., *The International Transportworkers' Federation: the Edo Fimmen era*, Amsterdam: IISG, 1997
Bob Reinalda, 'Interruption of internationalism: the ITF during World War One and its new start in 1919' in Reinalda, *International Transportworkers' Federation*
Bob Reinalda, 'The ITF and the non-European world' in Reinalda, *International Transportworkers' Federation*
Patrick Renshaw, *The General Strike*, Eyre Methuen, 1975
R.C. Rheiners, 'Racialism on the left: ED Morel and the "Black Horror" on the Rhine', *International Review of Social History*, 13, 1968
Joan Sangster, 'Crossing boundaries: women's organizing in Europe and the Americas 1880s-1940s' in Jonsson, Neunsinger and Sangster, *Crossing Boundaries*
Joan Sangster, 'Political tourism, writing and communication; transnational connections of women on the left, 1920s-1940s' in Jonsson, Neunsinger and Sangster, *Crossing Boundaries*
Thorsten Scheer, Josef Paul Kleihues and Paul Kahlfeldt, eds, *City of Architecture, Architecture of the City: Berlin, 1900-2000*, Berlin: Nicolai, 2000
Jonathan Schneer, *Ben Tillett. Portrait of a Labour leader*, Croom Helm, 1982
Mark Schorer, *Sinclair Lewis. An American life*, New York: McGraw Hill, 1961

Carl E. Schorske, *German Social Democracy 1905-1917. The development of the great schism*, Cambridge, Mass.: Harvard University Press, 1955

Bill Schwarz, '"The people in history". The Communist Party Historians' Group, 1946-1956' in Richard Johnson et al, eds, *Making Histories. Studies in history-writing and politics*, Hutchinson, 1982

Tedor Shanin, ed., *Late Marx and the Russian Road. 'Marx and the peripheries of capitalism'*, Routledge & Kegan Paul, 1983

Mark Shipway, *Anti-Parliamentary Communism. The movement for workers' councils in Britain, 1917-45*, Basingstoke: Macmillan, 1988

Jeffrey Skelley, ed., *The General Strike, 1926*, Lawrence & Wishart, 1976

Robert Skidelsky, *Oswald Mosley*, Macmillan, 1981 edn

Robert Skidelsky, *Politicians and the Slump. The Labour government of 1929-1931*, Macmillan, 1967

Quentin Skinner, 'Interpretation, rationality and truth' in Skinner, *Visions of Politics. Volume one: regarding method*, Cambridge: CUP, 2002

Sheldon Spear, 'Pacifist radicalism in the post-war British Labour Party: the case of E.D. Morel, 1919-24', *International Review of Social History*, 23, 2, 1978

Henry Srebrnik, *London Jews and British Communism 1935-1945*, Valentine Mitchell, 1995

E.D. Steele, 'Imperialism and Leeds politics, c. 1850-1914' in Derek Fraser, ed., *A History of Modern Leeds*, Manchester: MUP, 1980

Alexander Stephan, ed., *Americanization and Anti-Americanism. The German encounter with American culture after 1945*, New York and Oxford: Bergahn Books, 2005

Richard Stites, *Revolutionary Dreams. Utopian vision and experimental life in the Russian revolution*, New York: OUP, 1989

Mary Stocks, *Ernest Simon of Manchester*, Manchester: MUP, 1963

Brigitte Studer, *Un parti sous influence. Le parti communists suisse, une section du Komintern 1931 à 1939*, Lausanne: L'Age d'Homme, 1994

Geoffrey Swain, 'Was the Profintern really necessary?', *European History Quarterly*, 17, 1987

Marvin Swartz, *The Union of Democratic Control in British Politics during the First World War*, Oxford: OUP, 1971

Mark Swenarton, *Homes Fit for Heroes. The architecture and planning of early state housing in Britain*, Heinemann, 1981

Duncan Tanner, *Political Change and the Labour Party 1900-1918*, Cambridge: CUP, 1990

Robert Taylor, 'Citrine's unexpurgated diaries, 1925-26: the mining crisis and the national strike', *Historical Studies in Industrial Relations*, 20, 2005

Robert Taylor, *The TUC: from the General Strike to New Unionism*, Basingstoke: Palgrave, 2000.

E.P. Thompson, *William Morris. Romantic to revolutionary*, Lawrence & Wishart, 1955
Andrew Thorpe, *The British Communist Party and Moscow, 1920-43*, Manchester: MUP, 2000
Andrew Thorpe, 'Nina Fishman's Arthur Horner and labour and political biography', *Socialist History*, 38, 2011
Andrew Thorpe, 'Stalinism and British politics', *History*, 83, 1998
Wayne Thorpe, *'The Workers Themselves'. Revolutionary syndicalism and international labour, 1913-1923*, Dordrecht: Kluwer Academic Publishers, 1989
Charles Tilly, *Popular Contention in Great Britain 1758-1834*, Cambridge, Mass. & London: Harvard University Press, 1995
Dona Torr, *Tom Mann and his Times. Volume one: 1856-1890*, Lawrence & Wishart, 1956
Reiner Tosstorff, *Profintern. Die Rote Gewerkschaftsinternationale 1920-1937*, Paderborn: Schoeningh, 2004
Reiner Tosstorff, 'Unity between "Amsterdam" and "Moscow"? Edo Fimmen's relationship to the communist trade union movement' in Reinalda, *International Transportworkers' Federation*
Chushichi Tsuzuki, *H.M. Hyndman and British Socialism*, Oxford; OUP, 1961
Chushichi Tsuzuki, *Tom Mann, 1856-1941. The challenges of Labour*, Oxford: OUP, 1991
H.A. Tulloch, 'Changing British attitudes to the United States in the 1880s', *Historical Journal*, 20, 4, 1977
Rozina Visram, *Asians in Britain. 400 years of history*, Pluto, 2002
Graham Walker, *Thomas Johnston*, Manchester: MUP, 1988
Peter Weiler, *Ernest Bevin*, Manchester: MUP, 1993
Eric D. Weitz, *Creating German Communism 1890-1990: from popular protest to socialist state*, Princeton University Press, 1997
Alice Wexler, *Emma Goldman; an intimate life*, New York: Pantheon Books, 1984
Alice Wexler, *Emma Goldman in Exile. From the Russian Revolution to the Spanish Civil War*, Boston, Mass.: Beacon Press, 1989
Joseph White, 'Syndicalism in a mature industrial setting: the case of Britain' in van der Linden and Thorpe, *Revolutionary Syndicalism*
Joseph White, *Tom Mann*, Manchester: MUP, 1991
Stephen White, *Britain and the Bolshevik Revolution. A study in the politics of diplomacy 1920-1924*, Macmillan, 1979
Stephen White, 'British Labour in Soviet Russia, 1920', *English Historical Review*, 1994
Kevin Whitston, 'Worker resistance and Taylorism in Britain', *International Review of Social History*, 42, 1997
John Willett, *The New Sobriety. Art and politics in the Weimar period 1917-1933*, Thames & Hudson, 1978
Andrew J. Williams, *Labour and Russia. The attitude of the Labour*

Party to the USSR, Manchester: MUP, 1989

Andrew J. Williams, *Trading with the Bolsheviks. The politics of East-West trade 1920-39*, Manchester: MUP, 1992

Philip M. Williams, *Hugh Gaitskell. A political biography*, Cape, 1979

Elizabeth Williamson et al, *The Buildings of Scotland: Glasgow*, Penguin, 1990

Philip Williamson, *Stanley Baldwin. Conservative Leadership and National Values*, Cambridge: CUP, 1999

John Carter Wood, *The Most Remarkable Woman in England. Poison, celebrity and the trials of Beatrice Pace*, Manchester: MUP, 2012

George Woodcock, *Anarchism. A history of libertarian ideas and movements*, Harmondsworth: Penguin, 1975 edn

George Woodcock and Ivan Avakumović, *The Anarchist Prince. A biographical study of Peter Kropotkin*, New York: Schocken Books edn, 1971

T. Woodhouse, 'The working class' in Derek Fraser, ed., *A History of Modern Leeds*, Manchester: MUP, 1980

Matthew Worley, *Labour Inside the Gate. A history of the British Labour Party between the wars*, IB Tauris, 2008 edn

A.W. Wright, *G.D.H. Cole and Socialist Democracy*, Oxford: OUP, 1979

Jonathan Zeitlin, '"Rank and filism" and labour history: a rejoinder to Price and Cronin', *International Review of Social History*, 34, 1989

Jonathan Zeitlin, '"Rank and filism" in British labour history: a critique', *International Review of Social History*, 34, 1989

Timeline

	Purcell	British labour movement	National and International politics
1870-9	(1872) Born Hoxton, 3 November		
1880-9		(1884) H.M. Hyndman's Democratic Federation becomes the SDF (later SDP)	
			(1887) Trial and execution of Haymarket martyrs, USA
	(c1888) 'Converted' to socialist movement		(1888) International trade union congress, London 1890-9
1890-9	(1891) Joins London French Polishers' Union		
	(1893) Propaganda work for Legal Eight Hours and International Labour League	(1893) ILP formed	(1893) Zurich congress of Second International
			(1894) First exchange of fraternal delegates between TUC and AFL
	(c1895-6) Joins SDF		
	(1896) Delegate to London congress of Second International		(1896) London congress of Second International
	(1897) Marries Sarah Fidler		
	(1898) London French Polishers amalgamated into ASFP, AAP as general secretary		
1900-9	(1900) Moves to Manchester with ASFP	(1900) Labour Representation Committee formed	

Timeline

	Purcell	British labour movement	National and International politics
			(1901) Assassination of US president McKinley
	(1902) Delegate to Manchester and Salford Trades Council	(1902) Mosely industrial commission to USA (1902) NAFTA formed	
			(1904) International Union of Woodworkers formed
	(1905-7) First of several stints as chairman or vice-chairman of MSTC		(1905) Massacre of peaceful demonstrators in St Petersburg ('Bloody Sunday')
	(1906) Elected Salford city councillor	(1906) January general election returns twenty-nine LRC MPs including NAFTA-sponsored candidate James O'Grady; LRC becomes the Labour Party	
			(1907) International anarchist congress, Amsterdam
	(1909) Withdraws from LRC nomination West Salford		
1910	(January) Defeated as socialist parliamentary candidate West Salford		
		(May) Tom Mann returns to Britain	
	(July) Addresses Manchester meeting with Tom Mann: 'the best thing I was ever associated with'		
	(November) Chairs first conference of ISEL, Manchester	(November) Troops shoot on demonstrators at Tonypandy	
	(December) ASFP amalgamation with NAFTA, Purcell as trade organiser		

Timeline

	Purcell	British labour movement	National and International politics
1911		(September-October) 'Socialist unity' conference: SDP merges into BSP	
1912		*Miners' Next Step* published by Unofficial Reform Committee	
1913		(September) 'Triple Industrial Alliance' of Miners, Railwaymen's and Transport Workers' unions initiated through resolution of MFGB	(September-October) International syndicalist congress, London
	(November) Organises support for thirteen-week. Furnishing Trades' lockout begins, High Wycombe		
	(December) Fails to stand for re-election as Salford city councillor		
1914			Majority of socialist parties support their governments on the outbreak of European war
1915		(March) NAFTA anti-war manifesto signed by Bramley and Gossip	
		(September) McKenna budget introduces duties on select imported luxury goods	
1916			
1917	(March) Welcomes first Russian revolution at Manchester meeting	Fred Bramley elected TUC assistant secretary	(March) 'February' revolution in Russia overthrows Tsarism
			(November) 'October' revolution in Russia inaugurates Bolshevik rule

Timeline

	Purcell	British labour movement	National and International politics
1918	(September) Attends TUC as NAFTA delegate	(January/February) Labour Party adopts new constitution	
		(spring) National Federation of Building Trades Operatives formed without NAFTA participation	
			(November) Revolution in Germany, end of First World War
1919		(January) London (later national) Hands Off Russia committee formed	
	(February) Attends meeting of Belfast strike committee		(March) Communist International founded
		(July) Building subsidies introduced under Addison Housing Act	(July) IFTU re-established at Amsterdam; Fimmen and Oudegeest appointed joint secretaries
		(July–Sept) Partial national lockout of Furnishing Trades	
			(August) Promulgation of Weimar republic in Germany
	(September) Elected to TUC parliamentary committee (later general council)		
1920		(January) Manchester Building Guild formed	
	(May–June) Member British Labour delegation to Soviet Russia		
			(June) Zinoviev announces 'Red Industrial International'
	(July–August) Attends CPGB foundation congress as delegate of South Salford BSP	(July–August) CPGB founded	(July–August) Comintern Second Congress

	Purcell	British labour movement	National and International politics
1921		(August) Council of Action threatens general strike over intervention in Russia	(November) Second International relocates to London
		(January) British Bureau of 'Provisional International Council of Trade and Industrial Unions' (RILU) issues first manifesto	
			(February-March) Suppression by Bolsheviks of Kronstadt rising and Menshevik government in Georgia
		(April) Triple Industrial Alliance collapses on 'Black Friday'; Robert Williams expelled from CPGB	
		(June) National Building Guild established, Manchester	(June-July) Comintern Third Congress signals switch to united front
		(September) TUC general council formed	
1922		(January) Transport & General Workers' Union formed	
	(February) Attends conference of five west European socialist parties, Frankfurt		
	(February) Furniture and Furnishing Guild established; Purcell is secretary		
		(March-June) National engineering lockout	(March) Conference of the 'three internationals', Berlin
			(June-August) 'Show trial' of Social Revolutionaries, Moscow

Timeline

	Purcell	British labour movement	National and International politics
		(November) Ramsay MacDonald elected Labour Party leader	(November) Henry Ford's *My Life and Work* published in Britain
			(November-December) Comintern Fourth Congress
		(December) Second National Guilds Conference	
1923	(January) Furniture and Furnishing Guild wound up		(January) French occupation of the Ruhr; German hyper-inflation
			(May) British government's 'Curzon ultimatum' to the Soviets
			(May) LSI founding congress, Hamburg
			(November) Edo Fimmen forced into resigning as IFTU secretary
	(December) Elected MP for Coventry	(December) General election produces no overall majority; Labour the largest party	
1924	(January) Succeeds Margaret Bondfield as TUC chairman	(January) First (minority) Labour government formed	(January) Death of Lenin Soviet embassy re-established at Chesham House
			(April) Dawes plan for repayment of reparations
		(May) Snowden's first Labour budget repeals McKenna duties	
	(June) Confirmed as IFTU president		(June) IFTU Vienna Congress
			(June-July) Fifth Comintern congress
		(August) Wheatley Housing Act based on consultations with building industry	(August) Bolsheviks put down rising in Georgia

Purcell	British labour movement	National and International politics
	(August) National Minority Movement formed	
(September) Chairs Hull TUC	(September) Emma Goldman arrives in London	
	(September) Tomsky addresses Hull TUC as fraternal delegate	
(October) Loses parliamentary seat in Coventry	(October) General election returns Conservative majority; Baldwin government formed	
(November-December) Chairs TUC delegation to Soviet Russia		(December) Death of Samuel Gompers

1925

Purcell	British labour movement	National and International politics
	(March) *Sunday Worker* launched	
(April) Launches *Trade Union Unity* with George Hicks and Edo Fimmen		
(June) Wins Forest of Dean by-election		(May) Shanghai general strike
	(July) First Commonwealth Labour Conference	
	(July) Government agrees temporary coal subsidy following threatened TUC embargo ('Red Friday')	
	(September) Scarborough TUC signals support for left policies; Ernest Bevin elected to general council	
	(October) Fred Bramley dies; replaced as TUC secretary by Walter Citrine	
(October-November) Fraternal delegate to AFL, Atlanta City, followed by American speaking tour	(October) Arrest and conviction of twelve communist leaders on sedition charges	

Timeline

	Purcell	British labour movement	National and International politics
1926		(March-April) *Daily Mail* 'trade union mission' to USA	
	(April-May) Chairs TUC Ways and Means Committee (later Strike Organisation Committee)		
		(May) General Strike called and called off	
		(May) Emma Goldman leaves Britain	
	(May-November) Fundraising activities for the miners including two visits to Continental Europe	(May-November) Continuing miners' lockout	
			(June) Russian unions condemn 'betrayal' of General Strike
		(September) Publication of ILP's Living Wage policy	
		(September) Bournemouth TUC rejects criticisms of Russian unions	
1927		(January) TUC conference of executives to consider General Strike	
			(February) League Against Imperialism founding conference, Brussels
			(June) Condemnation of Soviet reprisals following shooting in Warsaw of ambassador Voikov
	(August) Causes storm with presidential address to IFTU Paris congress; removed as IFTU president		(August) IFTU Paris congress; Purcell removed as president and Oudegeest as secretary
	(November-March 1928) TUC delegation to India	(November) Government appoints Simon Commission on India	

	Purcell	British labour movement	National and International politics
1928	(May) Fails to secure election as NAFTA delegate to TUC; loses eligibility for TUC general council		
	(May) Withdraws nomination as IFTU president; succeeded by Citrine		(July–September) Sixth Comintern Congress confirms turn to independent revolutionary leadership
1929			(March) Meerut arrests, India
			(April) Adoption of first Five Year Plan, USSR
	(May) Contests Moss Side in general election; loses	(May) Election produces no overall majority; Labour forms second minority government	
	(September) Full-time secretary Manchester and Salford Trades Council		
1930-9	(1931) Organises 'People's Congress', Manchester	(1931) Fall of second Labour government	
	(1933) Third visit to the USSR		(1933) Nazism in power in Germany; destroys labour movement
			(1934) Kirov murder prelude to Soviet terror
	(1935) Dies in Crumpsall, 24 December	(1935) Webbs publish *Soviet Communism*	
		(1936) Citrine publishes *I Search for Truth in Russia*	(1936) First Moscow show trial
			(1937) Suicide of Tomsky

Index

Ablett, Noah, 33
Abramovich, Rafail, 126, 162, 180, 291
Accrington, Lancs, 37, 39
Adler, Friedrich, 120, 125, 138-9, 143, 156, 163, 172, 177, 282, 295
All-Russian Central Council of Trade Unions (ARCCTU), 147
All-Russian Co-operative Society (Arcos), 266
Allen, Clifford, 117, 119, 121, 126, 174
Allen, Jim, *Days of Hope*, 12
Alliance Cabinet-Makers' Association (ACMA), 34, 44
American Federation of Labour (AFL), 58, 114, 169, 205, 209, 220, 222, 284, 294
  AAP as fraternal delegate (1925), 140, 199, 218-21, 282, 283
  and German labour movement, 217-18,
  and TUC, 217-22
anarchism/anarchists, 29, 115, 118, 130, 161, 163-4, 183
  international congresses (1907), 161; *see also* individual anarchists
Anglo-Russian Parliamentary Committee (ARPC), 53, 71, 129, 295
Appleton, W.A., 94, 222
Armitage, J.R., 81, 85
Arnold, Matthew, 213-14, 216

Arnot, Robin Page, 71, 235
Astor, Lady, 183-4
Attlee, Clement, 286, 296
Austria/Austrians
  communist party, 138
  Social Democratic Labour Party, 138, 172
Aveling, Edward, 28

Baikalov, Anatoly, 292, 295
Baldwin, Roger, 165-6
Baldwin, Stanley, 13, 16, 84, 175, 204-5, 208, 222
Barnes, Alfred, 204-5, 22
Barron, Thomas 207, 210
Bath constituency, 81
Beauchamp, Joan, 72
Beaverbrook, Lord, 166
Beech, Dick, 117
Belfast
  furnishing trades in, 47
  general strike (1919), 47, 53
Berkman, Alexander, 118-20, 156-60 *passim*, 166, 171, 183, 188 n.95
Berlioz, Joanny, 137
Bettmann, Siegfried, 82
Bevin, Ernest, 13, 35, 86, 102 n.172, 222
  as architect of General Strike, 252-7
  ideas of solidarity and solidarity actions, 239, 243-7, 264
  role in General Strike, 233-4, 257-61, 267
  and TUC general council, 92-3, 244-6

biography, trade unionists', compared and discussed, 13-18, 158, 233, 293, 306-7
'Black Friday', 64, 67, 243, 248
blacklegs, 44, 85, 249; *see also* furnishing trades
Bondfield, Margaret, 23, 86, 116, 168, 216, 222, 246
Borodin, Mikhail, 71
Bowerman, C.W., 91
Bowman, Guy, 31, 90
boxing, AAP and, 28
boycott as union tactic, 38, 44, 108
Brailsford, H. N., 49, 126, 139, 163, 165, 175, 178, 211, 214, 216
Bramley, Fred, 19, 87, 89, 112, 116, 139, 169, 179, 207, 223, 241, 246
  biographical details, 35, 293
  internationalist attitudes, 49-50, 52,
  as NAFTA organiser, 36, 38-40, 43-5
  as TUC assistant secretary and secretary, 91-5, 113
  and TUC Russian delegation, 1924, 128-36, 174-5
  and Workers' Educational Association, 104
Bristol, 35, 294
Bristol North constituency, 81
British Committee for the Defence of Political Prisoners in Russia, 156, 161-6, 169, 170-1
British Drama League, 183
British Socialist Party (BSP), 32, 66-7, 71-2, 117
Brockway, Fenner, 283, 286, 289, 296
Bromley, John, 23, 70, 130, 249, 254, 259, 262, 267
Brown, J.W.,136, 220, 281-3, 289
Bryan, William Jennings, 159

building industry/building trades, 33, 74-5, 206-8, 213
Building Trades Operatives, National Federation of (NFBTO), 37, 74, 255
Building Trade Workers, Amalgamated Union of (AUBTW), 92, 253, 255, 277 n.233
  in General Strike, 261
  in Germany, 207-8
  and Labour Party, 80
  Operative Bricklayers' society, 73, 74
Building Guild, National, 72, 74, 76-7, 89
  London, 73
  Manchester, 73-4
Bukharin, N.I., 118
bureaucracy and leadership in trade unions, ideas of and debates around, 14, 17-18, 32-4, 36, 40-1, 168
Burns, John, 243
Buxton, Charles Roden, 117
Buxton, Dorothy, 176
Buxton, Noel, 79, 117, 119

Campbell, J.R., 85
Canadian Trades and Labour Congress, 217
Čapek, Karel and Josef, 210
Carlyle, Thomas, 51
Carnegie, Andrew, 216
  steelworks, 213
Charles, Fred, 170, 183
Chernov, Victor, 122
Chicherin, G.V, 117, 119
China, 112, 140
  AAP and, 282-6
Church, Richard, 214
Churchill, Winston, 15, 87, 256
Citrine, Walter, 16, 87, 130, 222, 234, 282
  and TUC, 19, 234, 293-6,
  General Strike and strike

preparations, 242, 247-51, 253, 255-61,
knighted, 294
and Soviet Russia, 179, 294-6, 306
Clarion Van, 35
Clay, Harold, 253, 255-7
Clynes, J.R., 248
Coates, W.P., 71, 78, 129, 178, 295
Coates, Zelda Kahan, 71, 179
Cole, G.D.H., 15, 64, 73, 209-10, 235, 238-9, 293
Cole, Margaret, 15
Colton, Jim, 172, 183
Colyer, W.T., 198, 203, 212, 215-16
'Common Rule', as union device, 47, 112, 141, 177
Commonwealth Labour Conference (1925), 70-1, 140, 282
Communist International or Comintern (CI), 54, 66, 68, 283
   a force for fratricidal division, 173
   a force for moderation, 133
   relations with British communists, 71-2, 164, 240, 295
   'twenty-one conditions', 123-4
Communist Party of Great Britain (CPGB), 120, 124, 126
   AAP and, 10, 32, 53-4, 65, 66-72 *passim*, 78-9, 81, 262, 265, 286
   anti-Americanism, 212, 215
   'babes' in Tomsky's eyes, 71, 128
   Class Against Class, 290-1
   congresses (1920), 67; (1924), 70, 71
   and general strikes, 238-40, 251
   and imperialism, 142

Conley, Andrew, 74
Connolly, James, 29

Cook, A.J., 10, 11, 14, 23, 67, 70-1, 89, 141, 239, 241, 243, 246-7, 254, 260, 262-5, 267, 291
co-operative movement, co-operative congresses, 38
Co-operative Employees, 36
   in Russia, 119
Coppock, Richard, 33, 73, 74, 89, 102 n.172
Cornelissen, Christian, 115
Coventry
   constituency, 81-5, 88, 175
   engineering guild, 192 n.198
Cowey, Ned, 26, 29
craft unionism and craft ideals, 74-5, 99 n.101
   and Americanism, 206-9, 212-13
Cramp, C.T., 102 n.172, 201
Crane, Walter, 20
Crosland, C.A.R., 212
Crossman, Richard, 88
'Curzon ultimatum' (1923), 125-6
Czolgosz, Leon, 158-9

Daily Express, 166
Daily Herald, 112, 130, 179, 245, 256, 296
Daily Mail, 204-5, 216, 220
Daily Worker
   London, 291
   New York, 219
Daniel, C.W., 172
Davies, S.O., 239
Dawes Plan, 127, 175, 203, 226 n.47
Debs, Eugene, 219
Dilke, Charles, 87
Dock, Wharf, Riverside and General Workers, 81
Dockers' Union, 51
Douillet, Joseph, 138
Dublin
   furnishing trades in, 47
   lockout (1913), 46
Dubreuil, Hyacinthe, 203, 212, 217

Dutt, R. Palme, 10, 24, 65, 68, 70, 71, 83, 139, 201, 289
  and Americanism, 210-11, 222

Electrical Trades Union (ETU), 250, 255
Ellis, Havelock, 162, 182-3
Elsbury, Sam, 76, 98 n.59
embargo, as union tactic, 238-9, 245, 248, 250-3, 262, 264, 266-7
engineering, engineering workers
  Amalgamated Engineering Union (AEU), 74, 241, 244
  Amalgamated Society of Engineers (ASE), 204, 237
  proposed engineering guild, 175
Ervine, St John, 214-15
Evans, Glyn, 71
Ewer, W.N., 160

Fabians/Fabianism, 20, 51, 73, 125-6, 142, 199, 213-14; see also Webbs, Sidney and Beatrice
fascism, as possible future, 198
Feakins, W.B., 216
Fimmen, Edo, 70, 111, 113-14, 126-7, 129, 137, 139-40, 282, 284, 306
Findlay, Alan, 130, 226 n.59
Finer, Herman, 210-11, 214-15
Firth, A.A., 259
Ford, Henry, and Fordism, 201-2, 210
  My Life and Work, 202, 214, 220
Forest of Dean
  constituency, 10, 78, 85-8, 93, 265, 290-1
  Forest of Dean Miners' Association, 86, 266-7
Foster, W.Z., 33-4, 38, 78, 160
France and French, 296
  Confédération générale du travail (CGT), 26, 31, 78, 115, 203, 281, 291
  revolution, parallels with Russia's, 171, 180, 182
  socialists, 282
  syndicalists, 78, 115
Free Speech Defence and Maintenance Committee, 70
Freedom, 167, 171
French Polishers, Amalgamated Society, 28, 35, 36, 38
Furnishing Trades Association, National Amalgamated (NAFTA), 12, 19, 86, 89, 91, 114, 139-40, 206, 213, 238, 283, 290-2
  AAP and, 290-1
  blacklegs and strikebreakers, 37-9, 45
  and building trades, 74-5, 92, 98 n.73
  and furnishing guild, 74-6
  in General Strike, 257
  immigrants and migrant workers, 45-6, 112
  industrial disputes, 37, 39-41, 44-5, 46-7, 74-5
  'industrial union' of furnishing trades, 34-5, 36-8
  internationalism, 43-8, 95, 177, 286, 289
  opposition to First World War, 48-52, 182
  Jewish members and branches, 45-6, 53, 119
  Joint Industrial Council, 41-2
  Labour Party and parliamentary activities, 40, 78-82
  leaders and officers, 35-6
  organisation of women workers, 38-9
  and Russian unions, 290
Furniture and Furnishing Guild (FFG), 65, 73-5, 89, 99 n.101

Gallacher, William, 71
Gast, John, 15-17
general elections (1906), 80;

(1924), 85; (1945), 80, 88; *see also* individual constituencies and candidates
General Federation of Trade Unions (GFTU), 50-1, 94, 222
General Workers, National Federation of, 51
Georgia, 124, 134, 143, 169, 179
Germany and Germans, 214, 296
 coal industry, 141
 communist party, 155 n.277, 202
 crisis (1923), 68
 labour movement, 110, 198, 235
 Allgemeiner Deutscher Gewerkschaftsbund (German confederation of trade unions, ADGB) 154, 206, 209, 291-2
  and AFL, 217-21,
  and IFTU, 113-14, 115, 127, 281-2
  and TUC, 130, 138
 building unions and building guilds, 207-8
 conceptions of marxism and modernity, 200, 202-3
 wartime attitudes to and relations with, 48-52
 within NAFTA, 46, 48, 112
Gillies, William, 156
Gitlow, Benjamin, 219
Glasier, Katherine Bruce, cited, 20, 306
Goldman, Emma, 10, 18, 34, 134, 178, 180-4, 236, 240, 292
 and anarchist movement, 159-61, 163-4, 167-73
 anglophobia, 173-4
 biographical details, 156-61
 campaign for Russian political prisoners, 161-73 *passim*
 in Spanish civil war, 194 n.264
Gompers, Samuel, 174, 216-18, 220
Gosling, Harry, 93
Gossip, Alex, 35, 41-2, 44, 49, 52-3, 67, 82, 102 n.172, 121, 219, 222, 256-7, 290-1
Gotz, Abram, 134
Graham, Duncan, 79
Graham, William, 210
Gramsci, Antonio, 199, 201, 202, 209
Grassmann, Peter, 129, 218, 282
Green, William, 218-19, 222
Grenfell, Harold, 132
guild socialism and guild socialists, 10, 65, 72-8, 125, 134, 206-7, 305; *see also* individual supporters and organisations

Haden Guest, Leslie, 117, 119
Hallsworth, Joseph, 286-7
Ham, Harry, 213
Hamilton, M.A., 216
Hands Off Russia, *see* Anglo-Russian Parliamentary Committee
Hardie, Keir, 29, 35, 78, 115, 216, 236-7, 249
Hardy, George, 53, 219, 251
'Haymarket martyrs', 158, 167
Haywood, Bill, 169
Henderson, Arthur, 14-15, 86, 125, 251
Henderson, Will, 250
Herzen, Alexander, 197
Hicks, George, 23, 74, 102 n.172
 and communism/CPGB, 70, 72, 93, 264
 social and political ideas, 207, 209
 and solidarity actions, 239, 241, 243-6, 255, 262
 and TUC, 92, 137
 fraternal delegate to AFL (1926), 221
 and Russia, 179, 294-5
 as TUC 'left', 257, 260
High Wycombe, building trades in, 39-41, 44-5, 47
Hillquit, Morris, 219

Hirsch, Julius, 208
Hobson, J.A., 139
Hobson, Samuel, 66, 72-4, 76-7, 97 n.40, 100 n.103, 251
House of Industry, 305
Hodges, Frank, 23, 81
Holdsworth, Alfred, 171
Holdsworth, Ethel Carnie, 171
Howell, George, 86
Hunecker, James, 161
Hunter, Ernest, 107-8
Hutt, Allen, 70, 137, 139, 256, 264
Huysmans, Camille, 113
Hyndman, Henry Mayers, 29-31, 42, 51, 89, 117, 294

Ibsen, Henrik, *An Enemy of the People*, 160-1, 166-7, 174
imperialism and the British Empire
  AAP's attitudes to, 288-9
Independent Jewish Cabinet Makers' Association, 46
Independent Labour Party (ILP), 28, 87, 95, 215, 217, 264
  and general strike, 236-7
  and international socialism, 29, 10, 126
  Labour Leader/New Leader, 125, 292
  Living Wage policy, 210-11, 287
  Socialist Review, 124, 199, 215
  and Soviet Russia, 117, 120, 124-6, 129, 132, 162-5, 180, 292, 296
India, 140
  AAP and TUC delegation to (1927-8), 93, 111, 143, 286-7
  All-India Trade Union Federation, 290
  All-Indian Trades Union Congress (AITUC), 217, 286, 289
  Indian National Congress and 'Swarajists', 50-1, 288-9
  Meerut conspiracy trial, 289-91, 295

Simon Commission, 286
India League, 287
Industrial Syndicalist Education League (ISEL), 25, 27, 31, 69, 73, 79, 90, 108, 168, 236
Inkpin, Albert, 31, 243, 293
Internationals
  conference of 'three internationals' (1922), 122
  First, 44, 107, 135-6
  'golden', 109
  Second, 107, 125
    congresses and conferences, Zurich (1893), 115; London (1896), 26-7, 28-9; Geneva (1920), 68; Frankfurt (1922), 67, 69, 106, 113, 124; *see also* Labour and Socialist International
  syndicalist, 78
    congress (1913), 78, 108, 168
  Third, *see* Communist International
  'two-and-a-half' or Vienna, 128
International Class War Prisoners' Aid (ICWPA), 70, 93, 180
International Committee for Political Prisoners, 165
International Co-operative Alliance, 108
International Federation of Trade Unions (IFTU), 10, 92, 94, 107, 113-15, 135-7, 217-18, 220-1, 288-9
  and British labour movement, 78, 110, 114, 116, 124-5, 129, 169, 263, 281-2
  congresses, London (1920), 124; Vienna (1924), 129; Paris (1927), 268, 281-5
  Purcell as president, 23, 114, 281-2
  and Russia/communism, 53, 116, 124, 126-7
International Labour

Organisation (ILO), 107, 200, 288, 295
International Miners' Federation 141
International Textile Workers' Federation, 106-7
International Trades Union Review, 94
International Transportworkers' Federation (ITF), 111, 120, 127, 129, 139, 284
Internationalism, *see* labour internationalism
Inter-Parliamentary Union, 219
Ireland and the Irish, 45, 46-7, 48
Irving, Dan, 35
Izvestia, 10, 130

Japan, 197
Jewish workers, anti-semitism and the labour movement, 45-6, 81
Jewson, Dorothy, 82
Joad, C.E.M., 214
Johnston, Tom, 142, 288
Jones, Mardy, 80
Jouhaux, Léon, 130, 154 n.254, 281-2, 291
Joynson-Hicks, William, 171-2
Justice, 294
Jute and Flax Workers' Union, 288

Kamenev, Lev, 118, 122, 125, 128
Kautsky, Karl, 198-200, 202-3, 206, 218
Keell, Thomas, 167
Kelly, Harry, 160, 168, 183
Klishko, Nikolai, 119
Krasin, Leonid, 117, 125-6, 199
Kropotkin, Peter, publications and influence, 15, 161
Kropotkin, Sophie, 169

Labour, 295
Labour and Socialist International (LSI), 124-6, 134, 138, 180
    and British labour movement, 138, 282
    Hamburg conference (1923), 124, 126
labour internationalism, 18, 43-50, 49-50, 52-3, 85, 106-16 *passim*, 138-41, 218, 284-5, 294
    AAP's ideas of, 88, 111
    First World War, attitudes to, 51-2
Labour Magazine, 93, 124, 156, 178, 215, 292, 293, 295
Labour Monthly, 23, 65, 72, 83, 91, 133, 136, 220, 241, 290, 305
Labour Party, 64-6, 68, 71, 156
    Advisory Committee on International Questions (ACIQ), 132, 176
    Commonwealth Labour Group, 141-2, 288
    conferences (1922), 124; (1925), 245; (1935), 260
    governments (1924), 64, 78-80, 84-5, 93-4, 125, 127, 132-3, 161, 172-3, 241; (1929-31), 115, 209, 291
    Parliamentary Labour Party (PLP), 78-80
    'Trade Union Group', 80
labour protectionism, 47, 84-5, 112-13, 141, 286-7
Labour Research Department (LRD), 70, 72, 93, 120, 256, 265
Lafargue, Paul, 28
Lancashire and Cheshire Federation of Trades Councils, 90
Lansbury, George, 10-11, 13, 19, 72, 79, 85, 128, 137, 142-3, 159, 178-9, 289, 292, 296
    in General Strike, 260
Lansbury's Labour Weekly, 132, 178, 245
Larkin, James, 33

Laski, Harold, 162-3, 165, 167
Lawrence, Susan, 178, 182, 260
Leacock, Steven, 216
League Against Imperialism (LAI), 142, 283, 289
Lee, H.W., 294-5
Leeds
  anti-war convention (1917), 53
  South-East parliamentary constituency, 45
Legal Eight Hours and International Labour League, 28
Legien, Carl, 50, 206
Leipart, Theodor 48, 206
Lenin, V.I., 77, 117, 119, 120, 123, 131, 136, 160
  described, 120
  Imperialism, 139
  The State and Revolution, 120
Levi, Paul, 106
Lewis, Sinclair, 214
Liverpool, furnishing trades in, 47
Lloyd George, David, 176
Lombard, Alfred, 263
London, Jack, 212
London
  AAP's activities in, 27-8
  furnishing trades in, 44-7
London French Polishers, 28
Losovsky, Alexander, 68, 118, 120, 123, 127, 128, 135-6, 174-5, 291
Lovett, William, 34-5, 48, 107
Luxemburg, Rosa, and mass strike, 235, 238, 252

Macarthur, Mary, 168
McDonald, James, 205
MacDonald, Ramsay, 10-11, 13, 29, 51, 113, 125, 217
  as Labour leader and premier, 23, 79, 82, 86, 94-5, 126-9, 132, 156, 245, 289
McDonnell, A.R., 132
McKenna Duties, 84-5, 141

McKinley, US President William (1901), assassinated 158-9, 168, 216
Mahon, John, 306
Mainwaring, Sam 236
Malatesta, Enrico, 161
Manchester and Salford, 75, 82
  AAP's activities in, 29-32, 40, 42, 45, 51, 53, 73-4, 79, 90-1, 236
  furnishing trades in, 45-6
  Labour Representation Committee, 90
Manchester and Salford Trades Council (MSTC), 19, 90, 114
  AAP secretary, 291
  Moss Side constituency, AAP and, 291
Mann, Tom, 10-11, 13-15, 115, 215, 216, 243, 288, 306
  AAP and, 19, 64-5, 70, 89
  in China (1926-7), 283
  and general strike, 234-8, 240, 255, 257
  links with CPGB and ancillaries, 67, 69
  and Red Friday, 245-7
  syndicalist ideas and activities, 25, 26-7, 29-31, 33, 39, 90
Markiewicz, Constance, 46
Marx, Eleanor, 28
Marx, Karl, 20
  and imperialism, 140
Marxism, in Britain and Germany compared, 199-209 *passim*
Mass-Observation, 296
Maxton, James, 85, 180, 292
May Day, as mass action, 238
Meakin, Walter, 117
Mellor, William, 72
Melnichansky, G., 131, 179
Menon, Khrishna, 287
Menshevism/Mensheviks, 117, 126, 134, 138, 154 n.254, 291; *see also* Georgia
Merrheim, Alphonse, 203

Mertens, Corneel, 129
Mexico, 221
Michels, Robert, 34, 183
Middleton, George 74, 76
Middleton, J.S., 250, 296
Mill, John Stuart, 20
Milne-Bailey, Walter, 250
miners and coalfields, 42, 79, 175
  Miners' Federation of Great Britain (MFGB), 140, 179, 244, 246-7
  solidarity, actions and advocacy, 248-9
  and TUC (1926), 250-1, 262-3
  Miners' Minority Movement, 86, 266
  nationalisation, 248
Miners' Next Step, 32-3
Morel, E.D., 49, 109, 112-13, 127-9, 132-3, 175, 178, 288, 292
Morison, S.E., 163
Morizet, André, 116
Morning Post, 255
Morris, William, 206, 209, 210, 212-13
Morrison, Herbert 71, 292
Mosely, Alfred, industrial commission to USA, 203-4, 205, 207, 213
Mosley, Cynthia, 210
Mosley, Oswald, 86, 210
Mosses, William, 205, 220
Mother Earth, 159
Mountjoy, Timothy, 86-7
Mukhina, Vera, 297
Münzenberg, Willi, 142, 283
Murphy, J.T., 32, 237

National Council of Labour Colleges, AAP and, 104 n.229
National Federation of Women Workers, 116
National Guilds Council, 74, 76
National Guilds League (NGL), 72-4, 164
  second conference (1923), 76

National Left Wing Movement, 72
National Minority Movement, 68-72, 86, 130, 219, 251, 266, 278 n.245, 286, 291
National Socialist Party (NSP), 51, 117
National Transport Workers' Federation, 31
National Unemployed Workers' Committee Movement (NUWCM), 237
National Union of General and Municipal Workers (NUGMW), 179
Nearing, Scott, 84, 223, 297
Netherlands/Dutch
  as international functionaries, 113
  Social Democratic Labour Party (SDAP), 114
Nettlau, Max, 174, 180
Nevinson, Henry, 162
New Economic Policy (NEP), 123, 133, 202, 292
Newbold, J.T. Walton, 71, 128-9, 222-3
Nietzsche, Friedrich, 160, 173
No Conscription Fellowship, 49
Norwich, 164

O'Grady, James, 35, 40, 45-6, 49, 51, 53, 75, 79, 81, 114, 127, 284
Oudegeest, Jan, 113-15, 123, 129, 135-8, 282-3
Owen, William C., 167

Pankhurst, Emmeline, 114
Pankhurst, Sylvia, 53, 164, 216
Paton, John, 260
Patternmakers' Association, United, 203
People's Convention, 80
People's Russian Information Bureau, 53

Perlman, Selig, 221
Pethick-Lawrence, Emmeline and Frederick, 162
Petrov, Peter, 295
Petrovsky, D.E., 71
Plebs and Plebs League, 215, 239
Piano Workers' Guild, 76
Pollak, Oscar, 156, 172, 294
Pollitt, Harry, 10, 13, 67, 68, 71, 80, 169, 175, 262, 264, 291, 293, 295-6
  imprisoned (1925-6), 70, 141, 240
  Minority Movement secretary, 69
Ponsonby, Arthur, 127-8
Post Office Workers' union, 74
Pouget, Emile, 26
Preobazhensky, E., 177
Price, Morgan Philips, 126
printing trades, 256
  London Society of Compositors, 256
  Typographical Association, 116
Pugh, Arthur, 246
Purcell, A.A.
  as 'claim-making performer', 307-8
  early career and biographical details, 27-32, 89
  councillor and council elections, 29, 32, 79
  parliamentary elections and career, 11, 29-30, 45, 65, 78-88 *passim*, 281, 283, 305; *see also* individual constituencies
  historiographical standing, 10-17
  oratory and discourse, 42-3, 83-4, 261-2
  as union negotiator, 42, 241
Purcell, May, 179
Purcell, Sarah, née Fidler, 28, 87-8
Purkis, Stuart, 98 n.59

Quaile, Mary 102 n.172, 179

Radek, Karl, 117-18
rail workers, 236
Railway Clerks' Association, 259
Railwaymen, National Union of (NUR), 36, 179, 247, 253
  and solidarity actions, 248-9, 264
Rakovsky, Christian, 127-8, 162
Ratcliffe, S. K., 210, 216
rationalisation, 201-3, 207-8
'Red Friday' (1925), 141, 204, 235, 238, 245, 248, 250
Red International of Labour Unions or Profintern (RILU), 68-9, 71, 118, 124, 127, 219, 237, 283, 289, 291
  British Bureau, 68-9
  Latin bureau, 137
'Restriction of Numbers', trade unions device, 112, 141, 177
Rhondda, Lady, 165
Richill, Co. Armagh, 47-8
robots, workers as, 208, 210, 221
Robson, W.A., 210
Rothstein, Andrew, 129
Rothstein, Theodore, cited, 107
Rousseau, Jean-Jacques, cited, 215
Rowan, Jim, 255
Roy, M.N., 139
Ruskin, John, 206, 209, 212
Russell, Bertrand, 65, 117, 143, 161-2, 164, 165-6, 178, 181, 216
Russia/USSR
  AAP, TUC and, 28, 52-3, 69, 94-5, 114-15, 120-3, 178, 282, 292, 294-5, 297
  and America(nism), 197-9, 201-2, 222-3
  attractions to left, 12, 164, 180-2
  Cheka and political repression, 119, 122-3, 124, 134, 162-3, 170-1, 290, 292, 295
  communist party, 11, 134

embassies and diplomats, 71, 178, 292, 295, 296
  Goldman and Berkman in, 156-7
  'Group of Social Democrats in London', 292
  revolutions (1905), 198; (1917), 53
  solidarity actions with, 235
  trade union movement, 118, 120-2
  support for British miners (1926), 263
  trading and commercial relations with, 75, 77, 174-8, 192 n.198
  tsarist regime opposed or defended, 51, 114, 158-9, 197-8
  workers' and union delegations, 179, 296, 306
    British Labour delegation (1920), 23, 52, 53, 68, 77, 81, 116-23 *passim*, 157, 175
    TUC delegation (1924), 23, 69, 71, 114, 129-38 *passim*, 160, 169-70, 295
Russia Today, 297

Sacco and Vanzetti case, 180
Saklatvala, Shapurji, 10, 13, 219
Salford, 29
  Salford South constituency, 29-30, 82; see also Manchester and Salford
  Salford West constituency, 29
Samuel, Herbert, 263
  Samuel Memorandum, 259
Sassenbach, Johannes, 217, 221, 263, 282, 286
Seaham constituency, 86
Shaw, George Bernard, 28, 117, 119, 142, 182
Shaw, Tom, 106-7
Shinwell, Emmanuel, 79
Shop Assistants' Union, Amalgamated, 27, 167-8

Shoreditch, borough council, 28
Simon, Ernest, 82
Sinclair, Upton, 212
Sinn Fein, 46
Skinner, Herbert, 116-17, 122
Smillie, Robert, 10, 103 n.181, 158
Smith, Gus, 48
Smith, Herbert, 10, 42-3, 130, 246, 263, 267
Snowden, Ethel, 116, 118, 122
Snowden, Philip, 84, 125
Social Democratic Federation (SDF)/Social Democratic Party (SDP), 28-9, 30-2, 35, 45, 51, 66, 89, 156, 162, 205, 294; see also British Socialist Party
Socialist League, 164, 167, 170
socialist representation committees, 30-1
Solidarity, 237
Sombart, Werner,
  on America, 198
  on general strike, 237
Sorel, Georges, 25-6
  and general strike, 235, 237
South Wales Miners, organisation and activities, 32-3, 48-9, 57 n.82, 180-1
Stalin, J.V., 11, 120, 127, 134, 160, 198, 292
state and social reform, AAP's attitudes to, 30, 39-40, 52, 77-8, 287-8, 305
Steffens, Lincoln, 223
Stendhal (Henri Beyle), 173, 197
Stewart, Arthur, 31
Stockport constituency, 81
strikes and lockouts
  Belfast (1919), 47, 53, 241, 242
  Dublin lockout (1913), 46
  engineering lockout (1922), 91
  general strikes, examples and advocacy, 235-42, 248
    AAP's ideas concerning, 238, 240-2, 268

General Strike (British, 1926), 11, 43, 64, 184
  AAP's role in, 233-4, 252, 254, 257-61, 306
  extended to press, 255-7
  inception of, 247-59 *passim*
  Liverpool (1911), 27
  Locomen's (1924), 241
  miners' lockout (1926), 262-7
  railway (1919), 248, 256
  Singer strike, Clydebank (1911), 205
  of transport workers (1911), 27
  see also boycott, embargo, blacklegs, individual trades and trade unions
Struve, Peter, 138
Sun Yat-Sen, 285
Sunday Times, 171
Sunday Worker, 10-11, 16, 72, 86, 239, 251, 264-5
Swales, Alonzo, 70, 87, 102 n.172, 103 n.181, 137, 141, 176, 218-19, 245, 246, 262, 284, 291-2
syndicalism, syndicalists, 30, 32-4, 64-5, 74, 78-9
  AAP's syndicalist outlook and activities, 24-7, 36-43, 52, 89-90, 236
  and idea of general strike, 233-7

Tailor and Garment Workers' union, 74
Tanner, Jack, 57 n.76, 67, 89, 117, 120, 237, 248
Tarnow, Fritz, 207, 219-20, 222
Taylor, Frederick W., Taylorism and scientific management, 201-3, 210, 222
Thomas, J.H., 23, 94, 114, 125, 127, 176-7, 246, 249, 257-8, 260-1, 264, 266
Thurtle, Ernest, 142
Tillett, Ben, 28, 31, 51, 93, 95, 103 n.181, 104 n.228, 106, 128-30, 137, 190 n.143, 191 n.171, 222, 226 n.147, 246, 262, 306
Time and Tide, 165
Times, The,171
Tocqueville, Alexis de, 173, 197
Tolstoy, Leo, 210
Tomkins, Alf, 283, 290, 292
Tomsky, Mikhail, 71, 118, 122-3, 128-9, 131, 133, 135, 143, 160, 179, 217, 223, 266, 297, 306
Toole, Joe, 29
Tortelier, Joseph, 115
Tracey, Herbert, 143, 156, 250, 256
Trade Union Unity, 66, 70, 93, 136-7, 264-5
trades councils, AAP and, 19, 29-30, 38, 90-1
Trades Disputes Act (1927), 80, 267-8
Trades Union Congress (TUC), 84, 176, 209
  AAP and, 40, 42, 82-3, 89-95 *passim*, 241, 264-6, 290-1
  and AFL, 217-22
  Anglo-Russian trade-union committee, 11, 43, 95, 247, 265-6
  British Worker (1926), 256, 293
  and communism, 69, 124
  congresses (1913), 50; (1917), 91; (1918), 40; (1922), 243; (1923), 243; (1924), 71, 83, 94, 129, 135, 136, 141, 217, 237, 243-4; (1925), 87, 135, 141, 177, 179, 223, 239, 245, 283, 297; (1926), 222, 266; (1933), 292
  fraternal delegates, 217
  general council (parliamentary committee), 70, 91-5, 205, 292
    as co-ordinator of solidarity actions, 238-9, 243-4, 249-52
  and IFTU, 107, 110
  India and Indian Affairs Committee, 286-7, 289-90

Industrial Review, 293
and international trade, 176-7
and Labour Party, 80, 92-5, 124, 156, 172-3
  Council of Action (1920), 236
  National Council of Labour, 295
'lefts', identified and depicted, 11, 243, 257-8, 260, 292
parochialism (alleged), 107
Special Industrial Committee/ Negotiating Committee (1925-6), 245, 258-9, 262
Strike Organisation Committee (1926), 11, 234
and trades councils, 90-1
Ways and Means Committee (WMC), 251-2, 254-5, 258
Trades Union Guild Council, 74
transport workers
  Transport and General Workers' Union (TGWU), 85-6, 92, 244-7, 253, 257, 261, 264
  and industrial alliance(s), 248
  strikes and solidarity actions, 253, 259, 277 n.233; *see also* strikes and lockouts
Transport Workers' Federation, 249
Tressell, Robert, 206
Trevelyan, Charles, 133, 243
'Triple' or 'Industrial' Alliance, 37, 65, 236, 242-8, 264
Troelstra, P.J., 28
Trotsky, Leon, 11, 115, 118, 127, 131, 160
Turner, Ben, 116-18, 260, 266
Turner, John, 27, 130, 163-4, 167-72, 174, 182, 195 n.267, 216, 295

Union of Democratic Control (UDC), 49, 109, 116, 126-7, 132-3, 169, 175, 292
United States/USA, 93
  AAP visits (1925), 10-11, 215-23 *passim*, 297
  anarchist activities in, 157-60, 167-8
  anti-communism in, 215
  attitudes of British and European left towards, 196-215 *passim*
  Baldwin government's mission to (1926), 222
  Daily Mail, 'Trade Union Mission' to (1926), 204-5, 216, 220
  syndicalism, 25-6
USSR, *see* Russia

Vandervelde, Emile, 124, 143
Varley, Julia, 102 n.172,
Venereal Disease, National Committee for Combating, 91
Voice of Labour, 168

Wagner, Martin, 208
Wallhead, Dick, 81, 117, 122, 128
Warwick, Countess of, 30, 81, 163
Washington Post, 219
Watkins, Nat, 69, 266
Webb, Beatrice, 64, 88, 113, 125-6, 173, 194 n.264, 197-8, 210, 213-14, 222, 296
Webb, Sidney, 64, 87, 124
Webbs, Sidney and Beatrice, 11, 18-20, 30, 33, 84, 91, 236, 284, 287, 308
  Constitution for a Socialist Commonwealth of Great Britain, 134
  History of Trade Unionism, 20, 168
  Industrial Democracy, 47, 111-12, 207
  Soviet Communism, 296-7, 305-6
Wedgwood, Josiah, 161, 162-3, 166, 180, 182
Weir, William, 205-6, 216
  Weir steel house, 206

Wellock, Wilfred, 210-11, 216
Wells, H.G., 160, 165, 196-8, 209, 215, 217
Wertheimer, Egon, 208, 222
West, Rebecca, 163, 165-6
Wheatley, John, 10
  Housing Act (1924), 94, 207
Whitechapel and St George's constituency, 80
Wignall, James, 85-6
Wilkinson, Ellen, 287, 289
Williams, Jack, 87, 266-7
Williams, Robert, 23-4, 52, 67-8, 81, 117-24 *passim*, 127, 179-80, 241, 249
Wills, Jack, 78
Wintringham, Tom, 252
Wise, E.F., 176

Woodworkers, Amalgamated Society of (ASW), 21, 92, 104
Woodworkers, International Union of (IUW), 44, 48, 206, 219, 222
Woodworkers' Union, German, 206
Workers' Weekly, 71, 85

Yorkshire Evening News, paean to Bevin, 257-60
Young, George, 117, 132-3, 138-9, 143, 163

Zinoviev, G.E., 68, 128, 283
'Zinoviev Letter' (1924), 95, 133, 166

Bolshevism and the British left: concluding thoughts

The studies comprising *Bolshevism and the British Left* have offered an exploration and reflection on the British labour movement's reception of Bolshevik ideas and material influences in the period between the two world wars. This was the period of the Labour Party's emergence in its modern form as the main institutional focus of the British left, and it has given rise to a particularly extensive historiography. The metaphor of Labour's forward march is a familiar one; and the story of these decades is often read backwards, as if it were preordained that other possible roads or detours would necessarily be closed off. One reason for reviewing the period through the prism of attitudes to the Bolsheviks is that it reveals a picture that is at once much richer, more complex and less teleological.

In its different way, each of the three studies has been more concerned with issues of ideology and political culture than with foreign affairs as traditionally conceived. The volumes have certainly registered the role of key institutions like the political parties of the left and the trade-union and co-operative movements. But their underlying method has nevertheless been biographical or prosopographical: that is, they have sought to explore these movements through the career paths of those on whose human capital they depended. Other studies in the field have tended to be framed within a foreign-policy context, and the most effective have been those deploying the particular skills of the diplomatic historian. None is the work of a historian with a primary interest in politics and society in early twentieth-century Britain, and it is from this distinctive perspective that the issues of Bolshevism and the British left have been approached here.

From this approach a number of insights have followed. First, the focus on human capital makes it clear that human capital alone has always been an insufficient basis on which to construct a political career path at any but the most rudimentary level. This was a particular focus of the first of these volumes, *Labour Legends and Russian Gold*. Here the contentious business of 'Moscow gold' was for the first time addressed within a wider political context, extending to the funding of the Labour Party as well as the Communist Party and exploring issues of independence, patronage and professionalisation as these were manifested through competing forms of funding and resourcing – issues that are strangely neglected in mainstream accounts of Labour politics. Despite their rather different focus, the two subsequent volumes supplied abundant supporting evidence. Political careers like those of the Webbs and A.A. Purcell simply cannot be conceived of without the support respectively of Beatrice Webb's independent income or Purcell's employment by his union. There can be no adequate study either of activist minorities or of political elites that does not address this most basic consideration.

The second insight was the exposure of a veritable web of interconnections between movements and periods that are often constructed as if entirely distinct from each other. Different political lives encompassed different affiliations and intellectual influences, at different stages of their political development. Often there were patterns of affinity or association that manifestly cut across the familiar institutional demarcations, like those of the Labour leader Lansbury with his communist children. The prosopographical method is one that can usefully be applied to any period of political history. Nevertheless, it offers particular illumination in a context such as this. Between the establishment of the first British socialist organisations in the early 1880s and the election of a majority Labour government some sixty years later, this period saw the one tectonic shift that has occurred in the modern British party system, as the Labour Party came from nowhere to supplant the Liberals as a party of government. In part this was a generational shift; but after the sharper jolt to party allegiances after 1914, the interwar period was one of unprecedented flux in respect of the primary political affiliations of activists, voters and politicians alike. The Labour Party hardly had a national organisation to speak of until 1918; and even after that it took the best part of a decade to establish the most basic party disciplines. This was the period in which Sidney Webb first spoke of the inevitability of gradualness, as Labour accumulated voters and supporters with what briefly seemed an irresistible momentum. One could hardly have shipped these hundreds of candidates and millions of voters into the country unobserved. That Labour's boundaries were more porous during this period than is sometimes suggested is a simple matter of historical record.

A third insight arises from the fact that the impact of Bolshevism upon the British left coincided with this period of organisational flux. In the first of these volumes, the contrast was drawn with the German case, in which a well-organised mass socialist party was deeply and irrevocably split over the issue of communism and the Russian revolution. Splits did of course occur in Britain too, in organisations like the British Socialist Party and the Independent Labour Party. Across the labour movement as a whole, however, there was no such cleavage over the issue of Russia. Of course, the positive reactions described in these volumes have to be counterbalanced with the informed and plausible hostility of figures like MacDonald and later Citrine. Nevertheless, in the delicate reconciliation that had to be effected between the labour movement's culture of pluralism and its ethos of unity, it was the critic of Soviet Russia who in some periods experienced the greater sense of constraint. Readers will probably be familiar with the later period of Britain's wartime alliance with the USSR, when George Orwell famously had such problems in finding a publisher for *Animal Farm*. Twenty years earlier, we have seen, Emma Goldman had encountered a similar reluctance to be shaken out of what she regarded as a Russian superstition. The difference in this earlier period was that this was an intensely partisan commitment that set the labour movement as a whole against the Conservatives – who were also displacing the Liberals from the other side. Where Bolshevism in other countries primarily served as a line of cleavage within the labour movement, in Britain, paradoxically, it played its part in consolidating Labour's distinct political identity at the crucial moment of its emergence as a party of government.

Bolshevism and the British Left may also be regarded as an exercise in transnational labour history. For some labour historians, a transnational approach has lately seemed a way out of the impasse or 'crisis' of their field that loomed so large in the early 1990s. Though communism, with its strongly international character, might have been thought particularly suited to such an approach, in practice a truly transnational communist history has been slow to develop. Instead, access to vast communist archives at first gave rise to a 'centre-periphery' debate that largely focused on the extent to which individual communist parties – the 'periphery' – were disciplined instruments of the communist 'centre' in Moscow. Whatever this implied in respect of communist parties themselves – and in Britain the exchanges were less than illuminating – the wider impact of this first attempt at a socialist society was largely discounted, as the relationship of Bolshevism and the British left became projected onto the communists alone. The teleological view of British Labour was in this way compounded by a sort of insularity, and the projection of this most alluring of transnational influences onto just one of the groups that experienced its fascination.

The volumes began with a simple image, to which Goldman among others subscribed, in which the international influence of communism appears as a conspiracy wholly dependent on Moscow's financial support. There is no attempt in these volumes to downplay such material considerations. Studies of the cultural cold war make much of diverse agencies funded either from the East or from the West. And within the indigent subworld of the British left, relatively small amounts of support could offer crucial leverage to those supportive of the Soviets against their detractors. More specifically, they allowed the consolidation of the CPGB as the most significant rival to the Labour Party from its left. Nevertheless, commitments like those of the Webbs, Purcell and a host of other figures cited in these volumes demonstrate how unequal such explanations are to the wider influence that Bolshevism had on the British left. In the case of the Webbs and Purcell, the biographical method allows us to trace the roots of pro-Soviet attachments in habits of thought and attachment dating well back into the late nineteenth century. Through the reconstruction of wider milieux, political environments and forms of intellectual exchange, the individual life may thus be regarded as a site on which the social in all its complexity is played out, according to dynamics which are never entirely captured within any single institution.

Through the Webbs and Purcell one also gets a sense of the possible diversity of encounters between Bolshevism and the British left. The differences in social and political character between these quintessential Fabian intellectuals and the sometime syndicalist and campaigning trade unionist hardly need be laboured. But there is also, of course, a crucial difference in the timing of their enrolment in the ranks of fellow-travellers. Perhaps a parallel may be drawn with the distinction which historians of British fascism make between those initially drawn to fascism as the diehards of the domestic class war and Oswald Mosley's later programmatic fascism, conceived as response to economic crisis and the incapacity to deal with it of the second Labour government. One should not make too much of the analogy between these intransigents of the right and those whose radicalisation drew them to the left. Nevertheless, there was a distinct shift that is identifiable with these same conjunctures: from the almost instinctive class-based solidarity which some felt as soon as they heard of the Russian revolution, and which underpinned Labour's Russophilia of the 1920s, to the more systematic exposition of Bolshevism as alternative, whose largest if not most impressive monument was the Webbs' *Soviet Communism*. For some, including a new cohort of intellectual recruits, this meant adhesion to the CPGB, which for the first time mapped out its own planners' vision of a 'Britain without capitalists'. For others it meant the bringing to bear of Soviet argument and example on what might be described as the programmatic Labourism to which so much effort was devoted in the period following the collapse of MacDonaldism in 1931. Arguably the last such wave of pro-Sovietism was that of the war years, and by the late 1960s and 1970s those irrecoverably influenced by it can be traced moving into influential positions in the trade unions or on the Labour backbenches.

Surveying the British left from this particular perspective exposes the odd skeleton in the cupboard, and offers a challenge to more schematic or teleological narratives, as well as the sorts of normative exclusion on which they largely depend. Given that these were the years of Labour's proverbial forward march, and of the achievement of a delimited British version of social democracy, it also raises important issues regarding Britain's wider political culture as this was reconfigured in an age of mass democracy. In particular, it raises issues about the role of party, into which the energies of so much of the left were for the time being largely channelled. In two crucial ways, this was clearly exclusionary in its consequences. Organisationally, it meant the gradual imposition of a managed party structure, in which competing institutional supports and career routes were progressively marginalised in favour of professionalised representation, for which in turn traditional qualifications and connections increasingly provided a necessary entry point. Politically, it meant the resolution of a heterodox and amorphous utopianism into the limited but realisable commitments epitomised by *Labour's Immediate Programme* (1937) and the similar statements of legislative intent that were to follow. Often this was described as a process of maturation or coming of age. 'An Opposition need not be a party', wrote Bernard Shaw as Labour set up its national organisation; 'a Government must be if it is really to govern and propagate its species'.[1] The achievements of the Attlee years should hardly be underestimated as we look back from our present political vantage point. The problem nevertheless remains, of what might also have been lost when so many things remained that needed to be Opposed – including, not least, the unravelling of so many of those very achievements.

In the first of these volumes I referred at the outset to what I described as the strangely conservative and exclusive notion of a British political tradition. Among students of British politics the concept continues to be invoked in what is usually a somewhat reductionist and inadequately historicised way. In some of its articulations, the notion of a top-down, elitist conception of democracy is central to this tradition, and there is indeed no lack of evidence for such a view in some of the chapters here. What, of course, is more problematic is the collation of such features into a traditionary narrative that embodies that same perspective. If all traditions are to some extent invented, they may also represent a form of recovery, restitution and contestation – very much in the spirit of the British marxist historians, who also represented one of the intersections between Bolshevism and the British left. This is not to say that critical and dissenting voices should simply be celebrated: if, in respect of Bolshevism, they were no more deluded than Thompson's 'deluded follower of Joanna Southcott', the human costs of such delusions were in the end incomparably greater. Nevertheless, it is in countering the unfolding of teleologies that require the disinvention of these alternative voices that a project like the present one may serve a purpose.

NOTE

1   Shaw to C.P. Trevelyan, 14 March 1918 in Dan H. Laurence, *Bernard Shaw. Collected letters 1911-1925*, Max Reinhardt, 1985, p. 542.